John and Thomas—
Gospels in Conflict?

Princeton Theological Monograph Series

K. C. Hanson, Charles M. Collier, and D. Christopher Spinks,
Series Editors

Recent volumes in the series:

Lowell K. Handy
Psalm 29 Through Time and Tradition

D. Seipl and Frederick W. Weidmann, editors
Enigmas and Powers

Stanley D. Walters
Go Figure!

Mark W. Hamilton et al., editors
Renewing Tradition

Scott A. Ellington
Risking Truth

David A. Ackerman
Lo, I Tell You a Mystery

Lloyd Kim
Polemic in the Book of Hebrews

John and Thomas—
Gospels in Conflict?

Johannine Characterization and the Thomas Question

Christopher W. Skinner

Foreword by Francis J. Moloney, SDB

PICKWICK *Publications* · Eugene, Oregon

JOHN AND THOMAS—GOSPELS IN CONFLICT?
Johannine Characterization and the Thomas Question

Princeton Theological Monograph Series 115

Pickwick Publications
A Division of Wipf and Stock Publishers
199 W. 8th Ave., Suite 3
Eugene, OR 97401

www.wipfandstock.com

ISBN 13: 978-1-60608-614-8

Cataloguing-in-Publication data:

Skinner, Christopher W.

John and Thomas—gospels in conflict? : Johannine characterization and the Thomas question / Christopher W. Skinner ; Foreword by Francis J. Moloney, SDB.

xxii + 248 p. ; 23 cm. Includes bibliographical references and index.

Princeton Theological Monograph Series 115

ISBN 13: 978-1-60608-614-8

1. Bible. N.T. John—Criticism, interpretation, etc. 2. Bible—Criticism, Narrative. 3. Gospel of Thomas (Coptic Gospel)—Criticism, interpretation, etc. I. Moloney, Francis J. II. Title. III. Series.

BS2615.2 S55 2009

Manufactured in the U.S.A.

For Tara, with gratitude for your patience with this project and with my many shortcomings. Though your endless sacrifices go unnoticed by those on the outside, I am ever reminded of how much you have brought into my life.

Contents

Foreword

The Fourth Gospel has always been something of an enigma for critical New Testament scholarship. The major challenge that faced the early critics was to identify the sources for a life of Jesus. The Gospel of Mark, quickly recognized as the earliest Gospel, was seen as the best source for the life of Jesus, and the primary source for the other so-called Synoptic Gospels. But what of the Gospel of John? Although more conservative critics attempted to show a link between Matthew, Mark, Luke, and John, and dipped into John for elements that might serve for a construction of the historical Jesus, most took the position that it was too "mystical" to be associated with mainstream early Christianity. Indeed, in the light of its highly developed presentation of Jesus as Logos, Son of God, and Christ, some more radical critics located its composition in the sub-apostolic period (second Christian century) or even in the third Christian century.

A decisive event in Johannine studies was the publication of Rudolf Bultmann's *Das Evangelium des Johannes* in 1941. Behind Bultmann's brilliant and challenging existentialist reading of the Johannine text lay a theory of the sources used by the Evangelist to compose the Gospel. According to Bultmann, he used a Synoptic-like source for some of the narrative, a "Signs Source," which contained the unique Johannine miracles, a collection of gnostic revelatory discourses that provided material for the lengthy Johannine discourses, and the original work of the Evangelist who welded all this material into a coherent and powerful whole. After the work of the Evangelist, a figure Bultmann called the Ecclesiastical Redactor worked through the text, bringing its dangerous (gnostic?) tendencies into closer relationship with mainstream Christian tradition, especially as it is reflected in the Pauline literature and the Synoptic Gospels. The text as it has been delivered into the Christian tradition is from the hands of the Ecclesiastical Redactor.

From that epoch-making moment, the interpretation of the Johannine text has been dominated by a search for its sources. It must be said that most Johannine scholarship across the latter half of the twentieth century has either supported (a minority) or sought to disprove the work of Bultmann. The two leading commentators of this period, Rudolf Schnackenburg (1965–1984) and Raymond E. Brown (1976–1980), are good examples of this. Both reject the Bultmannian source theories, but both accept that sources shaped the Gospel. For Schnackenburg, some form of early Gnosticism can be traced, while for Brown, sectarian Judaism is the dominant "source."

But these approaches to the story of the life, teaching, death, and resurrection of Jesus were challenged in the final decades of the second millennium. Following a widespread movement within the study of literature as such, the work of R. Alan Culpepper—*Anatomy of the Fourth Gospel: A Study in Literary Design* (1983)—opened the floodgates for a never-ending series of studies of the Gospel of John as literature, and especially as a "story" in its own right. There are various names given to this approach to the Johannine text, as there are various methods employed. Most commonly, it is called narrative criticism. It studies the narrative as a whole utterance, and asks little or nothing about the sources that might have been used to provide the details found in the story or its literary shape. A number of such studies of the Gospel of John appeared across the 1980s and 90s, but a full-scale commentary (in three volumes) using this method was Francis J. Moloney's *Belief in the Word: Reading the Fourth Gospel, John 1–4* (1993), *Signs and Shadows: Reading John 4–12* (1996), and *Glory Not Dishonor: Reading John 13–21* (1998).

However, as I have long insisted with my students and attempted to recognize in all my subsequent work, it is not enough to uncover the literary and theological design of a document from the past. The questions asked by the traditional historical-critical approach to the Gospels remain: What were the world, and the situation in that world, that produced this "story"? It is intellectually dishonest to describe literary and theological features of any ancient text without situating those features meaningfully within a given time and place. This must continue to be done for the Fourth Gospel, whatever method one uses in its interpretation.

The work of my former doctoral student, Dr. Christopher Skinner, finds its place within this rapid historical overview of Johannine scholarship, and makes a significant contribution to the contemporary debates, along the lines just suggested. The search for "sources" behind the Fourth Gospel has continued, despite the emergence of newer methods that tend to ignore them. One of the sources already identified as possible by Bultmann, and further developed by the posthumous publication of the commentary of Ernst Haenchen, *Das Johannesevangelium* (1980), was the *Gospel of Thomas*. For both Bultmann and Haenchen (among others) this text reflected an early stage of gnostic dualism also found in the Fourth Gospel. However, more recent scholarly activity has focused more intently on the *Gospel of Thomas* and other literature from the early centuries of Christianity, asking different questions. This work has been very well summarized in the study that follows, and I encourage the reader to reflect on it carefully. Given the critical stance that the author of the Fourth Gospel consistently takes against the figure of the disciple Thomas (see John 11:16; 14:5; 21:2), and especially in the dramatic final scene of John 20 (vv. 24–29), a number of scholars argue that one of the elements that influenced the writing of this life of Jesus was a polemic with very early Christian traditions that depended on Thomas.

The study that follows engages seriously with this fascinating contemporary approach to the Gospel of John. Aware of the depth and scope of the debate, Skinner provides a fair and accurate description of current scholarship; both those who advocate dependence upon Thomas traditions, and those who oppose it. The bulk of his work, however, is dedicated to a study of the "characterization" of a number of figures who interact with Jesus during the Johannine story. Skinner asks if Thomas is the only such follower of Jesus who is dealt with somewhat critically. After a detailed study of the characterization of Thomas, he goes on to show that a parallel process of characterization is used for the presence of Peter, Andrew, Philip, Judas (not Iscariot), and the disciples as an unnamed group. Having dealt with characters who, side-by-side with Thomas, are regarded as disciples of Jesus, he then turns to examine the roles of Nicodemus, the Samaritan woman, Mary, and Martha. What appears from the study of each of these characters is that no one is spared from a certain negativity on the part of Jesus. It appears that there may be a wider Johannine agenda that shows, through the presentation of the way each of the major characters in the Gospel relates to Jesus and responds to him, that what God does in and through Jesus transcends human expectation.

Christopher Skinner's valuable study is a fine example of an approach to the Johannine text that recognizes the importance of *both* the literary *and* the historical worlds that shape the story. It respects the contribution of those who argue for the Gospel as John as a reaction to currents in the early church best reflected in Thomasine literature, but shows that a focus upon the disciple Thomas's response to Jesus is too limited a perspective upon which to approach an understanding of the Gospel as a whole. I am glad to have been associated with this fine study, and trust that it will make an important contribution to both Johannine and Thomasine studies in the future.

Francis J. Moloney, SDB
Salesian Province Centre
Ascot Vale, Victoria, Australia

Preface

THIS BOOK IS A REVISED VERSION OF MY DOCTORAL DISSERTATION, which was written at the Catholic University of America between 2005 and 2007. It has sometimes consumed my interest and has at other times been the bane of my existence. Therefore, I consider it no small thing that you are holding this book in your hands. It is nothing less than a feat of perseverance.

I am keenly aware of the fact that a work such as this is not merely the result of one person's effort. There are a number of people who have contributed to the present volume, even if their ideas are not contained on the pages that follow. I want to thank first the members of my dissertation committee—Francis T. Gignac and Janet Timbie—for their thoughtful guidance during the process of completing this project. I also want to thank Frank J. Matera who significantly shaped my thinking during my time at Catholic University. I spent substantial time with four outstanding doctoral students during my time in Washington, DC. I was privileged to learn from and alongside my fellow *Moloneyschule* members, Kelly Iverson, Sherri Brown, Gregg Morrison, and the Rev. Dan Claire. Special thanks go to my *Doktorvater*, Francis J. Moloney. Frank, I consider it one of the great privileges of my young academic career to have been molded by your brilliant scholarship, your measured demeanor, your masterful direction, and your (occasional) sharp scolding.

I am also thankful to Michael J. Gorman and the administration of St. Mary's Seminary and University in Baltimore, Maryland. St. Mary's provided me with an opportunity to test many of my thoughts and ideas in my Gospel of John seminar in the fall of 2006. St. Mary's also provided me with a faculty research grant in the summer of 2007, which enabled me to complete this book. Since 2001 I have served on the full-time staff of Perry Hall Baptist Church in Baltimore. It has been a supportive environment, and my coworkers and church members have encouraged my efforts. In particular, I want to recognize the Rev. Jim Foreman, who has provided me not only with his friendship but also with a forum for the ridiculous and many reminders that I should not take myself so seriously. Thanks, Jim.

I would also like to thank K. C. Hanson and the editorial staff at Wipf and Stock for their willingness to publish this book in the Princeton Theological Monograph Series. Thanks are also due to the Rev. Jason Poling, who read the entire manuscript and commented carefully on a myriad of issues. His reflective comments have sharpened my expression and clarified my own thinking. Any mistakes or oversights that remain in the present volume are solely my responsibility.

Completing a work like this has the potential, if left unchecked, to be especially hard on a family. I am glad to say that my children, Christopher, Abby, and Drew, were often a welcome interruption and necessary comic relief at many turns in the writing process. The reminder that children are more important than ideas put this book and its ideas into proper perspective more than once. My parents, Robert and Linda Boyette, have also been a constant source of love, support, and encouragement over the years.

Most importantly, I want to express my appreciation for my wife, Tara. Her patience, perseverance, insight, and quiet understanding have attended this whole process. Without her I could not have completed this book and I would not have wanted to continue this sometimes crazy, often beautiful, and always interesting journey. This book is lovingly and affectionately dedicated to her.

Christopher W. Skinner
Abingdon, Maryland
February 2009

Abbreviations

AB	Anchor Bible
ABRL	Anchor Bible Reference Library
ACNT	Augsburg Commentaries on the New Testament
ANTC	Abingdon New Testament Commentaries
ASV	American Standard Version
ABR	*Australian Biblical Review*
BBB	Bonner biblische Beiträge
BBR	*Bulletin for Biblical Research*
BDAG	Bauer, W. F. W. Danker, W. F. Arndt, and F. W. Gingrich., *A Greek-English Lexicon of the New Testament and Other Early Christian Literature.*, 3rd ed. Chicago, 2000
BDB	Brown, F., S. R. Driver, and C. A. Briggs. *Hebrew and English Lexicon of the Old Testament.* Oxford, 1907
BDF	Blass, F., A. Debrunner, and R. W. Funk. *A Greek Grammar of the New Testament and Other Early Christian Literature*
BETL	Bibliotheca ephemeridum theologicarum lovaniensum
BHS	*Biblia Hebraica Stuttgartensia.*, Edited by K. Elliger and W. K. Rudolph. Stuttgart, 1983
Bib	*Biblica*
BibInt	*Biblical Interpretation*
BIS	Biblical Interpretation Series

BJRL	*Bulletin of the John Rylands University Library of Manchester*
BNTC	Black's New Testament Commentaries
BRev	*Bible Review*
BTB	*Biblical Theology Bulletin*
BSac	*Bibliotheca sacra*
CBQ	*Catholic Biblical Quarterly*
CBQMS	Catholic Biblical Quarterly Monograph Series
CEV	Contemporary English Version
CJT	*Canadian Journal of Theology*
ConBNT	Coniectanea biblica: New Testament Series
DJG	*Dictionary of Jesus and the Gospels*, edited by J. B. Green and S. McKnight. Downers Grove, 1992
DRev	*Downside Review*
EgT	*Eglise et théologie*
ESV	English Standard Version
ETL	*Ephemerides theologicae lovanienses*
EvT	*Evangelische Theologie*
ExpTim	*Expository Times*
FF	Foundations and Facets
HKNT	Handkommentar zum Neuen Testament
HR	*History of Religions*
HTCNT	Herder's Theological Commentary on the New Testament
HTR	*Harvard Theological Review*
HTS	Harvard Theological Studies
ICC	International Critical Commentary
Int	*Interpretation*
JA	*Journal asiatique*
JBL	*Journal of Biblical Literature*
JECS	*Journal of Early Christian Studies*

JETS — *Journal of the Evangelical Theological Society*
JSNT — *Journal for the Study of the New Testament*
JSNTSup — Journal for the Study of the New Testament: Supplement Series
JSOTSup — Journal for the Study of the Old Testament: Supplement Series
JTS — *Journal of Theological Studies*
LNTS — Library of New Testament Studies
NA^{27} — *Novum Testamentum Graece*, Nestle-Aland, 27th ed.
NAB — New American Bible
NASB — New American Standard Bible
NCB — New Century Bible
Neot — *Neotestamentica*
NET — New English Translation
NHMS — Nag Hammadi and Manichean Studies
NICNT — New International Commentary on the New Testament
NIDNTT — *New International Dictionary of New Testament Theology*, edited by C.olin Brown. 4 vols. Grand Rapids, 1975–1985
NIV — New International Version
NLT — New Living Translation
NovT — *Novum Testamentum*
NovTSup — Supplements to Novum Testamentum
NRSV — New Revised Standard Version
NTD — Das Neue Testament Deutsche
NTS — *New Testament Studies*
OLA — Orientalia lovaniensia analecta
P.Oxy. — Oxyrhynchus Papryi
PRSt — *Perspectives in Religious Studies*
RB — *Revue Biblique*

RevExp	*Review and Expositor*
SBLDS	Society of Biblical Literature Dissertation Series
SBT	Studies in Biblical Theology
SecCent	*Second Century*
SHR	Studies in the History of Religions (supplement to *Numen*)
SJT	*Scottish Journal of Theology*
SNTSMS	Society for New Testament Studies Monograph Series
Str-B	Strack, H. L., and P. Billerbeck., *Kommentar zum Neuen Testament aus Talmud und Midrasch*. 6 vols. Munich, 1922–1961
TDNT	*Theological Dictionary of the New Testament*., Eedited by G. Kittel and G. Friedrich., Ttranslated by G. W. Bromiley. 10 vols. Grand Rapids, 1964–1976
Tg. Neo.	*Targum Neofiti 1*
Tg. Yer.	*Targum Yerusalmi 1*
ThTo	*Theology Today*
TS	*Theological Studies*
TynBul	*Tyndale Bulletin*
UBS[3]	*Aland, K., M. Black, C. M. Martini, B. M. Metzger, A. Wikgren, The Greek New Testament*, United Bible Societies, 3rd ed.
VC	*Vigiliae christianae*
VCSup	Supplements to Vigiliae christianae
WTJ	*Westminster Theological Journal*
WUNT	Wissenschaftliche Untersuchungen zum Neuen Testament
ZNW	*Zeitschrift für die neutestamentliche Wissenschaft und die Kunde der älteren Kirche*

Introduction

In recent years, the *Gospel of Thomas* has been a topic of great interest for biblical scholars and historians of early Christianity, though little consensus has been reached on many of the important issues in Thomasine studies.[1] There is a recent and important trend in the study of the *Gospel of Thomas* that sees the Fourth Gospel as a response to its theology. This hypothesis is beginning to exercise increasing influence in current critical scholarship and demands a careful evaluation of the merits and deficiencies of its arguments. The present study addresses and raises questions about the assumptions upon which this hypothesis rests.

Many of the ideas raised in this current discussion have their origin in the scholarship of Helmut Koester, the first serious voice to suggest that the traditions contained in the *Gospel of Thomas* may have predated and even served as source material for the canonical Gospels. Early in his evaluation of the evidence, Koester set forth several lines of argumentation, suggesting that portions of the Johannine sayings tradition were related to similar sayings found not only in the *Gospel of Thomas* but also in the *Apocryphon of James* and the *Dialogue of the Savior*—two other treatises found at Nag Hammadi.[2] This led to subsequent publications where Koester openly advocated an early dating of the *Gospel of Thomas* and the possibility that earlier forms of sayings from the *Gospel of Thomas* were used by the authors of the canonical

1. Throughout this book when Thomas is italicized it refers to the *Gospel of Thomas* and when not italicized it refers to the character Thomas in the Fourth Gospel.

2. See e.g., Helmut Koester, "Dialog und Spruchüberlieferung." For an expansion of his original thesis, see also "Gnostic Writings as Witnesses." With a few exceptions, scholars did not begin to interact widely with the *Gospel of Thomas* until the early 1960s, yet even as far back as 1965 Koester proclaimed, "New sources from recent discoveries, first of all the (coptic) [*sic*] Gospel of Thomas, must be considered on par with the canonical writings, and they cannot be depreciated by reason of their non-canonical nature" ("ΓΝΩΜΑΙ ΔΙΑΦΟΡΟΙ," 283).

Gospels.[3] Koester's substantive and impressive interaction with a broad range of ancient texts has helped lay the groundwork for a new trajectory in biblical scholarship and has significantly informed the discussion of *Thomas*'s place vis-à-vis the canonical Gospels.[4]

In recent years, two of Koester's former students—Gregory J. Riley and Elaine Pagels—have assumed the mantle, generating both scholarly and popular publications that address the relationship and origins of the *Gospel of Thomas* and the Fourth Gospel.[5] Both Riley and Pagels assume a conflict between the Johannine and Thomasine communities that led to the composition of at least part of the Fourth Gospel. According to both scholars, John's Gospel contains an outward response to certain "heretical" ideas expressed in the *Gospel of Thomas* and is thus consciously anti-Thomasine in its theological outlook.[6] In addition to the publications of Riley and Pagels, April D. DeConick has also written extensively on the relationship between *Thomas* and John, sharing many of the same assumptions as Riley and Pagels.[7]

3. See, for instance, Koester's introductory comments on the *Gospel of Thomas* in James Robinson, *Nag Hammadi Library*, 124–26. For a more recent and developed treatment, see Koester and Patterson, *Ancient Christian Gospels*, 75–124. Here they suggest that the author of the Johannine literature directs a polemic against a number of Jesus traditions located in the *Gospel of Thomas*.

4. In 1971, Koester and James M. Robinson published an important book entitled *Trajectories through Early Christianity*. The book was a compilation of four previously published articles (two by each author) along with four new essays (also two by each author). The volume was driven by the assumption that historical discoveries and developments in our understanding of NT backgrounds render terms like "heresy" and "orthodoxy" inadequate. Rather, an appreciation for the intricate web of continuity and diversity among the early "Christian" communities opens new doors of historical investigation that shed light on the complexity of early Christianity and its many expressions—both kerygmatic and literary.

5. Cf. Riley, *Resurrection Reconsidered*; Pagels, "Exegesis of Genesis 1"; idem, *Beyond Belief*.

6. John's Gospel ultimately became part of the "orthodox" canonical tradition within early Christianity, while the *Gospel of Thomas* did not. Thus, the term "heretical" is used here against the backdrop of that developing "proto-orthodoxy" expressed in the Fourth Gospel.

7. Cf. DeConick, "John Rivals Thomas," 303–11; idem, "'Blessed Are Those,'" 381–98; idem, *Seek to See Him*, 72–73. One of DeConick's more recent publications, *Recovering the Original Gospel of Thomas*, discusses her conception of the "rolling corpus" of the *Gospel of Thomas*. She argues that the Thomas-sayings tradition began with authentic sayings of Jesus and went through a number of accretions before taking on a final form that was influenced by christological developments in the early second century. See also another recent volume by DeConick, *Original Gospel of Thomas in Translation*.

For all three authors, the seemingly negative characterization of Thomas in the Fourth Gospel is an important element in helping them validate their arguments for the existence of such a conflict. The relationship between *Thomas* and John is an important question, but it should be noted at the outset that this study is concerned not with this relationship per se. Rather, this study is concerned to question some elements of the approach undertaken by Riley, Pagels, DeConick, and others who embrace their assumptions. Their theories of gospel origins are based at least partially upon a community conflict that reveals itself through the not-so-subtle "polemic" of Thomas's negative characterization in the Fourth Gospel. Thus, for purposes of both clarity and brevity, the basic position advocated by Riley, Pagels, DeConick, and others will be referred to as the *community-conflict hypothesis* throughout the remainder of this book.

All three scholars make important contributions to the discussion that should not be minimized. However, there are other elements in their respective presentations that should give the interpreter some reason for reservation. The present study proceeds from the conviction that the questions raised concerning Thomas in the Fourth Gospel can and should be asked of other characters in the narrative. A narrative-critical analysis of characterization in the Fourth Gospel can provide insights into the Fourth Gospel's complex web of narrative foci. It can also provide multiple examples where characters are pitted against Jesus for the purpose of allowing the Johannine Jesus to speak authoritatively.

In light of these issues, the present study will proceed as follows: chapter 1 will trace the major movements in the study of the *Gospel of Thomas* and its relationship to the Fourth Gospel, at the same time attempting to situate the community-conflict hypothesis in the overall historical context of Thomasine studies. The discussion there will attempt to demonstrate not only the lack of consensus on many important areas in Thomasine studies, but also that many proposals that seek to identify authoritatively *Thomas's* place in the complex world of early Christianity rest on tenuous footing.

Chapter 2 will outline the suppositions and the methodology that will be applied throughout the remainder of the book. By considering the intricacies of the narrative approach to characterization, this chapter will also lay the foundation for a critique of the use of narrative methodologies by Riley, DeConick, and Pagels.

Chapters 3–6 will apply the previously stated methodology to different characters in the Fourth Gospel. Chapter 3 will focus specifically on the characterization of Thomas in John's Gospel with a view to understanding Thomas's role in relation to the Johannine Jesus. Here I will also interact with the views of Riley, DeConick, and Pagels regarding Thomas's portrayal in the Fourth Gospel. Chapter 4 will apply the same methodology to the character of Peter in John 1, 6, 13, 18, and 21. Chapter 5 will consider other disciples that are presented in a manner similar to Thomas and Peter. This will include a consideration of Philip (John 1, 6, 14), Andrew (John 1, 6), Judas (not Iscariot) (John 14), and the disciples as a representative group (John 4, 11). Chapter 6 will focus on other characters that are not disciples but nevertheless demonstrate the same trait of incomprehension. These include Nicodemus (John 3, 7, 19), the Samaritan woman (John 4), and the sisters Martha and Mary (John 11–12).

The conclusion will seek to develop the overall picture of Johannine characterization that emerges from the previous four chapters. In addition, the discussion will attempt to demonstrate the Fourth Gospel's consistency in using characterization as a means of developing the plot and providing opportunities for the Johannine Jesus to speak authoritatively to the literary audience. The study will conclude by examining the community-conflict hypothesis once again in light of the conclusions of the previous chapters. We turn now to an examination of the history of scholarly research on the *Gospel of Thomas*.

1

Historical Overview

The *Gospel of Thomas*: A Historical Sketch

FOR SOME TIME THE *GOSPEL OF THOMAS* HAS BEEN AT THE CENTER OF serious deliberations among those with interests in the developments of earliest Christianity.[1] Because of its potential to shed light on discussions ranging from trajectories within early Christianity to the most recent quests for the historical Jesus, the *Gospel of Thomas* has achieved importance in the academic community in recent years. However, *Thomas* scholars have not been able to provide a satisfactory answer to three important questions. The first question concerns the date of the earliest composition of the *Gospel of Thomas*. Mutually exclusive theories abound in present scholarship and there appears to be no consensus on the horizon. The second question concerns the relationship of *Thomas* to the canonical Gospels. As with the dating of *Thomas*, prominent scholars promote theories that are incompatible with one another; again a scholarly consensus appears unlikely in the near future. The third question concerns the theological outlook of the *Gospel of Thomas*. This question has sparked as much disagreement as the previous two questions. Together, these three questions raise a number of difficulties for the student of *Thomas*. Complicating matters even further, these questions have not ordinarily been discussed separately, giving rise to a scholarly tendency in which the answers to all three questions are almost inextricably linked. A close examination of the secondary

1. Throughout this book I will use the terms "*Thomas*" and "John" to refer to the *Gospel of Thomas* and the Fourth Gospel, respectively. Each term is used in accord with current scholarly discourse and neither is meant to imply anything with respect to authorship.

literature on the *Gospel of Thomas* reveals that, generally speaking, a given scholar's answer to one of these questions dictates that scholar's conclusions with respect to the other two.

Very early in the academic study of the *Gospel of Thomas*, many scholars assumed that the document's theological outlook was gnostic. A survey of the early literature on *Thomas* reveals that this conclusion was often based on the fact that the *Gospel of Thomas* was found among a group of overtly gnostic texts.[2] This is not as determinative as it was usually portrayed to be. After all, the first known commentary on the Fourth Gospel was written by the second-century gnostic Heracleon, and the Nag Hammadi codices included copies of Plato's *Republic* and the *Sentences* of Sextus—hardly gnostic compositions. Nevertheless, the assumption of *Thomas*'s inherently gnostic outlook has tended to color the perceptions of those scholars who, noticing parallels to the canonical Gospels, assumed *Thomas*'s dependence upon the canonical Gospels and in turn assigned to *Thomas* a date somewhere between the late second and early third centuries.[3] Historically, the perceived interconnection among these three questions can be demonstrated.

Other scholars have followed the approach of Helmut Koester, who sought to establish the antiquity of the *Thomas*-sayings tradition by examining important noncanonical literature. Still others have based

2. Many early works were quick to label *Thomas* as a gnostic or proto-gnostic source. These include, among others: Grant and Freedman, *Secret Sayings of Jesus*; Wilson, *Studies in the Gospel of Thomas*; Gaertner, *Theology of the Gospel According to Thomas*; Kasser, *L'Évangile selon Thomas*; Turner and Montefiore, *Thomas and the Evangelists*; Leipoldt, *Evangelium nach Thomas*; and Summers, *Secret Sayings of the Living Jesus*. The classification of *Thomas* as a gnostic text amounted to, in many instances, a theological knee-jerk reaction, effectively delaying questions that are being more freely discussed in recent dialogues about *Thomas*'s theological outlook.

3. Basing his work on the assumption that *Thomas* was gnostic and later than the canonical Gospels, Gaertner (*Theology of the Gospel According to Thomas*, 35, 42), offered the following conclusions: "Characteristic of many of the logia of the *Gospel of Thomas* is the fact that they *combine* different New Testament sayings of Jesus in a way for which, however, we have no equivalent in the New Testament. For example Logion 14 is a *combination* of sayings from the Sermon on the Mount, Matt. 6, from the Commissioning Discourses, Lk. 10 and Matt. 10, and from the pronouncement on purity and impurity, Mk. 7.15 . . . The occurrence of these '*compound texts*' in the *Gospel of Thomas* must be treated as one element in a process which can be proved to have been very common during the 2nd and 3rd centuries. Furthermore, we ought to take into consideration that these logia may reflect various attempts at *harmonizing the Gospels*" (emphasis added). Gaertner's conclusions are just one example of such thinking among early scholars working on *Thomas*.

their arguments for the antiquity of the *Thomas*-sayings tradition on an examination of earlier Greek fragments found at Oxyrhynchus.[4] In any case, when an early date has been assigned to *Thomas*, that date has been used to demonstrate *Thomas*'s independence from the canonical corpus and then further used to deny a connection to the later theological development of Christian gnosticism.[5] Again, the interconnection of answers to these three questions in the scholarly literature is evident. An awareness of this trend in previous scholarship points to the present need for careful examination of each question on its own terms.

Over its sixty-year history of scholarship, the *Gospel of Thomas* has been identified as a late anthological compilation, belonging to a period sometime between the second and third centuries,[6] and a very early

4. In the late 1890s, a number of previously unknown *logia Iesou* were discovered among the Greek Oxyrhynchus papyri. B. P. Grenfell and Hunt found Greek fragments that turned out to be *logia* from a Greek version of the *Gospel of Thomas*. They published their findings in a pamphlet entitled *Logia Iesou, Sayings of Our Lord*. The French scholar H.-Ch. Puech ultimately made the connection between the Greek *logia* and the Coptic *Gospel of Thomas*. He found that *P.Oxy.* 1 contained fragments of *logia* 26 through 33; *P.Oxy.* 654 contained fragments of *Thomas*'s incipit through *logion* 7 as well as *logia* 24 and 36; *P.Oxy.* 655 contained fragments of *logia* 36 through 39. See Puech's detailed study, "Une collection des paroles de Jésus." Both Emil Wendling (*Die Entstehung des Marcus-Evangeliums*, 53–56) and Rudolf Bultmann (*History of the Synoptic Tradition*, 31) sought to demonstrate the more primitive nature of the logion from *POxy.* 1, 6 vis-à-vis the synoptic version found in Mark 6:1–6. For a comprehensive discussion of the *logia* and an extensive bibliography, see Fitzmyer, *Essays on the Semitic Background*, 355–433.

5. Stevan Davies has been a pioneer in seeking to establish all three of these views. In his book, *The Gospel of Thomas and Christian Wisdom*, Davies presented the first substantive challenge to the view that *Thomas* was a gnostic text. In addition to this, he proclaimed in 1992, "A *consensus* is emerging in American scholarship that the *Gospel of Thomas* is a *text independent of the synoptics* and that it was *compiled in the mid to late first century*. It appears to be roughly as valuable a primary source for the teachings of Jesus as Q, and perhaps more so than the Gospels of Mark and John. Today many of those seriously concerned with the historical Jesus, with determining the most original forms of the sayings of Jesus, or with the study of the parables turn to the *Gospel of Thomas* for information as readily as to the Synoptics" ("Christology and Protology," 663; emphasis added). While Davies's use of the term "consensus" overstates the case, the early dating of *Thomas* as well as the independence of *Thomas* from the canonical corpus are both widely accepted conclusions among a significant cross-section of critical scholarship.

6. In his introductory comments on the *Gospel of Thomas*, Beate Blatz writes, "We can only say that *there is much in favour of the view that Thomas originated about the middle of the second century* in eastern Syria" (Schneemelcher, *New Testament Apocrypha*, 1:113; (emphasis added). Blatz does allow, however, for the possibility of

text, easily placed within the 70s to 80s CE.[7] In addition, *Thomas* has been thought to be dependent on the Synoptics,[8] the Gospel of John,[9] and even the Diatessaron.[10] Other scholars have identified *Thomas* as independent of the canonical Gospels[11] and, in some instances, as source material for the canonical Gospels.[12] As regards its compositional tongue, it has been argued that *Thomas* was originally written in Greek,[13] Coptic,[14] or in Syriac or Aramaic.[15] As regards its genre and theological outlook, *Thomas* has been described as a gnostic or proto-

a first-century dating. Many early writers on the *Gospel of Thomas* placed the document in the second century. For instance, Gaertner (*Theology of the Gospel According to Thomas*, 271) comments that "[h]itherto there has been a fair measure of agreement over the date AD 140–150, and no one has shown any desire to refer it to any earlier period." More recently Marvin Meyer (*Gospel of Thoma*, 10) has written, "Since the earliest of the Greek Oxyrhynchus fragments has been assigned a date of around 200 CE, the Gospel of Thomas must have been composed during the second century or even the latter part of the first century CE."

7. Patterson, *Gospel of Thomas and Jesus*, 113–20. Many current publications addressing the relationship between *Thomas* and the Synoptics have sought to challenge the previously held consensus that Mark is the earliest gospel and have thus replaced Mark with *Thomas*. This jockeying for chronological primacy has been a foundational element of many of the more recent publications arising from the so-called Third Quest for the historical Jesus.

8. This was true of many of the earlier studies cited above; see n. 2.

9. Sell, "Johannine Traditions in Logion 61," 24–25.

10. Quispel, "L'Évangile selon Thomas"; idem, *Tatian and the Gospel of Thomas*; idem, *Makarius, das Thomasevangelium*. Quispel was also adamant that the *Gospel of Thomas* was not a gnostic document. See also Perrin, *Thomas and Tatian*. Differing slightly from Quispel's original thesis, Perrin posits *Thomas*'s indirect dependence on the Synoptics by way of the Syriac Diatessaron. Perrin also argues for an original Syriac version of the *Gospel of Thomas*.

11. As stated above, much of this thinking goes back to the scholarship of Helmut Koester. More recent publications, following Davies's *Gospel of Thomas and Christian Wisdom*, argue for the independence of *Thomas* from the Synoptics and John.

12. Davies discusses at length Mark's dependence on the *Gospel of Thomas*. See his article "Mark's Use of the Gospel of Thomas."

13. While not a true "consensus" position, this view currently enjoys fairly wide acceptance. Most *Thomas* scholars view the Oxyrhynchus finds as evidence of a Greek *Vorlage* for the *Gospel of Thomas*.

14. Garitte, "'Logoi' d'Oxyrhynque."

15. See, for instance, Guillamont, "Sémitismes dans les logia de Jésus"; idem, "Sémitismes dans l'Évangile selon Thomas"; Quispel "Gospel of Thomas and the New Testament"; idem, "Some Remarks on the Gospel of Thomas"; Drijvers, "Facts and Problems"; Layton, *Gnostic Scriptures*, 377; Perrin, "NHC II,2 and the Oxyrhynchus Fragments."

gnostic text,[16] a type of Jewish-Christian wisdom literature,[17] a Jewish-Christian gospel tradition,[18] and an example of Christian mysticism.[19] In short, "consensus" is a term rarely used with confidence where the *Gospel of Thomas* is concerned.[20] In fact, it is difficult to imagine a topic of greater scholarly importance with less agreement on the most important of issues. An awareness of this fact helps to stress to an even greater degree the very delicate nature of many current attempts to locate the *Gospel of Thomas* definitively within early Christianity.

The present study is concerned with a recent scholarly trend that seeks to establish a concrete connection between the *Gospel of Thomas* and the Fourth Gospel. Specifically, some scholars have sought to identify a *Sitz im Leben* in the Johannine and Thomasine communities where mutually exclusive theologies are in competition with each other. Therefore, a more focused historical overview of scholarly views on the relationship of *Thomas* and John will help situate the present discussion in a wider historical framework. The following outline will proceed chronologically through the history of Thomasine scholarship, noting major developments in, and departures from, consensus views.

The Relationship between *Thomas* and John: A Historical Sketch

In 1959 the first English translation of the *Gospel of Thomas* was published.[21] Much of the early discussion of the *Gospel of Thomas* revolved around its relationship to the synoptic Gospels. However, in 1962 Raymond Brown published an important article devoted to examin-

16. Grant and Freedman, *Secret Sayings of Jesus*; Wilson, *Studies in the Gospel of Thomas*; Gaertner, *Theology of the Gospel According to Thomas*; Kasser, *L'Évangile selon Thomas*; Turner and Montefiore, *Thomas and the Evangelists*; Leipoldt, *Evangelium nach Thomas*; and Summers, *Secret Sayings of the Living Jesus*.

17. The influential work of Stevan Davies (*Gospel of Thomas and Christian Wisdom*) is the reference point for any serious discussion of this topic. Davies's convincing arguments offered the first serious alternative to understanding *Thomas* as a gnostic document. See also the pertinent sections in Siverstev, "Gospel of Thomas and Early Stages."

18. Quispel, "Qumran, John and Jewish Christianity," 144–46.

19. DeConick, *Seek to See Him*.

20. An ascetically oriented, Syrian provenance for the *Gospel of Thomas* is one area of near consensus in current Thomasine studies.

21. Guillamont et al., *Gospel According to Thomas*.

ing the relationship between *Thomas* and the Fourth Gospel.[22] Brown dealt extensively with the language and images of the Coptic *Gospel of Thomas* and the Greek version of the Fourth Gospel. His guiding observation was that the literature generated to that point on the *Gospel of Thomas* had failed to address what he saw as the very important question of the relationship between the two works.[23] Citing this lacuna as his motivation for writing, Brown went on to survey fifty-five logia from the *Gospel of Thomas* that appeared to have verbal, conceptual, or theological parallels with the Fourth Gospel.[24] From there he attempted to elucidate further the relationship between the two works. He concluded that the Johannine parallels in the *Gospel of Thomas* were evidence of *Thomas*'s dependence upon the Fourth Gospel. But that dependence, he argued, was not direct. Instead, he postulated that the *Gospel of Thomas* was influenced by Johannine teaching through at least one and possibly more "Gnostic, incipiently Gnostic, or semi-Gnostic" intermediaries.[25]

However useful Brown's treatment may otherwise have been, his discussion was tainted by the unsubstantiated assertion that *Thomas* was written later than the Fourth Gospel. Brown has been criticized by a number of scholars for taking such an important question for granted without offering proper validation.[26] While he was merely reflecting the consensus of the day regarding the later date of *Thomas*, Brown's

22. Brown, "Gospel of Thomas and St. John's Gospel."

23. He did cite Grant and Freedman, *Secret Sayings of Jesus*; Doresse, *L'Évangile selon Thomas*; and Kasser, *L'Évangile selon Thomas* as laying the initial foundation for his study inasmuch as each provided lists of potential parallels between the *Gospel of Thomas* and the Fourth Gospel.

24. Brown was also interested, but only peripherally, in *logia* that paralleled other portions of the corpus belonging to the "Johannine school," specifically 1 John and Revelation.

25. Brown, "Gospel of Thomas and St. John's Gospel," 177.

26. Davies (*Gospel of Thomas and Christian Wisdom*, 106–16) evaluates Brown's article at length, roundly criticizing his assumptions. Likewise, Gregory Riley (*Resurrection Reconsidered,* 2–3) notes that "Brown assumes for no stated reason that the Gospel of Thomas is a work later than the Gospel of John, and then proceeds to 'demonstrate' its dependence on John. Yet so great are the difficulties in finding dependence that he concludes that there were at least two, and perhaps several intermediaries between John and the Gospel of Thomas." He comments further that "his investigation and conclusions show no *direct* influence at all. *Indirect* influence through two (or several) intermediaries can be claimed for almost any two similar texts of debatable date, in either direction of dependence." For an outline of the more important criticisms of Brown's approach, see Dunderberg, "Thomas' I-Sayings and the Gospel of John," 35–38.

failure to demonstrate this assertion left the door wide open for later criticisms as well as suspicion of his findings regarding *Thomas* and John. However, for at least a decade and a half Brown's study, despite its flaws, served as the starting point for every subsequent discussion of the *Gospel of Thomas* and the Fourth Gospel.

In the early years after the publication of Brown's article, very little was written on the relationship between *Thomas* and the Fourth Gospel, though several writers did assume, affirm, or seek to expand Brown's original thesis. For instance, in a 1969 article devoted to text-critical issues in *Thomas*, Miroslav Marcovich concluded by writing that "the [*Gospel of Thomas*] was inspired by John, as R. E. Brown has shown, and probably to an extent *even greater than he recognized*."[27]

Using Brown's article as his starting point, Jesse Sell published an article in 1980 building largely upon his own 1976 dissertation, in which he argued that there were eight sayings in *Thomas* that revealed a dependence upon the Fourth Gospel.[28] Sell, however, went a step beyond Brown in arguing for *Thomas*'s direct dependence upon the Gospel of John. He wrote, "I am convinced that knowledge of much of the Johannine tradition was almost certainly one of the *many* factors which influenced the development of the text of GT . . . I find echoes of fifty-three separate verses from *seventeen different chapters of John*, strongly reflected in these eight sections of GT."[29] Still, by 1980, no serious rebuttal of Brown or treatment of the evidence he surveyed was attempted, as Sell himself mentioned at the outset of his article.[30] In the early 1980s, however, scholars began not only to question Brown's approach but also to reject his conclusions.

In 1983, Stevan Davies published his groundbreaking work, *The Gospel of Thomas and Christian Wisdom*, in which he challenged many of the major consensus positions held at that time. He questioned the idea that *Thomas* was a gnostic document as well as the notion that *Thomas* was a later work dependent on the canonical Gospels. Most im-

27. Marcovich, "Textual Criticism on the Gospel of Thomas," 74; emphasis added.

28. Sell, "Johannine Traditions"; idem, "Study of the Self-Predication Statements." The eight *logia* identified by Sell are *Gos. Thom.* prologue, 8, 13, 28, 38, 43, 91, 92.

29. Sell, "Johannine Traditions," 25, 27.

30. "The enormous secondary literature on [the *Gospel of Thomas*] contains only one detailed study of the possible relationship between GT and the Fourth Gospel [viz., Brown's]" (Sell, "Johannine Traditions," 25).

portantly for the present study, he disputed the claim that the *Gospel of Thomas* was influenced by the Fourth Gospel. Interacting in some detail with Brown's thesis, Davies considered Brown's suggestions as to how *Thomas* could have been influenced by Johannine ideas. He then concluded that Brown was in error about the Johannine impact on *Thomas* and theorized that the *Gospel of Thomas* had its origins in the nascent Johannine community. His conclusions are worth citing at length:

> If we assume that the sayings of Jesus in the Gospel of John were in part derived from sayings of Jesus such as are found in the synoptics, then the oral preaching of the early Johannine community must have contained sayings of Jesus modified in a Johannine way, but less modified than the sayings now preserved in John. One would expect then that a document which remained from the period of the oral preaching of the Johannine communities and which Thomas used would have been a sayings collection, as Thomas is . . . In fact, if we try to imagine what a sayings collection underlying Thomas from an early stage of the Johannine community would look like, it would look very much like Thomas itself . . . There are ideas in Thomas that do not appear in John, and vice versa. It may, however, be correct to see in the later Johannine writings a developed and transformed version of Thomasine Christianity. Thomas may have been utilized in early Johannine preaching, before Johannine Christianity reached its full development and before the detachment of the Johannine trajectory from the synoptic trajectory took place.[31]

Therefore for Davies, not only does *Thomas* not depend upon John, but the similarities between the two gospels can be accounted for by the assumption that early Johannine preaching drew largely upon the sayings tradition reflected in the *Gospel of Thomas*. Davies's work was indeed important for Thomasine scholarship in general as well as for the discussion of the relationship of *Thomas* to the Fourth Gospel.

So far, our historical sketch has covered the span of twenty-four years from the first English translation of *Thomas* in 1959 to the work of Stevan Davies in 1983. During that period other developments in the study of Christian origins were yielding ideas that would raise challenging questions about the origin of the entire canonical-sayings tradition.

31. Davies, *Gospel of Thomas and Christian Wisdom*, 115–16.

The influence of Helmut Koester on this discussion has already been briefly traced above. His impact on the dialogue is significant and extends as far back as 1965. During the period surveyed, there was a steady shift from the view that *Thomas* was written later than and dependent upon the Fourth Gospel to a view that the Fourth Gospel is later than and possibly dependent upon *Thomas*. This brings us to Riley, DeConick, and Pagels, who not only build upon the foundation laid by Koester and James M. Robinson but also capitalize on the opportunity afforded by the current state of the debate (that is, the shift to thinking of *Thomas* as an early document in a position to influence the Johannine-sayings tradition).[32] Though Pagels has been addressing related topics in her publications for a number of years, her specific focus on John and *Thomas* is recent. Therefore, it is appropriate to continue our chronological survey with Riley's work.

Riley's "Debate over Resurrection"

The publication of Gregory Riley's dissertation in 1995 opened a new phase in the discussion of John's relationship to *Thomas*.[33] Riley's treatment brought many of the theories related to gospel origins to the forefront and explicitly built his arguments upon that framework. No longer was the idea of an early Christian conflict engendering a polemical treatise relegated to a passing suggestion or discussion in a footnote. Rather, Riley's work helped establish this as a serious position among a broader range of biblical scholars. Whereas previous discussions had dealt extensively with important noncanonical literature by making the occasional connection with canonical literature, Riley rooted the conflict in the very heart of Christian "orthodoxy," the Gospel of John.[34]

In his treatment of this topic Riley concentrates on what he regards as competing views of the resurrection, attempting to demonstrate that

32. Though Riley, DeConick, and Pagels have offered the most extensive presentations of this theory, a handful of other American scholars who argue along similar lines. See, for instance, Johnson, "Gospel of Thomas 76:3 and Canonical Parallels," 322–24; Valantasis, *Gospel of Thomas*, 19; and Attridge, "'Seeking' and 'Asking,'" 295–302. For a comprehensive overview of this entire discussion focused on answering the question of the John-*Thomas* relationship, see Dunderberg, *Beloved Disciple in Conflict?*

33. Riley, *Resurrection Reconsidered.*

34. The Fourth Gospel played a central role in the development of Trinitarian and christological doctrines in the early church and was used extensively by the early church fathers and the ecumenical councils.

the *Gospel of Thomas* refutes the idea of the bodily resurrection of Jesus as well as the eschatological bodily resurrection of Jesus's followers.[35] This is countered, he argues, by the Fourth Gospel's emphasis on the bodily resurrection of both Jesus and his followers. The outward teaching on bodily resurrection in the Gospel of John is therefore, for Riley, a conscious response to this glaring error in the *Gospel of Thomas*. He argues further that in the Fourth Gospel Thomas is consistently portrayed in a negative light—the clearest example of this characterization occurring in the resurrection narrative (viz., the "Doubting Thomas" passage of John 20). This overall characterization, he says, reveals a Johannine polemic against Thomas and the flawed resurrection theology embraced by his community. Riley concludes that the two communities "were in close spiritual proximity to one another" and in continual dialogue about their differing theological presentations.[36] This, he writes, accounts for both the similarities and the differences found in their respective theologies.

For Riley, the Fourth Gospel clearly directs a polemic against two main characters: John the Baptist and Thomas. He sees the presentation of John the Baptist in John's Gospel as a symbol of the conflict between the followers of John and the proto-orthodox followers of Jesus. In the same way, "Doubting Thomas" is a character created by John and reveals a theological conflict between the Johannine Christians and the Thomasine Christians.[37] The supposed "anti-Baptist" polemic of the Fourth Gospel has been discussed for some time, but for Riley, John the Baptist and Thomas are the two paradigmatic characters placed strategically in key locations of the Fourth Gospel for polemical purposes.

One of the more enigmatic passages Riley addresses is the saying in *Gos. Thom.* 71, ⲡⲉϫⲉ ⲓ̅ⲥ̅ ϫⲉ ϯⲛⲁϣⲟⲣϣ̅ⲣ̅ ⲙ̅ⲡⲉⲉⲓⲏⲉⲓ ⲁⲩⲱ ⲙ̅ⲛ̅ ⲗⲁⲁⲩ ⲛⲁϣⲕⲟⲧϥ, "Jesus said, 'I will destroy this house and no one will be able to rebuild it.'"[38] There are parallels to this saying in the canonical tradition, and Riley interprets the differences between the *Thomas* saying and the

35. Riley is also concerned, but only peripherally, with the *Book of Thomas* and the *Acts of Thomas*—other literature arising from the *Thomas* tradition within early Christianity.

36. Riley, *Resurrection Reconsidered*, 177.

37. Ibid., 74–82, esp. 78.

38. All translations of ancient texts in this study are the author's unless otherwise indicated.

Johannine parallel in light of the conflict he envisions.[39] Examining this logion in comparison with the temple saying in John 2:19 ("Jesus answered them, 'Destroy this temple and I will raise it in three days'"), Riley notes a number of similarities and differences.

In both versions, Riley begins, the saying is attributed to Jesus. However, in John 2:19 the "destroyers" are "the Jews" to whom Jesus is speaking, in contrast to the *Thomas* version where Jesus himself is the "destroyer." Another difference is found in the use of the word ΗЄΙ, "house," in *Thomas* in place of ναός, "temple," in John. A third important difference between the texts is the missing reference to "three days" in the *Thomas* version. Riley interprets these similarities and differences in the two versions as evidence of an ongoing dispute in the sayings tradition over the idea of literal bodily resurrection. He writes,

> Jesus is the destroyer in *Thomas*. Again, this is the heart of the revolutionary charge, and the central hazardous point. John, in allowing Jesus to utter the saying, changed the role of destroyer from Jesus to "the Jews": Jesus tells the Jewish authorities to destroy the temple. *Thomas* allows Jesus to claim directly that he will destroy. This again points to a non-literal meaning for the saying.[40]

Essentially, Riley contends that a Jesus saying related to the expectation of Jesus's bodily resurrection began to circulate in early Christian circles; subsequently, *Thomas* Christians, in an effort to deny the bodily resurrection of Jesus, altered that saying to reflect the Thomasine idea of a spiritual resurrection. Then, the Johannine tradition constructed the figure of Thomas to attack this idea explicitly, while also addressing it implicitly in texts like John 2:19. Thus, for Riley, the Fourth Gospel shows an awareness of *Thomas's* theology and more importantly responds to and attempts to counter teachings in the *Thomas*-sayings tradition.[41]

39. Parallel sayings are found six different places in the canonical literature: Mark 14:58; 15:29; Matt 26:61; 27:40; John 2:19; and Acts 6:14.

40. Riley, *Resurrection Reconsidered*, 148–49.

41. Davies raises a number of important objections in his critical review for *RBL* of Riley's *Resurrection Reconsidered*. Davies builds his critique upon the observation that Riley's argument is rooted in a "complex and highly speculative thesis" (n.p.).

DeConick's "Dispute over Salvation"

In an essay written and delivered roughly contemporaneously with Riley's dissertation, but not formally published until 1997, April D. DeConick argued similarly to what Riley presented in his dissertation. Seeing the Johannine characterization of Thomas as a "fool," a "dunce," and a "faithless one," she too argued for a community conflict.[42] Working backwards from her conclusion of Johannine-Thomasine conflict, she outlined the dispute more fully in 2001 in an essay entitled, "John Rivals Thomas: From Community Conflict to Gospel Narrative."[43] There she wrote that the Fourth Evangelist's "criticism of Thomas specifically among the disciples is probably not arbitrary given the fact the Gospel of Thomas promotes a type of vision mysticism . . . [I]t is likely that [the Fourth Evangelist's] stories about Thomas are dramatizations of an actual dialogue in which the Johannine Community was engaged with the Thomas group."[44] As with Riley's view, DeConick sees Thomas's appearance in the narrative as evidence of John's polemical stance against the sayings tradition behind the *Gospel of Thomas*.

While DeConick disagrees with Riley's characterization of the conflict between the two communities as focused on resurrection, she nevertheless asserts a very real conflict between the two.[45] For DeConick, the root of the conflict (or "discursive field" of their dispute) is soteriological.[46] Specifically, she writes that the Fourth Gospel polemicizes against a *Thomas* tradition that promotes the idea of disciples seeking visions through ecstatic ascent. This is, she writes, at odds with the Johannine teaching on the necessity of faith apart from sight and is clear evidence of John's response to the *Thomas*-sayings tradition.

DeConick argues that a knowledge of mystical traditions stood behind sayings 15, 27, 37, 50, 59, 83, and 84 of the *Gospel of Thomas*.

42. See her discussion in DeConick, "Blessed Are Those Who Have Not Seen," 387–89.

43. Idem, "John Rivals Thomas," 303–11.

44. Ibid., 307.

45. DeConick ("Blessed Are Those," 391) writes: "The main issue in all three of these [Thomas] episodes [in the Fourth Gospel] is one of *identity*, not Jesus' corporeality as some have suggested." The accompanying footnote references Riley's *Resurrection Reconsidered* as the most recent work offering this purportedly mistaken suggestion.

46. DeConick distinguishes between the wider "religio-social horizon," or the specific religious community John is concerned to dispute, and the "discursive field," or the particular point of conflict between the two groups ("Blessed Are Those," 383).

Specifically, saying 59 (ⲡⲉϫⲉ ⲓ̅ⲥ̅ ϫⲉ ϭⲱϣ̄ⲧ ⲛ̄ⲥⲁ ⲡⲉⲧⲟⲛϩ ϩⲱⲥ ⲉⲧⲉⲧⲛ̄ ⲟⲛϩ ϩⲓⲛⲁ ϫⲉ ⲛⲉⲧⲙ̄ ⲙⲟⲩ ⲁⲩⲱ ⲛ̄ⲧⲉⲧⲛ̄ ϣⲓⲛⲉ ⲉⲛⲁⲩ ⲉⲣⲟϥ ⲁⲩⲱ ⲧⲉⲧⲛⲁϣ ϭⲙϭⲟⲙ ⲁⲛ ⲉⲛⲁⲩ; "Jesus said, 'Look at the Living One while you are alive lest you die and seek to see Him and are unable to do so'") is a paradigmatic passage for DeConick. She writes that this saying reflects a pre-mortem experience that "may anticipate death or an eschatological journey but which must be achieved in the believer's lifetime."[47] She sees four specific passages in the Fourth Gospel as direct condemnations of this element in *Thomas*'s theology. Specifically, John 1:18 ("No one has ever seen God"), 3:13 ("No one has ascended into heaven except he who descended from heaven"), 5:37 ("The Father who sent me has himself witnessed concerning me; you have never heard his voice nor seen him"), and 6:46 ("No one has seen the Father except the one who is from the Father; he has seen the Father") are supposed to represent explicit polemical responses to this aspect of *Thomas*'s theology.[48]

Much like Riley, DeConick sees the culmination of John's anti-*Thomas* polemic in the negative characterization of Thomas in the Fourth Gospel. The basis for DeConick's conclusions can be found on the lips of the Johannine Jesus in John 20:29: "Blessed are they who *have not seen* and *yet have believed*"—a clear response, she argues, to Thomas's declaration that seeing is believing.[49]

Pagels's "Disagreement over Creation"

The publications of Elaine Pagels on the relationship between *Thomas* and John follow chronologically those of both Riley and DeConick, even though her place in the broader discussion extends much farther back than either of these two scholars. Though some of her more recent publications focus specifically on the relationship between the *Gospel of Thomas* and the Gospel of John, Pagels has been generating important works based upon theories of early Christian conflict for more than twenty-five years. In 1979, she published the acclaimed work *The Gnostic Gospels*, where she argued at length that many intra-Christian conflicts could be seen when examining the Nag Hammadi literature

47. Idem, "John Rivals Thomas," 305.

48. Idem, "Blessed Are Those," 382.

49. Ibid., 390–91; emphasis added.

against the NT writings.[50] She found that much early Christian literature, both gnostic and orthodox, was replete with polemics directed at other "Christian" sects that held differing theological views. She concludes the book by writing,

> It is the winners who write history—their way. No wonder, then, that the viewpoint of the successful majority has dominated all traditional accounts of the origin of Christianity. Ecclesiastical Christians first defined the terms (naming themselves "orthodox" and their opponents "heretics"); then they proceeded to demonstrate—at least to their own satisfaction—that their triumph was historically inevitable, or, in religious terms, "guided by the Holy Spirit." But the discoveries at Nag Hammadi reopen fundamental questions. They suggest that Christianity might have developed in very different directions—or that Christianity as we know it might not have survived at all. Had Christianity remained multiform, it might well have disappeared from history, along with dozens of rival religious cults of antiquity.[51]

In some of her more recent work, Pagels builds upon this thinking and shares some of the important conclusions that are found in the works of both Riley and DeConick. Specifically, she applies this understanding of multiform expressions of Christianity to the relationship between the *Gospel of Thomas* and the Fourth Gospel and finds a conflict between the two groups rooted in a different theological approach to Genesis 1.

In a 1999 article, she expands on the community conflict envisioned by Riley and DeConick by finding yet another area of anti-*Thomas* sentiment in the Fourth Gospel. She sees a Johannine polemic against Thomasine Christianity rooted in competing views of the creation narrative.[52] According to Pagels, the overall message of *Thomas* is rooted in its underlying exegetical approach to the creation narrative. The prologue of John's Gospel, she argues, is a polemical response to *Thomas*'s incorrect (by Johannine standards) theological understanding of Genesis 1. She writes,

> We do not know, of course, whether or not John actually read the text we call the *Gospel of Thomas*; but comparison of the

50. Pagels, *Gnostic Gospels*.

51. Ibid., 142.

52. Pagels, "Exegesis of Genesis 1."

> Johannine prologue with the above-mentioned cluster of Thomas sayings suggests that he knew—and thoroughly disagreed with—the type of exegesis offered in Thomas. As we suggest, John's author not only was aware of this clash of traditions but actively engaged in polemic against specific patterns of Genesis exegesis he intended his prologue to refute.[53]

For Pagels, John takes issue not only with *Thomas*'s theological understanding of Genesis 1, but most especially with *Thomas*'s exegesis of the creation narrative. Like Riley and DeConick, her view pits the two gospels (and the two communities that stand behind them) in fundamental theological disagreement with each other.

Pagels sees references to the Genesis creation account in *Thomas* sayings 4, 11, 18, 19, 37, 49, 50, 77, 83, 84, and 85.[54] She also finds allusions in sayings 22, 24, 61, and 70.[55] Her coverage of the topic proceeds through a number of the above sayings in an effort to provide a comprehensive look at *Thomas*'s exegesis of Genesis 1.

Basing her approach on the assumption that the *Gospel of Thomas* has a carefully ordered arrangement, she begins with the promise in *Thomas*'s first logion ("whoever finds the meaning of these sayings will not taste death") and proceeds to draw out *Thomas*'s systematic—though not syllogistic—teaching on the restoration of creation.[56] Further, her exegesis is specifically rooted in a view that *Thomas* intends readers to pursue a baptismal ritual that will restore the initiate to a form of Adamic paradise.[57] After systematically examining the various Genesis references in *Thomas*, she concludes,

> Our evidence suggests, then, that Thomas's theology and anthropology do not depend upon some presupposed, generic "gnostic myth." Instead, as Schenke previously suggested and subsequent research has confirmed, the source of this religious

53. Ibid., 479.

54. Ibid., 481.

55. Ibid.

56. She writes, "Let us begin from the opening of Thomas's Gospel, adopting the hypothesis that the sayings are not randomly arranged, but carefully ordered to lead one through a process of seeing and finding 'the interpretation of these sayings' (log. 1). This is not to suggest, however, that the author follows an obvious or syllogistic rationale" (ibid.).

57. Pagels's basis for this assumption is found in the conclusions offered by Smith, "Garments of Shame."

> conviction is, quite simply, exegesis of Genesis 1—and, as we have seen, exegesis that follows a pattern both widely known as varied in the ancient world. Such exegesis connects the *eikōn* of Gen 1:26–27 with the primordial light (or: light/*anthrōpos* of Gen 1:3), to show that the divine image implanted at creation enables humankind to find—by means of baptism—the way back to its origin in the mystery of primordial creation.[58]

These conclusions provide her with the basis upon which to claim that John's prologue represents a polemic against Genesis exegesis adopted by the community associated with Thomas. Thus, there is found yet another area of implicit early Christian, and specifically Johannine-Thomasine, disagreement in the pages of the Fourth Gospel.

Although it is not evident in her discussion of Genesis exegesis in John and *Thomas*, Pagels agrees with Riley and DeConick on the explicit literary evidence of John's anti-Thomas polemic. In her 2003 bestseller *Beyond Belief*, she develops her portrait of the community conflict in forty-three pages, concluding with a discussion of Thomas's negative characterization in John.[59] She concludes that "John may have felt some satisfaction writing this scene [viz., the 'Doubting Thomas' passage]; for here he shows Thomas giving up his search for experiential truth—his "unbelief"—to confess what John sees as the truth of his gospel: the message would not be lost on Thomas Christians."[60] Once again, Thomas appears to be the theological "whipping boy" for the proto-orthodox author of the Fourth Gospel.

Synthesis of the Community-Conflict Position

While differing a bit in their respective presentations, Riley, DeConick, and Pagels all agree on several fundamental points: (1) the Thomasine and Johannine communities were embroiled in disputes over the person and message of Jesus; (2) these disputes are evident in the polemical stance of the Fourth Gospel toward multiple elements of *Thomas*'s teaching; (3) at least part of the Fourth Gospel was written in response to certain elements of *Thomas*'s theology; and (4) this anti-*Thomas* polemic is most clearly seen in the negative portrayal of Thomas in the Fourth Gospel. This final point represents the clearest and most important evidence of

58. Pagels, "Exegesis of Genesis 1," 488.

59. Pagels, *Beyond Belief*, 30–73.

60. Ibid., 72.

John's anti-*Thomas* polemic, though each scholar makes a sustained case for other evidence in the Fourth Gospel. In the end, the case for a John-*Thomas* conflict cannot be made apart from each scholar's view on the role of the Thomas character in the Fourth Gospel.

The consideration of these three scholars and their views brings our historical overview to the present day. Thus, from at least 1995 to the present, the view that John's Gospel is, or contains, a conscious response to the *Gospel of Thomas* has been gaining momentum, has enjoyed a hearing among biblical scholars and historians of early Christianity, and is growing in influence among American scholars.[61]

The foregoing historical sketch was undertaken with the purpose of introducing the community-conflict hypothesis advocated by Riley, DeConick, and Pagels, and situating that hypothesis in the overall context of *Thomas* studies.[62] Before moving forward the work of one more scholar must be introduced into the discussion.

Ismo Dunderberg and the Beloved Disciple

To this point the most comprehensive scholarly work engaging this recent theory has been that of Ismo Dunderberg. In a series of articles[63] that subsequently became the basis for his book *The Beloved Disciple in Conflict?*, Dunderberg drew together the arguments of

61. Dunderberg (*Beloved Disciple in Conflict*, 5) comments that this view has failed to catch on among European scholars.

62. Two additional studies that were omitted from the above overview deserve brief mention. These works have been separated because they are difficult to situate in the context of the categories provided in the discussion. Both Hans-Martin Schenke ("Function and Background of the Beloved Disciple") and James H. Charlesworth (*Beloved Disciple*) have written in order to demonstrate a concrete connection between the Beloved Disciple and the Johannine figure named Thomas. The conclusions offered by these two works have not found widespread acceptance in the academic community, but their intriguing suggestions deserve brief consideration. While both works argue for a clear connection between Thomas and the Beloved Disciple, the two authors go about it quite differently. Schenke argues that the Beloved Disciple is a "redactional fiction who functions to give the Fourth Gospel the appearance of being authenticated and written by an eyewitness" ("Function and Background," 116). Charlesworth argues that the Beloved Disciple is a historical person who should be equated with the disciple known as Thomas (*Beloved Disciple*, 418–19). For a systematic consideration of the arguments posed by both scholars, see Dunderberg, "Thomas and the Beloved Disciple."

63. Material from his articles "John and Thomas in Conflict?," "Beloved Disciple in John," "Thomas' I-Sayings and the Gospel of John," and "Thomas and the Beloved Disciple" was reworked and constitutes the substantive discussion of the book.

Riley, DeConick, Pagels in an attempt to provide a comprehensive answer to the question of *Thomas*'s relationship to the Fourth Gospel. However, in his analysis Dunderberg shows more concern for historical issues, and his engagement in literary discussions focuses more on the potential interrelationships of the Gospels of John and *Thomas*. He makes much of the role of a Beloved Disciple in the two gospel traditions but focuses very little on specific literary and theological issues as they develop in the Fourth Gospel.

The approach taken here is steadfastly concerned with characterization in the Fourth Gospel, and though Dunderberg's approach is different in focus his work largely serves as the impetus for the present study. At one turn of his discussion he writes, "[T]he Johannine picture of Thomas is negative, but in a manner similar to that of most other figures of the Johannine story world. Thomas is not the only follower of Jesus in John who understands him poorly; most other characters do this as well. Should we, then, posit early Christian groups behind all other followers of Jesus rebuked by him?"[64] He correctly notes that many characters in the Fourth Gospel have difficulties understanding Jesus, but he makes no attempt to demonstrate this. This passing suggestion raises interesting questions to which Dunderberg never returns, and since he makes no attempt to validate this assertion, it is my aim to further his thesis by providing a systematic study of uncomprehending characters in the Fourth Gospel. Thus, in what follows I proceed under the conviction that Dunderberg's rejection of the community-conflict hypothesis is basically correct and can be bolstered by an examination of the other uncomprehending characters of the Fourth Gospel. This study does not intend to be the final word in the John-*Thomas* debate as much as it seeks to build upon the scholarship and helpful suggestions provided by Dunderberg. Thus, the narrative work that follows is meant to be of benefit to those working on the John-*Thomas* question as well as those applying literary methods to the study of the Fourth Gospel.

Now that the major assumptions of the community-conflict hypothesis have been outlined against the wider backdrop of *Thomas* scholarship in general, and the contributions of Dunderberg in particular, it is possible to proceed to a discussion of the methodological approach that will be used throughout the remainder of this study.

64. Dunderberg, *Beloved Disciple in Conflict?*, 66.

2

Characterization and the Fourth Gospel

In the previous chapter I analyzed the views of Riley, DeConick, and Pagels in order to get a clearer picture of the assumptions driving their respective methodologies. Each author is driven by historical-critical assumptions that show a concern for the world behind the text,[1] specifically the complex world of early Christianity. Each author also incorporates narrative-critical assumptions that address the world in the text,[2] specifically the use of a character for rhetorical and polemical purposes. Since this study is concerned to test the claims of the community-conflict hypothesis regarding the characterization of Thomas in the Gospel of John, I am especially concerned here with the worlds *in* and *in front of* the text of the Fourth Gospel.

The approach adopted in this study is based upon the assumption that, despite its historical elements[3] and literary apo-

1. Schneiders devotes an entire chapter of her *Revelatory Text* to the discussion of this approach to the biblical text. She defines the "world behind the text" as "a window on the ancient world through which one can discern, to some extent, the author(s) and her or his historical, theological, and ideological agenda as well as the community to which the text was originally addressed and the ancient world in which that community lived" (113).

2. Schneiders (ibid., 132–56) refers to this as the world *of* the text. She describes it concisely as the "text of linguistic system and mirror" (ibid., 113), which is essentially the world reflected in the events of the story.

3. A great deal has been written both denying and asserting the historical reliability of the Fourth Gospel. The trend in more recent historical Jesus studies has been to deny that there is much historical value in John's Gospel. There have been other attempts, however, to make a sustained case for the general historical reliability of John. See, for instance, Blomberg, *Historical Reliability of John's Gospel*. For an approach that recognizes and seeks to balance both the literary and historical elements of the Fourth Gospel, Moloney, "Fourth Gospel and the Jesus of History." See also the section in Fortna and Thatcher, *Jesus in the Johannine Tradition*, 35–101, entitled "The Fourth Gospel and Jesus," which consists of chapters about situating John's Gospel in history,

rias,[4] the Fourth Gospel displays a remarkable literary unity. This unity allows the text to be read as an autonomous narrative as well as a work of art.[5] An appreciation for both the literary unity and the artistry of the text has the potential to provide many substantive insights into the rhetorical strategy behind the Gospel's message. These insights are drawn from the methodologies of contemporary literary scholars that have been integrated into the discipline of biblical studies.

Over the last three decades biblical scholarship has been increasingly open to the application of contemporary literary theory to the narratives of the Hebrew Bible and the NT.[6] The history of this important development does not need to be reviewed here, but several important elements need to be outlined, as they figure prominently in the following chapters.

The Gospel of John was composed by a real author for an original audience of real readers. Much of the original context of the Fourth Gospel is foreign to the modern reader who is unfamiliar with Koiné

---

historical traces in the Fourth Gospel's Palestinian awareness, and general thoughts on the historical reliability of the Gospel.

4. The so-called *aporias* of John's Gospel have been a topic of serious discussion among Johannine scholars. The term is taken from the Greek ἀπορία, "perplexity" (BDAG, s.v. ἀπορία) indicating a "difficult passing." Passages identified as *aporias* appear to represent a seemingly displaced unit or an untidy literary seam. The earliest publications on the issue of Johannine *aporias* were Schwartz, *Aporien im vierten Evangelium* (1907); and Lewis, *Disarrangements in the Fourth Gospel* (1910). In the context of discussing Johannine composition and sources, Fortna (*Fourth Gospel and Its Predecessor*, 1–11) addresses the import of the Johannine displacements. See also the chapter in Brown, *Introduction to the Gospel of John*, 41–89, entitled "The Unity and Composition of the Fourth Gospel" for a historical overview of scholarly views on sources behind the Fourth Gospel.

5. To speak of the "autonomy" of the narrative is to assert that the story is able to stand on its own without assistance from the stories related by the Synoptic evangelists or other noncanonical gospel writers.

6. General introductions to biblical narrative and reader-response criticisms include Alter, *Art of Biblical Narrative*; Bar-Efrat, *Narrative Art in the Bible*; Berlin, *Poetics and Interpretation of Biblical Narrative*; Fokkelman, *Reading Biblical Narrative*; Kermode, *Genesis of Secrecy*; McKnight, *Postmodern Use of the Bible*; Moloney, *Beginning the Good News*; idem, "Narrative Criticism of the Gospels"; Powell, *What Is Narrative Criticism?*; Sternberg, *Poetics of Biblical Narrative*; and Tolmie, *Narratology and Biblical Narratives*. Culpepper's seminal work, *Anatomy of the Fourth Gospel*, is the proper starting point for those interested in the early evolution of NT narrative criticism and its application to John's Gospel. His general approach has been systematically applied to the Fourth Gospel in three volumes by Moloney: *Belief in the Word*; *Signs and Shadows*; and *Glory Not Dishonor*.

Greek and with the societal norms and religious symbolism of the first century.[7] Still, the Fourth Gospel continues to resonate with modern readers in a way that reveals the universal qualities of John's story of Jesus. This does not mean that the reading experience is solely dependent upon the whims or perspectives of the modern reader (or the reader of any era), as some postmodern theories of reader-oriented criticism have argued.[8] To be sure, the "lenses" through which each reader sees the narrative are important. More important, however, is the significant interchange that occurs between what the text presents to the reader and what the reader brings to the text. Recognizing and balancing these elements of the reading experience is critical for the development of a responsible narrative-critical hermeneutic.

Historical-critical scholars have discussed primarily the world behind the text in order to discover what the text presents to the reader. The concept of authorial intent has been an important assumption driving the scholarship of many in historical-critical circles. While many of the insights of historical-critical scholarship are valuable and need to be incorporated into narrative reading strategies, authorial intent can-

7. Outi Lehtipuu speaks to this difficulty as it applies to the biblical narratives in general. He writes, "The interpretation of biblical narratives faces several obstacles. A major problem is the temporal distance between the modern readers and the origins of the biblical texts. Both the text itself and its extratextual context are alien to us. This creates at least two kinds of difficulties. First, the stories contain terms that are altogether strange to us. For example, what does the expression 'Abraham's bosom' (NRSV: 'side') mean? Or what kind of a place is Hades? Second, there are familiar terms that do not necessarily bear the same meaning as today. For example, do the conceptions 'rich' and 'poor' refer to the same kinds of socioeconomic realities as today? A great chasm has been fixed between our world and the world of the story by time and cultural changes, and we must be cautious not to give anachronistic meanings to familiar sounding conceptions found in ancient texts" ("Characterization and Persuasion, 74).

8. At the beginning of his first volume on biblical criticism and postmodernism, Fernando Segovia advocates just such an approach when he writes, "The essays that follow represent the contributions to the first stage of the project, dealing with diversity in the American scene as such. They represent that 'speaking in other tongues' within the Unites States itself that, I argued above, characterizes the most recent development in biblical criticism and reflects the postmodernist turn at large: *a world in which readers become as important as texts and in which models and reconstructions are regarded as constructions*; a world in which *there is no master narrative but many narratives in competition* and no Jerusalem but many Jerusalems; a world in which the fundamental problem lies not in the translation and dissemination of a centralized and hegemonic message into other tongues but rather in having the different tongues engage in critical dialogue with one another" (Segovia and Tolbert, *Reading from This Place*, 32; emphasis added). See also Adam, *What Is Postmodern Biblical Criticism?*

not be the only or even the most important assumption driving our understanding of the reading experience. Instead, a responsible reading strategy for the NT narratives should seek to balance the concerns of elements such as Greek grammar and syntax, textual details, and sociopolitical backgrounds (the concerns of historical critics) with an appreciation for literary elements such as rhetorical strategy, irony, and character development (the concerns of literary critics).

Literary critics have recognized that the text speaks to the reader through a construct known as the implied author. The implied author is "the author who emerges through the story, as opposed to the actual writer."[9] The implied author informs the reader of the succession of events, the interaction between characters, and any other action that takes place at a given time in the narrative. The real reader, in most instances, will never have contact with the real author of a given work, and this is certainly true of the modern reader's experience with the Gospel of John. The implied author then is that intratextual component of the narrative that emerges as the real reader encounters the events, characters, and temporal flow of the story.

I have already asserted the importance of balancing what the real reader brings to the text with what the text presents to the reader. While the real reader brings a host of experiences and perspectives to the text, there is in the text another intratextual phenomenon known as the implied reader.[10] The text speaks *through* the implied author *to* the implied reader with the real reader as a witness to that discourse. Chatman writes that the "counterpart of the implied author is the implied reader—not the flesh-and-bones you or I sitting in our living rooms reading the book, but the audience presupposed by the narrative itself. Like the implied author, the implied reader is always present."[11] Likewise, Moloney describes the implied reader as a "heuristic device used to trace the temporal flow of the narrative," and comments that

9. Bar-Efrat, *Narrative Art in the Bible*, 14.

10. There is a wealth of information concerning the implied reader in Staley, *Print's First Kiss*. While I find implausible Staley's thesis regarding the unreliability of the narrator and the victimization of the reader in John's Gospel, it is undeniable that this volume contains many other helpful insights related to narration and the implied reader.

11. Chatman, *Story and Discourse*, 149–50. For an insightful discussion of the reader and the narrative's effect on the reader through constructs like the implied reader, see Booth, *Rhetoric of Fiction*, 119–47.

the implied reader "emerges as a forward-looking textual effect that also knows and recalls what has happened and what has been revealed in the story so far."[12]

While the reading experience of each real reader will invariably be different, the implied reader within the narrative consistently perceives the message of the implied author correctly. In a manner of speaking, the implied reader "gets it right" every time.[13] The real reader witnesses the events as reported by the implied author to the implied reader. Through this exchange, the real reader experiences the rhetorical flow of the text.

This study will attempt to read individual pericopes in a way that will draw out the message of the Fourth Gospel in the exchange between the implied author and the implied reader, while at the same time drawing upon the insights of historical-critical scholarship. In what follows then, I will be concerned with the nuances of the Greek text,[14] textual criticism,[15] sociopolitical backgrounds, and other such factors, but only as they serve to inform the overall literary effect of the Fourth Gospel.

The remainder of this chapter will be divided into three sections. The first section will outline a general approach to understanding characterization in narrative literature. The second section will be devoted to a specific discussion of characters in the Fourth Gospel and how they fit into the narrative scheme provided by the implied author. The final section of this chapter will examine the importance of the Johannine prologue (1:1–18) for understanding and appreciating the array of characters presented in the Fourth Gospel. All of this will pave the way for a discussion of individual characters in the chapters that follow.

12. Moloney, "Who Is 'the Reader' in/of the Fourth Gospel?" 21.

13. Culpepper groups the implied reader into the category of "ideal narrative audience" and distinguishes that from a hypothetical narrative audience and the author's intended real audience. Arguing that the implied reader always properly perceives the implied author's message, he writes, "In John the ideal narrative audience adopts the narrator's ideological point of view, penetrates the misunderstandings, appreciates the irony, and is moved to fresh appreciations of transcendent mystery through the gospel's symbolism" (*Anatomy of the Fourth Gospel*, 208).

14. Unless otherwise specified, all references to the Greek text in this study are to NA^{27}.

15. All textual issues will be discussed from a consciously reasoned-eclectic position. Thus, each reading will be taken on its own merits and equal consideration will be given to external and internal criteria.

Defining Characterization: Clarifying Methodology

Increasingly, biblical scholars have been using literary methods to raise important questions about the nature of characters and characterization in biblical narrative. For instance, are readers to understand a character as a real person or as a mere construct of words and ideas?[16] Further, are characters to be understood as having a correspondence to reality, or are they to be viewed as plot functionaries guiding the story to a specific end and guiding the reader to a desired response?[17] In the case of the canonical Gospels, are readers to understand the characters as mere actants, as historical individuals, or as something altogether different?[18] These questions must be answered in order to set forth a general understanding of characterization in narrative literature and, more importantly, before proceeding to a focused discussion of Johannine characterization.

Purist, Realist, or Something Else?

The debate over "realist" and "purist" approaches to defining character is an important area of discussion among literary critics.[19] The realist ap-

16. Addressing this distinction, Chatman (*Story and Discourse*, 118) comments that the "equation of characters with 'mere words' is wrong. . . . Too many mimes, too many captionless silent films, too many ballets have shown the folly of such a restriction. Too often do we recall fictional characters vividly, yet not a single word of the text in which they came alive; indeed, I venture to say that readers generally remember characters that way." He goes on to argue the case for a middle ground between understanding characters as "words" and understanding them as real persons.

17. Marvin Mudrick ("Character and Event in Fiction," 211) writes, "One of the recurring anxieties of literary critics concerns the way in which a character in drama or fiction may be said to exist. The 'purist' argument—in the ascendancy nowadays among critics—points out that characters do not exist at all except insofar as they are part of the images and events which bear and move them, that any effort to extract them from their context and to discuss them as if they are real human beings is a sentimental misunderstanding of the nature of literature. The 'realistic' argument—on the defensive nowadays—insists that characters acquire, in the course of action, a kind of independence from the events in which they live, and that they can be usefully discussed at some distance from their context."

18. Culpepper (*Anatomy of the Fourth Gospel*, 105–6) provides a helpful discussion of this question.

19. Another way of describing this debate is to make a distinction between "mimetic" representations (i.e., representations of reality) or mere plot functionaries (i.e., actants that simply serve to continue the action of the plot). Chatman's discussion of these distinctions in *Story and Discourse*, 108–27, is the logical starting point for one

proach argues that characters "acquire an independence from the plot in which they occur, and that characters can be discussed apart from their literary contexts."[20] This means that in many instances characters are extracted from their narrative worlds and treated as real people in hypothetical situations in the real world. This approach is primarily associated with the Romantic writers of the nineteenth century,[21] and though it finds fewer advocates today among theoreticians it is quite common among those who discuss characterization at a popular or less technical level.

As an example, the realist approach might take Shakespeare's Hamlet, extract him from his literary setting, and place him hypothetically into a modern setting, all with the intent of asking, "How might Hamlet respond in such-and-such a situation?" Hamlet's psychological profile as revealed in the Shakespearean tragedy would be used to treat him as an autonomous individual in the twenty-first century. This approach would thus seek to analyze the character in question psychologically on the basis of what has been revealed about that character in his/her original literary setting.

On the opposite end of the spectrum is the purist approach, which rejects the idea that characters can be taken out of their literary contexts or viewed in hypothetical, nonliterary situations as autonomous individuals. Advocates of this view would argue that Hamlet is necessarily defined by the literary parameters, events, time period, and characters associated with his own story. Thus, to remove him from his literary setting would be to create an entirely new character.

The purist view is, at its most basic level, derived from an Aristotelian view of character. According to Aristotle, "action" is the most important element in any dramatic presentation and the secondary element in the drama is the agent who performs the action.[22] Practically speaking, the Aristotelian approach to characterization almost completely subjugates

wishing to gain a familiarity with a fair representation of both sides of the debate. See also Conway, *Men and Women in the Fourth Gospel*, 50–58, for a detailed discussion of this distinction using the terms "mimetic" and "functional."

20. Burnett, "Characterization and Reader Construction," 4.

21. Conway (*Men and Women*, 50) notes that this view "saw characters as more or less autonomous beings who possessed motives, values, and personality, all of which were open to analysis by the critic."

22. See the discussion of Aristotle's *Poetics* in Chatman, *Story and Discourse*, 108–10.

the character to the action performed, and in so doing reduces the character to the role of a formless agent. Chatman notes that "Aristotle's general formulation of character and characterization is not appropriate to a general theory of narrative, although, as usual, he provokes questions that cannot be ignored."[23] If Aristotle's categories raise the question of the character's importance, the modern purist approach builds on that foundation by raising the question of the character's autonomy apart from the narrative in which that character originally appears. Culpepper contributes a helpful point to this discussion:

> [W]e must face the question of the legitimacy of treating the people described in a historical writing as characters. If the evangelist drew upon oral tradition which derived from those who knew the various people involved in the story and told of events which actually happened, is it not blatant distortion to apply the canons of fictional literature to the study of these people? On the other side, does it not distort the concept "characterization" to apply it to the description of persons in historical or biographical literature? These questions bristle with difficulties. . . . We are presently interested in characterization as the art and techniques by which an author fashions a convincing portrait of a person within a more or less unified piece of writing. *Even if one is disposed to see real, historical persons behind every character in John and actual events in every episode, the question of how the author chose to portray the person still arises.*[24]

In that same vein, Scholes provides what is perhaps an overly forceful but necessary safeguard to overemphasizing the historicity of a given character in any narrative. He writes: "The greatest mistake we can make in dealing with characters in fiction is to insist on their 'reality.' No character in a book is a real person. Not even if he is in a history book and his name is Ulysses S. Grant."[25]

As helpful as the cautionary insights of Culpepper and Scholes are, they offer a position that so contrasts with the realist approach that a polarizing effect begins to emerge. This means that, as the views are presently formulated, one cannot simultaneously embrace the purist position and incorporate elements of the realist position, and vice versa. The two positions are formulated without any movement to the middle

23. Ibid., 110.

24. Culpepper, *Anatomy of the Fourth Gospel*, 105; emphasis added.

25. Scholes, *Elements of Fiction*, 17.

from either camp. Rimmon-Kenan identifies the quandary in the following way:

> Whereas in mimetic theories (i.e., theories which consider literature as, in some sense, an imitation of reality) characters are equated with people, in semiotic theories they dissolve into textuality. What remains? *If both approaches end up cancelling the specificity of fictional characters, though from different standpoints, should the study of character be abandoned, or should both approaches be rejected and a different perspective sought?*[26]

I propose here that the answer is not, as Rimmon-Kenan suggests, to reject both views, but rather to take the best of both and to create a middle ground. That middle ground should see a given character's correspondence to reality, and balance that with an understanding that each character is unique to, and ultimately a product of, his/her literary environment.[27] This means that no character can be understood as a "real" individual apart from his/her narrative framework but that (1) each is understood to possess a certain level of autonomy within the context of the narrative; and (2) every character reflects some correspondence to reality, even if he/she is not understood to be "real." If we approach characterization in this way, we will see that the characters of the Fourth Gospel create sympathy among the readers as they are continually pushed toward a decision.

Round, Flat, or Something Else?

In his classic work *Aspects of the Novel*, E. M. Forster asks and attempts to answer whether characters should be viewed as human beings, historical persons, or something else altogether.[28] Prefiguring the conclusions of the purist camp, Forster concludes that characters should not

26. Rimmon-Kenan, *Narrative Fiction*, 33; emphasis added.

27. Chatman (*Story and Discourse*, 119) ably expresses this "middle ground" when he writes that "a viable theory of character should preserve openness and treat characters as autonomous beings, not as mere plot functions. It should argue that the character is reconstructed by the audience from evidence announced or implicit in an original construction and communicated by the discourse, through whatever medium."

28. "What is the difference between people in a novel and people like the novelist or like you, or like me, or Queen Victoria? There is bound to be a difference. If a character in a novel is exactly like Queen Victoria—not rather like but exactly like—then it actually is Queen Victoria, and the novel, or all of it that the character touches, becomes a memoir" (Forster, *Aspects of the Novel*, 71).

be extracted from the narrative and given unconditional autonomy.[29] However, Forster's deeper concern in posing the question is to understand how characters function with respect to the other elements of the narrative. It is in this context that he sets forth his well-known distinction between "round" characters and "flat" characters.[30]

According to Forster, "round" characters are those prominent figures in any story that display a host of potentially conflicting traits, while "flat" characters are predictable and one-dimensional. Using these categories, one might refer to the Jesus of John's Gospel as "round" inasmuch as he displays a host of emotional characteristics and complex motivations.[31] One might also refer to the uncomprehending characters of the Fourth Gospel as "flat" inasmuch as they are primarily defined by their consistent misperception of the mission and message of Jesus. To do this, however, would be to overstate the case.

While Forster's categories have proven to be helpful, many literary critics have found his dichotomy between round and flat characters to be problematic in that it too rigidly compartmentalizes characters that seem to exist on a larger literary spectrum. For this reason, the distinction between round and flat characters, though widely referenced, has fallen out of favor with many literary critics. Strict adherence to these two categories would, for example, fail to recognize the complexity in many of the minor characters found in the canonical gospels.[32]

Seemingly flat characters can express genuine insights and be momentarily transformed into characters with multiple round edges.[33] In the Fourth Gospel this is particularly true of Nicodemus, who early in

29. Ibid., 100.

30. Ibid., 103–25.

31. For instance, Jesus cleanses the temple in a fit of anger (2:1–22), weeps at the death of his friend Lazarus (11:35), and is continually driven by the Father's will (5:16–44; 6:35–51; 8:16–29; 10:14–18; 12:27–50, among other passages).

32. In recent years, a number of helpful publications have appeared that focus on the role of minor characters in the canonical Gospels. See, for instance, Williams, *Other Followers of Jesus*; Malbon, "Major Importance of Minor Characters"; and Conway, "Speaking through Ambiguity."

33. Rimmon-Kenan (*Narrative Fiction*, 61) comments, "A trait may be implied both by one-time (or non-routine) actions. . . . One-time actions tend to evoke the dynamic aspect of character, often playing a part in a turning point in the narrative. By contrast, habitual actions tend to reveal the character's unchanging or static aspect, often having a cosmic or ironic effect, as when a character clings to old habits in a situation which renders them inadequate."

the narrative displays an inability to comprehend Jesus's message and mission (3:1–15) but later appears as a follower of (or at least sympathizer with) the crucified Jesus (19:38–42). His seemingly flat characteristic of misperception is rounded by the narrator to indicate not just a new characteristic (i.e., belief) but rather a genuine, thoroughly Johannine transformation. Burnett expresses the issue well when he writes that it "seems best to speak of *degrees of characterization* in biblical texts, and to plot textual indicators on a continuum for any particular text, from words at one pole to 'persons' at the other pole."[34] This continuum must include at least three categories: (1) *agents*, which have little or no development and function essentially to advance the plot; (2) *types*, which have differing levels of character development and typically reveal a prominent, mainly static trait; and (3) *full-blown characters* with differing levels of direct and indirect characterization. Each of these individual categories must also be understood to exist on a continuum.

Characterization and Plot Development

Before moving to a focused examination of Johannine characterization, one further issue requires discussion—the relationship of characterization to the action of the story. Characters do not exist in a vacuum. Without action there is no need for and, in fact, there can be no characters.[35] The relationship of character to action is important because not only does a given character initiate, respond to, and interpret the action of the story, such action is often the indirect means by which the narrator portrays that character. A character can be described or developed explicitly (e.g., "the man went away sad because he was very rich" [Luke 18:23]) and can also be developed indirectly through speech and action. This means that the critic must pay particular attention to all activity within a narrative in order to weigh the significance of words and deeds for a given character's overall development.

While characters can be developed through direct description, this is rare in the Fourth Gospel. Two such examples of direct characterization in the Fourth Gospel apply to the figure Judas Iscariot. The first example is found in 6:70–71, where Jesus comments that one of his dis-

34. Burnett, "Characterization and Reader Construction," 19; emphasis added.

35. Henry James ("Art of Fiction") famously wrote, "What is character but the determination of incident? What is incident but the illustration of character?"

ciples is a "devil" (καὶ ἐξ ὑμῶν εἷς διάβολός ἐστιν). The ambiguity of this statement is cleared up in the following parenthetical aside of v. 71: "Now he said this about Judas, son of Simon Iscariot, one of the Twelve. For this one was about to betray him"; ἔλεγεν δὲ τὸν Ἰούδαν Σίμωνος Ἰσκαριώτου· οὗτος γὰρ ἔμελλεν παραδιδόναι αὐτόν, εἷς ἐκ τῶν δώδεκα.

A second example is found in 12:4–6 where Judas is again presented in a negative manner, this time with increasing specificity. In v. 4 his name is followed by three descriptive phrases. He is again mentioned as Judas, the Iscariot (ὁ Ἰσκαριώτης), one of Jesus's disciples (εἷς [ἐκ] τῶν μαθητῶν αὐτοῦ), the one who was about to betray him (ὁ μέλλων αὐτὸν παραδιδόναι). In v. 5 the reader learns of Judas's protest at Mary's anointing of Jesus's feet. He protests that Mary's actions represent a gratuitous wasting of resources in light of the needs of the poor. Verse 6 goes on to provide what is possibly the clearest example of direct characterization in the Fourth Gospel. There the reader is informed that Judas was not genuinely concerned with the poor (εἶπεν δὲ τοῦτο οὐχ ὅτι περὶ τῶν πτωχῶν ἔμελεν αὐτῷ), but that he was a thief (ἀλλ᾽ ὅτι κλέπτης ἦν), that he was keeper of the money box (καὶ τὸ γλωσσόκομον ἔχων), and that he would regularly steal from the money box (τὰ βαλλόμενα ἐβάσταζεν). In these three verses the reader gets a glimpse into Judas's position among the Twelve and the motivation behind his words and actions. The reader is also a witness to two specific examples of Judas's illicit activities: his present thievery and his future betrayal of Jesus. Such direct detail is rare in the Fourth Gospel where characters are concerned. More often, it is the reader's job to grasp each character's subtle nuances and respond appropriately. In John's Gospel, these nuances are typically found in the report of a given character's action, including elements of cognition and direct speech.

In the following chapters a strong emphasis will be placed on the dominant traits that arise from the reported speech, thoughts, and activity of each character. This approach will help to clarify that character's place on the continuum of characters (e.g., agent, type, full-blown character) and also reveal the implied author's hoped-for response by the reader to that character.

Approaching the Characters of the Fourth Gospel

In the Fourth Gospel, Jesus is the focal point from start to finish. He is the overarching concern of the story and is consistently portrayed in a developed and complex manner. He displays a broad range of emotions,[36] an awareness of things that neither the other characters nor the readers know,[37] and a driving motivation to remain steadfast in honoring the will of the "Father."[38] With respect to the continuum of characters discussed above, Jesus is the only true example of a full-blown character in the Fourth Gospel.[39] It is difficult, though not impossible, to regard Johannine characters other than Jesus as possessing any true autonomy within the narrative. This is because their appearance is often too brief to allow for substantial development by the narrator.[40] Though the Fourth Gospel is the only canonical account to provide extended narratives around particular figures, each character is still somewhat like a lesser planet in the Johannine solar system revolving around Jesus.[41]

From the outset of the Gospel, characters such as John the Baptist (1:26–36), Andrew (1:41), Philip (1:45), and Nathanael (1:49) demonstrate this truth. These characters and others appear simply to confess something significant about Jesus in a way that is consistent with or different from what has previously been revealed in the prologue (1:1–18). Though the narrator reports the direct speech and cognitive awareness of these early characters, there is little significance for them beyond their initial appearances. Therefore, whether these characters

36. Among other emotions, Jesus displays indignation (2:12–22), grief (11:33–37), and distress (12:27–33).

37. See 1:47–51; 4:16–19; 11:1–44; 12:27–33; 13:18–30.

38. See 5:16–44; 6:35–51; 8:16–29; 10:14–18; 12:27–50; 17:1–26.

39. Koester's three-dimensional model of Jesus's characterization is helpful. He identifies John's Jesus as a human being, a prophet, Messiah, and God incarnate. He writes, "This threefold pattern emerges repeatedly in Jesus' words to his friends and foes, showing that it is essential to the Gospel as a whole. Although interpreters sometimes give primary attention to one element, such as Jesus' divinity, each element has its own integrity, and it is through the interplay of all three aspects that the evangelist presents Jesus' identity and mission" (*Symbolism in the Fourth Gospel*, 39).

40. Culpepper (*Anatomy of the Fourth Gospel*, 102) points to this fact: "Most of the characters appear on the literary stage only long enough to fulfill their role in the evangelist's representation of Jesus and the responses to him."

41. These extended narratives appear in the wider context of Jesus's interactions with Nicodemus (3:1–21), the Samaritan woman (4:1–30), and the man born blind (9:1–41), to name just a few.

are identified as agents or types, they must necessarily be labeled as "minor characters."[42]

Scholars have approached the study of these minor characters from a number of different perspectives. Some have attempted to identify the so-called representative figures of the Fourth Gospel,[43] while others have examined the significance of anonymous characters alongside those who are identified by name.[44] Still others have examined the similarities and differences between John's male and female characters.[45] Each of these approaches offers something of value to the study of Johannine characterization, and while this study attempts to stand on the shoulders of those contributions, I aim to move in a slightly different direction. Before establishing that direction I must briefly consider the strengths and weaknesses of these prior approaches and assess their value for the present study.

Representative Figures in the Fourth Gospel

The tendency to regard Johannine characters as symbolic of a specific group or a greater spiritual reality has been pervasive in the history of exegesis on the Fourth Gospel.[46] There are a number of advocates of this position from differing methodological viewpoints, and there is not space here for a discussion of each. However, from a modern literary perspective this approach would regard each character as possessing one discernible, dominant trait (e.g., belief, unbelief) that highlights one aspect of a proper or improper response to Jesus. Culpepper comments,

42. Conway ("Speaking through Ambiguity," 324–41) provides a helpful analysis of the flaws in previous approaches to examining John's minor characters.

43. See, for instance, the chapter "Representative Figures" in Collins, *These Things Have Been Written*, 1–45; and Koester, *Symbolism in the Fourth Gospel*, 33–77.

44. See Beck, *Discipleship Paradigm*. See also Watty, "Significance of Anonymity in the Fourth Gospel." The helpfulness of this insightful study is remarkable in light of its brevity.

45. See especially Conway, *Men and Women in the Fourth Gospel*. See also, in chronological order: Brown, "Roles of Women in the Fourth Gospel"; Schneiders, "Women in the Fourth Gospel"; Rena, "Women in the Gospel of John"; Seim, "Roles of Women in the Gospel of John"; de Boer, "John 4:27: Women (and Men) in the Gospel." Dorothy Lee offers a compelling treatment of gender and symbol in her work *Flesh and Glory*.

46. See Collins, *These Things Have Been Written*, 1–8, for reflections on the history of such exegesis.

> When any of the minor characters conveys an impression of personhood it is usually the personification of a single trait: Thomas doubts, Pilate wrestles with the claims of truth and political expediency, Peter is impulsive, the Beloved Disciple is perceptive. . . . As a result, one is almost forced to consider the characters in terms of their commissions, plot functions, and representational value.[47]

Culpepper's comments are somewhat problematic for the present study in that they tend to foster a general acceptance of Forster's distinction between round and flat characters.[48] I briefly examined above the temporary rounding effect associated with some of the minor characters in the Fourth Gospel, a phenomenon that contrasts with Forster's categories and with the representative approach.

Conway has also pointed out some weaknesses in the representative approach. Most notably, she writes that those who have attempted to identify the central trait of these representative characters have often come away with widely divergent conclusions. If these representative characters are truly one-dimensional and transparent, one might expect these dominant traits to be discerned more readily.[49]

Indeed, many of John's characters are ambiguous at best and hold the potential to confound the reader. A prime example of this ambiguity is found once again in the presentation of Judas Iscariot. The representative approach might label Judas as a model of one whose loyalty to Jesus gives way to betrayal. But the reader has learned that Judas has been chosen by Jesus to be one of the Twelve and that he is also the one who would betray Jesus.[50] He is, in fact, presented as the betrayer from his initial appearance in the Gospel, raising the question of his legitimacy as a candidate for this group of disciples. How is the reader to interpret and respond to such ambiguity? These seemingly conflicting realities do not help the reader to identify definitively Judas's one dominant trait or symbolic significance.

In the end, the representative approach categorizes characters too narrowly in a way that fails to account for the complexity of many

47. Culpepper, *Anatomy of the Fourth Gospel*, 102.

48. In fact, Culpepper does use Forster's categories to inform his discussion of Johannine characters. See especially ibid, 102–3.

49. Conway, "Speaking through Ambiguity," 328.

50. Ibid., 330–31.

Johannine figures. In addition, there is no uniformity or unanimity among those who have sought to identify what these figures represent. However, this approach does help to affirm the previous conclusion that many Johannine characters have a tendency to remain relatively undeveloped and demonstrate a certain degree of flatness. This helpful insight will inform the methodology used in the following chapters.

Anonymous Characters in the Fourth Gospel

In a study of the role of anonymity in the Gospel of John, William Watty describes the remarkable precision displayed by the Fourth Evangelist in identifying characters in the Fourth Gospel by name, birthplace, parentage, etc.[51] In addition, Watty recognizes the way in which the Evangelist meticulously identifies places, defines Semitic terms, and possesses knowledge of events beyond the scope of any character in the narrative. Against that backdrop, Watty finds compelling the instances where concern for detail is conspicuous by its absence—this includes the nameless, faceless, but literarily significant characters in John's story.

The analysis of anonymous characters in the Gospel of John has identified a phenomenon quite different from what can be seen in much narrative literature. Very often in narrative literature anonymous characters are merely actants who help to guide the action of the story. This is particularly true in the Synoptics, where the absence of a name is often an indicator of unimportance. Noting this trend, Beck comments,

> [S]ome Fourth Gospel anonymous characters invert this tendency [in the Synoptics], occupy more textual space, and demonstrate narrative significance by their faith response to Jesus' word, a response of witness to the efficacy of his word. Among these anonymous characters are Jesus' mother, the Samaritan woman, the royal official in chapter 4, the infirm man in 5, the blind man in 9, and in spite of the textual problems raised by the pericope, the woman caught in adultery.[52]

Those who might otherwise be regarded as unimportant seemingly become models of Johannine faith that is greater than those who are named directly. The mother of Jesus is a poignant example of this. Though her name is given as Mary in the Synoptic Gospels, she is never

51. Watty, "Significance of Anonymity," 209–12.

52. Beck, *Discipleship Paradigm*, 2. Beck's article "Narrative Function of Anonymity" is a distillation of select portions of his dissertation.

directly named in John. Few would argue, however, that her role is an insignificant one. In fact, some have identified the mother of Jesus as the first true example of Johannine "faith" in the Fourth Gospel.[53] Though she is anonymous she ultimately becomes paradigmatic for belief—the Gospel's central theological emphasis.[54] Is it reasonable to conclude that the name of Jesus's mother was unknown or unimportant to an author who took the time to record the name of an actant such as Malchus, the servant whose ear was cut off at Jesus's arrest (18:10)? There must be some greater literary significance in John's use of anonymity.

From an analysis of John's nameless figures it is reasonable to conclude that anonymous characters are an important part of the Fourth Gospel's approach to characterization. The importance of anonymous characters in John's Gospel is a useful insight for the present study inasmuch as this study will examine characters with name and position (e.g., the disciples Thomas, Peter, Andrew, Philip, Judas [not Iscariot], a "ruler of the Jews" named Nicodemus, etc.) alongside an anonymous figure (the "woman of Samaria"). This reminder of the literary significance of John's anonymous characters will guide our reading of John 4 where Jesus interacts with the unnamed Samaritan woman.

Male and Female Characters in the Fourth Gospel

While other studies have been devoted to discussing the role of select male and female characters in John, Colleen Conway's dissertation provides the most comprehensive study to date of the literary effect created by John's use of male and female characters.[55] After a systematic study of John's important male and female characters, Conway concludes,

> [T]he mother of Jesus, the Samaritan woman, Martha and Mary of Bethany, and Mary Magdalene are presented in a positive light, but in the presentation of men there is no consistency. Three of the men, Nicodemus, Pilate, and Peter are presented

53. For instance, see Moloney, *Gospel of John*, 66–70. Raymond F. Collins (*These Things Have Been Written*, 158–82) also alludes to Mary's role as a model of faithful response to Jesus.

54. This theme pervades practically every chapter of the Gospel. An incomplete list of occurrences of πιστεύω used in reference to Jesus includes 1:7, 12; 2:23; 3:12–18, 36; 4:50, 53; 5:24, 46–47; 6:29–47; 7:38–39, 48; 8:24, 45–46; 9:35–38; 10:37–38, 42; 11:26–27; 12:11; 13:19; 14:1–2, 11–12; 16:9; 17:21; 19:35; 20:31. All but three chapters contain explicit references to belief in the mission and message of Jesus.

55. Conway, *Men and Women in the Fourth Gospel.*

> negatively, in clear contrast to the women, but two of them, the man born blind, and the Beloved Disciple play positive roles. Indeed, the man born blind turns out to be the most outstanding character of all, second only to Jesus.[56]

The present study is in substantial agreement with many of Conway's conclusions. Specifically, her conclusion that female characters are presented in a primarily positive way is quite helpful for the present study.

In what follows, I will examine six male characters (Thomas, Peter, Andrew, Philip, Judas [not Iscariot], and Nicodemus), three female characters (the Samaritan woman, Martha and Mary) and one male character group (the twelve disciples). I will not differ here from Conway's conclusion that female characters in the Fourth Gospel are presented in a positive light. Instead I will affirm and draw upon this important insight. This will help to demonstrate that the incidence of Johannine misunderstanding is not necessarily used for polemical purposes, which will in turn raise questions about the intellectual and spiritual failures of Thomas as he is understood by the community-conflict hypothesis. If female characters—who are consistently presented in a positive light—are also pictured as possessing a certain degree of spiritual incomprehension, then a case can be made that the Fourth Gospel is not specifically directing a polemic against any one character.

Uncomprehending Characters in the Fourth Gospel

Throughout the remainder of this study I will be considering named and anonymous, male and female characters that are undeveloped and primarily one-dimensional. Thus, I will draw upon the insights offered by those scholars surveyed above who have written on different elements of John's minor characters. However, the next four chapters of this study are specifically concerned with those characters that display in their interactions with Jesus a failure to understand some element of his message, mission, claims, or actions.

The role of misunderstanding in the Fourth Gospel has been thoroughly investigated.[57] Misunderstanding is important to the overall

56. Ibid., 201.

57. Paul D. Duke's revised dissertation, *Irony in the Fourth Gospel*, is the starting point for understanding how the Fourth Gospel uses situational irony to create misunderstanding. See also Leroy, *Rätsel und Missverständnis*; Carson, "Understanding

literary effect of the narrative and is often combined with verbal and/or situational irony to create a greater rhetorical effect. As much as Johannine misunderstanding has been discussed, there has not been a systematic treatment of Johannine misunderstanding as it applies to John's approach to characterization. Since the community-conflict position accuses the Fourth Gospel of directing a polemic against the *Thomas* tradition through the spiritually dull, uncomprehending character of Thomas, the examination of Thomas and other Johannine characters that exhibit a similar lack of comprehension seems especially pertinent. To evaluate properly the claims of the community-conflict hypothesis one must discern whether the characterization of Thomas is a Johannine anomaly or part of a wider literary pattern in the Fourth Gospel.

The greatest source of direct information about Jesus is found in the Gospel's prologue. These verses detail the origins and divine status of Jesus (1:1–2), his role in creation (1:3), his role as the light of humanity (1:5, 9), his position vis-à-vis John the Baptist (1:6–8; 15–18), his dominion over the created order (1:10–11), his rejection by "his own" (1:11), his incarnation and glory (1:14), and his revelation of the Father (1:18). These themes are woven throughout the remainder of the Fourth Gospel in a way that consistently points the implied reader back to the highly revealing prologue. Without the information provided in the prologue, the implied reader is destined to grope in the "darkness" that shrouds many of John's characters.

Each character in the narrative approaches Jesus with varying levels of understanding but no one approaches him fully comprehending the truths that have been revealed to the reader in the prologue. Thus, it is possible for the reader to evaluate the correctness of every character's interaction with Jesus on the basis of what has been revealed in the prologue. In order to gain a clearer understanding of how characters misperceive Jesus, we must look at what the reader already knows about Jesus. After an examination of these recurring themes it becomes clear that some characters simply misunderstand what Jesus is saying or doing and, in each case, the misunderstanding in question can be

---

Misunderstandings in the Fourth Gospel"; Hamid-Khani, *Revelation and Concealment of Christ*; Urban, *Das Menschenbild nach dem Johannesevangelium*; de Jonge, "Nicodemus and Jesus"; Richard, "Expressions of Double Meaning"; Smalley, "Johannine Son of Man Sayings"; and Schneiders, "History and Symbolism in the Fourth Gospel."

traced back to a truth that has been revealed to the implied reader in the prologue. With that in mind, this study will argue that Thomas is just one example of the uncomprehending Johannine character and that the so-called anti-Thomas polemic is just one stitch in a larger narrative tapestry that serves the literary purposes of the Evangelist. To validate this claim further I turn now to an examination of the prologue.

Johannine Characters and the Role of John's Prologue

The implied author (narrator)[58] of the Fourth Gospel is omniscient.[59] He continually expresses an inside view of events and appears to have access to information that is beyond the scope of all characters within the narrative.[60] For instance, he knows whom Jesus loves (11:5; 13:1–3, 23; 19:26; 20:2), what Jesus perceives (6:6, 15, 61, 64; 13:1; 19:28), and when Jesus is troubled (11:33, 38; 13:1). He provides information about the beliefs (2:11, 22; 20:8), suppositions (13:19; 20:15), and memories of the disciples (2:22; 12:16; 13:28; 19:35). Not only does he show an awareness of things the characters and implied reader do not know, but he also "tells us what none of the characters could easily convey to the reader."[61] The implied author is able to guide the implied reader skillfully through a maze of reported activities, interactions, and conversations in the Fourth Gospel largely because of the qualities of omniscience and reliability.[62] The implied author has the correct information in its entirety and faithfully—though not fully—disseminates that information to the

58. Literary critics typically distinguish between the narrator and implied author. Bar-Efrat (*Narrative Art in the Bible*, 14) comments that it is "customary to make a distinction between the (implied) author and the narrator. It is the latter who tells us what is happening and which character is speaking at any given time. The former becomes known to us through what the narrator says, through the speech of the characters (which is formulated by the author) and through the organization of the narrative materials, plot, time, space, etc." However, in the Fourth Gospel the two are indistinguishable. Therefore, the terms "implied author" and "narrator" will be used interchangeably throughout the remainder of this study.

59. See the insightful discussion of John's omniscient narrator in Pamment, "Focus in the Fourth Gospel."

60. On the omniscient narrator within and outside of the Fourth Gospel, see Culpepper, *Anatomy of the Fourth Gospel*, 21–26; Bar-Efrat, *Narrative Art in the Bible*, 17–23; Sternberg, *Poetics of Biblical Narrative*, 84–99.

61. Culpepper, *Anatomy of the Fourth Gospel*, 25.

62. Here I reject Staley's argument that the implied author victimizes the reader by providing unreliable information.

reader. In contrast to the implied author, the implied reader is highly informed but not omniscient. The implied reader is given privileged information that characters in the narrative do not possess, and because of this inside view the implied reader is in a position to evaluate properly every character's response to Jesus. Scholars have long recognized that the primary source from which the implied reader of the Fourth Gospel derives privileged information is the prologue (1:1–18).

John's prologue has been the topic of seemingly endless scholarly attention. Some scholars have discussed the prologue's stages of composition, often identifying pre-Christian hymns or formulae behind its final form.[63] Others have tried to identify the prologue's literary structure.[64] Still others have spent considerable space discussing the prologue's Hellenistic background,[65] Jewish background,[66] and christological import.[67] I am presently concerned with the literary purpose of the prologue as it relates to both the final form of the text and its rhetorical impact on the reader.

The prologue sets the theological and literary agenda for the remainder of the Fourth Gospel. The implied reader of the Fourth Gospel is able to comprehend the meaning of Jesus's origin and mission in a way that the characters in the narrative cannot. This allows the reader to interpret and evaluate the various responses to Jesus. Since everything in the narrative necessarily revolves around Jesus and a given character's (or reader's) response to him, this means that the Fourth Gospel and its

63. This is the case in the work of Rudolf Bultmann (and it is especially true of his epoch-making commentary on the Fourth Gospel, *Das Evangelium des Johannes* (originally published in German in 1941, translated into English and released as *The Gospel of John* in 1971). See also Robinson, "Relation of the Prologue"; Black, "Does an Aramaic Tradition Underlie John 1:16?"; Van der Watt, "Composition of the Prologue."

64. Culpepper, "Pivot of John's Prologue"; Staley, "Structure of John's Prologue"; Coloe, "Structure of the Johannine Prologue"; Hayward, "Holy Name of the God of Moses"; Viviano, "Structure of the Prologue"; Ridderbos, "Structure and Scope of the Prologue; La Potterie, "Structure du Prologue."

65. Tobin, "Prologue of John and Hellenistic Jewish Speculation."

66. Borgen, "Observations on the Targumic Character"; Boyarin, "Gospel of the Memra"; Ashton, "Transformation of Wisdom"; Hanson, "John 1:14–18 and Exodus 34"; Kysar, "Background of the Prologue"; Baarda, "John 1:17b"; Mowley, "John 1:14–18."

67. Brown, "Prologue of the Gospel of John"; Carter, "Prologue of John's Gospel"; Fennema, "John 1:18"; Pryor, "Of the Virgin Birth"; Painter, "John: Christology and the Fourth Gospel."

characters cannot be understood properly apart from the information provided in the prologue.

A number of themes are introduced in the prologue and those themes reappear throughout the Gospel in the discourses of Jesus. For instance, the term "life" (ζωή) appears twice in 1:4. This term reappears in Jesus's discussions with Nicodemus (3:15–16) and the Samaritan woman (4:14). Peter also uses the term at the end of the Bread of Life discourse in 6:68.[68] The next significant term in the prologue is "light" (φῶς), which occurs in 1:4, 5, 7, 8, and 9, and reappears in Jesus's conversations with Nicodemus (3:19–21) and with the disciples as they prepare to return to Judea (11:9–10).[69] Other important themes from the prologue include "witness" (μαρτυρία/μαρτυρέω, 1:7, 8, 15),[70] "the world" (κόσμος, 1:9, 10),[71] "truth"/"true" (ἀλήθεια/ἀληθινός, 1: 9, 14, 17),[72] "belief"/"to believe" (πιστεύω, 1:7, 12),[73] "his own" (ἴδιος),[74] and "glory" (δόξα).[75] Pamment comments that "characters use these concepts in slightly different ways, allowing the narrator to indicate their full range of meaning, and this is the purpose of the dialogues."[76] Throughout the narrative, characters appear as comprehending or uncomprehending to the degree that they grasp these themes from the prologue. As stated above, no one character fully grasps the truth behind these themes (except possibly the Beloved Disciple), and therefore every character is uncomprehending to a degree. However, several characters are explicitly presented as uncomprehending in order that

68. The term also occurs in 3:36; 4:36; 5:24, 26, 29, 39, 40; 6:27, 33, 35, 40, 47, 48, 51, 53, 54, 63; 8:12; 10:10, 28; 11:25; 12:25, 50; 14:6; 17:2, 3; 20:31.

69. See also 5:35; 8:12; 9:5; 12:35, 36, 46.

70. The nominal form appears in 1:19; 3:11, 32, 33; 5:31, 32, 34, 36; 8:13; 14; 17; 19:35; 21:24. The verbal form appears in 1:32, 34; 2:25; 3:11, 26, 28, 32; 4:39, 44; 5:31, 32, 33, 36, 37, 39, 7:7; 8:13, 14, 18; 10:25; 12:17; 13:21; 15:26, 27; 18:23, 37; 19:35; 21:24.

71. See also 1:29; 3:16, 17, 19; 4:42; 6:14, 33, 51; 7:4, 7; 8:12, 23, 26; 9:5, 39; 10:36; 11:9, 27; 12:19, 25, 31, 46, 47; 13:1; 14:17, 19, 22, 27, 30, 31; 15:18, 19; 16:8, 11, 20, 21, 28, 33; 17:5, 6, 9, 11, 13, 14, 15, 16, 18, 21, 23, 24, 25; 18:20, 36, 37; 21:25.

72. ἀλήθεια appears in 3:21; 4:23, 24; 5:33; 8:32, 40, 44, 45, 46; 14:6, 17; 15:26; 16:7, 13; 17:17, 19; 18:37, 38. ἀληθινός appears in 4:23, 37; 6:32; 7:28; 8:16; 15:1; 17:3; 19:35. ἀληθής appears in 3:33; 4:18; 5:31, 32; 6:55; 7:18; 8:13, 14, 17, 26; 10:41; 19:35; 21:24. ἀληθῶς appears in 1:47, 4:42; 6:14; 7:26, 40; 8:31; 17:8.

73. See fn 54 above.

74. See also 1:41; 4:44; 5:18, 43; 7:18; 8:44; 10:3, 4, 12; 13:1; 15:19; 16:32; 19:27.

75. See also 2:11; 5:41, 44; 7:18; 8:50, 54; 9:24; 11:4, 40; 12:41, 43; 17:5, 22, 24.

76. Pamment, "Focus in the Fourth Gospel," 73.

they might appear as foils for the teaching and activity of the Johannine Jesus. The narrator then uses the discourses of Jesus to shed light on the fuller meaning of these themes, often accomplishing this in a context where Jesus is instructing and correcting that character.

In the following chapters I will return to these themes and show how the uncomprehending characters fail to grasp them fully. I will also recognize several common elements in each pericope. First, Jesus speaks or acts in a way that is consistent with his mission from the Father, and does so in the presence of another Johannine character. Second, the character in question misperceives some element of Jesus's words or deeds in a way that requires instruction and/or correction. Third, Jesus speaks or acts again in an instructive and corrective way. Fourth, in each instance, one or more themes from the prologue are addressed, revealing the depth of the character's misunderstanding, which in turn more fully elucidates the truth about Jesus.

Because this study is concerned to examine Johannine characterization with a view to shedding light on another discussion (viz., the John-*Thomas* question) I will intentionally avoid overly technical terminology related to literary hermeneutics. My aim in the chapters that follow is to read the narrative closely while tracing the Fourth Gospel's presentation of uncomprehending characters. It is my hope that this approach will be helpful for illuminating the literary and theological purposes behind incomprehension as it is applied to characters in the Fourth Gospel, and that the results will prove helpful for the discussion of John's relationship to the *Gospel of Thomas*. I turn now to a consideration of Thomas in the Fourth Gospel, keeping in mind the methodology established above as well as the conclusions of Riley, DeConick, and Pagels.

3

Jesus and Thomas in the Fourth Gospel

> In John 11:16, as Jesus is departing to go to Bethany and raise Lazarus, Thomas speaks the desperate words, "Let us also go, that we may die with him." Thomas expects that not only he but Jesus and his fellow disciples will also die in Judea as Lazarus had died, where "the Jews" were just seeking to stone Jesus (11:8). Yet Jesus is not stoned, nor do any of the disciples die; instead one of Jesus's greatest miracles occurs in the raising of Lazarus. Thomas is here singled out by the author of John as the only one of the twelve disciples named; he is shown to be wrong, and wrong in the specific context of resurrection. In John 14:5, in response to a statement of Jesus, Thomas declares himself to be ignorant of both the (postmortem) destination and "way" of Jesus. In John 20:24–29, Thomas alone of the Eleven fails to see the risen Jesus; he is alone in his doubt, and alone in his demand to touch the wounds of Jesus; he alone is rebuked for unbelief. As a character in John, Thomas is cast as one who is wrong, ignorant and unbelieving.[1]

The disciple Thomas appears four times in the Fourth Gospel. He makes his first appearance in 11:16 where the disciples are discussing the fate of Lazarus. The reader sees Thomas a second time in 14:5 in the context of the so-called Farewell Discourse. In that chapter a literary pattern emerges in which Jesus addresses and corrects the disciples on four different issues. Thomas's third appearance in the narrative (20:24–28) is certainly the most well known of the four and is the one that has won him the label "Doubting Thomas." For Riley, DeConick, and Pagels, this pericope is of paramount importance for understanding the John-*Thomas* conflict they assert. Thomas's fourth and final appearance in 21:2 is nothing more than a passing mention in a list of

1. Riley, *Resurrection Reconsidered*, 78–79.

disciples present during one of Jesus's post-resurrection appearances. A cursory glance at these texts raises the initial question of Thomas's importance in the overall narrative scheme of the Fourth Gospel. With such a minor role in the Gospel, can Thomas be regarded as the impetus for the writing of all or of a significant part of the Fourth Gospel? In order both to assess Thomas's relative importance within the story and to establish the presence of a Johannine literary pattern, I will undertake an examination of the Fourth Gospel's "Thomas passages" in this chapter. Specifically, I will examine the first three pericopes in which Thomas appears: 11:1–16, 14:1–24,[2] and 20:24–28. Since the fourth appearance of Thomas lends little if anything to an overall view of Thomas's presentation in the Fourth Gospel, I will not consider it here. In what follows I will attempt to provide a close reading of the text, paying special attention to issues of characterization.

Jesus and Thomas in John 11:1–16

The Fourth Gospel, unlike the Synoptics, does not contain a specific account of the calling of the Twelve, though this is perhaps implied (cf. 6:67–71).[3] The reader of the Fourth Gospel sees the calling of a handful of disciples (Andrew in 1:40; Simon Peter in 1:41–42; Philip in 1:43; Nathanael in 1:45–50) as well as their repeated appearances in the narrative.[4] However, the reader has not been provided with a comprehensive list of the disciples called by Jesus or following him. Instead, at various turns in John's presentation, new voices emerge from the small band of Jesus followers. In ch. 11, Thomas is just such a voice. At nearly the halfway point of the Gospel, the reader meets Thomas for the first time. However, Thomas is not the only new character introduced in John 11. In

2. Thomas appears only in vv. 5–7 of this chapter, but since the remainder of the chapter consists of a pattern where Jesus instructs the disciples individually and corporately I have decided to extend the limits of the exegesis. This decision is meant to inform the discussion of this and future chapters in this study.

3. The Synoptic call narratives can be found in Mark 3:13–19; Matt 10:2–4; and Luke 6:12–16. It is unlikely that the Fourth Gospel's original audience would have read the text without an awareness of Jesus's small band of followers. In 6:67, 70, John shows an awareness of the tradition of the twelve disciples. For more on the historical situation surrounding the twelve disciples, see Meier, "Circle of the Twelve."

4. Andrew appears three times (1:40–45; 6:8; 12:22), Simon Peter appears six times (1:40–44; 6:68; 13:6–37; 18:10–27; 20:2–6; 21:2–21), Philip appears four times (1:43–48; 6:5–7; 12:21–22; 14:8–9), and Nathanael appears only twice (1:43–49 and 21:2).

fact, nearly every significant voice or action in the chapter comes from a character that is appearing or speaking for the first time. Thomas, Martha, and Mary all make their debut on the narrative stage in ch. 11 and each adds a considerable depth to the scenes depicted there.

In 11:1–16, Jesus speaks to the disciples about the death of Lazarus. He speaks of his death first in the veiled manner typical of Johannine discourse (Λάζαρος ὁ φίλος ἡμῶν κεκοίμηται, "Lazarus, our friend has fallen asleep"; v. 11) but then plainly announces his death in the wake of the disciples' failure to understand (Λάζαρος ἀπέθανεν, "Lazarus has died"; v. 14). After two brief conversations between Jesus and the disciples, Thomas expresses a desire to "die with him,"[5] a statement that effectively ends the literary unit as the group prepares to travel to Judea. As the narrative moves beyond v. 16, the reader eventually witnesses the seventh and final "sign" of the Fourth Gospel as Jesus raises Lazarus from the dead.[6] The raising of Lazarus reveals Jesus's power over death and, more importantly, foreshadows his own resurrection in ch. 20.[7] Thus, at the literary level, John 11:1–16 serves primarily to set the stage for the raising of Lazarus. Thomas, as will be demonstrated below, is merely a minor player in the pericope under consideration. This unit can be divided as follows:

5. The referent behind αὐτοῦ is debated. Is Thomas referring to Lazarus, Jesus, both? This question will be examined in greater detail below.

6. The other six *semeia* occur in 2:1–12 (changing of water to wine); 4:46–54 (healing of an official's son); 5:1–9 (healing at the pool of Bethesda); 6:1–15 (multiplication of loaves and fish); 6:16–21 (walking on the water); and 9:1–12 (healing of the man born blind). These are the seven signs traditionally identified by commentators on the Fourth Gospel. Andreas Köstenberger ("Seventh Johannine Sign") departs tendentiously from the traditional listing of Johannine *semeia* by replacing the walking on water (6:16–21) with the cleansing of the temple (2:13–22).

7. It is appropriate to see a progression in the signs of the Fourth Gospel. Jesus is pictured as going from possessing power over the elements (i.e., turning water to wine) to power over contracted illness (the healing at the pool of Bethesda), to power over congenital illness (the healing of the man born blind) to power over death (the resurrection of Lazarus that foreshadows Jesus's own resurrection). Such a progression in his signs reveals the comprehensive nature of Jesus's authority and helps to reinforce the Gospel's emphasis on his role as revealer of the Father to humanity.

1. Presentation of characters, time, setting, and events (11:1–6)
2. Discussions between Jesus and the disciples (11:7–16)
    a. Discussion about traveling to Judea (11:7–10)
    b. Discussion about the fate of Lazarus (11:11–16)

Presentation of the Situation (11:1–6)

Chapter 11 begins by providing several pieces of new information. The reader learns three important details about a previously unknown character: (1) he is named Lazarus, (2) he is from Bethany, and (3) he is sick. Significantly, the word order of the Greek text emphasizes the illness above the name or region (ἦν δέ τις ἀσθενῶν, Λάζαρος ἀπὸ Βηθανίας). This is important because in the present unit and the one that follows, the illness will be of greater importance to the developing plot. In this first verse, the reader also meets for the first time the two sisters of Lazarus, Mary, and Martha. These three siblings will be important players in the unfolding events of chs. 11–12.

It was asserted in the previous chapter that since Jesus is the only example of a full-blown character in the Fourth Gospel, it is not surprising that other characters have little direct characterization and often receive only a passing mention in the text. However, in light of the narrator's explicit affirmation that Jesus loves them (v. 5), it is somewhat surprising that the reader is learning of these siblings for the first time in the story. Other than the enigmatic "beloved disciple" passages,[8] this is the only place in the narrative where Jesus is explicitly described as loving individuals.[9] This fact heightens the reader's anticipation of what will happen as the story of Mary, Martha, and Lazarus moves forward.[10]

In v. 2 the narrator describes Mary of Bethany as ἡ ἀλείψασα τὸν κύριον μύρῳ καὶ ἐκμάξασα τοὺς πόδας αὐτοῦ ταῖς θριξὶν αὐτῆς,

8. The anonymous "disciple whom Jesus loved" is mentioned in chs. 13, 19, 21. Issues related to the identity and literary function of the Beloved Disciple will be discussed in an excursus in chapter 4.

9. There are, however, other instances in the Fourth Gospel where Jesus is depicted as loving corporate entities; e.g., Jesus loves "his own" in 13:1, and he commands the disciples to "love another as I have loved you [pl.]" in 15:12.

10. Though it is not a widely held scholarly opinion, some have identified Lazarus as the Beloved Disciple because he is the only male figure in the Fourth Gospel explicitly described as "loved" by Jesus. On this point, see the interesting reconstruction of Stibbe, *John as Storyteller*, 78.

"the one who anointed the Lord with oil and wiped his feet with her hair." The careful reader will realize that this event has not yet occurred in the Johannine narrative (it takes place in 12:1–9). This verse has been scrutinized by source critics and identified as one of the classic examples of Johannine aporia.[11] In addition, this verse has also been listed among the "asides" or "footnotes" of the Fourth Gospel.[12] Thus, some scholars see in this one verse the convergence of two uniquely Johannine literary elements. However, while this verse is a good example of a side comment to the reader, it need not be classified as an untidy literary seam or as the insertion of a later editor. In fact, the comment points forward to a meaningful event between Jesus and Mary, and builds further anticipation for the events that will occur beyond the present pericope. The reader should understand that the events to follow will be significant enough to serve as the impetus for Mary's later actions described in v. 2. In addition to building anticipation in the reader, Moloney suggests that this proleptic comment should be understood as a narrative gap that elevates Mary above her sister and highlights the key role Mary will play throughout chs. 11–12.[13]

In the first part of v. 3, the narrator reports that the sisters send Jesus a message about their brother's illness, and thus the reader learns of Lazarus's illness at the same time as Jesus. The narration of events at this stage creates a level of uncertainty and again builds anticipation for how Jesus will respond. This anticipation will reach an initial climax in v. 35 where the reader witnesses Jesus's response to the grieving crowds.

11. Brown (*Gospel According to John*, 1:421–23) encloses vv. 2, 5, and 13 of this pericope in parentheses. In reference to v. 2, he comments, "This verse is clearly a parenthesis added by an editor: it refers to a scene in ch. xii which has not yet been narrated; it uses the term 'Lord,' which John does not usually use of Jesus during the ministry when describing him in third person narrative." Other scholars who identify this as a later addition that interrupts the original text include Bernard (*Critical and Exegetical Commentary*, 2:372–73, Schnackenburg (*Gospel According to St. John*, 2:322), and Lindars (*Gospel of John*, 386–87). Bultmann (*Gospel of John*, 302) regards this verse as part of John's attempt to harmonize his account with the anointing story in Mark 14:3–9.

12. Tenney, in his important study of Johannine asides ("Footnotes of John's Gospel," 364), identifies 11:2 as a footnote (his term for the parenthetical comment in John) reflecting the "knowledge of Jesus." Tom Thatcher ("New Look at Asides," 434) also sees 11:2 as an aside and categorizes it as providing a "preliminary character label." For more scholarly reflections on this topic, see O'Rourke, "Asides in the Gospel of John."

13. Moloney, "Can Everyone be Wrong?" 510. For further reflections on the narrative roles of Martha and Mary, see Moloney, "Faith of Martha and Mary."

A second climax will follow at the point when Jesus summons Lazarus from the grave.

The vocative κύριε of v. 3b recalls the use of κύριον by the narrator in the previous verse and highlights the belief that Mary and Martha have in Jesus. This confession sets them squarely within the tradition of the Johannine disciples and other believers who refer to Jesus as κύριε throughout the narrative.[14] Notably the disciples use this term with reference to Jesus just a few verses later in this same pericope (11:12). In addition, Martha calls Jesus κύριε in 11:21, 27, as does Mary in 11:32. In 11:34, the sisters collectively refer to him using this term.

After receiving the message from Mary and Martha, Jesus comments in v. 4 that the sickness Lazarus has contracted is not "unto death" (αὕτη ἡ ἀσθένεια οὐκ ἔστιν πρὸς θάνατον). It is possible to understand the final clause in a resultative sense. In other words, πρὸς θάνατον could be taken to mean that Lazarus's sickness will not lead to his death. However, this is in fact what occurs.[15] Since Lazarus is ultimately raised from the dead, it is possible to understand πρὸς θάνατον in the sense that the sickness does not have a *final* result in death and so points forward to his imminent resurrection. It seems better, however, to combine these and to take πρὸς θάνατον as a clause expressing both purpose and result. This would indicate that there is a definite purpose behind the sickness, and that though it does initially lead to death it will result in death being overturned and God being glorified. This is further reinforced by the next two clauses, ἀλλ' ὑπὲρ τῆς δόξης τοῦ θεοῦ, "but for the glory of God," and ἵνα δοξασθῇ ὁ υἱὸς τοῦ θεοῦ δι' αὐτῆς, "that the son of God may be glorified through it."[16]

14. See, for instance, the use of κύριος by the crowds in 6:34, Peter in 6:68, and the man born blind in 9:36, 38.

15. "Jesus' statement [viz., the illness is not unto death], which is plainly contrary to the phenomenological facts since Lazarus' illness *will* lead to his own death and eventually to Jesus' death, opens up an ambiguity in the word 'death' by calling radically into question its presumed univocal reference to the end of earthly life. In some cases, what Lazarus will undergo as a result of natural causes and what Jesus will undergo as a result of human malice is not death. This is reinforced and a hint of the true answer is given in verses 5–10 . . . Therefore, whatever death means, nature and human intention cannot be regarded as its ultimate causes because what they bring about is in some sense not death; and they cannot bring about death at all except according to God's will and design" (Schneiders, "Death in the Community of Eternal Life," 49).

16. The ἵνα here is taken in its most natural sense of purpose. See BDAG, s.v. ἵνα. See also the discussion of ἵνα with the subjunctive in Wallace, *Exegetical Syntax of the New Testament*, 471–72.

Against this backdrop, it can be surmised that Lazarus's illness was not simply brought about by random forces but rather by the direct activity of God, that it might result in both resurrection and in the Father and Son receiving glory.[17] Though it does initially end in death, the illness culminates in resurrection and in celebration. Thus, the narrator emphasizes the purposeful activity of the Father as well as the intervention of the Son in and behind the sickness of Lazarus.

Verse 5 provides another example of a side comment to the reader and expands what has already been hinted at in v. 3.[18] The earlier message of Mary and Martha to Jesus is ἴδε ὃν φιλεῖς ἀσθενεῖ, "the one whom you love is sick." The narrator affirms that in addition to loving Lazarus, Jesus also loves his two sisters: ἠγάπα δὲ ὁ Ἰησοῦς τὴν Μάρθαν καὶ τὴν ἀδελφὴν αὐτῆς καὶ τὸν Λάζαρον.

Up to this point in the narrative most of Jesus's miraculous activities have occurred in the context of his itinerant wanderings.[19] The reader has not yet witnessed a specific example of Jesus traveling to a location specifically for the purpose of performing a sign. At a macro level Jesus's actions throughout the gospel are portrayed as motivated by love (love for the Father, love for humanity, etc.). However, this instance is clearly unique in the Fourth Gospel's presentation of Jesus's ministry, and once again this portrait of Jesus builds anticipation in the reader who waits to see how Jesus will respond.

What happens (or rather does *not* happen) is unexpected. The reader's anticipation is met with a surprising twist as Jesus decides to

17. Moloney appears to affirm this line of thinking when he writes, "As Jesus delayed, Lazarus had died in his absence. But *this is what Jesus wanted* so that the disciples might come to faith" ("Can Everyone be Wrong? 512; emphasis added).

18. Brown (*Gospel According to John*, 1:421) places parentheses around v. 5, indicating his exegetical decision that this is an aside to the reader. Tenney ("Footnotes of John's Gospel") does not include v. 5 in his list, while Thatcher ("New Look at Asides," 436) categorizes it as an aside that defines a "reminiscent character label."

19. Jesus performs his first sign while attending a wedding in Cana (2:1–11) and performs his second sign upon returning to Cana after ministering in Galilee and Samaria (4:46–54). The healing at the pool of Bethesda takes place as Jesus goes up to Jerusalem to celebrate a feast (5:1–17). The bread sign and the walking on water occur in the context of Jesus's ministry in and around the sea of Galilee (ch. 6). Finally, the healing of the man born blind occurs as Jesus is "passing by," καὶ παράγων, presumably still in Jerusalem (9:1). The raising of Lazarus is the only instance in the Fourth Gospel where Jesus travels to a specific location for the express purpose of performing a sign.

remain in the same unspecified location for an additional two days (v. 6). The reader has come to expect an immediate response from him in similar times of need or crisis,[20] and is therefore astonished at Jesus's inactivity and seeming apathy in the face of his friend's grave illness.

Discussion between Jesus and the Disciples (11:7–16)

In vv. 7–16, the disciples and Jesus enter into serious discussion about two issues. The first issue is Jesus's seemingly misguided desire to venture back into Judea so soon after having his life threatened there by the Jewish leadership (10:31–39). The second topic of discussion is the fate of Lazarus and its implications for their journey to Judea.

Discussion about Traveling to Judea (vv. 7–10)

Verse 7 begins with the words ἔπειτα μετὰ τοῦτο, "then after this." This is a subtle change from the characteristic use of μετὰ τοῦτο and μετὰ ταῦτα up to this point in the narrative.[21] τοῦτο likely refers to the two-day waiting period after Jesus received the news of Lazarus's sickness. The combination of explicit temporal markers ἔπειτα and μετὰ τοῦτο demonstrates a deliberate delineation of time and a slowing of narrative velocity from the terse depictions of words and actions in vv. 1–6.

After waiting for two days Jesus urges a return trip to Judea. The disciples express alarm at this suggestion since Jesus's last two forays into Judea nearly ended in death.

In ch. 8, Jesus faced off with the Jewish leaders and uttered words they deemed blasphemous. In 8:58 Jesus says, "Before Abraham was, I am." In typical Johannine fashion, the Jewish leaders failed to understand that he was speaking not chronologically but theologically.[22] They did not realize (as the reader does) that "I am," ἐγώ εἰμι, in Jesus's vernacular is a form of divine self-revelation intended to identify himself with YHWH. ἐγώ εἰμι is used throughout the Fourth Gospel in both

20. In each of the previous signs (with the walking on water as the sole exception), Jesus has acted immediately to change an outcome for those who are sick, dying, or otherwise in need.

21. μετὰ τοῦτο / μετὰ ταῦτα appears in 2:12, 3:22; 5:1, 14; 6:1; 7:1; 11:11; 13:7; 19:28, 38; and 21:1.

22. Just prior to Jesus's words they exclaim, πεντήκοντα ἔτη οὔπω ἔχεις καὶ Ἀβραὰμ ἑώρακας; From this statement the reader should gather that the Jewish leaders do not understand the theological or christological import of Jesus's claim.

predicated[23] and unpredicated[24] statements that help to illustrate the Fourth Gospel's complex christological presentation. Because of their misunderstanding, the Jewish leaders consider Jesus's words to be blasphemous and they pick up stones in order to stone him (8:59). Jesus, however, is able to escape.

After healing the man born blind (ch. 9) Jesus is once again at odds with the Jewish leaders. This leads to the events in ch. 10 where Jesus identifies himself as the "good shepherd" in an obvious contrast with the Jewish leaders who are "poor shepherds" of God's people. Once again, Jesus's words are judged to be blasphemous when in 10:30 he says ἐγὼ καὶ ὁ πατὴρ ἕν ἐσμεν, "I and the Father are one." At this, the Jews seize him and again pick up stones in order to kill him. He is able to escape a second time.

When in 11:8 the disciples protest, ῥαββί, νῦν ἐζήτουν σε λιθάσαι οἱ Ἰουδαῖοι, they are referring back to this second and most recent series of events in Judea (10:31–39). In light of this threat of violence from the Jewish leaders, it is interesting that in the beginning of ch. 11 Jesus and the disciples are in an undisclosed location. Throughout the story thus far, it has been the regular practice of the narrator to provide information about the physical setting of each occurrence in the Gospel.[25] A specific physical location in this instance is conspicu-

23. In 6:35, 48, Jesus proclaims, ἐγώ εἰμι ὁ ἄρτος τῆς ζωῆς, "I am the bread of life." In the same discourse, Jesus is pictured as saying in 6:41, ἐγώ εἰμι ὁ ἄρτος ὁ καταβὰς ἐκ τοῦ οὐρανου, "I am the bread that came down from heaven," and in 6:51, ἐγώ εἰμι ὁ ἄρτος ὁ ζῶν ὁ ἐκ τοῦ οὐρανοῦ καταβάς, "I am the living bread who came down from heaven." In 8:12 and 9:5, Jesus refers to himself as the light of the world (ἐγώ εἰμι τό φῶς τοῦ κόσμου). Other predicated ἐγώ εἰμι statements can be found in 8:23, 24, 28; 10:11, 36, 38; 11:25; 14:6; 15:1. Not everyone is convinced that these ἐγώ εἰμι statements carry the same force as the absolute ἐγώ εἰμι statements.

24. In addition to 8:58, the phrase ἐγώ εἰμι also appears without a predicate in 4:26; 8:24, 28; 13:19; 18:5, 8. Many modern translations remove the absolute nature of Jesus's statement from most of these passages by translating ἐγώ εἰμι as "I am he," "I am the one I claim to be," or some other variation. Interestingly, the NLT translates the ἐγώ εἰμι of 4:26 and 13:19 as "I am the Messiah," accompanied by an unsatisfying explanatory note about the wording of the original Greek.

25. From the very beginning of the Gospel, the reader learns that John's preaching took place in Bethany beyond the Jordan (1:28). From there Jesus ventures to Galilee (1:43), then moves to Cana (2:1–12), Jerusalem (2:13–25), Samaria (4:1–45), Cana (4:46–54), Bethesda (ch. 5), the sea of Galilee (6:1–58), Capernaum (6:59–71), and finally Jerusalem (7:1—10:39). Johannine scholars have long recognized the Evangelist's impressive knowledge of Palestinian geography.

ous by its absence. The reader is simply told in 10:40 that Jesus was staying "beyond the Jordan where John first baptized."[26] This nebulous description keeps the reader (outside the narrative) and the Jewish leaders (within the narrative) in the dark about where this conversation between Jesus and the disciples is taking place. While the location of these conversations is clearly outside of Bethany, neither the reader nor the Jewish leaders are privy to the exact location where they take place. This purposeful lacuna on the part of the narrator serves to highlight the intensity of the violence threatened by the Jewish leaders as well as the need for Jesus to seek physical separation from them.[27]

Jesus's reply to the disciples in v. 9 is not as clearly understood as is his desire to depart for Judea. His puzzling calculation of time (οὐχὶ δώδεκα ὧραί εἰσιν τῆς ἡμέρας;) and his self-evident statement about walking in the light (ἐάν τις περιπατῇ ἐν τῇ ἡμέρᾳ, οὐ προσκόπτει) are meant to draw upon the light/darkness imagery initially provided in the prologue. Specifically, Jesus's cryptic reply is meant to draw upon the events that occur during the feast of Tabernacles (7:1—10:21), and to highlight the christological significance of Jesus's ongoing battle with the Jewish leaders. As both the "light of humanity" that "shines in the darkness" (1:4, 5) and "the light of the world" (8:12; 9:5), Jesus prepares for a battle in Judea against the arrayed forces of darkness (i.e., sickness, death, and the Jewish leadership). As promised in the prologue, the darkness of death will not be able to overcome the light of life (1:5).[28]

The violence of 8:59 and 10:31 anticipates the violence that will result in the death of Jesus in his final return to Judea. This violence will be met in the end with Jesus's power over death and darkness. For now, the protest of the disciples is met with Jesus's veiled but triumphal

26. Brown makes a connection between the settings of 1:28 and 10:40 and suggests that 10:40 may have marked the original ending of the Gospel recounting Jesus's public ministry. See his pertinent comments in *Gospel According to John*, 1:44–45, 413–15.

27. Brown (ibid., 1:414), regards chs. 11–12 as a later editorial addition to the original Gospel outline that ended at 10:42. Bultmann (*Gospel of John*) along with Boismard and Lamouille (*L'Evangile de Jean*) also share this conclusion.

28. Ironic speech and double entendre are hallmarks of Johannine discourse. The term καταλαμβάνω in 1:5 should likely be understood in two senses: "the darkness has not *comprehended* it" (i.e., the light), and "the darkness has not *overcome* it." Each sense is consistent with what occurs throughout the Gospel. Those who are shrouded in darkness are unable to *comprehend* Jesus, the light of the world. And in the end, the darkness of death is not able to *overcome* the light of life as Jesus is raised from the dead. On the different translational possibilities, see BDAG, s.v. καταλαμβάνω.

hint of his victory over darkness in the near future with the raising of Lazarus. Moloney's comments on vv. 9–10 are instructive:

> Whatever may happen in the story that is yet to be told, Jesus is the light. Using the Jewish calculation of twelve hours for light of day and twelve hours for darkness of night, the disciples are told of the need to walk in the light of the world. Because of the lack of a full appropriation of the light that Jesus brings, the disciples must stumble because they have no light in them. The reader follows the progress of the disciples closely. Will these words of Jesus, the light of the world, enable them to recognize the victory of light over darkness?[29]

Jesus intends to enter Judea once again to show that the light is more powerful than the darkness of death to which his friend has succumbed.[30] The death of this friend becomes the next topic of conversation for Jesus and the disciples.

Discussion about the Fate of Lazarus (vv. 11–16)

After highlighting the contrasts between light and darkness, Jesus continues in v. 11 to provide the disciples with a concrete example of how light can overcome darkness. He informs the disciples that Lazarus has fallen asleep but that it is his intention to "wake him up," ἵνα ἐξυπνίσω αὐτόν. It becomes clear that this is Jesus's motivation behind wanting to travel again into Judea.

Jesus's veiled comment about Lazarus's death is completely lost on the uncomprehending disciples who assert that if Lazarus is merely sleeping, he will recover (σωθήσεται). Some modern translations render σῴζω as "get better"[31] or "recover."[32] Highlighting the deliberate ambiguity in the text, the NAB gives σῴζω its metaphorical sense by translating it "he will be saved." As these various translations illustrate, it is difficult to do justice to the complexity of the term in this verse. σῴζω in v. 12 should most likely be understood as a double entendre. Lazarus does eventually "recover" from his illness, but only because he is be "saved" (or "rescued") from death. Once again there is an instance

29. Moloney, *Signs and Shadows*, 158.

30. See the narrator's comment in the 1:5: "The light shines in the darkness and the darkness has not overcome/understood [κατέλαβεν] it."

31. E.g., NIV and NLT.

32. E.g., NASB, ESV, and NET.

where one cannot fully encapsulate John's ironic language with an economy of words.

As in the narrative aside found in 2:21, the narrator again turns explicitly to the reader and explains what Jesus's listeners have failed to grasp. Jesus is not speaking of sleep but of death. Because the disciples have not understood, Jesus plainly announces in v. 14 that Lazarus has died (Λάζαρος ἀπέθανεν) and indicates his joy (χαίρω, v. 15) that his disciples will now be able to witness the ultimate display of the light's dominion over darkness.[33]

In v. 7 Jesus announced his intent to travel into Judea by saying ἄγωμεν εἰς τὴν Ἰουδαίαν, "let us go into Judea." Here at the end of v. 15 Jesus utters the words ἄγωμεν πρὸς αὐτόν, "let us go to him." This second statement parallels his first, lexically and syntactically. In each discussion with the disciples Jesus has indicated a desire to depart (ἄγωμεν). In the first instance the reader learns of the region to which he desires to go (εἰς τὴν Ἰουδαίαν), and in the second instance the reader understands the reason why he desires to go (πρὸς αὐτόν).[34]

It should not be overlooked that Jesus's reason for not going earlier is explicitly stated in v. 15. The purpose behind this delay, he tells his disciples, is ἵνα πιστεύσητε. This is what does *not* happen, as the remainder of the chapter is dominated by the theme of failing to believe. Thomas's words come on the heels of Jesus's expressed hope that this situation will engender belief in the hapless disciples.

In v. 16 the reader is finally introduced to the disciple known as Thomas. The narrator describes him as Θωμᾶς ὁ λεγόμενος Δίδυμος.[35] Upon being introduced, Thomas affirms the two prior statements of Jesus's desire to leave. He says to his fellow disciples, ἄγωμεν καὶ ἡμεῖς ἵνα ἀποθάνωμεν μετ᾽ αὐτοῦ. The most natural reading of

33. Though the disciples have forgotten, the reader remembers that in 5:25 Jesus told the crowds, "Amen, amen, I say to you, the hour is coming and now is, when the dead will hear the Son of God's voice, and those who hear will live."

34. In the present context, for Jesus to go πρὸς αὐτόν is to depart with the purpose of bringing the "light" to Lazarus who has lapsed into the darkness of death.

35. Both the transliteration Θωμᾶς (from the Aramaic תאומא) and the Greek Δίδυμος mean "twin." In the *Gospel of Thomas* he is called ΔΙΔΥΜΟϹ ΙΟΥΔΑϹ ΘΩΜΑϹ, and in the *Book of Thomas the Contender* he is called ΙΟΥΔΑϹ ΘΩΜΑϹ. In later traditions (most notably in the *Acts of Thomas*) Thomas is regarded as the twin brother of Jesus. In *Acts of Thomas* 1, a distinction is made between Judas, the brother of James (presumably the same Jude to identify himself as the brother of James in the canonical epistle of Jude), and Judas Thomas, the twin brother of Jesus.

ἀποθάνωμεν μετ᾽ αὐτοῦ is surely in reference to the death of Lazarus, but there is some question as to the referent behind αὐτοῦ. The nearest referent in the text with which to connect αὐτοῦ is clearly Λάζαρος at the end of v. 14. In addition, at the end of v.15, Jesus, still speaking of Lazarus, states, ἄγωμεν πρὸς αὐτόν. Thus, it seems preferable, upon first glance, to link Thomas's use of αὐτοῦ with Lazarus. However, when all is considered it is not entirely clear that this is the best way to understand Thomas's words.

Two points need to be emphasized here, one with respect to resurrection and the other with respect to death. First, at the end of ch. 12 Jesus and the disciples make their way to Judea and Lazarus is raised from the dead. In the account of the raising of Lazarus there are some key terms that also appear in the account of Jesus's resurrection in ch. 20. For instance, μνημεῖον, "tomb" (11:17, 38; 20:1, 3, 4, 6, 11), λίθος, "stone" (11:38; 20:1), σουδάριον, "grave cloth" (11:44; 20:7) are just a few of the important terms and concepts that appear in both resurrection stories.[36] The reader hears the echoes and perceives the connection between the two accounts. All of this suggests that the reader is supposed to make a concrete connection between the raising of Lazarus and the resurrection of Jesus. After the raising of Lazarus there are no more *semeia* for the remainder of the Gospel. Jesus's last and greatest sign is the foreshadowing of his greatest act in the Gospel—his own resurrection.

Second, before resurrection can occur there must necessarily be death. This raises the question once again of the referent behind Thomas's use of αὐτοῦ in v. 16. It appears that αὐτοῦ is somewhat ambiguous inasmuch as the wider context intimates that the disciples feared *Jesus* would be killed upon returning to Judea. Just as their resurrections are connected, the deaths of Lazarus and Jesus are intimately bound to one another in the broader literary tapestry of the Fourth Gospel. Therefore, it seems plausible to assert that the words ἄγωμεν καὶ ἡμεῖς ἵνα ἀποθάνωμεν μετ᾽ αὐτοῦ are intentionally unclear and are supposed to nudge the reader into reflecting not only

36. John Pryor (*John: Evangelist of the Covenant People*, 48) dismisses this when he writes, "[O]ne may rightly object that such agreement [in wording] is only to be expected in two accounts dealing with the same subject." There is surely a stronger, even if a more subtle connection between the language and images of both resurrection passages than Pryor allows.

on the death of Lazarus but also on the imminent death of Jesus. The informed reader has already picked up on this theme and is therefore in a position to understand where the narrative is heading: just as Lazarus has died and will be revived, Jesus will also die and be raised.

Read in this way, Thomas's statement in v. 16 is laden with ambiguity. Whether Thomas's words are understood as a reference to dying along with Lazarus or with Jesus, it is clear that he has not understood that the mission to Judea is one to be characterized primarily by resurrection and *not* by death. Once again, anticipation begins to build in the reader. In the end, however, the disciples die neither with Lazarus (as he is raised to new life), nor with Jesus (as they eventually abandon him at his arrest). Thus, the anticipation that builds in the reader results in an unmet expectation similar to that of Jesus's inactivity in v. 6. The reader's unmet expectation, however, is overshadowed, at least initially, by Jesus's final *semeion* in the Fourth Gospel, the raising of Lazarus.

Thomas's words effectively end the unit as the reader awaits Jesus's next great act. The previous chapter of this study emphasized that in the Fourth Gospel there is little direct development for characters other than Jesus. That observation holds true in the present pericope in the character of Thomas, called Didymus. Here, Thomas serves as a foil, being used by the narrator to create a situation where narrative tension, irony, and misunderstanding point forward to the illumination given by the "light of the world."

Thomas Thus Far

In his first appearance, Thomas offers little substance to the discussion and he does not figure prominently in the events that follow. Even though the reader learns his name and hears his voice, Thomas does not stand out as a character of any great narratival significance. His lone proclamation in this pericope is nothing more than a launching point for the contrastive actions of Jesus in the remainder of ch. 11.[37] However, Thomas's role as an uncomprehending character begins in the unit just considered.

37. Throughout the rest of ch. 11, the lack of faith is an important theme. Thomas's incomprehension is a preface to the misunderstanding and unbelief displayed by Martha and Mary.

Jesus and Thomas in John 14:1–24

In ch. 14, Thomas enters onto the narrative stage of the Fourth Gospel for a second time. A number of important events have taken place in the intervening chapters from the first to the second appearance of Thomas. Following the raising of Lazarus at the end of ch. 11, Jesus is anointed by one of the sisters from Bethany (12:1–9) in a scene that provides the author an opportunity to have Jesus speak openly about his upcoming death. Throughout chs. 12–13, Jesus not only predicts his death but also his betrayal by two disciples while the Jewish leaders persist in their posture of unbelief toward Jesus.

Chapter 13 is the beginning of what scholars have traditionally called John's "Farewell Discourse."[38] Though that section of the Gospel is filled with seemingly disconnected material, many commentators see a thread of continuity woven throughout 13:1—17:26. It is widely recognized that these chapters comprise a fairly coherent farewell address meant to prepare the disciples for Jesus's departure.[39] This sort of farewell address is not uncommon in ancient literature.[40]

Neyrey outlines the nine elements of a typical farewell address, all of which are present in John 13–17: (1) announcement of death or departure, (2) review of the patriarch's life, (3) relationships to be maintained, (4) revelations of beneficial things to come, (5) predictions of future hard times, (6) exhortation to practice a group-specific virtue and to avoid a group-specific vice, (7) successor named, (8) legacy bestowed, and (9) occasionally a final prayer or blessing.[41] Having already alluded

38. This is widely recognized, with some variation, in the commentary tradition. See, among others, Neyrey, *Gospel of John*, 240; Schnackenburg, *Gospel According to St. John*, 3:6–89; and Carson, *Gospel According to John*, 476 (all of whom who see the Farewell Discourse beginning at 13:31); Kysar, *John*, 219; and Ridderbos, *Gospel of John*, 481 (both of whom see the Farewell Discourse beginning in 14:1 and extending through the end of ch. 17); Morris, *Gospel According to John*, 542; Keener, *Gospel of John*, 1:893; and Moloney, *Gospel of John*, 370 (all of whom see the discourse comprising all of ch. 13–17).

39. "Readers of John 13–17 quickly learn that this seemingly disorganized assemblage of materials makes excellent sense when viewed as a farewell address" (Neyrey, *Gospel of John*, 238).

40. Two biblical examples can be found in the Pentateuch: the farewell addresses of Jacob in Gen 49 and Moses in Deut 32. The *Testament of the Twelve Patriarchs* is the best extracanonical example of this type of farewell speech.

41. Neyrey, *Gospel of John*, 239. It is important to note that Neyrey does not suggest that these nine elements follow a specific chronology in any given farewell address.

to his death in 13:33 (element 1 in Neyrey's list), Jesus begins in ch. 14 to discuss his departure in more concrete terms. After the upheaval created by predictions of death and betrayal, Jesus speaks of his departure while offering words of comfort to the disciples. The unit under consideration can be broken down into the following substructure:

1. Jesus speaks of his departure (14:1–4)
2. Jesus corrects and instructs the disciples (14:5–24)
    a. Jesus addresses Thomas (14:5–7)
    b. Jesus addresses Philip (14:8–10)
    c. Jesus addresses the disciples (14:11–21)
    d. Jesus addresses Judas (not Iscariot) (14:22–24)[42]

Jesus Speaks of His Departure (14:1–4)

In two previous instances in the foregoing chapters, the reader has seen a "troubled" Jesus. After predicting his death, Jesus proclaims in 12:27, νῦν ἡ ψυχή μου *τετάρακται*, "Now my soul is *troubled*." Then, just before predicting his betrayal by Judas Iscariot, the narrator asserts in 13:21 that [ὁ] Ἰησοῦς *ἐταράχθη* τῷ πνεύματι, "Jesus was *troubled* in spirit." It is clear that the narrator wants the reader to regard these vulnerable moments as a picture of the inner turmoil Jesus experiences as a result of following the will of the Father toward the cross. It is ironic then, that Jesus expresses in these verses greater concern for the inner turmoil his disciples are experiencing at the announcement of his departure.

In the first half of v. 1, Jesus consoles the disciples, using the same term that has characterized his own psyche in the previous two chapters: μὴ *ταρασσέσθω* ὑμῶν ἡ καρδία, "Do not let your hearts *be troubled*." On the eve of his betrayal and arrest, when it would be entirely appropriate for Jesus to accept consolation from the disciples, he once again displays a selfless attitude of servanthood in his concern for them.[43]

In fact, his reconstruction of Jesus's farewell address locates these different elements in a very different order.

42. Philip, the disciples as a group, and Judas (not Iscariot) will all be considered in chapter 5 of this study. However, it is appropriate to discuss them here as well since their presence in ch. 14 can help to demonstrate the consistent literary pattern at work in John 14. In chapter 5 I will draw upon what is written in this section.

43. This attitude of selflessness is a concrete example of the kind of servitude Jesus called for in 13:1–17 when he washed the disciples' feet.

The second half of v. 1 reads, πιστεύετε εἰς τὸν θεὸν καὶ εἰς ἐμὲ πιστεύετε. A close reading of this statement raises a number of questions, since πιστεύετε (which appears twice) can be understood as either an indicative or an imperative. There are then, a number of options for how the verbs could be understood.

First, it is possible to understand both verbs as indicatives. This would cause them to be read as statements of fact: "You trust in God and you trust in me." This rendering, however, makes little sense in the context of a farewell speech where Jesus is preparing the disciples for his departure. It is better to regard at least one of the verbs as an imperative in light of the opening prohibition, μὴ ταρασσέσθω (v. 1a). We recall that element 6 of the farewell address as outlined by Neyrey is "exhortation to practice a group-specific virtue and to avoid a group-specific vice." The prohibition against being troubled then, suggests that an affirmative, hortatory imperative will follow.

In that light, a second option emerges as to how πιστεύετε could be read. Some translations[44] and commentators[45] understand both verbs as imperatives: "Trust in God, trust also in me." A third option, and the one I prefer here, is to read the first verb as an indicative and the second as an imperative: "You trust in God, trust also in me." The language and structure of v. 1b suggest a close identity between God and Jesus.[46] Thus, this rendering accords well with the Fourth Gospel's consistent emphasis on Jesus as the unique revelation of the Father. In addition, this rendering accords well with the fact that the Johannine disciples already appear to stand in some tradition within Judaism.[47] Since they

44. E.g., NIV, NASB, NLT, ESV, ASV. A notable exception among modern English translations is the NAB, which reads, "You have faith in God [indicative], have faith also in me [imperative]."

45. See, among others, Moloney, *Gospel According to John*, 392; Carson, *Gospel According to John*, 487; Stibbe, *John*, 152; Morris, *Gospel According to John*, 565. Keener (*Gospel of John*, 931) comments that both instances of πιστεύετε in 14:1 should be taken in the same mood and then suggests that imperative is "more likely."

46. Specifically, the structure of the words εἰς τὸν θεὸν καὶ εἰς ἐμέ seem to indicate a close connection, perhaps even an identification between the two prepositional phrases that are connected by καί. In this regard, Ridderbos (*Gospel of John*, 488 n. 23) comments, "The chiastically structured pronouncement coordinates two clauses ('believe in God,' 'believe in me') and makes the second (imperatival) clause dependent on the first (indicative)."

47. How else can one explain their knowledge of a "Messiah" (1:41) or "the one about whom Moses wrote and also the prophets" (1:45)?

have demonstrated a trust in God by following Jesus in the first place, it seems redundant for Jesus to exhort them to "trust in God." It is much more difficult, as the reader has already seen, for the disciples to trust in Jesus in the same way they trust in God.[48] At this point, it is appropriate to recall the words of the prologue where it is revealed that those who believe in his name are enabled to become true children of God (1:12–13). The sort of trust Jesus calls for in v. 1b has the potential to create an altogether different relationship for the disciples with both the Father and the Son. There is an entirely new level to that relationship that will be divulged in the following three verses.

In v. 3 the reader and the disciples learn that Jesus is departing to the dwelling place of God, otherwise identified in v. 2 as τῇ οἰκίᾳ τοῦ πατρός μου. In that "house," Jesus says, there are many dwelling places (μοναὶ).[49] The term μονή has a clear lexical connection to the important Johannine term μένω, "abide."[50] Though μένω has already appeared at various turns in the narrative, it will become even more prominent in the remainder of the Farewell Discourse (Jesus uses the term eleven times in ch. 15 alone). The use of this term with reference to an unseen dwelling suggests a greater permanence in the relationship between Jesus and his followers—one that extends beyond what trust in Jesus's name provides. The narrator has already informed the reader that trusting in Jesus's name gives one the authority to be a child of God. If this is true, the τόπος Jesus prepares must represent a final consummative stage in the relationship between the Father and his children.[51] After going away to the Father's house and preparing a place, Jesus insists that he will return to his disciples so that they may abide together in the same location (v. 3). Thus, the spiritual abiding that has characterized their relationship will culminate in their abiding together in the same location.

48. Of course, there is a fourth option for how the two verbs could be read. The first verb could be read as an imperative and the second could be read as an indicative. This would create an English rendering that reads, "Trust in God also as you trust in me." In addition to being a questionable translation on grammatical grounds, this rendering also seems untenable given the overall narrative context.

49. Cf. BDAG, s.v. μονή.

50. μένω is used forty times in the Fourth Gospel: 1:32, 33, 38, 39 (twice); 2:12; 3:36; 4:40 (twice); 5:38; 6:27; 7:9; 8:31, 35 (twice); 9:41; 10:40; 11:6, 54; 12:24, 34, 46; 14:10, 17, 25; 15:4 (three times), 5, 6, 7 (twice), 9, 10 (twice), 16; 19:31; 21:22, 23.

51. See the helpful discussion of this concept in Gundry, "In My Father's House."

Before being interrupted by three of his disciples, Jesus utters words that once again lead to misunderstanding. In v. 4, Jesus tells the disciples ὅπου [ἐγὼ] ὑπάγω οἴδατε τὴν ὁδόν,[52] "You know the way where I am going." This enigmatic statement catches the reader by surprise since none of Jesus's discourses have included a discussion of a particular ὁδός. The only other occurrence of ὁδός (besides its use in 14:4–6) is in the preaching of John the Baptist (1:23). Quoting the words of Isaiah 40:3, John proclaims that he is making straight the ὁδὸς κυρίου. There is therefore no reason for the reader to grasp fully Jesus's comment in v. 4, and there is equally no expectation that the disciples should understand Jesus's comment about a "way" to the Father's house. Thomas is about to affirm this by saying what everyone who is paying attention is already thinking.

Jesus Corrects and Instructs the Disciples (14:5–24)

In the wake of Jesus's statement in v. 4, a pattern of misunderstanding and correction emerges in the rest of the chapter. Thomas is the first to object to Jesus's words. After Thomas objects, Philip also demonstrates an inability to understand something Jesus has said. Once Jesus has addressed Philip he speaks to the disciples as a whole. During his address to the group, a third disciple—identified as Judas (not Iscariot)—finds himself unable to comprehend the spiritual truths behind Jesus's teaching. This pattern not only provides Jesus opportunities to set forth distinctly Johannine themes but also reinforces in the reader the impression that Jesus is widely misunderstood both by outsiders and insiders.

Jesus Addresses Thomas (14:5–7)

After Jesus's discussion of the "way" to the Father, Thomas speaks up and professes to be unaware of where Jesus is going. Acting as spokesman for the group, he claims corporate ignorance (οὐκ οἴδαμεν ποῦ ὑπάγεις), and as a consequence poses a logical question on behalf of the ignorant group (πῶς δυνάμεθα τὴν ὁδὸν εἰδέναι;). Thomas has

52. 𝔓^{66} A C^{3} D Θ Ψ $f^{1.13}$ 𝔐 lat sy sa ac^{2} read ὅπου ἐγὼ ὑπάγω οἴδατε καὶ τὴν ὁδόν *οἴδατε*. The external evidence for this reading is weighty but this longer text can be explained more easily on the basis of the distinction made by Thomas in v. 5 between *where* Jesus is going (ποῦ) and *how* to get there (πῶς). Thus, the second οἴδατε is likely a later addition meant to parallel Thomas's proclamation in v. 5 and thereby bring greater clarity to the text.

failed to understand that Jesus is once again speaking of his death and introducing his resurrection under the guise of his "return."

Two key elements from Thomas's previous appearance in the Gospel are present in this pericope: (1) Thomas says something that expresses his incomprehension of Jesus's message and/or mission, and (2) he once again speaks in a context where resurrection is addressed. This resurrection connection is hinted at by some commentators and is surely one of the centerpieces of Riley's argument regarding the negative portrayal of Thomas in John's Gospel.

The reader knows that the disciples have not heard Jesus teach explicitly about a "way" to the Father's house. Even though this is the case, the reader should see in this proclamation a display of incomprehension similar to that demonstrated by Thomas in 11:16. This becomes even clearer in the light of Jesus's next statement: ἐγώ εἰμι ἡ ὁδὸς καὶ ἡ ἀλήθεια καὶ ἡ ζωή. These words represent the most detailed ἐγώ εἰμι statement with a predicate in the Gospel. These concepts are connected and the narrator shows Jesus identifying himself as the embodiment of all three. ἀλήθεια and ζωή are both key terms from the prologue that appear throughout the narrative. Had Jesus been speaking of "truth" or "life," the reader and the disciples would have been more familiar with the concepts. In using ὁδός (v. 4), the narrator creates an opportunity to speak authoritatively to the literary audience while using the voice of Jesus. In this way, it appears that Thomas has been set up as a foil. Neither the characters nor the reader understand what Jesus means by ὁδός, but Thomas is the unlucky character who expresses what everyone else is thinking. When this happens, Thomas's role as an uncomprehending character develops even further.

Once again Jesus turns an opportunity to clarify his teachings into a chance to emphasize the unique nature of his relationship to the Father. To know one is to know the other (v. 7a). To see Jesus is to have seen the very representation of God (v. 7b). This second half of v. 7 is not as clear as Jesus would like it to be because it leads to another misunderstanding from the disciple named Philip.

Jesus Addresses Philip (14:8–10)

The reader has already seen Philip on several previous occasions in the story thus far. In addition to being one of the first disciples to follow Jesus (see 1:43–46), Philip speaks in the account of the bread sign

(6:6–8) and is also involved in bringing some Greeks who had come to the feast to see Jesus (12:20–22).[53]

Drawing upon Jesus's declaration to Thomas that to see him is to see the Father (v. 7b), Philip interrupts in v. 8 and asks Jesus to show them the Father (δεῖξον ἡμῖν τὸν πατέρα). Jesus's reply shows, once again, that he has not been understood by his followers. Barrett's comment on Philip's request is insightful: "His uncomprehending question here serves simply, according to John's method, to advance the argument. It implies separation between Jesus and the Father whereas in truth there is mutual indwelling."[54]

As in the previous pericope where Thomas failed to understand Jesus's teaching on the way to the Father, Philip's ignorant request is part of the literary method whereby the narrator keeps Jesus's discourse going. By having characters question, declare, or object in a spirit of misunderstanding, the narrator is, as Barrett puts it, simply "advancing the argument" of the discourse. In other words, the narrator is not "picking on" Thomas alone (as the advocates of the community-conflict hypothesis might argue), but rather is showing Philip to be an equally uncomprehending character. This trend of incomprehension will continue throughout the rest of ch. 14.

Jesus is incredulous at Philip's request and questions whether Philip knows him (τοσούτῳ χρόνῳ μεθ' ὑμῶν εἰμι καὶ οὐκ ἔγνωκάς με; v. 9) and believes in him (οὐ πιστεύεις ὅτι ἐγὼ ἐν τῷ πατρὶ καὶ ὁ πατὴρ ἐν ἐμοί ἐστιν; v. 10). If one were to accept Jesus's view of things, the unique, abiding relationship between Father and Son is seemingly self-evident, and should certainly be clear to those who have walked with him for nearly three years.[55]

In v. 10b Jesus declares that his words are not his own but that what he has spoken is directly from the Father. Throughout vv. 9–10 Jesus uses three different verbs of perception or cognition to describe how he uniquely unveils the Father to the world: to know (γινώσκω), to see

53. Philip's role as an uncomprehending character will be discussed in chapter 5. There I will examine his presentation in both chs. 6 and 14.

54. Barrett, *Gospel According to St. John*, 459.

55. The Fourth Gospel is the only canonical Gospel to have a chronology longer than a year. There are several Jewish feasts ("a feast of the Jews," 5:1; the feast of tabernacles, 6:7; the feast of dedication, 10:22) and each year of Jesus's ministry with the disciples is punctuated by an occurrence of the Passover (2:13, 23; 6:4; 13:1; 18:28). Jesus's words τοσούτῳ χρόνῳ μεθ' ὑμῶν should be understood against the backdrop of a lengthy ministry with the disciples.

(ὁράω), and to believe (πιστεύω). One might also infer from Jesus's comments about speaking words from the Father that a fourth verb is implied: to hear (ἀκούω). Those who can perceive any element of Jesus's message can experience a genuine representation of the Father. Even Jesus's works come directly from the Father (ὁ δὲ πατὴρ ἐν ἐμοὶ μένων ποιεῖ τὰ ἔργα αὐτοῦ).

The prologue informed the reader that Jesus was the unique revealer of the Father (1:18). Now the disciples are hearing what the reader has known all along. In all his words and deeds, Jesus comprehensively reveals the Father.

Jesus Addresses the Disciples (14:11–21)

Many translations keep v. 11 with the previous section, but in light of the emerging pattern it seems best to separate v. 11 from the Philip passage. The text does not explicitly say that Jesus turns to the disciples as a group and begins to address them. However, in vv. 9–10 Jesus spoke with Philip using singular verbs (ἔγνωκας, λέγεις, v. 9; πιστεύεις, v. 10). This indicates that he was speaking directly to Philip. In v. 11, Jesus switches to the plural πιστεύετε and continues to use plural verbs (αἰτήσητε, vv. 13, 14; ἀγαπᾶτε, τηρήσετε, v. 15; γινώσκετε, v. 17; θεωρεῖτε, ζήσετε, v. 19; γνώσεσθε, v. 20) until Judas interjects in v. 22. It seems then that the shift to plural verbs is a clear textual indication that Jesus is no longer speaking directly to Philip but to the entire group.

In 14:2 Jesus exhorted the disciples to trust in him the same way they trusted the Father. Here again in v. 11, Jesus exhorts the disciples to believe (πιστεύετε).[56] They are to embrace Jesus's teaching about the unique relationship between the Father and Son. If they are unable to believe on the basis of his word, Jesus points to the works he has performed (διὰ τὰ ἔργα αὐτὰ πιστεύετε).[57] This is not the first time Jesus has called his works as witness to his identity (see 5:16–23).

56. Carson (*Gospel According to John*, 495) comments that πιστεύετε does not carry the same force here as in v. 1. Instead, he argues that it should be taken in the sense of "Believe that what I have just said is true." At the literary level, this conclusion seems to present an unnecessary bifurcation of meanings behind πιστεύετε. The repetition of πιστεύω is intended to ring in the reader's mind, even if the context is not a direct command to exercise belief in Jesus in a salvific sense.

57. Moloney, in his three-volume literary reading of the Fourth Gospel (*Belief in the Word*; *Signs and Shadows*; *Glory Not Dishonor*), ably demonstrates the distinction

Throughout the depiction of Jesus's ministry in the Fourth Gospel, the author has used the double ἀμήν statement to punctuate a given teaching or pronouncement.[58] In v. 12, Jesus uses the double ἀμήν statement to emphasize, once again, the special relationship he and the Father enter into with the one who believes. Just as the Father and Son abide in one another and the Son is enabled by the Father, the one who believes will be enabled to do the very same deeds as Jesus after he departs to be with the Father.

The unqualified promises of vv. 13–14 seem rather astounding when taken at face value.[59] Of course, there is no suggestion that the Son ever asks or expects anything that is not consonant with the will of the Father. The special abiding relationship the Father and Son possess overrides the seizing of personal prerogatives by the Son. In the same way, Jesus says, those who ask ἐν τῷ ὀνόματί μου will get what they request. To ask in Jesus's name is to show evidence of a special abiding relationship like that displayed by the Father and Son (see 1:12–13). Abiding in Jesus's name prevents one from asking for something that is outside the will of the Father. Thus, whatever is asked for by the believer in Jesus's name is granted because it necessarily conforms to the will of God.

There is a subtle shift in subject matter in vv. 15–21. Once again, the reader can detect the creative shaping of the story in a way that advances the argument of Jesus's discourse.

Jesus turns in vv. 15–21 to a discussion of the παράκλητος he intends to send once he departs to be with the Father. In describing him as *another* helper (ἄλλον παράκλητον) Jesus subtly asserts that the advocate will be of the same kind and share common qualities that he and the Father possess. This other advocate Jesus identifies as the "spirit

---

in John's economy between belief on the basis of Jesus's works and belief on the basis of Jesus's word.

58. The double ἀμήν statement occurs twenty-five times in the Fourth Gospel. In addition to 14:12 it can be found in 1:51; 3:3, 5, 11; 5:19, 24, 25; 6:26, 32, 47, 53; 8:34, 51, 58; 10:1, 7; 12:24; 13:16, 20, 21, 38; 14:12; 16:20, 23; 21:18.

59. Verse 14 is not contained in X f^1 565 1009 1365 vg^{ms} $syr^{c, s, pal}$ arm geo along with a few other lectionary readings. Though it is more common to opt for the shorter reading as the original, the manuscript evidence is not weighty. In addition to the fact that the external evidence is not terribly strong, this problem may be explained away internally as an omission on the basis of homoioteleuton. The scribe in question may have accidentally skipped from the ἐάν at the beginning of v. 14 to the ἐάν at the beginning of v. 15. Thus, the inclusion of v. 14 seems to be the logical choice.

of truth," πνεῦμα τῆς ἀληθείας. Once again the reader is met with a theme from the Pprologue (ἀληθείας, 1:9, 14, 17). In this instance, Jesus is not simply dispensing truth through proclamation or miraculous activity. He intends to dispense truth in a form that will continually manifest itself among his followers. This other representative of the Father will abide *with* the disciples (παρ' ὑμῖν μένει, v. 17) and *in* them (ἐν ὑμῖν ἔσται, v. 17). The enduring presence of the παράκλητος will allow the disciples to continue abiding in Jesus's name even after he has gone to be with the Father.[60]

Throughout the Gospel Jesus has spoken of himself as the Son, and it has typically been with respect to his relationship to God, the Father. Though Jesus has not spoken of himself as a "father" to the disciples, he comments that he will not leave them as orphans (ὀρφανούς) in the world (v. 18). While most commonly referring to those "deprived of parents," ὀρφανός can also be used to describe one who is "without the aid and comfort of one who serves as an associate and friend."[61] Understood in this way, Jesus is letting the disciples know that he does not intend to leave them helpless after his departure. Following this statement he tells the disciples, ἔρχομαι πρὸς ὑμᾶς. How is the reader to understand this statement? Is Jesus speaking of the return after his departure to the Father (i.e., his resurrection)?[62] Is the reader to understand this as the Parousia? Or is Jesus speaking of the coming of the παράκλητος, which the reader has already learned is another representation of the qualities he and the Father share?[63] Perhaps this is aiming for a degree of specificity not intended by the text. Jesus has just promised that his enduring presence will be with the disciples in the form of the παράκλητος (14:16–17), and he has also informed them of his personal return after preparing a place for them (14:2–3). Jesus's statement that he will come to them is simply an affirmation that he will

60. In this regard, Moloney (*Glory Not Dishonor*, 43) comments, "Jesus' departure and the gift of the Paraclete, the spirit of truth, necessitate a distinction between Jesus and the Spirit. But what the Spirit does for the disciples is the prolongation and perfection of what Jesus does for them. In the Spirit-Paraclete, the absence of the physical Jesus is overcome."

61. BDAG, s.v. ὀρφανός. Cf. also Barrett, *Gospel According to St. John*, 463.

62. In 20:19, 24, 26, Jesus's resurrection appearances are spoken of in terms of his coming (in vv. 19, 24, the aorist form ἦλθεν is used, while the historical present ἔρχεται is used in v. 26).

63. Carson (*Gospel According to John*, 501–2) has a helpful treatment of the various views and how they have been resolved by other scholars.

not abandon them. No matter what, Jesus's followers will have access to his presence.

Just in case the disciples fail to realize, Jesus asserts that the departure he has been discussing since 14:1 is imminent. In v. 19 he states, ἔτι μικρὸν καὶ ὁ κόσμος με οὐκέτι θεωρεῖ. Jesus's sobering words need to be received seriously by the disciples. His departure is not only certain, it is also near.

The theme of Jesus's oneness with the Father has been prominent throughout the Gospel and particularly in this section of the Farewell Discourse. Verse 20 widens the scope of that relationship to include the disciples (ἐγὼ ἐν τῷ πατρί μου καὶ ὑμεῖς ἐν ἐμοὶ κἀγὼ ἐν ὑμῖν); then in v. 21 it is widened further to include not just the disciples but *anyone* who keeps faithfully the commandments of Jesus (ὁ ἔχων τὰς ἐντολάς μου καὶ τηρῶν αὐτὰς). This point is missed and once again a disciple professes misunderstanding.

Jesus Addresses Judas (Not Iscariot) (14:22–24)

For the third time in the chapter, a named disciple questions Jesus in a way that reveals misunderstanding.[64] First it was Thomas, then it was Philip. In these verses, the reader meets Judas for the first time. The reader has already met Judas the Iscariot, knows that he is the betrayer, and knows that he is not present among the disciples during this discourse. Therefore, the narrator is careful to identify the disciple as Ἰούδας, οὐχ ὁ Ἰσχαριώτης.

After Jesus's statement that he will reveal himself to those who keep his commands (v. 21), Judas, calling Jesus κύριε (v. 22), inquires as to why Jesus only intends to reveal himself to the disciples and not to the world. Judas, seemingly stuck on Jesus's words in vv. 19–20, has failed to grasp Jesus's progression from speaking of the disciples to speaking in v. 21 of *whoever* obeys (ὁ ἔχων). Further, by assuming that the disciples are the only ones to keep Jesus's commandments, Judas has misunderstood Jesus. It is not just the Twelve who will see Jesus. The scope of

64. Moloney (*Glory Not Dishonor*, 45) comments, "Judas' question, asking further clarification of a revelation to the disciples, which will not be given to 'the world' (v. 22), enables this subsection of the discourse to close with the same themes (vv. 23–24). As with the earlier questions (see vv. 5, 8) Judas asks for information already obvious to the reader. Jesus' revelation of himself, which is the sight of God's glory (see 1:14; 2:11; 11:4, 40), can only be given to those who are open to his word."

Jesus's revelation is widened to include whoever loves him, and those who do will necessarily keep his commandments (v. 23).The implied corollary to this is expressed in v. 24a: ὁ μὴ ἀγαπῶν με τοὺς λόγους μου οὐ τηρεῖ. This explanation draws a clear delineation between those who will occupy one of the dwelling places Jesus is preparing and those who will not. As in 14:10, Jesus finishes addressing Judas by reiterating that his words are directly from the Father.

Judas, like Thomas and Philip before him, stands out as an uncomprehending character. Though he has been in the company of Jesus for nearly three years, he is no closer to grasping the truths of Jesus's mission. The narrator has once again used one of the disciples to advance the argument of the chapter.

Thomas Thus Far

What can be gleaned about John's overall presentation of Thomas from the literary unit considered in the previous section? To begin with, it is clear from the foregoing discussion that Thomas is one element in a larger pattern. This stands in sharp contrast to some of the foundational assumptions of the community-conflict hypothesis. Here, the Fourth Gospel does not seem to be directing a polemic against Thomas alone. Rather, the disciples in general seem to be spiritually dull in regard to the teaching of Jesus.

In ch. 14, Thomas is again presented as an uncomprehending character just as he was in ch. 11. The difference here is that Thomas is one of three named disciples to misunderstand Jesus's teaching and to be characterized with a slant of negativity. It is nonetheless safe to conclude that the developing portrait of Thomas is a negative one. He has appeared twice and he has spoken twice. In each instance, Thomas has given little evidence of spiritual insight. The picture of Thomas in John is not yet complete. In order to complete the consideration of Thomas's portrait in the Fourth Gospel, the discussion turns now to Thomas's third appearance.

Jesus and Thomas in John 20:24–28

In this section I consider the third and most significant of Thomas's four appearances in the Gospel. Since Thomas's last appearance in the story a great deal has occurred. After completing the remainder of his Farewell

Discourse (chs. 15–17), Jesus has been arrested (18:1–11), questioned by Jewish rulers (18:12–24), brought before Pilate (18:28—19:16), crucified (19:17–42), and raised (20:1–10). In ch. 20 the resurrected Jesus makes a number of appearances. He manifests himself first to Mary Magdalene while still in the garden (20:11–18), then to the assembled disciples (20:19–23). With what the reader has already seen of Thomas, it is appropriate that his third appearance in the narrative is, like his first two appearances, in the context of resurrection.

In v. 24 the reader is informed that, of the Twelve, Thomas alone has failed to see the risen Jesus. This time, the narrator provides the most detailed introduction of Thomas in the narrative: Θωμᾶς δὲ εἷς ἐκ τῶν δώδεκα, ὁ λεγόμενος Δίδυμος, "Thomas, one of the Twelve, the one called Didymus" (or "Twin").[65] The reader again hears Thomas's name and surname and is reminded of his position among the group. This identification reminds the reader that Thomas is the disciple who has appeared at two previous points in Jesus's ministry. It also serves to point the reader back to those two previous passages.

The narrator goes on to report that Thomas was not present with the disciples when Jesus appeared to them (v. 24b). The reader may also infer from this comment that Thomas missed Mary's morning message to the assembled disciples about seeing the risen Jesus (v. 18) as well as Jesus's appearance that same evening (v. 19). Given the emotion-filled context, the imperfect ἔλεγον in v. 25 leaves the reader with the impression of a repetitive insistence: they were telling him (over and over again) ἑωράκαμεν τὸν κύριον.[66] Thus, the other disciples are insisting repeatedly that they have seen the risen Jesus. Contrast ἔλεγον with the narrator's comment that Thomas simply said (εἶπεν) he would not believe. The disciples' enthusiastic insistence on having seen a glorified Jesus is met with Thomas's cold dismissal of their message.

65. Riley (*Resurrection Reconsidered*, 100–114) argues that the use of "Didymus" is meant to identify Thomas to the Thomasine community.

66. This suggestion is based upon the category described by Wallace as the "iterative imperfect": "The imperfect is frequently used for *repeated* action in past time. It is similar to the customary imperfect, but it is not something that regularly recurs. Further, the iterative imperfect occurs over a shorter span of time" (Wallace, *Exegetical Syntax of the New Testament*, 546). Brown (*Gospel According to John*, 2:1025) understands ἔλεγον as a conative imperfect—"they *tried* to tell him." In either case, there is an emphasis on the effort exerted by the disciples in trying to convince Thomas of what they have seen.

In order for Thomas to believe that Jesus has been raised from the grave, he insists upon three criteria. He must be able to see the nail marks (ἐὰν μὴ ἴδω ἐν ταῖς χερσὶν αὐτοῦ τὸν τύπον τῶν ἥλων), thrust his hand into the nail marks (καὶ βάλω τὸν δάκτυλόν μου εἰς τὸν τύπον τῶν ἥλων), and thrust his finger into Jesus's side (καὶ βάλω μου τὴν χεῖρα εἰς τὴν πλευρὰν αὐτοῦ).[67] Apart from this, Thomas refuses to believe. In fact, the statement οὐ μὴ πιστεύσω (v. 25) is not a mere denial of certainty, but rather a denial of potentiality.[68] In short, apart from the criteria he demands, Thomas not only refuses to believe, he is unable. In this regard, Moloney comments,

> Thomas demands that Jesus be "touchable." As Mary wished to cling to Jesus' body, Thomas asks that he experience the risen body of the crucified one by seeing the nail marks and placing his finger into the wounds and his hand in Jesus' side . . . Thomas does not refuse the possibility of resurrection. He insists that the risen body of Jesus fulfill his requirements.[69]

Throughout the Fourth Gospel the reader has been treated to an array of characters that express belief in Jesus for different reasons. There are those characters that exercise belief in Jesus because of the word he speaks.[70] These characters are presented in a substantially positive light. Then there are those characters that believe because they have seen Jesus's works. These characters are presented in a substantially negative

67. The double use of βάλω is rather enigmatic in this context. Thomas is not describing a simple "touch" of Jesus's nail piercings and Jesus's side, but rather digital exploration. On this, Cf. BDAG, s.v. βάλλω.

68. "Emphatic negation is indicated by οὐ μή plus the *aorist subjunctive* . . . This is the strongest way to negate something in Greek. One might think that the negative with the subjunctive could not be as strong as the negative with the indicative. However, while οὐ + the indicative denies a *certainty*, οὐ μή + the subjunctive denies a *potentiality*" (Wallace, *Exegetical Syntax of the New Testament*, 468). See also BDAG, s.v. μή ("οὐ μή is the most decisive way of negativing someth. in the future").

69. Moloney, *Glory Not Dishonor*, 176.

70. The mother of Jesus is a primary example of one who believes on the basis of Jesus's words. She approaches Jesus in 2:3 with a problem. Even after Jesus rebukes her in 2:4, she turns to the servants and tells them, ὅ τι ἂν λέγῃ ὑμῖν ποιήσατε, "Do whatever he says to you." This statement is the first instance in the Fourth Gospel of one placing trust in the word of Jesus. Even in ch. 14 (discussed above) Jesus is exhorting his disciples to believe what they cannot see. The idea of believing in the word is a foundational Johannine theme.

light.[71] Thomas is about to become the example par excellence of one who believes on the basis of works.

A little more than a week after Jesus's appearances to Mary and the disciples (καὶ μεθ' ἡμέρας ὀκτώ), Jesus appears again to the assembled disciples, only this time Thomas is present (v. 26). Jesus speaks first to the group as a whole, bringing them a blessing of peace (εἰρήνη ὑμῖν = שלום אלכם). Then Jesus, possessing full knowledge of Thomas's earlier expression of doubt, speaks directly to Thomas's three criteria.

Jesus's words to Thomas in v. 27 consist of five imperatives in rapid succession. The first four are affirmative: (1) φέρε τὸν δάκτυλόν σου ὧδε, "extend[72] your finger here"; (2) ἴδε τὰς χεῖράς μου, "behold my hands"; (3) φέρε τὴν χεῖρά σου, "extend your hand"; and (4) βάλε εἰς τὴν πλευράν μου, "put it into my side." The fifth imperative is negative: μὴ γίνου ἄπιστος ἀλλὰ πιστός,[73] "Do not persist in unbelief but believe."

There is a logical connection between the first four commands and the last one. If Thomas follows Jesus's first four commands (to see, touch, and experience him), the fifth command (to cease unbelief) will naturally result. Thomas's earlier displayed an unwillingness to entertain the notion of Jesus's resurrection apart from seeing, touching, and experiencing him. Jesus now overcomes Thomas's objections by offering him the opportunity see, touch, and experience for himself. Now that the obstacles have been removed, πίστις is a possibility for Thomas.

Thomas's exclamation, "my Lord and my God" (v. 28), is an emphatic affirmation that he is no longer persisting in unbelief. The phrase ὁ κύριός μου καὶ ὁ θεός μου is a confessional Greek equivalent for the Hebrew יהוה אלהים.[74] In this simple exclamation, Thomas confesses

71. A prime example of this character group is the crowd whose hunger has been satisfied in 6:1–13. When they begin searching for Jesus the next day, he indicts their improper motivation by telling them, "Amen, amen, I say to you, you are seeking me not because you saw signs but because you ate from the loaves and were filled" (6:26). It is not the sign proper (the multiplication of the loaves) that has caused them to believe, but rather the end result of that sign (satisfying their hunger).

72. BDAG (s.v. φέρω) suggests "reach out" as a possible rendering of in v. 27.

73. DeConick ("Blessed Are Those Who Have Not Seen," 395) identifies (incorrectly in my estimation) this final command as a "rebuke." She appears to misunderstand the fundamental, logical connection between the string of imperatives.

74. The phrase יהוה אלהים appears approximately forty times in the OT. In the LXX the Greek phrase κύριος ὁ θεός regularly translates יהוה אלהים.

what the reader has known all along—Jesus is the unique revelation of the Father to humanity. He is the true, full, and physical manifestation of YHWH.

Jesus does not deny the truthfulness of Thomas's confession. Instead, he questions the source of Thomas's confession ὅτι ἑώρακάς με πεπίστευκας; He then points out the dichotomy between those who reach the same conclusion on the basis of works (in this case, Jesus's resurrection) and those who believe on the basis of Jesus's word: μακάριοι οἱ μὴ ἰδόντες καὶ πιστεύσαντες. This final statement in the conversation between Thomas and Jesus is important to a number of commentators for different reasons.

As discussed in chapter 1 of this study, the advocates of the community-conflict hypothesis see in Jesus's comment an indictment of Thomas that serves as a climax to the story and thus highlights the anti-Thomasine nature of the Fourth Gospel. Regarding v. 29, DeConick asserts, "Clearly, a conflict is set up here between the false hero, Thomas, who insists that a *visio Dei* is necessary, and John's hero, Jesus who rebuts this in favor of faith."[75] She continues,

> Thus I maintain that this story is not about bodily resurrection and must be distinguished from Luke 24:26. Rather the impetus of this story for the Johannine writer is encapsulated in the climactic saying attributed to Jesus which blesses those who have faith in Jesus even though they have not had a visionary encounter (20:29). Behind this articulation we can reconstruct the discursive field. For Johannine Christians faith in Jesus was the basis of their salvation, whereas for Thomasine Christians, the mystical visionary encounter was paramount. The discourse between these communities on this subject is preserved here from the perspective of the Johannine community which presents its "correct" version of soteriology that developed as a result of the discourse.[76]

Could it be that DeConick sees more in these two verses than is actually there, and that she finds in 20:29 exactly what she is looking for? Seemingly aware of this objection, she protests that her conclusions are "more than provocative" when one considers different elements

75. DeConick, "Blessed Are Those Who Have Not Seen," 395.

76. Ibid., 396.

of the *Gospel of Thomas*.[77] One problem with her solution, however, is that it makes much of unsubstantiated outside elements (a proposed conflict, elements of Thomasine soteriology, etc.) and not enough of demonstrable elements within the narrative (issues related to plot and characterization). It is not my intention at this point to offer a full critique of DeConick (or Riley and Pagels). For now, suffice it to say that DeConick's understanding of 20:29 isolates Thomas from the larger narrative. Her presentation does not account for other characters and themes, and thus fails to keep the larger narrative in view.

In contrast to the theories of Riley, DeConick, and Pagels, some recognize Thomas as a privileged character in that his pronouncement is the most complete christological confession in the narrative.[78] Throughout the story, a remarkable host of characters utter partially true but incomplete confessions in identifying Jesus. John the Baptist identifies him as the "Lamb of God" (1:29, 36) and "Son of God" (1:34). Andrew calls him the "Messiah" (1:41). Philip refers to him as "the one Moses wrote about in the Law and also the Prophets" (1:45). Nathanael tells Jesus that he is the "Son of God, the King of Israel" (1:49). Nicodemus ironically confesses that Jesus is a "teacher who has come from God" (3:2). The Samaritan woman recognizes that Jesus is a "prophet" (4:19) and later wonders aloud (with some doubt)[79] if Jesus could be the Messiah (4:29). The Samaritan townspeople proclaim that they have seen for themselves that Jesus is the "savior of the world" (4:42). After Jesus feeds the multitudes, some in the crowd confess, "This is truly the prophet who is to come into the world" (6:14). In ch. 7, "the prophet" (v. 40) and

77. Ibid.

78. Neyrey (*Gospel of John*, 330–31) comments, "But Thomas differs from all other characters in that he does not simply receive from others knowledge about Jesus. He is moved to make the most exalted acknowledgment of Jesus's status in the Fourth Gospel, 'My Lord and my God!' (20:28). Thomas earlier saw Jesus raise Lazarus from the dead, which at the time was a 'sign,' not a demonstration of Jesus' eschatological power (11:7–16). But with his access to the body of the Risen Jesus, he is schooled to acknowledge that Jesus indeed has God's eschatological power to 'have life in himself' and to 'lay down his life and take it again.' Now there is ample proof that Jesus is 'equal to God' and that he has God's two powers: creative ('God') and eschatological ('Lord')." In Rome the phrase "Lord and God" was used with reference to emperors. Against this backdrop, John may intend to create a contrast between Jesus and the emperor. On this, see Cassidy, *John's Gospel in New Perspective*.

79. Her question, μήτι οὗτός ἐστιν ὁ χριστός; is laden with reticence and may expect a negative answer. I will discuss this more when I examine the Samaritan woman in chapter 6 of this study.

"the Christ (Messiah)" (v. 41) are two opinions expressed by the crowds regarding Jesus's identity. After his healing, the man born blind calls Jesus a "prophet" (9:17). Every instance in this impressive list of titles ascribed to Jesus ultimately falls short inasmuch as it fails to recognize him as both "Lord" and "God." Therefore, Thomas receives the exalted position of being able to utter the truest and most complete christological confession in the Fourth Gospel. It is true that he professes belief only after seeing the risen Jesus, but so do the other disciples. Thomas is alone in his exalted proclamation that Jesus is κύριος ὁ θεός. Prior to seeing Jesus, Thomas is not in a position to offer such a confession. At that stage Thomas is a "final example [to the reader] of partial faith among foundational disciples stumbling toward faith."[80] When he finally sees Jesus, he fully affirms what no one else (other than the narrator in the prologue) has grasped.

It has also been suggested that Thomas is undergoing successive stages of faith in this last pericope.[81] Thus, his refusal to believe apart from sight and Jesus's statement about faith without sight are examples to those early readers of the text who, not having seen Jesus, found themselves struggling with the truth claims of the Gospel.

Read in this way, Jesus's words to Thomas in 20:29 become less about a polemic and more about one of the Gospel's main themes, belief in Jesus. When one considers the overall narrative and its many interwoven elements, it is much more likely that this Thomas pericope intends to address the reader *within the Johannine community* that is struggling with belief rather, than a group of readers or a particular theological system *outside the Johannine community*. This observation is strongly supported by the narrator's concluding comments in vv. 30–31.[82]

In a final, direct comment to the reader, the narrator reports that Jesus performed many other *semeia* that did not find their way into John's story.[83] Instead, the miraculous deeds recounted in the Fourth

80. Moloney, *Signs and Shadows*, 176.

81. Ibid., 177–78.

82. Carson (*The Gospel of John*, 660–61) comments that the combined μὲν οὖν of v. 30 is meant to connect vv. 30–31 with the preceding material. He writes, "The flow of thought seems to be: Those who have not seen the risen Christ and yet have believed are blessed; *therefore* this book has been composed, to the end that you may believe."

83. Here σημεῖα should probably be understood in a broader manner that encompasses more than just the seven "signs" presented to the reader. It should be broadened to include any element of Jesus's ministry recounted in the foregoing chapters. This is

Gospel (the ταῦτα of v. 21) have been chosen for a very specific purpose. The primary purpose is to engender belief in the readership. This final statement creates an *inclusio* with the prologue. *Belief* in Jesus's name (as in 1:12–13) culminates in the believer having *life* in his name (20:31). The reader must confess the same thing as Thomas without the benefit of sight enjoyed by Thomas.

Much has been made of the use of πιστεύω in v. 31. First, there is a textual problem in the verse. Some witnesses contain the present subjunctive πιστεύητε (𝔓^{66vid} ℵ* B Θ 0250 892^{s} *l* 2211) while others contain the aorist subjunctive πιστεύσητε (ℵ^{2} A C D L W Ψ $f^{1.13}$ 33 𝔐). The external attestation for both readings is fairly good, with the range of witnesses being slightly stronger for the aorist subjunctive reading. However, on internal grounds, this problem is more difficult to solve since there is some debate as to how the change in tense would influence the interpretation of the verse.

A great deal is also made of how the tense would impact the meaning and thus the translation of the verb. The aorist subjunctive, as the argument goes, would imply belief for the first time, whereas the present subjunctive would have reference to ongoing belief.[84] Some scholars suggest that this would have an impact on whether or not the Gospel is being addressed primarily to those who already believe or to those who do not. However, when one considers that in the Fourth Gospel πιστεύω is used in the present tense to refer both initial faith and ongoing faith,[85] and that the aorist is without nuance in this regard, it is unlikely that such a rigid distinction can be maintained.[86]

Going back to the textual problem, the bracketed sigma is obvious testimony to the significant disagreement among the members of the committee responsible for editing the text and textual apparatus. The

---

a more likely way to understand the connection between σημεῖα in v. 20 and ταῦτα ("these things") in v. 21.

84. On this, see Fee, "On the Text and Meaning of John 20:30–31," in *To What End Exegesis? Essays Textual, Exegetical, and Theological*. See also Carson, "Purpose of the Fourth Gospel"; idem, "Syntactical and Text-Critical Reflections on John 20:31."

85. For example, in 9:38 the man born blind confesses with the present tense πιστεύω in the context of initial belief. By contrast, the aorist ἐπίστευσαν is used in 2:23 to describe initial faith in Jesus.

86. A particularly helpful discussion of this textual issue can be found in the text-critical appendix of the *New Testament: New English Translation / Novum Testamentum Graece*, 844.

evidence for the aorist subjunctive reading is negligibly better, and since the question cannot be fully determined by appealing to internal evidence, I opt here for the reading πιστεύσητε (though, as already stated, I am not convinced that it significantly informs how we understand the nature of "belief" in v. 31).

In the end, the reader sees that the belief expressed by Thomas has been the focus of the narrator all along. In vv. 30–31, the reader (at whatever stage of "belief") is now called to that same confession. Thomas is thus an erring character whose status is raised by being the first to confess truly Johannine faith.

Conclusion

Throughout this chapter I have sought to offer a close reading of the text while paying particular attention to the manner in which Thomas is characterized in the Fourth Gospel. It is important to emphasize once again that this study is not concerned primarily with the relationship between the Gospels of John and *Thomas*. Here I am interested specifically in testing the claims of the community-conflict hypothesis regarding John's supposed polemic against Thomas.

After examining the presentation of Thomas in the Fourth Gospel it is possible to offer a few points of synthesis. First, it is undoubtedly the case that Thomas is (as described by Riley, DeConick, and Pagels) consistently depicted in a less-than-flattering light. The reader hears Thomas speak on three different occasions, and each time he says something that (a) shows that he has missed the point, and (b) offers a contrast to what the reader knows or expects. In this way, Thomas is a prime example of an uncomprehending character.

Second, in all three contexts in which Thomas and Jesus interact, the theme of resurrection is involved. I thus affirm portions of the thesis advocated by Riley in his examination of Thomas's presentation in John. It is clear that Thomas appears as an uncomprehending character in three different contexts associated with resurrection. Each time Thomas speaks he betrays an inability to perceive truths related to the mission and message of Jesus, and each instance is related to the resurrection of either Lazarus or Jesus.

This is a particularly interesting element of Thomas's characterization in the Fourth Gospel because it shows stages in the development of his understanding of resurrection. He goes from a stage of missing the point altogether ("Let us go also that we may die with him," 11:16; "We do not know where you are going, how can we know the way?" 14:5) to a middle stage of imposing his own standards upon belief in Jesus's resurrection ("Unless I see the wounds. . . , 20:25) to a final stage of complete Johannine faith ("My Lord and my God," 20:28).

Third, and significantly, this synthetic portrait of Thomas reveals that his overall impact on the narrative is rather unimpressive. He appears three times, utters a paltry fifty-seven words, and in each appearance he is used merely as a foil to help the narrator make his point from the mouth of Jesus. In this light, it remains difficult to imagine a scenario in which the author of the Fourth Gospel is writing primarily in response to Thomasine ideas but where the character of Thomas plays such a minimal role in the broad scope of the narrative.

As the above synthesis shows, I have not taken a position that disagrees entirely with the positions advocated by Riley, DeConick, and Pagels. If I agree with certain salient points made by the advocates of the community-conflict hypothesis, what keeps me from fully embracing that position? It is correct to argue that the Fourth Gospel presents Thomas as uncomprehending and somewhat foolish. It is also correct to argue that he is consistently presented in a negative manner. I recognize here that these two claims of the community-conflict hypothesis are generally valid. But what am I to make of the claim that Thomas's confession and Jesus's corrective in 20:29 represent the climax of the Gospel, thereby singling out Thomas as the primary focus of a Johannine polemic?

Before this question can be addressed properly, other Johannine characters must be examined. Once complete, the overall picture of characterization in the Fourth Gospel will help provide a comprehensive critique of the community-conflict position and its respective adherents.

A look back at the quotation from Riley at the beginning of this chapter recalls the words, "Thomas is cast as one who is wrong, ignorant and unbelieving."[87] As previously stated, I am in substantial agreement with this final statement of Riley's quotation. Within the overall narrative framework of the Fourth Gospel, Thomas is a good example of one who is *wrong*, *ignorant*, and *unbelieving*. In this way, Riley has provided

87. Riley, *Resurrection Reconsidered*, 79.

three very helpful categories. However, Thomas is eventually redeemed, as the most exalted christological confession in the narrative belongs to him.

However, a critical question arises in light of Riley's statement: Is Thomas the only one to be "wrong, ignorant, and unbelieving"? Using these three categories, I move forward posing another question: Are there other wrong, ignorant, and unbelieving Johannine characters, and, if there are, what does this tell us not only about the Fourth Gospel but also about the assumptions behind the community-conflict hypothesis?

At this point in our discussion it is appropriate to turn to another character who, like Thomas, appears in numerous situations in the Fourth Gospel, is a named disciple of Jesus, and is, in some ways, an equally conspicuous example of an uncomprehending character. Like Thomas, this character has also been described by a number of scholars as the recipient of a significant Johannine polemic. Chapter 4 turns now to a discussion of Peter in the Fourth Gospel.

4

Jesus and Peter in the Fourth Gospel

> Peter is a complex figure in the Fourth Gospel, but the interpreter must take care not to confuse the Matthean (or synoptic) Peter with his counterpart in John. By considering the way in which Peter is characterized only in the Fourth Gospel, it becomes apparent that he is a man who has come dangerously close to being placed outside the Johannine pale.[1]

In comparison to Thomas, Peter figures more prominently in John's Gospel. He appears twice as frequently (chs. 1, 6, 13, 18, 20, 21) and speaks almost twice as often.[2] In the Fourth Gospel, Peter is the most prominent of Jesus's disciples, with the possible exception of the Beloved Disciple. In addition to being an important figure in the Fourth Gospel, Peter is the unquestioned leader of the disciples in the Synoptic tradition. Despite such prominence in the canonical Gospel traditions, Peter has received a considerable amount of negative press among Johannine scholars over the last three decades. So strong is this sentiment that it has become commonplace to speak of the "anti-Petrine" stance of the Fourth Gospel.

Not all scholars agree that the Fourth Gospel is anti-Petrine in its outlook. There are two major schools of thought on the role of Peter in the Gospel of John. On one end of the spectrum is the view represented by scholars such as Oscar Cullmann[3] and Raymond E. Brown,[4] as well as the Petrine dialogue group (consisting of Roman Catholic

1. Droge, "Status of Peter in the Fourth Gospel," 311.

2. Compare Thomas's fifty-seven words in the Greek text with the ninety-nine words ascribed to Peter.

3. Cullmann, *Peter: Disciple, Apostle, Martyr.*

4. Brown, *Gospel According to John*, 2:1006–7.

and Lutheran scholars).[5] This position regards the Johannine portrait of Peter as more or less on an equal plane with that of the Beloved Disciple. While these scholars recognize that Peter's role in the Fourth Gospel is somewhat diminished when compared to his overall presentation in the Synoptics, they nevertheless reject the notion that John's Gospel is anti-Petrine. In this regard, Cullmann writes that the Fourth Gospel

> nowhere attempts to deny directly the special role of Peter within the group of disciples. It only has the tendency to lessen this role, in so far as it seeks to show that beside the unique position of Peter there is the somewhat different special role of the "Beloved Disciple."[6]

He goes on to write that it is "only the exclusive nature of Peter's unique position that is opposed; in other respects *the different character of the role* of the two men is emphasized."[7]

In short, this view contends that the Beloved Disciple and Peter are equal in terms of supremacy but different in terms of their roles. In his commentary on the Fourth Gospel, Brown uses these categories when he writes,

> Peter is not the special hero of the Johannine writer. The Beloved Disciple has that role; and the writer takes special interest in showing the Beloved Disciple's "*primacy of love*," a superiority that does not exclude Peter's possessing *another type of primacy*.[8]

This line of thinking begins by acknowledging that the Beloved Disciple (rather than Peter) is the apostolic "hero" figure in John's Gospel, but it stops short of admitting that Peter is deprecated to any significant degree.

5. In the early 1970s a national dialogue between Roman Catholic and Lutheran biblical scholars and theologians was convened to discuss Peter's presentation in the NT. With Raymond Brown, Karl P. Donfried, and John Reumann as editors, the conclusions of the group were published under the title, *Peter in the New Testament*.

6. Cullmann, *Peter*, 27.

7. Ibid.; emphasis added.

8. Brown, *Gospel According to John*, 2:1006–7; emphasis added. The term "primacy" often has connotations that reach beyond the realm of biblical studies and into the realm of ecclesiological discussions. Therefore, I have used the term "supremacy" above in order to avoid confusion.

On the other end of the spectrum are scholars such as Eric L. Titus,[9] Graydon F. Snyder,[10] Arthur H. Maynard,[11] and Arthur Droge,[12] who see a negative picture of Peter in the Fourth Gospel. These scholars believe that the portrait of Peter in the Fourth Gospel is driven by an anti-Petrine polemic. Consider the following quote from Maynard:

> The accumulated evidence makes it very difficult to understand the view of Brown, Cullmann, and others that the Beloved Disciple is not put above Peter, but that they simply are given different roles: one superior in authority and the other superior in personal relationship to Jesus. This is close to the situation in the Appendix [viz., ch. 21], but in the body of the Gospel Peter is made to appear in very bad light, indeed. This Gospel apparently came from a community that wanted nothing to do with the primacy of any one man, not even Peter![13]

Those who embrace this position see in the Fourth Gospel a noticeable polemic against Peter that, by means of direct contrast, results in an exaltation of the Beloved Disciple—the embodiment of Johannine Christianity. While these scholars do not envision a conflict between the communities associated with Peter and John, their suggestion of an anti-Petrine polemic in the Fourth Gospel both anticipates and lays the groundwork for the scholarship of those who advocate the community-conflict hypothesis. The suggestion of a driving polemic informs both the anti-Thomasine and the anti-Petrine views of the text. The result is a considerable overlap in the assumptions and conclusions arising from the advocates of both theories.

Just as the publications of Riley, DeConick, and Pagels informed the discussion in the previous chapter, so will the questions raised by these two competing strands of scholarship inform the background behind the discussion in this chapter. The examination that follows will test the claims of both positions (i.e., the position advocated by Cullmann and Brown, and the anti-Petrine position) by examining the role of Peter in the Fourth Gospel. This chapter will consider Peter's role in 1:35–42; 6:60–71; 13:1–38; 18:1–27; and 20:1–10. These sections will

9. Titus, *Message of the Fourth Gospel*, 220.

10. Snyder, "John 13:16," 5–15.

11. Maynard, "Role of Peter in the Fourth Gospel."

12. Droge, "Status of Peter in the Fourth Gospel."

13. Maynard, "Role of Peter in the Fourth Gospel," 546.

be followed by an excursus on the Beloved Disciple and an examination of John 21.[14]

Jesus and Peter in John 1:35–42

The reader meets Peter for the first time in 1:35–42 on the day following the Baptist's proclamation that Jesus is the "Lamb of God" (1:29) and "Son of God" (1:34).[15] In 1:36 the Baptist proclaims for a second time that Jesus is the "Lamb of God," but this time his proclamation occurs in the presence of two unnamed disciples. Since the reader has not yet been told that John has disciples, this information provides a link to the events of the previous day (vv. 29–34) and helps to explain why the two disciples so willingly follow Jesus (v. 37). So begins a series of encounters between Jesus and his first followers in the Johannine narrative. The exegesis of this first pericope will proceed according to the following structural breakdown:

1. Jesus and two unnamed disciples (1:35–39)
2. Jesus, Andrew, and Peter (1:40–42)

Jesus and Two Unnamed Disciples (1:35–39)

Having heard the Baptist exalt Jesus three times (1:29, 34, 36), two of the Baptist's disciples leave him and begin to follow Jesus. When the two unnamed disciples approach Jesus he asks, τί ζητεῖτε; "what do you seek?" (v. 38a).[16] In response they call him "Rabbi" and ask him where he

14. Though there is a near consensus in Johannine studies that ch. 21 is a later addition to the Fourth Gospel, the presentation of Peter in that chapter is illuminating in a number of ways. Peter's "reinstatement" appears to append a pro-Petrine ending to the Fourth Gospel, but further investigation suggests that the reader is still to regard the Beloved Disciple as the figure with which to identify. For a study that disagrees that John 21 is a later addition, see Minear, "Original Functions of John 21."

15. Several commentators remark that another day may be implied between the events of vv. 40 and 41. Most prominently among them is Boismard (*Moïse ou Jésus*, 79–81), however, this reckoning of time seems to go against the grain of the narrator's consistent pattern of enumerating explicitly these first few days of Jesus's ministry (see 1:29, 35, 43; 2:1). Boismard is able to overcome this problem by opting for the reading πρωΐ, "in the morning," in v. 41, but he can only arrive at this conclusion by applying a questionable variant (that does not appear in a single extant Greek MS!) to create another day in the narrative.

16. Stibbe (*John's Gospel*, 1) perceptively notes that this question is repeated by the risen Jesus to Mary Magdalene in 20:15 (τίνα ζητεῖς;), and thus forms an *inclusio* at the macro level of the story.

is staying (v. 38b). The use of "Rabbi" here by the two disciples is simply honorific and does not yet show any spiritual insight on their part. Their reverence for Jesus at this stage of the story would be consonant with the high praise their teacher has thrice ascribed to Jesus. However, in subsequent verses, some of the early Johannine disciples demonstrate a remarkable awareness of Jesus's messianic significance.[17]

Since John appears in the prologue (1:6, 15) where he is specifically identified as ἀπεσταλμένος παρὰ θεοῦ (1:6a), the reader knows that his testimony about Jesus as the "Lamb of God" and the "Son of God" is not only true but also from God. Thus, the first named character in the Gospel other than the λόγος confirms what has been revealed in the prologue. In the following section of this pericope Andrew will offer the story's second confession of Jesus's messianic status, which will prove significant inasmuch as it agrees with the evaluative point of view shared by the narrator and by God.[18]

Jesus, Andrew, and Peter (1:40–42)

After his initial conversation with Jesus (1:38–39), Andrew (the only one of the two previously unnamed disciples to be named)[19] seeks his brother in order to inform him that he and the other disciple have found the Messiah (1:41b).[20] The reader is supposed to catalog this confession with information revealed in the prologue, information provided by

17. The narration of events over these first few days of ministry unveils a number of titles ascribed to Jesus by those who become his earliest disciples. For instance, Andrew remarks that Jesus is the "Messiah" (1:41), Philip calls him "the one about whom Moses wrote in the Law, and also the prophets" (1:45), and Nathanael calls him the "Son of God, the king of Israel" (1:49). This portrait contrasts with the synoptics where the disciples progress over time in their understanding of who Jesus is (compare, e.g., Mark 4:35–41 and its parallel passages).

18. Though θεός is mentioned a number of times, the reader does not hear God speak in the prologue. God's viewpoint is nevertheless implied in the narrator's description of the λόγος.

19. The identity of the other unnamed disciple has long been a topic of debate in Johannine studies. Some have argued that there is a connection between this unnamed disciple and the Beloved Disciple that appears later in the narrative. Others have argued that the question is an irrelevant foray into issues on which the narrative intends to remain silent. For comment on both sides of the issue see Neirynck, "Anonymous Disciple in John 1."

20. This verse and 4:25 are the only instances in the NT where the term "messiah" appears in transliterated Greek. Typically, a form of Χριστός is used for the Hebrew term משיח.

John the Baptist, and the confessions that will appear in the rest of the chapter. In this way, a nascent Johannine Christology begins to unfold before the reader.

After identifying Andrew by name, the narrator refers to him as the brother of Simon Peter (v. 40a). This introduction is noteworthy because the reader has yet to encounter a character named Simon Peter. The preliminary mention of Peter, who is unknown to the reader, is similar to the narrator's comment about Mary of Bethany in 11:2. The reader hears Mary's name and is "reminded" of her significant deed before she makes an appearance in the narrative.[21] The mention of Peter in v. 40 can be regarded as sure evidence that his reputation was already established among the original readers of the Fourth Gospel and that he was the better known of the two brothers among the early Christian communities.[22]

A textual problem raises questions about the interpretation of v. 41. The text of NA[27] reads εὑρίσκει οὗτος *πρωτον* τον ἀδελφὸν τὸν ἴδιον Σίμωνα, "he *first* found his own brother Simon" (contained in 𝔓[66.75] ℵ[2] A B Θ Ψ $f^{1.13}$ 892 al sy[p.h]). The adverbial use of the neuter adjective πρῶτον would imply that the first thing Andrew did after speaking with Jesus was to find his brother and tell him about Jesus.

Another reading (attested by the original hand of Sinaiticus as well as the majority of Byzantine mss) has πρῶτος in the place of πρῶτον. This reading would have the adjective modifying Ἀνδρέας and would thus indicate that Andrew was *the first to go find* his brother Simon. Brown comments that many who have opted for this reading have seen an implication that the other unnamed disciple (presumably John) went *second* to find his brother (presumably James).[23] This series of assumptions not only places the sons of Zebedee (known from the synoptic

21. Mary's anointing of Jesus's feet is mentioned in the chapter before the reader witnesses it. This not only indicates the original reader's familiarity with the tradition of a woman anointing Jesus's feet, but also serves as a prolepsis pointing forward to a significant event and elevating Mary in the eyes of the reader. Schnackenburg (*Gospel According to St. John*, 1:310 n. 81) comments that this "shows that the matter has been frequently spoken of before Christian hearers."

22. This is noted by a number of commentators. See, among others, Brown, *Gospel According to John*, 1:75; Schnackenburg, *Gospel According to St. John*, 1:309–10; Carson, *Gospel According to John*, 154; Moloney, *Gospel of John*, 61; and D. M. Smith, *John*, 72.

23. Brown, *Gospel According to John*, 1:75.

tradition) into the Fourth Gospel[24] but is also thought to lend credibility to the traditional connection between John, the son of Zebedee and the author of the Fourth Gospel.

A third reading (Latin *mane*) is found in a handful of Old Latin manuscripts and implies the Greek πρωΐ ("in the morning"). This reading eliminates altogether the ambiguity of the first two readings and would indicate that another day has begun, which may accord well with the reckoning of time in v. 39.[25]

Of the three readings, πρῶτον is the best option since it (1) is the most difficult reading of the three, and (2) is attested by the broadest range of early, quality witnesses. In light of this reading, the reader understands that Andrew, after conversing with Jesus, immediately finds his brother with the intent of taking him to meet Jesus (v. 42a).

Little narrative time passes between the first mention of Simon Peter to the reader (v. 40) and the first meeting between Jesus and Simon Peter (v. 42b). In addition, little narrative time passes between Jesus's first encounter with Simon and the changing of his name to Cephas. In the Matthean tradition, Peter's name is changed after a period of ministry that culminates in the so-called Great Confession at Caesarea Philippi (see Matt 16:13–20). In the Fourth Gospel, Peter's name change occurs almost as soon as both the reader and Jesus encounter him for the first time.

In 1:40 the narrator introduces this new character as Σίμωνος Πέτρου. Two verses later Jesus identifies him as Σίμων ὁ υἱὸς Ἰωάννου (v. 42c).[26] Then, after looking at him (ἐμβλέψας αὐτῷ), Jesus proclaims, σὺ κληθήσῃ Κηφᾶς (v. 42d).

24. While they do not appear in the body of the Gospel, the sons of Zebedee are mentioned in the appendix (οἱ τοῦ Ζεβεδαίου, 21:2).

25. The narrator indicates that Jesus's initial conversation with the two unnamed disciples took place at about the tenth hour (ὥρα ἦν ὡς δεκάτη, i.e., about four o'clock). Those who opt for the third reading (*mane* = πρωΐ) take this to mean that it was late afternoon when the disciples inquired about Jesus. Assuming they followed Jesus's direction to "come and see" (v. 39a), Andrew would have arisen early the next morning to find his brother. As helpful as this suggestion is in both eliminating ambiguity from the text and in following the pattern of days described by the Evangelist, it assumes too much. In addition, the reading suffers much, especially given its very poor external attestation.

26. The reading ὁ υἱὸς Ἰωνᾶ, "son of Jonah," is found in A B^2 Δ Ψ $f^{1.13}$ 𝔐. However, the reading ὁ υἱὸς Ἰωάννου is accepted here on the basis of (1) better external evidence and (2) the likelihood that the variant reading arose out of a desire to assimilate

Jesus's pronouncement in v. 42d points forward proleptically to the significance Peter's character will hold later in the narrative. For the reader, Jesus's words are a bold announcement of what Peter will become. However, the future κληθήσῃ should not be understood (as some have argued) as an indication of a future name change. Rather, the reader should understand that the name change takes place instantaneously.[27] In support of this claim is the observation that from this point forward in the story, every subsequent appearance of Simon contains the name Peter.[28] Jesus has named him "Rock," and as the story moves forward the reader expects to see him become that "Rock."

The changing of names from Σίμων (Hebrew שמעון, "God has heard")[29] to Κηφᾶς (Aramaic כיפא, "crag" or "rock"),[30] is surely signifi-

the present text to Matt 16:17 (Σίμων Βαριωνᾶ). By this reckoning, both texts would refer to Peter as "Simon, son of Jonah." The difference between the Johannine and Matthean readings should not be held as evidence of disagreement over the name of Peter's father inasmuch as both Ἰωάννης and Ἰων(ν)ᾶ are regarded as Greek variations of the same Hebrew name. On this assertion, see the reading Ἰωάναν for Jonah in 1 Chr 26:3 (LXX).

27. There is some discussion as to how the future (κληθήσῃ, v. 42b) should be understood. Schnackenburg (*Gospel According to St. John*, 1:311) argues that it should be read as a Semitic future of volition ("You shall [in the future] be called Rock"), indicating what Peter would become rather than an instantaneous change. Bultmann (*Gospel of John*, 71) argues similarly. However, both Barrett (*Gospel According to St. John*, 182) and Brown (*Gospel According to John*, 1:80) argue that the name change is instantaneous, citing analogous constructions in the LXX as evidence (see the similar use of οὐ plus καλέω in the future tense of Gen 17:5, 15). The latter argument is more convincing and is strengthened by the recognition that the name "Peter" appears in every one of his remaining appearances throughout the Gospel.

28. He is called "Simon Peter" in 6:8, 68; 13:6, 9, 24, 36; 18:10, 15, 25; 20:2, 6; 21:2, 3, 11, 15, 17, and simply "Peter" in 1:44 (his first mention after 1:42!), 13:8, 37; 18:11, 16, 17, 18, 27; 20:3, 4; 21:3, 7, 17, 19. Throughout the remainder of the Fourth Gospel he never appears as simply "Simon."

29. It is noteworthy that in Acts 15:14, Simon Peter is referred to as Συμεών (another Greek variant of Σίμων).

30. Schlatter (*Evangelist Johannes*, 56) suggests that the name might have been spelled קיפא in Galilean Aramaic. This may have been the case in light of the fact that Greek *kappa* often transliterates the Hebrew/Aramaic *qoph* (see BDF, s.v. 39). It has been pointed out by a number of commentators that *petros* is not an exact equivalent for *kēphā'* and this is thought to raise some difficulties. For more discussion on the philological background and significance of the name Cephas, see the chapter entitled, "Aramaic *Kēphā'* and Peter's Name in the New Testament," in Fitzmyer, *To Advance the Gospel*, 112–24. The proper name Cephas as a designation for Peter is attested elsewhere in the NT only in the writings of Paul (see Gal 1:18; 2:9, 11, 14; 1 Cor 1:12; 3:22; 9:5; 15:5).

cant, though the narrator does not stop to comment on the significance of the name change. Instead, in typical Johannine fashion, the narrator turns to explain to the reader that Κηφᾶς is the Aramaic equivalent of Πέτρος.[31]

In the biblical tradition there is great importance attached to the changing of one's name. In antiquity, an individual's name was thought to be an indicator of both character and destiny. This is nowhere more evident than in the book of Genesis, where the patriarchs undergo name changes that serve to identify their status in God's economy. For example, Abram ("Great Father") becomes Abraham ("Father of Multitudes," Gen 17:5) and Jacob ("Deceiver") becomes Israel ("One Who Strives with God," Gen 32:28). The significance of the name change in these two examples, however, is already explicit in the various contexts dealing with the patriarchs and their actions before God. By contrast, at this stage in the Johannine narrative the context is not illuminating and the significance of the name change is not immediately clear. Instead, the reader must continually look forward in order to appreciate the significance of Simon's name change.[32] By examining this event, the reader understands that the name is both related to something Jesus recognizes in Peter[33] and a prediction of what Peter will become.[34] In

31. Bart Ehrman ("Cephas and Peter," 463–74) argues that despite the explicit connection between Cephas and Peter in John 1:42, the two names did not refer historically to the same person. He writes, "From the early second century on, a number of sources maintain that Cephas and Peter were two different persons. Some of these sources claim that both belonged to the Twelve, others place Peter among the Twelve and Cephas among the Seventy, yet others leave the matter unresolved" (ibid., 466). This suggestion is not unique to Ehrman. The Cephas-Peter relationship was questioned in a number of publications in the first three decades of the twentieth century. Cf., e.g., Lake, "Simon, Cephas, Peter"; Goguel, *Foi à la résurrection de Jésus*, 272–75; and Riddle, "Cephas-Peter Problem." In response to Ehrman's article, Dale C. Allison ("Peter and Cephas") argues persuasively that Peter and Cephas are to be regarded as the same person.

32. Moloney (*Belief in the Word*, 69) remarks that the reader "needs to wait for the further developments that will take place through the story." In addition, see Moloney's article, "Function of Prolepsis." Though it is focused on John 6 and we are dealing here with John 1, the article contains a number of illuminating insights as to how the implied author continually points the reader forward through the use of prolepses.

33. In this regard, Brown (*Gospel According to John*, 1:76) comments, "Neither *Petros* in Greek nor *kēphâ* in Aramaic is a normal proper name; rather it is a nickname (like American 'Rocky') which would have to be explained by something in Simon's character or career."

34. Carson asserts that "[t]his is not so much a merely predictive utterance as a declaration of *what Jesus will make of him*" (*Gospel According to John*, 156; emphasis added).

this way, the verb κληθήσῃ (taken as a divine passive) is a signal to the reader that something God-wrought is going to occur in Peter's life as the story progresses.

Needless to say, this interaction between Jesus and Peter is a good sign for the early development of Peter's character. That Jesus, the protagonist and hero of the story, deals with Peter in this manner at their first meeting is significant for the unfolding narrative. From this first encounter between Jesus and Peter, it is safe to say that the reader's initial impression of Peter is quite positive.

Jesus and Peter in John 6:60–71

Peter makes his second appearance in the Fourth Gospel in 6:68, on the day following Jesus's multiplication of loaves for the five thousand (cf. 6:1–15). There the reader hears Peter speak for the first time in the story and in a manner that, like John (1:29, 34, 36) and Andrew (1:41) before him, agrees with the evaluative point of view of both the narrator and God.

John 6 contains some of the more enigmatic words in the Fourth Gospel, and as a result the chapter has caused a number of interpretive difficulties for Johannine scholars.[35] There are significant questions about the eucharistic imagery of the so-called Bread of Life discourse,[36] the relationship between vv. 51c–58 and vv. 60–65,[37] the relation of the Johannine bread miracle tradition to the similar tradition in the Synoptics,[38] and a number of source-critical questions.[39] Without mini-

35. Moloney (*Johannine Son of Man*, 87) begins his discussion of the chapter by commenting that "John 6 must stand as a testing ground for every endeavour to explain the Fourth Gospel in a coherent fashion. Any scholar who turns to the Fourth Gospel finds himself faced with the immense problems which arise from this chapter."

36. See Barrett (*Gospel According to St. John*, 281–85) for a discussion and an overview of opinions on whether or not the "bread of life" discourse should be regarded as Eucharistic.

37. For a summary of scholarly proposals on this question, see Moloney, *Johannine Son of Man*, 87–107.

38. This is the only miracle story to appear in all four canonical Gospels. See the pertinent reflections on this issue in Carson, *Gospel According to John*, 267; and Barrett, *Gospel According to St. John*, 271.

39. Among others, Lincoln (*Gospel According to St. John*, 210) comments, "The abrupt change of setting from Jerusalem to crossing the Sea of Galilee has led many to suggest that his new episode would most naturally follow on from the end of chapter 4 and that the sequence of episodes in the narrative must have transposed the chapter

mizing the importance of these issues, the exegesis here will focus on Peter's role and the significance of this pericope for the reader's growing impression of Peter.

John 6 narrates a series of events over a two-day span, which culminates in two mutually exclusive responses to Jesus by his "disciples."[40] In 6:1–13, the reader is given the details of the temporal, spatial, and situational settings of Jesus's multiplication of the loaves and fish. Following the events at Bethesda (ch. 5), Jesus and his disciples are on the other side of the sea of Galilee when a large crowd begins to gather. After a brief conversation between Jesus and Philip about where to buy food to feed the gathered multitude, Jesus is introduced to a boy with five barley loaves and two fish. These meager resources become the manifold provision of God as Jesus multiplies the food into a feast for the five thousand. This fourth *semeion* in the Gospel causes the awestruck crowd to offer another in a growing list of confessions in John's story: "Truly, this is the prophet who is to come into the world" (v. 14). In response to the wondrous provision the zealous crowd endeavors to take Jesus by force and make him king. Aware of their intentions, Jesus withdraws from them.

That evening Jesus's disciples set sail on the sea without him. As they struggle through a difficult wind and tempestuous waters, Jesus walks out to them on the water (vv. 16–19). Jesus's walking on water is almost universally regarded as the fifth *semeion* of John's Gospel. When the disciples see Jesus they become afraid, but after he reassures them (ἐγώ εἰμι· μὴ φοβεῖσθε, v. 20),[41] the disciples willingly accept Jesus into the boat. All of the activities narrated in these verses occur on the first of two days recounted in ch. 6. In 6:22, a new day begins

---

order for purposes of their analysis. There is, however, no actual textual evidence for a different order and this view may well be over-concerned with geographical issues at the expense of thematic links. Whether or not 6.1 was originally linked with some other passage in an earlier edition of the Gospel, it makes excellent sense that the evangelist has placed the self-contained unit of 6.1–71 where he has."

40. In 6:60–71 there is an increasing specificity on the part of the narrator regarding Jesus's "disciples." Two groups emerge in this unit: one group simply referred to as "many of his disciples," and another group known as "the Twelve." The former represents a falling away on account of Jesus's message. The latter represents an acceptance of his message, mission, and person.

41. The narratival and theological significance of absolute ἐγώ εἰμι statements in the Fourth Gospel is discussed below.

(τῇ ἐπαύριον), and this day carries the reader through the remaining events of the chapter.[42]

As the next day begins, a portion of the remaining crowd seeks Jesus and travels to the locale where he and his disciples have landed (vv. 22–24).[43] This sets the stage for vv. 25–59, which comprise the Bread of Life discourse. The discourse takes shape as Jesus interacts with a mixed crowd that interjects on six occasions: (1) v. 25, "Rabbi, when did you get here?"; (2) v. 28, "What must we do to accomplish the works of God?"; (3) v. 30, "What sign do you give that we may see and believe you?"; (4) v. 34, "Sir, give us this bread always!" (5); v. 42, "Is this not Jesus, the son of Joseph . . . ?"; and (6) v. 52, "How can this man give us his flesh to eat?" Each of the six interjections from the crowd introduces a new line of thinking on the topic of the "bread from heaven" and draws upon important imagery from the OT.

In an interesting twist, the reader learns that, in addition to those who witnessed the multiplication of loaves, the crowd also consists of οἱ Ἰουδαῖοι (see vv. 41, 51). The reader again senses that "the Jews" are ever lurking behind the scenes of the story, ready to interrogate and accuse Jesus.[44]

At several turns in the discourse Jesus's words lead to confusion and spark outrage. In the final section of the discourse (vv. 53–59) he proclaims that his listeners must "eat his flesh" and "drink his blood" in order to have eternal life. This saying produces the two opposing responses to Jesus that occur in vv. 60–71.[45] One group falls away on

42. After 6:22, there is no indication of a temporal change until the μετὰ ταῦτα of 7:1.

43. I describe this group as "a portion of the remaining crowd" for two reasons. First, the phrase ὁ ὄχλος ὁ ἑστηκὼς πέραν τῆς θαλάσσης (6:22) seems to narrow the previous description of the group as ὄχλος πολύς (6:2). It appears to refer to those from the ὄχλος πολύς that remained in that region the following day. Second, scholars have been quick to comment upon the great unlikelihood of 5,000 men navigating the waters of the Sea of Tiberias at the same time.

44. "The Jews" play a notorious role in the Fourth Gospel as the perpetual antagonists and enemies of Jesus. The term οἱ Ἰουδαῖοι appears seventy-one times in the narrative, and normally in a negative sense after they develop a full-blown hostility toward Jesus in John 5.

45. There is some question as to whether the disciples are reacting to Jesus's words in vv. 53–55 or to the earlier portion of his discourse (vv. 21–51). Moloney (*Signs and Shadows*, 60) comments that regardless of which portion of Jesus's speech is identified, "[t]he reader is aware that the disciples have reached a crucial moment. They have heard 'the word' of Jesus; how will they respond?"

account of this saying, and the other draws closer to Jesus. In this pericope, Peter is again presented in a positive light. The following exegesis divides vv. 60–71 into two units:

1. "Many disciples" respond to Jesus's hard saying (6:60–66)
2. Jesus questions "the Twelve" (6:67–71)

"Many Disciples" Respond to Jesus's Hard Saying (6:60–66)

This section begins (πολλοὶ . . . ἐκ τῶν μαθητῶν αὐτοῦ, v. 60) and ends (ἐκ τούτου πολλοὶ ἐκ τῶν μαθητῶν αὐτοῦ, v. 66) with the response of "many disciples" to the words of Jesus in the preceding section. Previously, the narrator has spoken in general terms of a crowd (ὁ ὄχλος, 6:24) that was searching for Jesus. It is clear from the overall context that some members of that crowd are the recipients of Jesus's address. In addition, the reader learned in v. 41 that οἱ Ἰουδαῖοι were grumbling against Jesus because of his words about being the "bread from heaven." Now in v. 60 the reader sees "many disciples." The reader must assume that the crowd to whom Jesus has been speaking includes at least three different groups: those from the crowd, members of "the Jews," and Jesus's own disciples. Thus, Jesus's audience consists of those who are sympathetic to his words and those who are not.

In v. 60 "many disciples" react negatively to Jesus's teaching on "eating his flesh" and "drinking his blood," commenting that those instructions are difficult to accept (σκληρός ἐστιν ὁ λόγος οὗτος) and questioning their ability to "hear" Jesus's instructions (τίς δύναται αὐτοῦ ἀκούειν;).[46] Aware that his words are troublesome to these disciples, Jesus asks two questions. The first question, τοῦτο ὑμᾶς σκανδαλίζει; (v. 61b), is followed by a second, more difficult question, ἐὰν οὖν θεωρῆτε τὸν υἱὸν τοῦ ἀνθρώπου ἀναβαίνοντα ὅπου ἦν τὸ πρότερον; (v. 62).

Jesus's second question is problematic because it consists of the protasis of a third-class conditional statement without an apodosis.[47] This is a form of ellipsis typically referred to as aposiopesis. In this

46. It is unclear as to whether the verb ἀκούω should be understood as "obey," "understand," or "listen" in this verse. All three options are viable in the present context, though BDAG (s.v. ἀκούω) opts for the nuance, "to pay attention to by listening."

47. On the function and significance of the third class condition, see Wallace, *Exegetical Syntax of the New Testament*, 696–97.

construction the apodosis is not supplied but is thought to be understood easily by the reader. Failure to achieve a scholarly consensus on v. 62 has shown that the implied apodosis is not as easily understood as one might wish.[48] The interpretation taken here views the ellipsis as a continuation of the line of thought introduced in Jesus's first question (τοῦτο ὑμᾶς σκανδαλίζει;). The implied apodosis thus carries the implication, "Would you still be offended?"

A key reason why the disciples fail to grasp and accept what Jesus is saying is that they have taken his words about "eating flesh" and "drinking blood" on an earthly (viz., "fleshly") level. So Jesus condemns the flesh as useless (ἡ σὰρξ οὐκ ὠφελεῖ οὐδέν) and then affirms that his words are not flesh but spirit and life (v. 63). The reader has the privileged position of knowing what the prologue has to say about the relationship of the λόγος to ζωή ("in him was life and that life was the light of humanity," 1:4) and to σάρξ (though his origins are heavenly, Jesus "became flesh" in order to dwell among his own, 1:14). The present disciples, however, do not have this insight and will ultimately depart in ignorance.

The inability of the disciples to understand Jesus ultimately gives way to their unbelief, which Jesus confirms in v. 64. This is followed by another narrative aside where the reader is told that Jesus knew ἐξ ἀρχῆς (cf. ἐν ἀρχῇ, 1:1, 2) not only who would not believe in him but also who would betray him. This statement brings together two future realities for Jesus that will culminate in the passion narrative. He is going to be betrayed by one of his disciples and ultimately rejected by his own (cf. οἱ ἴδιοι αὐτὸν οὐ παρέλαβον, 1:11).

In the end, this group of disciples decides that Jesus's "hard saying" is ultimately too difficult to accept and they depart from following him (v. 66). Drawing upon the imagery of the prologue, Stibbe comments that the λόγος of God has himself become the σκληρὸς λόγος for these departing disciples and, in many ways, for the reader.[49]

48. For an overview of scholarly opinion on how to read the ellipsis, see Moloney, *Johannine Son of Man*, 120–23; idem, *Gospel of John*, 83–86.

49. "Perhaps the most revealing moment in these chapters—as far as the characterization of Jesus is concerned—is after the lengthy dialogue in 6:25–59. Just after Jesus has preached his homily on 'Manna from heaven' in the Capernaum synagogue (6:59), many of his disciples say, 'This is a hard teaching. Who can accept it?' The phrase translated 'hard teaching' is *sklēros logos*. It is a phrase which functions as a perfect title for Jesus who, in prologue of John's Gospel, is called God's *Logos*. In John 5–10, Jesus is

In John 6 the reader has seen οἱ Ἰουδαῖοι harass Jesus and οἱ μαθηταί depart from him. There is one remaining group in the chapter: οἱ δώδεκα. This group responds appropriately to Jesus's revelations and in the process Peter emerges as a spokesman for and leader of the group.

Jesus Questions "the Twelve" (6:67–71)

Aware of the exodus of many "disciples," Jesus turns to "the Twelve" and asks if they intend to depart as well (6:67). The reader is arrested by the narrator's mention of "the Twelve." Outside of this chapter, this designation for Jesus's closest followers occurs only one other time in the Fourth Gospel (20:24, where Thomas is identified as "one of the Twelve"). From the perspective of early Christian tradition, this designation reveals the Evangelist's awareness of a tradition of "the Twelve." From the perspective of the unfolding story, it reveals a third group and thereby another possible response to Jesus's words in the Bread of Life discourse.

In answer to Jesus's question, Peter confesses that Jesus has the "words of eternal life" (6:68), recalling the truth of what Jesus has just stated in v. 63 about his words being "spirit and life." Peter's confession also recalls the prominent theme of "belief in Jesus's word," which runs throughout 2:1—4:54. In that unit a handful of characters, including the mother of Jesus (2:5), the Samaritans (4:39), and the royal official (4:50), believe Jesus on the basis of his word. By contrast, Nicodemus (3:4, 9) fails to believe because he does not understand Jesus's words. At this stage of the narrative Peter fits squarely within the tradition of those who believe in Jesus's word. Peter also proclaims that Jesus is the "Holy One of God" (6:69). With these words the reader has another confession to add to the growing list of Johannine christological affirmations.

John 6 ends with Jesus's prediction of a future betrayal by one of the Twelve. Again, in typical Johannine fashion, the narrator turns to the reader and eliminates the suspense: Judas, the son of Simon the Iscariot, is the future betrayer.

As for Peter, the two previously mentioned elements of his confession affirm truths about Jesus that reflect what the reader has already learned in the prologue. Peter correctly identifies Jesus's relationship to

truly the *Sklēros Logos*, the Difficult Word. He is difficult in both his movements and his language. He is not an easy person to grasp, either at the level of comprehension or at the level of apprehension" (Stibbe, *John's Gospel*, 24).

ἡ ζωή (ἐν αὐτῷ ζωὴ ἦν, 1:4) and ὁ θεός (ὁ λόγος ἦν πρὸς τὸν θεόν, 1:1b) allowing him to stand out as a good example of a Johannine character with spiritual insight. After Peter's second appearance in the narrative the reader's impression of him remains quite positive.

Jesus and Peter in John 13:1–38

Following his first two appearances, Peter is off to a good start in the eyes of the reader. In John 13, however, Peter's character begins to take a turn that sets him on an increasingly negative trajectory throughout the remainder of the story. At the beginning of ch. 13, Jesus washes the disciples' feet, an act that not only prefigures his service on the cross but also invites the disciples to join the "household" of God.[50] Peter fails to comprehend the significance of this act and a series of misunderstandings results.

After the footwashing, the disciples and Jesus share a meal, at which time Jesus predicts that he will be betrayed by one of the Twelve.[51] When Jesus informs the disciples that he is going away and that they will be unable to follow, Peter protests that he will lay down his own life for Jesus. Once again Peter's naïve misunderstanding is met with Jesus's correction, only this time it accompanies a prediction of Peter's denial.

At the level of characterization, this chapter is dominated by the themes of devotion and betrayal. In the end, Judas will betray Jesus in a way that leads to his arrest, but the reader understands that Peter's denial makes him a betrayer on par with Judas Iscariot.

In addition to literary questions, there have been serious questions raised about the seemingly disjointed nature of this chapter. A number of detailed reconstructions of the chapter's compositional

50. On this point, see the insightful study by Coloe, "Welcome into the Household of God." Coloe argues that Jesus's actions in washing his disciples' feet are a profound Near Eastern symbol of welcoming one into a household. Through this action, Jesus is welcoming the disciples into the household of the Father—a theme Jesus will introduce in the chapter following the footwashing. Coloe's argument goes a bit too far in identifying the footwashing as a Johannine *semeion* (p. 415). Nevertheless, there are a number of helpful insights in her essay that should be considered seriously.

51. The term οἱ δώδεκα is not used in this pericope, but the reader learned in 6:70–71 that the betrayer will come from within the Twelve. Jesus speaks of the Twelve in v. 70: οὐκ ἐγὼ ὑμᾶς τοὺς δώδεκα ἐξελεξάμην; καὶ ἐξ ὑμῶν εἷς διάβολός ἐστιν. The narrator then explains in v. 71: ἔλεγεν δὲ τὸν Ἰούδαν Σίμωνος Ἰσκαριώτου· οὗτος γὰρ ἔμελλεν παραδιδόναι αὐτόν, εἷς ἐκ τῶν δώδεκα.

history have been suggested.[52] It is possible, however, to make sense of the chapter by approaching it as a unified narrative. In an article on John 13:1–20, Schneiders provides a particularly fine example of this approach.[53] She writes,

> First, in the interpretation that follows, the text from John will be treated primarily as a *work* rather than as an object. This implies that the text is viewed not primarily as something to be analyzed but as a human expression which functions as a mediation of meaning; that the purpose of studying the text is not to decompose it into its constituent elements in order to account for its genesis but to appropriate the meaning of the text in its integrity; that the objective of interpretation is not empirically verifiable propositions about the historical-critical references of the text, but the dialectical illumination of the meaning of the text and the self-understanding of the reader.[54]

In accord with Schneiders's basic presuppositions, this section will address some of the pertinent source critical questions while remaining focused on the final form of the text.

The uniquely Johannine double ἀμήν statement occurs across John 13, which allows the structure of the chapter to be discerned more readily. This distinctive Johannine literary feature occurs in vv. 16, 20, 21, 38. In vv. 16 and 20 the double ἀμήν is used to close out a specific literary unit and punctuate the teaching of Jesus on the topic at hand.[55] In vv. 21 and 38 the double ἀμήν is used to create an *inclusio* that frames a third unit that also sets it apart from the other two (vv. 1–17 and 18–20). With these structural elements in mind, the exegesis of ch. 13 will proceed as follows:

52. See the discussions in Boismard, "Le Lavement des pieds"; Schnackenburg, *Gospel According to St. John*, 3:10–14; Segovia, "John 13:1–20"; Weis, "Footwashing in the Johannine Community," esp. 301–6); Wojciechowski, "Source de Jean 13.1–20."

53. Schneiders, " Foot Washing (John 13:1–20)."

54. Ibid., 76–77.

55. The double ἀμήν statement occurs in v. 16 but the unit does not end until v. 17. The statement is meant to introduce two related statements of Jesus, "one concerning the relationship between servant and master (v. 16) and another about knowing and doing (v. 17)" (Moloney, *Glory Not Dishonor*, 9).

1. Jesus washes the disciples' feet (13:1–17)
    a. Jesus begins to wash the disciples' feet (13:1–5)
    b. Peter protests (13:6–11)
    c. Jesus explains the footwashing (13:12–17)
2. Jesus reveals God (13:18–20)
3. Jesus predicts betrayals by Judas and Peter (13:21–38)
    a. Jesus predicts Judas's betrayal (13:18–30)
    b. Jesus predicts Peter's denial (13:31–38)

Jesus Washes the Disciples' Feet (13:1–17)

The passion nears its climax as Jesus begins his final discourse in chs. 13–17.[56] Here Jesus prepares the disciples for his departure by washing their feet. This display of service and humility foreshadows his service on the cross, but for the Twelve it culminates in misunderstanding and correction.

Jesus Begins to Wash the Disciples' Feet (13:1–5)

John situates the events of this chapter just before the Passover (πρὸ δὲ τῆς ἑορτῆς τοῦ πάσχα, v. 1). A number of significant events have already occurred in the Fourth Gospel during the different Jewish feasts, though Passover is easily the most prominent feast in John's presentation.[57] Throughout the Gospel there are a handful of references to Jesus observing the Passover, and Jesus himself is condemned at the very moment lambs are being prepared for it (19:12–16). The association between John the Baptist's pronouncement in 1:29, 36 and Jesus's condemnation in 19:14 is not lost on the reader.[58]

56. There is no little debate about the literary parameters of Jesus's final discourse. Not all scholars agree that it begins in ch. 13. Many believe the discourse begins at 13:1, others argue for 13:31 as the beginning, while still others regard 14:1 as the starting point. For more discussion on this, see n. 38 in chapter 3.

57. Jesus celebrates the Passover in 2:13; 6:4; 11:55—12:1, and the events of chs. 18–20 occur during Passover. The Feast of Tabernacles (or Booths) is mentioned in 7:2 and the Feast of Dedication (Hanukkah) is mentioned in 10:22. Overall John is quite at home situating Jesus's ministry in the context of the theologically significant Jewish feasts.

58. For more discussion of the significance of John the Baptist's "Lamb of God" affirmation and its narratival connection to the Passover sacrifice, see Brown, *Gospel*

It has become common to read v. 2 in a way that suggests the evening meal was already underway.[59] Bultmann, however, points out that it is not necessary to understand δείπνου γινομένου in this manner, preferring instead to translate it as "on the occasion of the meal."[60] Coloe comments that Bultmann's suggestion accords well with the cultural practice of having guests wash their feet prior to the evening meal.[61] In addition, this rendering also makes better sense of the awkward intrusion of clauses reporting the knowledge of both Judas and Jesus (vv. 2b–3).

With full knowledge that his departure is near, Jesus desires to demonstrate the extent of his love toward the disciples.[62] Providing the reader with an internal view, the narrator offers a number of details related to the thoughts and perceptions of Judas and Jesus and thus points toward the coming battle between light and darkness as the events of the evening move forward.

First, the narrator reports that the devil (τοῦ διαβόλου) has already convinced Judas Iscariot to betray Jesus. This statement is meant to recall Jesus's earlier comment to the Twelve in 6:70: οὐκ ἐγὼ ὑμᾶς τοὺς δώδεκα ἐξελεξάμην; καὶ ἐξ ὑμῶν εἷς διάβολός ἐστιν. A vast majority of commentators recognize in 13:2 a Semitic idiom ("to put in mind")[63] which leads to an understanding of this phrase that is

According to John, 1:58–63; Carson, *Gospel According to John*, 147–50; Smith, *John*, 68–70. See also Skinner, "Another Look at the Lamb of God."

59. The NIV, NASB, ESV, NAB, and NRSV all render the verse in a way that indicates dinner was in process. In addition to the translation issue, there is also a textual problem in this verse. The reading γενομένου is attested to by 𝔓[66] ℵ[2] A D Θ $f^{1.13}$ 33 𝔐 lat. This reading would indicate that the meal had already been completed and, considering the context, would be the more difficult reading. In the end, the reading γινομένου, supported by ℵ* B L W Ψ 070 579 1241, enjoys better manuscript support and should most likely be retained.

60. Bultmann, *Gospel of John*, 465 n. 2.

61. Coloe, "Welcome into the Household of God," 406–7. She cites Luke 7:44 as a NT example of this practice.

62. This phrase is rendered "loved them to the end" by a number of translations (NRSV, NAB, ESV, NASB). The NIV's rendering, "he showed them the full extent of his love" is good but it fails to make τέλος explicit. There is surely an intended connection between the εἰς τέλος here and Jesus's use of τετέλεσται in 19:28. In the end, it is difficult to render this verse into English without breaking it up into multiple phrases or adding an explanatory gloss.

63. The construction can be seen in Job 22:22 (LXX): καὶ ἀνάλαβε τὰ ῥήματα αὐτοῦ ἐν καρδίᾳ σου, "and lay up these words in your heart." The corresponding

expressed in Barrett's translation: "the devil had already made up his mind that Judas should betray him."[64] Embracing this interpretation, Culpepper points out that the καρδία of the devil rather than of Judas is the object of βάλλω εἰς.[65] At the same time, the reader learns that Jesus knows "everything has been handed over to him by the Father," and that just as he has come from the Father (cf. 1:1–2) he will soon return to him. This sets up a critical contrast between the heart/mind of the devil (v. 2) and the heart/mind of Jesus (vv. 1, 3).[66]

In v. 4 Jesus arises from the meal (ἐγείρεται ἐκ τοῦ δείπνου),[67] removes his outer garments (τίθησιν τὰ ἱμάτια), and takes a towel (λαβὼν λέντιον) to wrap around his waist. The narrator's use of τίθημι and λαμβάνω (here and in v. 12) calls the reader's attention back to the image of the "good shepherd" in 10:11–18. There, Jesus comments that the Good Shepherd lays down his life (τὴν ψυχὴν αὐτοῦ τίθησιν, 10:11, 15, 17, 18) in order to take it back up again (ἵνα πάλιν λάβω αὐτήν, 10:17, 18). The use of τίθημι also recalls the words of Jesus in 11:34 when he inquires about the burial place of Lazarus: ποῦ τεθείκατε αὐτόν; The language of the text in this section points back to the Good Shepherd discourse (where there is the "laying down" and "taking up" of life) and the encounter with Lazarus (where death and burial are explicit) and looks forward to the crucifixion and resurrection of Jesus. In this way, Jesus's actions are symbolic and prophetic, highlighting the ultimate extent of his servitude. In this regard Barrett comments, "When Jesus lays aside his garments in preparation for his act of humility and cleansing he foreshadows the laying down of his life."[68]

Hebrew phrase is ושים אמריו בלבבך. Another example from the LXX which does not have a counterpart in the MT is 1 Sam 29:10: καὶ λόγον λοιμὸν μὴ θῇς ἐν καρδίᾳ σου, "and do not put an evil word in your heart."

64. Barrett, *Gospel According to St. John*, 439. See also Schnackenburg, *Gospel According to St. John*, 3:6–17; Morris, *Gospel According to John*, 614; Moloney, *Glory Not Dishonor*, 13 n. 39; Culpepper, "Johannine *hypodeigma*," 136. Brown translates the idiom as "*The devil had already induced Judas*, son of Simon, the Iscariot, to betray Jesus" (*Gospel According to John*, 2:548; emphasis added).

65. Culpepper, "Johannine *hypodeigma*," 136.

66. Here we understand that the terms εἰδώς (used in reference to Jesus in vv. 1, 3) and καρδία (used in reference to the devil in v. 2) imply perception or cognition.

67. This should not necessarily be taken to mean that the meal is in progress but only that each member in attendance has already taken his place at the table.

68. Barrett, *Gospel According to St. John*, 439. Brown (*Gospel According to John*, 2:551) also sees potential parallels between the present text and 10:11, 15, 17, 18.

Verse 5 indicates that Jesus begins to wash and dry the disciples' feet. Here, Peter appears for a third time in the story, and this time the impression he leaves upon the reader is not as positive as in his previous two appearances.

Peter Protests (13:6–11)

Jesus comes to Simon Peter and an abrupt break in the footwashing occurs. At first, Peter seems surprised by Jesus's actions: κύριε, σύ μου νίπτεις τοὺς πόδας; (v. 6). It is not appropriate at this point to regard Peter's question as a protest. If that were the case the reader might expect Peter's question to begin with μή. Instead, there is a progression in Peter's speech from surprise to outright objection.

Aware of Peter's inability to understand the significance of this event, Jesus addresses him for the first time in this conversation, seeking to comfort him with the assurance that, though he is unable to understand now, he will understand at a later time (μετὰ ταῦτα). Jesus's statement recalls three prior instances in the narrative where the disciples do not comprehend something Jesus has said or done until after his departure (see 2:17, 22; 12:16).[69] This motif of "now" and "after" pervades several episodes in the Gospel and creates a tension between the time of Jesus's ministry (the "now") and the post-resurrection situation of the disciples (the "after"). Throughout the story the reader has observed the disciples' lack of understanding in the "now" and has been

---

Schnackenburg (*Gospel According to St. John*, 3:18) however, disagrees, writing that, "Since the evangelist concentrates all his attention on the following conversation between Jesus and Peter, any attempts to provide a further interpretation are out of the question here. It is, for example, not possible to construct, from the verbs used for taking off and putting on the outer garment (τιθέναι, place, and λαμβάνειν, take) a background relationship with 10:17f, where the same verbs are used for Jesus's laying down and taking up his life."

69. In the "after" the disciples understand the significance of the Scripture, "Zeal for your house will consume me" (2:17). Only in their post-resurrection setting do they grasp the connection between the OT citation and the actions of their teacher. The disciples also remember and realize in the "after" that when Jesus spoke of raising the temple in three days that he was speaking of the temple of his body (2:22). The narrator says that this causes them to believe. In addition, the disciples understand the theological import of Jesus's triumphal entry only after he is "glorified" (12:16). This theme contributes greatly to the overall sense in the Fourth Gospel that those closest to Jesus do not comprehend his mission.

informed by the narrator of their remembrances and understanding in the "after."[70] On this motif in the present unit Moloney comments,

> The footwashing is part of God's design for Jesus, and Simon Peter's objections indicate that he is imposing his understanding on Jesus's actions. There is a lack of openness to the revelation of God's ways in Jesus's words and deeds. Jesus's response balances Simon Peter's ignorance in the "now" of story time against the "afterward" of plotted time, when he will understand. Something will happen between "now" and "afterward" that will change Simon Peter. A gap has been created, but the reader has been provided with sufficient information to suspect that "the hour" and Jesus's loving his own to the end are part of the intervening events.[71]

It is noteworthy for the present discussion that Jesus specifically states that Peter does not understand the import or meaning of the footwashing (v. 7). In the reader's most recent experience with Peter (6:68) he was perceptive and spiritually aware. Here, he begins to surprise the reader with a series of grave misunderstandings.

Peter is not reassured by Jesus's comment that he will understand "later" and in v. 8 registers an official protest: οὐ μὴ νίψῃς μου τοὺς πόδας εἰς τὸν αἰῶνα. The combination of οὐ μὴ and εἰς τὸν αἰῶνα underscores the intensity of Peter's protest.[72] Peter does not object to footwashing in general. It is the idea of having his feet washed by Jesus that is utterly unacceptable to him.[73] He fails to understand why Jesus has done what is typically reserved for servants.

70. Richard B. Hays ("Reading Scripture in Light of the Resurrection") argues that the narrator's report of these post-resurrection "remembrances" of the disciples provides the reader with a hermeneutical lens through which to read the entire Gospel. He writes, "Thus in John 2:13–22 the story of Jesus's death and resurrection is posited as the key that unlocks the interpretation of Scripture. Retrospective reading of the Old Testament after the resurrection enables Jesus's disciples to 'believe' in a new way both the Scripture and Jesus's teaching and to see how each illuminates the other . . . The figural correlation between the psalmist's prayer and the story of Jesus illuminates both in unexpected ways" (224).

71. Moloney, *Glory Not Dishonor*, 14.

72. As observed in the previous chapter, the combination of οὐ and μή with the aorist subjunctive is the strongest way to negate something in Greek and denies the potentiality of an action. See Wallace, *Exegetical Syntax of the New Testament*, 546.

73. "Peter's difficulty is not with having his feet washed *per se*, but with having them washed by Jesus. Peter perceives this as a degrading act for Jesus to perform, for it was customary in Peter's society that a slave would bring a bowl of water and a person would wash his/her own feet" (Coloe, "Welcome into the Household of God" 408).

In response to Peter's protest, Jesus replies a second time in the context of this conversation and declares that if Peter rejects the footwashing he can have no μέρος with Jesus. Often translated "part," the term μέρος likely refers to a portion or share of an inheritance—a concept upon which Jesus will elaborate in 14:2–3.[74]

Once again, however, Peter does not understand what Jesus means and responds by asking Jesus to wash his feet, head, and hands. Peter fails to see the symbolism in the washing of his feet and focuses rather on the act itself. If the act of washing brings one into union with Jesus, Peter wants more than a footwashing. He desires that his entire body be cleansed. The reader cannot doubt Peter's sincerity but at this point is beginning to question his ability to comprehend the spiritual truths Jesus is elaborating. On three different occasions in this conversation, Peter has demonstrated an inability to understand Jesus's actions (the footwashing) and words (his explanation of the footwashing).

In v. 10, Jesus replies to Peter for a third time in the conversation in a way that addresses his misunderstanding. There is in this verse a difficult textual issue. As it stands, the textual tradition supports two major readings, one of which has a number of minor variations. The phrase εἰ μὴ τοὺς πόδας ("except for the feet"), which is retained in NA^{27}, is found in the vast majority of witnesses including B C* D (K) L W Ψ f^{13} 892 *al* it vg^{cl} syh Or^{txt}. At least one important witness omits the phrase (א) but the external attestation for the NA^{27} reading is clearly superior.

On this textual issue the interpreter is also faced with a number of internal considerations. Though it is often common to opt for the shorter reading, Lincoln comments that a predominant interpretation of this passage causes the longer phrase to be regarded as the *lectio difficilior*.[75] Thus, there appears to be a conflict between two sets of internal evidence. On the difficulties involved in using internal criteria to resolve this issue, Lincoln comments,

74. See BDAG, s.v. μέρος. Brown (*Gospel According to John*, 2:565–66) comments, "The eschatological use of *meros* for eternal reward is found elsewhere in the Johannine writings (Rev xx 6, xxi 8, xxii 19). This interpretation of *meros* in v. 8 is reinforced by the fact that Jesus speaks of a heritage 'with me.' . . . Therefore, it is clear that the footwashing is something that makes it possible for the disciples to have eternal life with Jesus. Such emphasis is intelligible if we understand the footwashing as a symbol of Jesus' salvific death."

75. Lincoln, *Gospel According to St. John*, 364 n. 1.

> There is probably no escaping some form of circularity here, since overall interpretation of the passage is *both affected by and affects which text is adopted*. It seems best, however to begin with the better-attested longer reading and to attempt to make sense of the passage in this form.[76]

The interpretation taken here recognizes the validity of Lincoln's argument and retains εἰ μὴ τοὺς πόδας.

Jesus informs Peter that he, along with the other disciples, is already "clean." He does, however, add one qualification: ἀλλ' οὐχὶ πάντες. In what is probably to be regarded as a parenthetical statement, the narrator adds in v. 11 that Jesus knew who was going to betray him. The reader knows as well. Having already been introduced to Judas Iscariot on two previous occasions (6:71, 12:4), the reader is well aware that Judas is ὁ μέλλων αὐτὸν παραδιδόναι.

As Jesus finishes this conversation and washes the other disciples' feet, there is no attempt to exonerate Peter from this series of three related misunderstandings. In fact, the narrator does not return to the discussion. The reader's previous impression of Peter has been challenged in this unit but is not completely lost. Though Peter remains in his incomprehension there will be future opportunities for him to observe and understand Jesus's words and deeds.

Jesus Explains the Footwashing (13:12–17)

After the discussion with Peter, Jesus finishes washing the disciples' feet and once again dons his outer garments (v. 12). He then begins to explain the significance of what he has just done.[77] Whoever calls him κύριος and διδάσκαλος must be willing to follow his example of servitude (vv. 14–15). This is reinforced by his appeal to the generally accepted maxim, "A slave is not greater than his master, nor a messenger than the one who sent him" (v. 16).

In v. 17, Jesus again appeals to their understanding of what he has just said. In v. 1, the reader learned that "Jesus knew (εἰδὼς) that his hour had come." Likewise, in v. 3, the reader is told the "Jesus knew (εἰδὼς) that the Father had handed everything over to him." With the

76. Ibid.; emphasis added.

77. He prefaces the explanation with the question γινώσκετε τί πεποίηκα ὑμῖν; However, the reader understands that the disciples do not understand, thus necessitating the ensuing explanation.

knowledge that comes from the Father, Jesus serves his disciples. In the same way, at the end of v. 17 Jesus encourages the disciples to follow his example and act upon what they know (οἴδατε).[78]

Ultimately, the disciples do not "know" or "understand." The reader thus discerns the overall failure of the disciples to grasp the significance of what Jesus has explained and its connection to his prior and future acts of service (i.e., the footwashing and the cross, respectively).

Jesus Reveals God (13:18–20)

After indicating that his prior statement in v. 17 does not apply to all the disciples, Jesus affirms that his betrayal is in accord with the fulfillment of Scripture. In support of the claim that his betrayal fulfills Scripture is Jesus's citation of Psalm 40:10: ὁ τρώγων μου τὸν ἄρτον ἐπῆρεν ἐπ' ἐμέ τὴν πτέραν αὐτοῦ.[79] Foretelling the event not only validates the truthfulness of Jesus's message but also (and more importantly) helps reinforce in the disciples a belief in Jesus's status as the unique revealer of the Father to humanity (ἵνα πιστεύσητε ὅταν γένηται ὅτι ἐγώ εἰμι, v. 19).[80]

78. The use of οἶδα and ποιέω draws a connection between Jesus's knowing (εἰδώς, vv. 1, 3) and "doing" (see the verbs associated with Jesus's activity in vv. 4–5) and his exhortation to the Twelve in v. 17: εἰ ταῦτα οἴδατε, μακάριοί ἐστε ἐὰν ποιῆτε αὐτά. On the connection between these two episodes, Moloney (*Glory Not Dishonor*, 9) writes, "At the close of the section, after the solemn double 'amen,' Jesus tell the disciples that, in their relationship to him as his servants and sent one (v. 16), they are called to repeat exactly what the 'master' has done:

If you *know* THESE THINGS
blessed are you
if you *do* THESE THINGS (v. 17)."

79. The LXX (Ps 40:10b) reads ὁ ἐσθίων ἄρτους μου ἐμεγάλυνεν ἐπ' ἐμὲ πτερνισμόν. Among other changes in the citation, the verb ἐσθίω has been replaced by τρώγω, possibly to reflect the language of John's eucharistic passage (ch. 6). This term appears four times in the "bread of life" discourse (ὁ τρώγων; 6:54, 56, 57, 58), and there is much discussion about whether or not this passage has some connection to the Johannine eucharistic material. For opposing views, see Barrett (*Gospel According to St. John*, 444–45) who regards the change to τρώγω as an explicit eucharistic link, and Schnackenburg (*The Gospel According to St. John*, 3:26) who sees no special connection to John 6.

80. When translating this verse into English, some prefer to insert the term "Messiah" after "I am" (e.g., NLT). The NRSV, NIV, NASB, ESV, and NET Bible render this phrase "I am he." Of the modern translations, the NAB alone gets it right: "so that when it happens you may believe that I AM." The concept of Davidic Messiah thought

Much has been written on the absolute use of ἐγώ εἰμι in the Fourth Gospel. Before one can discuss the absolute use of ἐγώ εἰμι here or in the LXX, one must undertake an examination of the Hebrew phrase אני הוא (or אנכי הוא). An understanding of this phrase has the potential to provide insight into the Fourth Gospel's use of ἐγώ εἰμι.

Within the different expressions of Judaism prior to and during the first century C.E., the name of God was an important and often delicate issue. The name of Israel's God as revealed to Moses was יהוה (which appears to be a form of the verb היה "to be").[81] Over time, reverence for the name of God within Judaism led to the abandonment of the divine name in social and religious discourse. On the Jewish reverence for the divine name, Dodd writes,

> In Judaism after the Old Testament period the gradual withdrawal of the name יהוה from public use, and the ultimate suppression of its pronunciation, was accompanied (whether as cause or as consequence or as both) by a growing sense of the extreme power and sanctity of the actual name—the המפורש שם as it came to be called, meaning properly, it appears, the name as distinctly pronounced according to its letters and sounds, though other, sometimes fanciful, explanations of the term were offered.[82]

As a result of this withdrawal, the circumlocution אני הוא begins to be used as a substitute for the divine name. However, this phrase is not only used in Judaism after the OT period (as Dodd noted) but also in a number of passages in the OT. Several important examples appear in Second Isaiah:

1. Isa 43:10:

אתם עדי נאם־יהוה ועבדי אשר בחרתי למאן תדעו ותאמינו
הוא לפני לא־נוצר אל ואחרי לא יהיה
לי ותבינו כי־אני

---

to be implied by Jesus's citation of Ps 41:10, while present in the Synoptic tradition, is foreign to the context of the Fourth Gospel.

81. In response to Moses's question about how to respond to the Israelites if they ask for God's name, the Lord responds: אהיה אשר אהיה, "I am that I am" (Exod 3:14). In the following verse, the Lord's instructions continue: "Thus you shall say to the sons of Israel, YHWH (יהוה) has sent me to you."

82. Dodd, *Interpretation of the Fourth Gospel*, 93.

"You are my witnesses," says the Lord, "and my servant whom I have chosen, in order that you might know and believe that *I am* (he). No god was formed before me and there shall be none after me."

2. Isa 43:25:

אנכי אנכי הוא מחה פשעיך למעני וחטאתיך לא אזכר

"I, *I am* (he) who blots out transgressions for my own sake and will remember your sins no more."

3. Isa 48:12:

אלי יעקב וישראל מקראי אני־הוא אני ראשון אף אני
אחרין שמע

"Hear me O Jacob, and Israel whom I have called: *I am* (he). I am the first and I am the last."

4. Isa 52:6:

לכן ידע עמי שמי לכן ביום ההוא כי־אני־הוא המדבר הנני

"Therefore, my people will know my name, thus, on that day, that *I am* is speaking. Behold, here I am."

In each of the above instances, the phrase אני הוא (or אנכי הוא) is translated with an absolute ἐγώ εἰμι in the corresponding LXX passages.[83] Schnackenburg writes, "Since these passages show so clear a reference to the Old Testament revelation formula, and no other parallels can be found for this absolute use (without any more detailed description or explanation by a metaphor), they are in themselves proof of Old Testament influence."[84] In addition, Dodd assesses the lexical evidence and concludes that in 13:19

> It is difficult not to see here an allusion to the divine name אני הוא. The implication would seem to be that God has given His own Name to Christ; and this is actually stated in xvii. 11. We may further recall that the Name is associated in the Old

83. There is an example in Isa 45:18 where אני יהוה is rendered ἐγώ εἰμι in the LXX.

84. Schnackenburg, *Gospel According to St. John*, 2:84. In this commentary Schnackenburg has a detailed excursus entitled "The Origin and Meaning of the ἐγώ εἰμι formula" (2:79–89) where he discusses a range of pertinent issues.

> Testament with the glory of God . . . Thus the eternal glory of God is given to Christ, and in the same act the Name of God is glorified. This would seem to be the presupposition of the use by Christ of the divine name ἐγώ εἰμι = אני הוא.[85]

In light of this evidence, it seems best to regard John's absolute use of ἐγώ εἰμι as an explicit allusion to the divine name.[86] Thus, the λόγος, the revealer of the Father (1:18) who possesses a unique position vis-à-vis God (cf. 1:1), also possesses the name of God. Throughout the remainder of the Gospel, the absolute use of ἐγώ εἰμι adds christological depth to the reader's experience.

After this revelation of his divine name, Jesus emphasizes his connection with those who accept him (v. 20a) and reiterates the connection between himself and the Father (v. 20b). The double ἀμήν statement of v. 20a brings this unit to a close. Verses 18–20 become the centerpiece of ch. 13 as vv. 1–17 emphasize the connection between knowing and doing and vv. 21–38 focus on the future betrayals of Jesus by two of his own.

Jesus Predicts His Betrayal by Judas and Peter (13:21–38)

In vv. 1–17 the reader saw Jesus display his devotion to the disciples. The present unit sets up a sharp contrast to that devotion when Jesus predicts betrayal by two of his friends. The reader, whose two prior experiences with Judas have brought with them the ominous promise of betrayal, is not shocked at Jesus's revelation to the Twelve. However, the prediction of Peter's threefold denial is a significant source of surprise for the reader. Each subsection in this literary unit is focused on one of these two betrayals.

Jesus Predicts Judas's Betrayal (13:21–30)

What has been implied two previous times in the story is now spelled out explicitly for the disciples in v. 21: ἀμὴν ἀμὴν λέγω ὑμῖν ὅτι εἷς ἐξ ὑμῶν παραδώσει με. Jesus, troubled in spirit, informs the Twelve that one among them—the one who was previously called a "devil"—

85. Dodd, *Interpretation of the Fourth Gospel*, 95–96.

86. In addition to the works already cited, see the entries in *TDNT*, 2:398–400; *NIDNTT*, 2:278–81.

will betray him. Upon hearing this statement the disciples are at a loss (ἀπορέω) and begin speculating as to who the betrayer might be.[87]

In v. 23 the reader meets the "disciple whom Jesus loved" for the first time.[88] This character is commonly called "the Beloved Disciple" in modern scholarly discourse on the Fourth Gospel. From this point forward, when the reader encounters Peter, the Beloved Disciple is usually present.[89]

In this instance, the Beloved Disciple is seated next to Jesus and leaning against his side (ἐν τῷ κόλπῳ τοῦ Ἰησοῦ, a description that recalls the words of prologue where Jesus is εἰς τὸν κόλπον τοῦ πατρός, 1:18). This may be an initial clue that the Beloved Disciple is the character with whom the reader should primarily identify.

Here, Peter appears again and is once more cast as uncomprehending. In this regard, Culpepper comments:, "At this point the Beloved Disciple is introduced. Peter, *who obviously does not understand what Jesus has said*, signals for the Beloved Disciple to ask Jesus who he was talking about."[90] Peter attempts to use the Beloved Disciple as an intermediary in approaching Jesus for further information. Filled with curiosity about the betrayer, Peter asks the Beloved Disciple to find out the identity of the person about whom Jesus is speaking. The Beloved Disciple asks (v. 25) and Jesus answers (v. 26), but curiously the Beloved Disciple never reports the answer to Peter. Nevertheless, the reader is informed that Judas Iscariot is the betrayer. By receiving the dipped morsel, Judas confirms the prophetic pronouncement uttered by Jesus when he quoted Ps 41:10 (40:10 LXX). Also by receiving (rather than rejecting) the morsel, Judas's actions become even more despicable. It would be one thing for Judas to reject the morsel and then betray Jesus.

87. BDAG, s.v. ἀπορέω. Recognizing the inherent difficulties in rendering this term into English, the NET Bible translates ἀπορούμενοι using two words, "worried and perplexed."

88. It is possible, though not certain, that the narrator intends the unnamed disciple with Andrew (1:37–40) to be regarded by the reader as the Beloved Disciple.

89. The only time they are separated throughout the remainder of the Gospel is in chs. 18–19. A critical contrast is set up between Peter (ch. 18) who denies Jesus, and the Beloved Disciple (ch. 19), the only member of the Twelve to draw near to Jesus's cross. They are together at the empty tomb and in ch. 21. Some believe the "other disciple" in 18:15 should be understood as the Beloved Disciple. On this suggestion, see Brown, *Introduction to the Gospel of John*, 189–91.

90. Culpepper, "Johannine *hypodeigma*," 145; emphasis added.

Entering into table fellowship with him and then departing to betray him is a different thing altogether.

Verse 27 begins a chain of activity that sets the events of Jesus's passion in motion. When Judas receives the bread, Satan (ὁ σατανᾶς = διάβολος) immediately takes control of him. Jesus then commands him to take care of his business quickly. The reader was previously informed that the devil had decided that Judas would betray Jesus (v. 2).[91] That plan culminates in Judas being overtaken by Satan. He is now directed by a satanic agenda to betray Jesus and hand him over to the religious leaders.

In another of many side comments to the reader, the narrator indicates that the disciples (including Peter and the Beloved Disciple) do not understand Jesus's comment to Judas (vv. 28–29).[92] Some think Jesus's statement has to do with Judas's position as keeper of the money box, while others assume he is directing Judas to purchase something for the feast.

In accord with Jesus's command (ὃ ποιεῖς ποίησον τάχιον, v. 27) Judas departs immediately (ἐξῆλθεν εὐθύς, v. 30). At that instant in the narrative Judas becomes an outsider. As the narrative presses forward, he is not present for Jesus's Farewell Discourse. He cannot lay claim to the comfort Jesus offers the disciples, nor can he appropriate one of the prepared dwelling places (14:2–3) or the benefits of Jesus's prayer of intercession (17:6–19). After he approaches Jesus in the garden (18:1–11) the narrator makes no attempt to exonerate Judas or, as other NT narratives do (Matt 27:1–10; Acts 1:12–18), explain his remorse or the manner of his death. Judas simply fades from the picture.

Once again the narrator leaves a situation without addressing any progression in the disciples' understanding of Jesus's message. As far as the reader is concerned, the disciples (including Peter) remain in the dark.

Jesus Predicts Peter's Denial (13:31–38)

On the heels of Judas's departure Jesus begins to explain his glorification. Jesus has spoken of his glory on a number of previous occasions

91. This conclusion is based upon the previous interpretation of the Semitic idiom in 13:2 (nn. 63 and 64 above).

92. Moloney (*Glory Not Dishonor*, 23) comments that οὐδεὶς ἔγνω is a reference to the "overwhelming and universal ignorance of the disciples," and that "this includes the Beloved Disciple (v. 28)."

in the narrative.[93] Here, his glorification is explicitly tied to his betrayal and death. The "hour" for which the reader has been waiting has finally arrived.[94]

In v. 33 Jesus informs the disciples that he will be going away and they will not be able to join him. He will elaborate on this topic in 14:1–12. For now he reiterates what he earlier told the Jewish leaders in 7:33: οὐ δύνασθε ἐλθεῖν.

It has already been stated that there have been protracted discussions about this chapter's redactional history, and much of it works under the assumption that the chapter is disjointed in its content. The love commandment in v. 34 is one example of an apparent interruption in the flow of the text. Smith's comments in this regard are helpful:

> Jesus now give his disciples the love commandment, which characterizes his teaching, but there is no immediate preparation or build-up to it. Indeed, Jesus has been discussing his glorification and departure from his disciples (vv. 31–33), and after the command (vv. 34–35) that subject is resumed (vv. 36–38). At first glance, the love command may seem to be an interjection or interpolation. Yet, coming as it does at the conclusion of the narration of Jesus's actions at the meal, particularly the footwashing, and before the longer discourses with the disciples (chaps. 14–16), it is appropriately placed. *What Jesus has demonstrated he now commands.*[95]

Therefore the "new commandment" to love another as Jesus has loved is a look back at the footwashing and a look forward to the crucifixion. And, to love "as Jesus loves" implies laying down one's life for others.

As in the instances of the betrayer's identity (vv. 24–25), Peter's ignorance shows again when he asks Jesus, ποῦ ὑπάγεις; (v. 36a). Jesus refuses to answer and reinforces what he has earlier said in v. 33—the disciples cannot come to where he is going. His hour has come and his glorification entails a departure to the Father who sent him. Ironically, Jesus does indicate that the disciples will be able to follow later. Again,

93. The theme was introduced in the prologue in 1:14. The reader sees Jesus "reveal his glory" in 2:11. Then, in 8:50, 54; 11:4, 40; 14:13; 16:14; 17:4, 5, 10, 22, 24, Jesus speaks of the glory he and the Father share that will ultimately be revealed in his betrayal, crucifixion, and resurrection.

94. Jesus has previously spoken about his "hour" in 2:4; 4:21, 23; 5:25, 28; 7:30; 8:20; 12:23, 27.

95. Smith, *John*, 258–59; emphasis added.

the reader perceives the interplay between the "now" of narrated time and the "after" of the post-resurrection period. The sincerity of Peter's proclamation is challenged by the statement that what Jesus does and says now cannot be understood until after Jesus's hour has passed. Because Peter does not understand this truth, he ignorantly protests that he is willing to lay down his life for Jesus.

Peter's insistence that he will lay down his life for Jesus is met with a sarcastic question (τὴν ψυχήν σου ὑπὲρ ἐμοῦ θήσεις) and Jesus's contradiction of Peter's proclamation (ἀμὴν ἀμὴν λέγω σοι, οὐ μὴ ἀλέκτωρ φωνήσῃ ἕως οὗ ἀρνήσῃ με τρίς, v. 38). In light of Peter's sincerity throughout the story thus far, the prediction of his denial is somewhat shocking to the reader. Peter will fail to lay down his life for Jesus and thus fail to love as Jesus loves. If, as stated above, an implication of Jesus's love command (v. 34) is to lay down one's life willingly, Peter is cast as one who will not keep Jesus's command.

For the third time in this chapter, the narrator moves forward without stopping to comment further on the episode of misunderstanding. Here Jesus continues speaking in ch. 14 in a way that is meant to bring the disciples comfort at the announcement of his departure. Peter is not exonerated of his spiritual incomprehension by the narrator and the reader does not hear from him again until Jesus's prophecy of denial comes true. The previously positive picture of Peter is beginning to change.

Peter Thus Far

In John 13, Peter is characterized as sincere but uncomprehending. To borrow two of the adjectives Riley previously applied to the character of Thomas, Peter is beginning to appear both ignorant and wrong in ch. 13.[96] It is too soon to say that the reader has developed a negative

96. Culpepper's summary of ch. 13 reinforces not only the point of our discussion here but also the focus of this study: "Our reading of this chapter, though it has dealt with only certain aspects of the text, has shown that the chapter presents a coherent development of the contrast between Jesus's knowledge and the disciples' *lack of understanding*. This contrast is fundamental to the plot of the entire Gospel. Jesus has come as Word incarnate to reveal the Father (1:18). His revelation is light in darkness, but his own do not receive him. Even *the disciples do not understand* until after his death . . . Because *Peter does not understand* that the hour of Jesus's death has come, *he cannot understand* the footwashing, and he is not ready to lay down his life" ("The Johannine *hypodeigma*," 147; emphasis added.

picture of him. Instead, the reader moves forward with measured ambivalence, still waiting for Peter to become the "rock" alluded to in ch. 1, but uncertain as to whether he will muster the necessary understanding of Jesus's mission.

In the first pericope (13:1–17), he does not understand the significance of the footwashing and vociferously protests before Jesus. On three different occasions in the conversation Peter is corrected and instructed by Jesus. This leads to no improvement in the situation as he persists in misunderstanding. At this stage of the chapter the narrator does not comment on Peter's failure but simply moves on.

In the second pericope (13:18–38), Peter displays ignorance regarding Jesus's betrayer (vv. 22–25) and his departure (vv. 36–37). In a final climactic moment in the chapter, Peter's previously unquestioned sincerity is met with a sober prediction of his future denial of Jesus. Peter is not only in the dark about Judas's betrayal, but is equally ignorant of his own capacity to betray Jesus.

Jesus and Peter in John 18:1–27

At the conclusion of the Farewell Discourse, Jesus and the disciples depart across the Kidron Valley (18:1). In an unnamed garden the events of Jesus's final night and day begin to unfold. Judas Iscariot, earlier dispatched to complete his commission "quickly" (13:27), leads Roman soldiers and a detachment from the chief priests and Pharisees to arrest Jesus in the garden. After a brief struggle, Jesus is taken to the Jewish authorities. While Jesus is inside facing the Jewish leaders, Peter is outside denying that he knows Jesus. Thus, the two predictions of betrayal from ch. 13 are realized.

The exegesis of 18:1–27 will proceed as follows:

1. Betrayal and confrontation (18:1–11)
    a. Betrayal by Judas in a garden (18:1–3)
    b. Jesus confronted by the mob (18:4–11)
2. The trial of Jesus and Peter's denial (18:12–27)
    a. Jesus taken to Annas (18:12–14)
    b. Peter's first denial (18:15–18)
    c. Jesus questioned by Annas (18:19–24)
    d. Peter's second and third denials (18:25–27)

Betrayal and Confrontation (18:1–11)

Jesus has finished addressing the disciples during their final meal (13:1–17:26). The group now ventures out into a garden where the earlier prediction of betrayal by one of Jesus's friends now comes to pass.

Betrayal by Judas in a Garden (18:1–3)

The narrator informs the reader that the disciples and Jesus have departed across the wadi of the Kidron (v. 1) and have made their way into an unnamed garden. At this point in the accounts by Mark and Matthew, Jesus retreats to the Mount of Olives and specifically enters a garden in Gethsemane to pray.[97] Luke also situates the events on the Mount of Olives (22:39–46) but does not specifically mention Gethsemane.[98]

An important element of the Synoptic presentation of Jesus in the garden is his prayer of angst just prior to his arrest. This is noticeably absent in the Johannine account.[99] Unlike the drawn-out Gethsemane scenes in the Synoptics, the Johannine garden scene develops quickly as there is a perceptible change in narrative velocity from 17:26 to 18:1–11.[100] At the end of ch. 17, Jesus has been speaking for an extended

97. See Mark 14:32–42; Matt 26:36–46.

98. All four accounts refer to same general area. The term "Gethsemane" (used by Mark and Matthew) is a transliteration of the Aramaic גת שמני, "oil press," and may be used in reference to an olive grove on one side of the Mount of Olives. This location accords well with Luke's description of the events occurring on τὸ ὄρος τῶν ἐλαιῶν, "the Mount of Olives" (22:39). The Johannine reference to a garden across the wadi of the Kidron shows John's familiarity with the Gethsemane tradition. More important for our discussion, however, are John's differences from the Gethsemane tradition. For more information on the similarities and differences between the canonical accounts, see *DJG*, "Gethsemane."

99. In the Synoptic tradition Jesus pleads with the Father to deliver him from what he is facing. His prayer in the Markan account is, "Take this cup from me, yet not what I will, but what you will" (14:36). The prayer in the Matthean account is essentially the same with a few grammatical improvements: "My Father, if it is possible, may this cup be taken from me. Yet not what I will, but what you will" (26:39). In Luke, Jesus prays, "Father, if you are willing, take this cup from me; yet not my will, but your will be done" (22:42). John's Gospel offers a strong contrast to the Synoptic tradition's angst-filled prayer. In John 12:27 a defiant Jesus proclaims, "Now my soul has become troubled. And what shall I say, 'Father deliver me from this hour?' But for this very reason I came to this hour."

100. In the Johannine account there is an interesting parallel. In 18:11 Jesus speaks of the cup (τὸ ποτήριον) he must drink. In each of the Synoptic accounts Jesus prays that the cup (τὸ ποτήριον in all three Gospels) may be taken from him.

period, and during that time the narrative has slowed significantly. In 18:1 the action picks up quickly as Jesus goes out (ἐξῆλθεν) across the Kidron Valley (v. 1a) and goes into (εἰσῆλθεν) a garden (v. 1b), leading to an acceleration of activity from there.

The differences between John's depiction of this episode and the Synoptic tradition are striking. The absence of the name Gethsemane is far from the most drastic difference between the two traditions. In contrast to the Synoptics, Jesus is not filled with inner turmoil as he awaits the arrival of his "hour," nor does he turn to the Father in prayer as he does three times in the Synoptics. Instead, Jesus has prayed extensively just prior to his arrival in the garden (cf. Jesus's prayer of John 17) and Jesus appears to be confident during the confrontation in the garden. He is in charge at all times in dealing with the arresting party.

Though the reader has not witnessed any activity in this garden, the narrator explains that Judas knows the location because it has been a regular meeting place for Jesus and the disciples (v. 2). Judas appears accompanied by an unlikely pairing of groups.[101] With him are a Roman cohort (τὴν σπεῖραν)[102] and a delegation of temple officers sent from the chief priests and Pharisees (ἐκ τῶν ἀρχιερέων καὶ ἐκ τῶν Φαρισαίων ὑπηρέτας).[103] From this description the reader understands that there is a host of enemies conspiring to oppose Jesus. Jesus faces opposition from one of his own (Judas), from the Jewish leaders (with whom he has been at odds throughout the entire narrative), and from a new group (representatives of the Roman government).

Historically, this specific combination of forces is unlikely, though some collusion of Roman and Jewish forces is plausible. Nevertheless, within the story this combined mob is a picture of how the forces of darkness have arrayed to battle Jesus, the light of the world. In that same vein, the group comes, under the cover of night, with lanterns (φανῶν) and torches (λαμπάδων).[104] In an ironic twist, they have come bringing

101. Brown's discussion of the historical, literary, and theological issues raised by this verse is particularly helpful. See Brown, *Death of the Messiah*, 1:248–52.

102. A Roman cohort was a military unit with a capacity of 600 soldiers.

103. The term ὑπηρέτης commonly refers to "one who functions as a helper" and occurs frequently in the contexts where a subordinate capacity is implied. See BDAG, s.v. ὑπηρέτης. In this instance, the term is likely referring to servants of the Sanhedrin in whom were vested some policing authorities.

104. Both terms can be used to refer to a torch. BDAG (s.v. λαμπάς) suggests that when used together, φανοί should be understood as "lanterns."

their own illumination to take the light of the world into their custody. The text also indicates that the assembled group has weapons (ὅπλων). The clear implication is that they are prepared to take Jesus by force if necessary.

Jesus Confronted by the Mob (18:4–11)

Aware of all that will happen to him, Jesus approaches the delegation and asks whom they are seeking. This question and the answer that follows (Ἰησοῦν τὸν Ναζωραῖον, v. 5a) provides Jesus another opportunity to emphasize his unique connection to the Father (λέγει αὐτοῖς· ἐγώ εἰμι, v. 5b). Once again, it is hard to regard ἐγώ εἰμι as anything other than a comment on Jesus's role as the unique revelation of the Father to humanity who has been given the very name of the Father.

The second half of v. 5 provides a parenthetical comment to the reader that indicates that Judas, the betrayer, is standing in the midst of the delegation (εἱστήκει δὲ καὶ Ἰούδας ὁ παραδιδοὺς αὐτὸν μετ' αὐτῶν). This is the last reference to Judas Iscariot in the Fourth Gospel. He has fulfilled his role within the story and he disappears from the scene without further comment from the narrator.

Jesus's absolute ἐγώ εἰμι statement causes the assembled group to move back (ἀπῆλθον εἰς τὰ ὀπίσω) and fall to the ground (ἔπεσαν χαμαί). The irony of this response is not lost on the reader who understands that as the unique representation of God to humanity, Jesus is deserving of their prostration. At this response, Jesus once again asks whom they are seeking (v. 7), and reiterates his earlier self-identification: ἐγώ εἰμι. As in the previous occurrences of ἐγώ εἰμι in the Gospel, this identification should be taken in the sense that emphasizes the connection between Jesus and YHWH.[105]

The repetition of ἐγώ εἰμι three times in a span of four verses (vv. 5b, 6a, 8a) is undoubtedly meant to keep the concept in the front of the reader's mind. It also helps to establish Jesus's control over the narrated events in the garden. He boldly identifies himself and then instructs the mob to release the disciples (ἄφετε τούτους ὑπάγειν, v. 8b). In another narrative aside, the reader is informed that Jesus's words (οὓς δέδωκάς μοι οὐκ ἀπώλεσα ἐξ αὐτῶν οὐδένα) are prophetic and the reader recalls three of Jesus's earlier proleptic pronouncements:

105. See the above exegesis of John 13:19.

1. 6:39:	τοῦτο δέ ἐστιν τὸ θέλημα τοῦ πέμψαντός με, ἵνα πᾶν ὃ δέδωκέν μοι μὴ ἀπολέσω ἐξ αὐτοῦ, ἀλλὰ ἀναστήσω αὐτὸ ἐν τῇ ἐσχάτῃ ἡμέρᾳ. "This is the will of the one who sent me, that I should not lose one of all those he has given to me, and I will raise them up on the last day."
2. 10:28:	κἀγὼ δίδωμι αὐτοῖς ζωὴν αἰώνιον καὶ οὐ μὴ ἀπό–λωνται εἰς τὸν αἰῶνα καὶ οὐχ ἁρπάσει τις αὐτὰ ἐκ τῆς χειρός μου. "And I give them eternal life and they will never perish and no one will snatch them from my hand."
3. 17:12:	ὅτε ἤμην μετ᾽ αὐτῶν ἐγὼ ἐτήρουν αὐτοὺς ἐν τῷ ὀνό–ματί σου ᾧ δέδωκάς μοι, καὶ ἐφύλαξα, καὶ οὐδεὶς ἐξ αὐτῶν ἀπώλετο εἰ μὴ ὁ υἱὸς τῆς ἀπωλείας, ἵνα ἡ γραφὴ πληρωθῇ. "When I was with them I protected them and guarded them by the name that you have given me. And not one of them has been lost except for the son of perdition, that the scripture might be fulfilled."

All three passages bear upon the interpretation of 18:9, but 17:12 is of particular importance because it is the only one of the three passages to provide a qualification: the "son of perdition," ὁ υἱὸς τῆς ἀπωλεί–ας, will be lost.

A predominant view among Johannine scholars is that the reader should regard Judas Iscariot as ὁ υἱὸς τῆς ἀπωλείας.[106] The only other occurrence of this phrase in the canonical literature is in 2 Thess 2:3 where it is a reference to Satan (cf. also 2 Thess 2:8–9, where ὁ υἱὸς τῆς ἀπωλείας is referred to as "the lawless one" and is connected explicitly with Satan). The reader has heard Jesus refer to Judas as a devil (6:70), seen the devil take over Judas's mind (13:2), and seen Satan enter into him (13:27). Therefore, it appears that when Judas

106. Cf. for instance, Morris, *Gospel According to John*, 728; Lincoln, *Gospel According to St. John*, 437; Schnackenburg, *Gospel According to St. John*, 3:182; and Hoskyns, *Fourth Gospel*, 501.

betrays Jesus, he is not the responsible party. In addition, Judas has his feet washed by Jesus (13:12) and shares the morsel at dinner (13:26–27). Judas has participated fully in the fellowship of those the Father has given to Jesus to care for and protect. Arguing that ὁ υἱὸς τῆς ἀπωλείας is Satan rather than Judas, Moloney writes,

> The only figure in the story Jesus could not care for is Satan, who planned a betrayal (see 13:2). But Jesus washed the feet and shared the morsel with Judas, despite Satan's designs. Nevertheless, Satan entered Judas (see 13:27) "that the scripture might be fulfilled" (17:12c), and the reader recalls 13:18. There is a divine order in the events of the life and death of Jesus beyond the control of Jesus. The Son of Perdition is beyond the control of Jesus, but he was given the disciples to care for . . . Jesus has kept and cared for them all, including Judas . . . He now asks the Father to be "father" to all the disciples, including Judas.[107]

As attractive as this interpretation is, it runs into an insurmountable problem in the light of Jesus's use of αὐτούς in 17:12. Jesus prays, "When I was with them (μετ᾽ αὐτῶν) I protected them (αὐτοὺς) and guarded them by the name that you have given me. And not one of them (οὐδεὶς ἐξ αὐτῶν) has been lost except for (εἰ μὴ) the son of perdition, that the Scripture might be fulfilled." The qualifying phrase εἰ μὴ following ἐξ αὐτῶν makes it clear that ὁ υἱὸς τῆς ἀπωλείας is among those who have been given to Jesus by the Father. Even though Judas has been under the control of Satan, he (rather than Satan) is among those given to Jesus by the Father. Thus the reader must identify Judas, on some level, as ὁ υἱὸς τῆς ἀπωλείας. Carson offers what is perhaps an acceptable mediating position when he writes that John 17:12 probably "portrays Judas Iscariot as a horrible precursor belonging to the same genus as the eschatological 'son of perdition,' just as in 1 Jn. 2:18, 22; 4:3 John portrays the heretical teachers he there confronts as of a piece with the antichrist."[108]

In any case, the Fourth Gospel does not stop to comment nor does it return (as do Matt 27 and Acts 1) to report on Judas after the betrayal. In the present context Judas may be among those for whom Jesus provides release in the garden, but the reader knows that Judas will not escape the condemnation of God. On the other hand, Peter and the

107. Moloney, *Glory Not Dishonor*, 115.

108. Carson, *Gospel According to John*, 563.

other disciples are granted release from the imminent police action of the mob, though Peter's actions in v. 10 reveal once again a fundamental misunderstanding of Jesus's mission. If Jesus is going to return to the Father, he must be arrested by the delegation of police and soldiers. This is the way to the cross, which for the Johannine Jesus is the way back to the Father.

Instead of departing, however, Peter pulls his sword and strikes Malchus,[109] the servant of the high priest, cutting off his right ear.[110] Jesus rebukes Peter for his impetuous action by commanding him to put his sword away and by pointing out that he must fulfill the will of the Father (τὸ ποτήριον ὃ δέδωκέν μοι ὁ πατὴρ οὐ μὴ πίω αὐτό; v. 11).[111] As discussed above, Jesus's use of τό ποτήριον parallels an important element of the Synoptic accounts of Jesus's prayer on the Mount of Olives and reveals the Evangelist's familiarity with the Gethsemane tradition. Jesus's question to Peter is the climactic moment in this scene and, as in previous scenes, there is no response from Peter and no explanation by the narrator. The setting shifts without a word about Peter's misunderstanding of the situation. In the end, the narrator may intend an implicit criticism of Peter's inability to see the divine destiny of Jesus.

The Trial of Jesus and Peter's Denial (18:12–24)

As the mob leaves the garden, Jesus is bound, taken into custody, and brought before the Jewish leadership. While Jesus is inside being questioned by Annas, Peter is outside being questioned by those who are standing around and warming themselves. A critical contrast develops between the actions of Jesus and Peter. Jesus speaks boldly before those who have authority to condemn him, while Peter cowers in the presence of a little girl and a slave (18:17, 26). Jesus confesses the truth, while Peter denies it, consequently disavowing Jesus. Even the prior confession of Jesus (ἐγώ εἰμι, vv. 5b, 6b, 8a) stands in contrast to Peter's

109. An interesting element of the narrative is John's identification of the servant as Malchus. This raises questions about John's naming of seemingly insignificant characters while other important characters are left anonymous (e.g., Jesus's mother, the Samaritan woman, etc.).

110. On the significance of Peter cutting of the *right* ear, see the discussion in Brown, *Gospel According to John*, 2:812.

111. When οὐ μή is combined with the subjunctive to form a question, the resulting clause has the force of an affirmation. On this, see BDF, para. 365.

denials (οὐκ εἰμί, vv. 17, 25). Thus the scenes in this literary unit are replete with a series of characteristic Johannine dualisms. There is also an alternating pattern of interchange between the events surrounding Jesus and Annas (vv. 12–14, 19–24) and the events surrounding Peter (vv. 15–18, 25–27). This shifting back and forth helps the narrator create a dramatized irony as the events on the "inside" (Jesus before Annas) contrast sharply with those on the "outside" (Peter in the courtyard).

Jesus Taken to Annas (18:12–14)

Though Jesus has willingly given himself up, the cohort, their commanding officer (χιλίαρχος),[112] and the temple police seize and bind him (v. 12). Their destination is the house of Annas, the father-in-law of Caiaphas the high priest.[113] The reader met Caiaphas on a previous occasion (11:49–52) where he spoke ironically of the importance of one man dying for the nation. While the context of Caiaphas's statement is the political expediency of having Jesus die instead of the Jews undergoing Roman persecution, the narrator informs the reader that this statement also beautifully encapsulates the mission of Jesus (i.e., one dying on behalf of the many). The narrator's mention of Caiaphas is meant to remind the reader that Jesus's death will be efficacious for the nation.

112. The term χιλίαρχος was the technical term for the commander of a thousand (see BDAG, s.v. χιλίαρχος), even though the cohort only consisted of 600 soldiers.

113. In v. 19, the narrator comments that the high priest questioned Jesus (ὁ οὖν ἀρχιερεὺς ἠρώτησεν τὸν Ἰησοῦν). Then, in v. 24 the reader learns that it is Annas who has been questioning him. There are different attempts to explain this seeming contradiction. Mahoney ("New Look at an Old Problem") argues on text-critical grounds that the text can be understood to refer to Caiaphas. He concludes, "Finally, the answer, then, to our opening question is: St. John records a private, informal enquiry by Caiphas the high priest in the presence of Annas. At its conclusion Caiphas departed to another part of the palace where the Sanhedrin was assembling. Then Annas, who remained after the departure of Caiphas, sent Jesus to him for a formal religious trial" (p. 144). This fanciful reconstruction is intriguing, but unwarranted and unsupported by the textual evidence. Another approach is provided by Staley ("Subversive Narrator/Victimized Reader"), who argues that this is one of the many attempts by the narrator to misinform the implied reader purposely. There are instances, however, where former high priests (as Annas was) are referred to as ἀρχιερεύς. Therefore, this element of the text is to be regarded neither as a factual error nor a subversive literary technique.

Peter's First Denial (18:15–18)

While Jesus is inside being questioned by Annas, Simon Peter and "another disciple," ἄλλος μαθητής, are following at a distance. The other disciple is acquainted with the high priest and is able to gain access to the courtyard (v. 15).[114] Eventually Peter (v. 16) gains access to the inside when the other disciple speaks to a slave girl who watches the door and Peter is allowed to enter. The introduction of this slave girl provides Peter his first opportunity to confess or deny Jesus. As he enters the courtyard, the slave girl inquires of him, μὴ καὶ σὺ ἐκ τῶν μαθητῶν εἶ τοῦ ἀνθρώπου τούτου; Her question expects a negative answer and that is exactly what Peter provides. By replying οὐκ εἰμί, Peter not only denies Jesus but also utters words that stand out against the threefold appearance of ἐγώ εἰμι in vv. 5–8.

This scene ends with a side comment from the narrator. A group of characters, including slaves and guards, are warming themselves by the fire in the courtyard of the high priest (v. 18a). The narrator comments that Peter is μετ᾽ αὐτῶν (v. 18b), a phrase which recalls the presence of Judas among the members of the arresting party (Ἰούδας ὁ παραδιδοὺς αὐτὸν μετ᾽ αὐτῶν, v. 5). The connection between the betrayals of Judas and Peter that was so vividly drawn in ch. 13 is reemphasized in this scene. The irony here is that, while Jesus is inside facing the judgment by the Jewish leaders, Peter is outside in subtle collusion with those who oppose Jesus. Even when Peter is on the inside (in the courtyard with the other disciple), he remains on the outside because he is "with them."

Jesus Questioned by Annas (18:19–24)

The setting now flashes back to Jesus's interview before Annas. Annas questions Jesus about his disciples and his teaching. In his response Jesus reverses the order from Annas's question and addresses his teaching (ἐδίδαξα, "I taught," v. 20) and his disciples (τοὺς ἀκηκοότας, "those who have heard," v. 21), respectively.

With regard to his teaching Jesus first comments that he has spoken openly: ἐγὼ παρρησίᾳ λελάληκα τῷ κόσμῳ (v. 20). This is not merely a reference to Jesus's public teaching but points back to the pro-

114. For historical speculation on how the other disciple could have been γνωστὸς τῷ ἀρχιερεῖ, cf. Brown, *Gospel According to John*, 2:841.

logue and reminds the reader that Jesus—the unique representation of the Father—has come into the world to enlighten a humanity that has not recognized him (cf. 1:9–10). Jesus's use of the perfect λελάληκα in v. 20 is likely intensive, indicating the ongoing implications of past completed activity.[115] In this case, there are continuing implications of Jesus's activity of speaking τῷ κόσμῳ.

Not only has Jesus spoken to the world, he reminds Annas in v. 20 that he has taught publicly in synagogue (ἐδίδαξα ἐν συναγωγῇ) and in the temple courts where Jewish people were known to congregate (ἐν τῷ ἱερῷ, ὅπου πάντες οἱ Ἰουδαῖοι συνέρχονται). The change in tense in v. 20 from the perfect (λελάληκα) to the aorist (ἐδίδαξα) is significant because it signals the end of Jesus's ministry of proclamation to the Jews. As a rule, Jesus taught πάντοτε in synagogue and temple courts. This is no longer the case. His ministry to them is complete. However, the word is still available τῷ κόσμῳ.[116]

Because Jesus has spoken openly there should be no question about the substance of his message. Instead of answering these questions, Jesus instructs Annas to ask those who have heard him teach. Taking Jesus's words as a sign of insolence toward the office of high priest, one of the officers strikes Jesus on the face and asks if his words are appropriate.[117] Jesus responds, "If I have spoken evil (εἰ κακῶς ἐλάλησα), bear witness concerning the evil.[118] But if I have spoken well (εἰ δὲ καλῶς [ἐλάλησα implied]), why do you strike me?" (v. 23). The reader knows that Jesus has consistently "spoken well" in providing the truth of God. That truth has not been accepted and the soldier provides no justification for the slap. The resultant action is that Annas sends Jesus bound to the current high priest, Caiaphas (v. 24).

115. On the intensive (resultative) perfect, see Wallace, *Exegetical Syntax of the New Testament*, 574–76.

116. "The perfect tense, placed in close proximity with the aorist *edidaxa* indicates that although the teaching of Jesus to 'the Jews' has come to an end, the word of Jesus is still available. Something began in the past, and its consequences are still abroad" (Moloney, *Glory Not Dishonor*, 134).

117. On reverence for the high priest, Brown (*Gospel According to John*, 2:827) notes, "An attitude of propriety was demanded by Exod xxii 28: 'You shall not revile God nor curse [say something wrong of] a ruler of your people.' It is not unheard of that an attendant at a trial might be carried away to act against a prisoner."

118. In the LXX, the phrase "to speak evil", λαλεῖν κακῶς, translates the Hebrew קלל, "to curse," in contexts associated with blasphemy. See Lev 19:14 (οὐ κακῶς ἐρεῖς); 20:9 (ὃς ἂν κακῶς εἴπῃ); and Isa 8:21 (καὶ κακῶς ἐρεῖτε).

Peter's Second and Third Denials (18:25–27)

While Peter is still "with them," an unidentified group within the courtyard asks whether he is one of Jesus's disciples. As with Peter's first denial, the question expects a negative answer and again Peter provides one: οὐκ εἰμί (v. 25). Without a break in the action Peter is questioned for a third time about his relationship to Jesus. This time a relative of Malchus (18:10) poses the question with the expectation of an affirmative answer: οὐκ ἐγώ σε εἶδον ἐν τῷ κήπῳ μετ' αὐτοῦ; (v. 26). The last words of the question recall Peter's presence with those in the courtyard and again draw the intended contrast. Will Peter confess to having been μετ' αὐτοῦ or will he deny it and remain μετ' αὐτῶν? Having heard Jesus's prediction in ch. 13, the reader is not surprised that Peter denies knowing Jesus for a third time. After the third denial the cock crows immediately. As with Judas, the narrator does not stop to report Peter's remorseful reaction (as do the Synoptics).[119] Instead, the story presses forward. In denying Jesus, Peter has failed to honor the love commandment and has become a betrayer on the level of Judas Iscariot.

Throughout the unit Jesus has been inside confessing truth while Peter has been outside denying Jesus. The inside/outside imagery is not lost upon the reader. Peter is not only a betrayer on the level of Judas; he has persisted in being an outsider.

Peter Thus Far

In the third and fourth passages examined in this chapter (13:1–38; 18:1–27) there are the parallel elements of unbelief, misunderstanding, and the absolute use of ἐγώ εἰμι by Jesus. In addition, Peter, who began his journey in the Fourth Gospel as a strong (1:42) and faithful (6:68) follower, is now shown to be fragile, impulsive (in cutting off Malchus's ear, 18:10), and unbelieving (in seeking to thwart the Father's plan by force, 18:10–11). He further demonstrates an inability to be faithful (in denying Jesus, 18:15–18, 25–27) and to love as Jesus loves (in his failure to lay down his life—a clear implication of Jesus's love commandment in 13:34–38).

119. In Mark 14:72, after the cock crows a second time, Peter remembers and weeps. In Matthew 27:75 Peter hears the cock crow and weeps bitterly. In Luke 22:62, Jesus is in a position to make eye contact with Peter as he remembers the prophecy. Peter responds with remorse and sorrow. In all three accounts Peter's emotions represent a literary attempt to exonerate Peter.

In John 18, Peter appears as an impetuous, cowardly disciple who fails once again to understand the nature of Jesus's mission. His forceful resistance of the arresting party in the face of Jesus's willingness to surrender indicates his misunderstanding of Jesus's manner of returning to the Father. In fulfillment of Jesus's prophecy (13:38), Peter denies three times knowing Jesus. This demonstrates unbelief and a lack of love. After the events of chs. 1 and 6, the reader remains ambivalent about Peter but surprised by this drastic turn in his characterization. Nevertheless, the reader is still aware of Peter's sincerity and awaits the fulfillment of Jesus's promise in 1:43. Despite his denials, Peter has heard Jesus's words and will have another opportunity for redemption.

Jesus and Peter in John 20:1–10

The last time the reader saw Peter was on the occasion of his third denial (18:26–27) and his final words in the text were words of denial (οὐκ εἰμί, 18:25). Since that time there has been no mention of Peter and no attempt to absolve him of the responsibility of denying Jesus three times. Nevertheless, Peter retains the important status he has achieved throughout the Gospel. This is evident in that after Mary's discovery of the empty tomb Peter is the first recipient of the news (v. 2). Despite his recent indiscretions Peter remains chief among the small group of the followers of Jesus.

The reader, who has witnessed Jesus's crucifixion and is well aware of the resurrection imagery used throughout Jesus's last discourse, expects Jesus's "return" from the Father. This expectation is met at the beginning of ch. 20. Jesus returns and validates the mission he has spoken of throughout the Fourth Gospel. My exegesis of 20:1–10 will divide the unit as follows:

1. Mary Magdalene witnesses the empty tomb (20:1–2)
2. Peter and the Beloved Disciple at the tomb (20:3–10)

Mary Magdalene Witnesses the Empty Tomb (20:1–2)

Verse 1 begins with the typical Johannine practice of providing the spatial and temporal settings of the pericope. It is now early on the first day of the week. The narrator makes sure to point out that these events take place σκοτίας ἔτι οὔσης, "while it was still dark" (v. 1a). The reader recognizes the theological motif of darkness and its association with unbelief throughout the Fourth Gospel.[120] Specifically, the reader recalls the words of the prologue: "The light shines in the darkness but the darkness has not overcome it" (1:5). The light of the world has seemingly been extinguished by the proceedings of the previous few days, but the events at the empty tomb will confirm the triumph of the Light of the World over the darkness.

Mary Magdalene, whom the reader has only just met at the foot of the cross in 19:25, is the first to venture to the tomb of Jesus.[121] Upon arriving she notices that the stone has been rolled away from the entrance. The terse description provided by the narrator (βλέπει τὸν λίθον ἠρμένον ἐκ τοῦ μνημείου) makes it appear that Mary's immediate response is not to investigate the tomb but rather to run directly to the disciples. She remains, for the moment ἐν σκοτίᾳ.

In particular, Mary finds Simon Peter and the Beloved Disciple and reports to them about the tomb. Her report to the two disciples is, ἦραν τὸν κύριον ἐκ τοῦ μνημείου καὶ οὐκ οἴδαμεν ποῦ ἔθηκαν αὐτόν (v. 2b). In Mary's words there is a noticeable interchange between the unidentified "they" (implied in ἦραν) and the "we" (implied in οἴδαμεν). The reader knows what has happened but Mary does not. In fact, for Mary the idea of resurrection does not even come to mind. She is in the "darkness" of unfaith. Further, Mary's we/they language helps to reinforce the outsider/insider distinction initially created in ch. 14.[122] Her report leads to immediate action on the part of the two disciples.

Peter and the Beloved Disciple at the Tomb (20:3–10)

In v. 3 the two disciples depart *toward* the tomb (ἐξῆλθεν οὖν . . . καὶ ἤρχοντο εἰς τὸ μνημεῖον). In addition, v. 4 reports that as they make

120. Cf. e.g., 1:5; 3:2; 6:17; 9:4; 8:12; 11:10; 12:35, 46; 13:30; 19:39.

121. Mary appears in the passion and resurrection narratives of all three synoptics (Mark 15:40, 47; 16:1; Matt 27:56, 61; 28:1; Luke 24:10). She also appears earlier in Luke's Gospel (8:2), where it is reported that Jesus cast seven demons out of her. Mary Magdalene is not a prominent figure in the Fourth Gospel. However, in light of her appearance in the Synoptic resurrection traditions, it is unlikely that she was unknown to the original readership of John.

122. Moloney (*Glory Not Dishonor*, 159) comments, "For Mary Magdalene there are two groups involved: the "they" who have taken away (*ēran*) the corpse of the Lord and the "we" who do not know (*ouk oidamen*) where they have laid it."

their way to the tomb they are running together (ἔτρεχον δὲ οἱ δύο ὁμοῦ). The picture of the two disciples in vv. 3–4 contrasts with the description of Mary Magdalene who in v. 2 runs away from the tomb (*τρέχει* οὖν καὶ ἔρχεται πρὸς Σίμωνα κτλ.). The running to and fro pictured in these first few verses generates an element of excited frenzy within the scene.

As the two disciples are running, the Beloved Disciple passes Peter and arrives first.[123] That the Beloved Disciple arrives first, and Peter second, is thought by some to be evidence of the anti-Petrine polemic. Should this, however, be regarded as a "race," as some have presumed?

The reader knows of the Beloved Disciple's position as the disciple par excellence in the Fourth Gospel (cf. 13:23–26; 19:25–27).[124] Throughout the Gospel the reader has also seen Peter in a position of leadership over the disciples—though his example has not always been exemplary. In this instance, however, both disciples run away from the situation of darkness and unfaith evident in Mary's words and depart toward the tomb, the place of faith associated with God's intervention in the story. The Beloved Disciple remains the figure with whom the reader is to identify primarily. Nevertheless, Peter remains the "Rock," and this movement from unfaith and misunderstanding to faith and comprehension begins the consummation of Jesus's promise to Peter in 1:42. I will argue below that ch. 21, though widely regarded as a later addition, is ultimately the story's full consummation of Jesus's promise to Peter in ch. 1.

The Beloved Disciple is the first of Jesus's disciples to witness the linen cloths lying inside the empty tomb. The text says that the Beloved Disciple observes the tomb but cautiously stops short of entering (οὐ μέντοι εἰσῆλθεν, v. 5). By contrast Peter reaches the tomb second and enters (εἰσῆλθεν εἰς τὸ μνημεῖον, v. 6).

The description of what Peter sees in the tomb is much more detailed than what the Beloved Disciple witnesses. The latter simply sees κείμενα τὰ ὀθόνια, "the strips of linen cloth there" (v. 5). Peter, on the other hand, sees τὰ ὀθόνια κείμενα, "the strips of linen cloth there" (v.

123. Some see this as a race to the tomb. See Tilborg, *Imaginative Love in John*, 101–2; and Bauer, *Johannesevangelium erklärt*, 229.

124. Following this section is an excursus on the Beloved Disciple. The conclusions of that excursus provide background on the present discussion of Peter vis-à-vis the Beloved Disciple.

6b), τὸ σουδάριον ὃ ἦν ἐπὶ τῆς κεφαλῆς αὐτοῦ, "the towel which had been upon his head" (v. 7a), and notices that it "it was not with the strips of linen cloth but rolled up in a place by itself" (v. 7b). Despite this wealth of information, the narrator does not comment on Peter's response to what he has witnessed. Whereas Peter's response to seeing the empty tomb is not indicated by the narrator, the reader is explicitly told that the Beloved Disciple "saw and believed" (v. 8). It is hard to miss the contrasts created by this presentation of the two disciples. While both disciples move toward genuine Johannine faith, the narrator continues to elevate the Beloved Disciple.

In v. 9 the reader is again struck by the now-and-after tension that runs throughout the story. The reader is told that both disciples still did not understand the Scripture (οὐδέπω γὰρ ᾔδεισαν τὴν γραφὴν) that Jesus must rise from the dead. As in four previous instances (2:17, 22; 12:16; 13:7), the reader understands a truth in the narrated time of the story that the disciples will not fully understand until after Jesus's post-resurrection appearances. Neither disciple knows the Scriptures, and neither has seen the resurrected Jesus. However, both disciples are moving toward faith. Still, the narrator wants the reader to remember specifically that the Beloved Disciple "believes." This is not necessarily an indication that Peter did not believe, but once again we see the Johannine emphasis on the Beloved Disciple vis-à-vis Peter. The unit closes with the comment that the disciples went back to their homes (v. 10). This movement sets the stage for the future appearances of the risen Jesus to the Twelve.

Peter Thus Far

In John 20, Peter is cast as a disciple who moves from darkness toward light and from unfaith toward faith. In his previous two appearances, Peter had failed to understand Jesus's symbolic actions (the footwashing, 13:1–20), explicit teaching about his departure (13:24–38), nonresistance to his departure (18:10–11), or the importance of laying down one's life as implied by the love command (18:15–18, 25–27; cf. 13:34–35). Nevertheless, when he along with the Beloved Disciple hears the report of the empty tomb, he responds by moving toward the location of God's entrance into the story (20:3–10).

In this unit Peter regains some of the luster from previous scenes and is on his way toward becoming the "Rock" alluded to in 1:42. He shows a level of trust and spiritual comprehension, but he has not yet been fully restored in the eyes of the reader. We await the events of ch. 21 for Peter's full restoration.

I suggest here that, in light of the previously considered Thomas passages, Peter is a second (and more significant) example of an uncomprehending character in the Fourth Gospel. Even though he starts out in an extremely positive light in the eyes of the reader, his failures and frailties reveal a persistent inability to understand Jesus's mission and message. However, to argue for an anti-Petrine polemic without considering the similar characterization of other characters in the Gospel is to overlook the same aspects as the advocates of the community-conflict hypothesis. Before the discussion of Peter in the Fourth Gospel can be concluded, his relationship to the Beloved Disciple and his role in ch. 21 must be considered.

Excursus on the Beloved Disciple

Throughout the history of scholarship on the Fourth Gospel there has been no shortage of theories attempting to identify the Beloved Disciple. The traditional view that the Beloved Disciple was the son of Zebedee who, for whatever reason, chose to remain anonymous, is no longer generally accepted.[125] Others have identified Lazarus,[126] Thomas,[127] and even Matthias (from Acts 1:21–26)[128] as the Beloved Disciple. Most of these reconstructions, however, have been focused on the identity of the historical figure behind this mysterious character.[129] Here I am

125. A classic volume in support of this traditional view is Edwards, *The Disciple Who Wrote These Things*.

126. Filson, "Who Was the Beloved Disciple?" See more recently Stibbe, *John as Storytelle*, 77–82.

127. Schenke, "Function and Background of the Beloved Disciple"; and Charlesworth, *Beloved Disciple*. A more detailed description of these works can be found in n. 62 of chapter 1.

128. Titus, "Identity of the Beloved Disciple."

129. Brown (*Introduction to the Gospel of John*, 189–99) has addressed the historical and authorship issues at length. He writes, "If John of Zebedee was the author of the Gospel, he was almost surely also the BD [Beloved Disciple]. However, if he was the BD, he was not necessarily the author of the Gospel. And he might have been neither . . . No matter who the BD was personally, was the author (i.e., the writer) the BD? If not, who

concerned not as much with identifying the historical Beloved Disciple (assuming there was one)[130] as with determining the role he plays in the Gospel.

The Beloved Disciple is specifically mentioned six times in the Fourth Gospel (13:23, 25; 19:26; 20:2; 21:7, 20), and his presence may be implied in two other passages (1:35, 39; 18:15 [twice]), though this is the topic of considerable debate. The question that will be considered here is, what impact does his presence have on the scenes in which he appears and on the Gospel as a whole? In what follows I will examine elements of two episodes in which "another disciple" appears (1:35–42; 18:15–18) and three episodes in which the Beloved Disciple is explicitly identified (13:21–38; 19:25–27; 20:3–10). The final section of this chapter will consider the presentation of both Peter and the Beloved Disciple in ch. 21.

An Unnamed Disciple in John 1:35–42

This pericope was examined in greater detail in the above exegetical overview of the Gospel's first Peter passage. The events of vv. 35–42 occur on the third of four days recounted after the prologue.[131] On that day the reader learns that John has followers, and as he stands with two of those unnamed disciples (v. 35) he identifies Jesus as the "Lamb of God" for a second time (v. 36; cf. 1:29). This causes the two disciples to follow Jesus and inquire where he is staying. When Jesus beckons them to "come and see" (v. 38), the text indicates that both disciples willingly follow.

Little if any concrete information can be gleaned from the reader's experience with the unnamed disciple. In fact, the reader meets the disciple only indirectly as part of a twosome. The disciple never appears alone in this unit, is simply identified as ἄλλος μαθητής (as in 18:15), and does not speak independently of the other. Further, it seems that the narrator consciously avoids mention of the other disciple after nar-

was he?" (p. 191). See also idem, *Community of the Beloved Disciple*, 31–34.

130. Schnackenburg (*Gospel According to St. John*, 3:375–88) undertakes a detailed examination of scholarly proposals, internal evidence, and issues of authorship related to the Beloved Disciple in an excursus entitled "The Disciple Whom Jesus Loved."

131. A first day is implied in 1:19 where the reader hears the Baptist testify. Then the phrase τῇ ἐπαύριον, "the next day," appears in 1:29, 35, 43. Therefore, four days are delineated in vv. 19–51.

rating his initial appearance. Instead, the focus turns to Andrew (v. 40) and subsequently to Simon Peter (vv. 41–42).

For the purposes of the story, this first pericope establishes the existence of an unnamed disciple who, along with Andrew, was a follower of John the Baptist and decides to follow Jesus. More information is needed to discern the mysteries behind this character. Apart from further information, it is perhaps impossible to discern whether the other disciple is to be equated with the "disciple whom Jesus loved."

The Beloved Disciple in John 13:21–38

For all intents and purposes, John 13 contains the first appearance of the Beloved Disciple in the Fourth Gospel. In 20:2 the "other disciple" known from John 18 (and possibly ch. 1) is implicitly connected with the "disciple whom Jesus loved" (see the conflation, τὸν ἄλλον μαθητὴν ὃν ἐφίλει ὁ Ἰησοῦς).[132] It is not until the appendix that this connection is made explicit (cf. 21:20). These passages likely represent later redactional activity that intends to clarify previously unclear elements from earlier strata of the Gospel.

As with 1:35–38, this pericope has also been discussed above in some detail. It was argued above that Peter fails to understand both the prediction of Judas's betrayal and his request for further information about the betrayer. The narrated activity of John 13 begins not only Peter's movement from a previously positive presentation but also the narrator's consistently positive portrait of the Beloved Disciple. First, he is explicitly described as ὃν ἠγάπα ὁ Ἰησοῦς (v. 23b). This is an important designation because in the Gospel the phrase is used only of Mary, Martha, and Lazarus (ch. 11). No other member of the Twelve is referred to in this manner.

Second, the narrator's first description of this disciple is his position of honor at the table: ἀνακείμενος εἷς ἐκ τῶν μαθητῶν αὐτοῦ ἐν τῷ κόλπῳ τοῦ Ἰησοῦ (v. 23a).[133] This description is likely meant to recall the prologue's description of the Logos as μονογενὴς θεὸς ὁ ὢν εἰς τὸν κόλπον τοῦ πατρὸς (1:18). In v. 25 the narrator also refers to the Beloved Disciple as ἐπὶ τὸ στῆθος τοῦ Ἰησοῦ. Therefore

132. The phrase ἄλλος μαθητής is used by itself in 20:3, 4, 8.

133. This phrase is used in Pliny's *Epistles* (4.22.4) to refer to the place of honor at a feast.

the implied closeness between Jesus and the Beloved Disciple at the latter's first appearance in the story leaves a considerable impression upon the reader.

A third, less explicit element of the Beloved Disciple's initial portrait emerges as the narrator juxtaposes him with Peter. Peter's desire for knowledge (v. 24) and inability to obtain it without an intermediary stand out against the Beloved Disciple's proximity to Jesus and his ability to ask Jesus directly and receive an answer (vv. 25–27).

In this first appearance, the Beloved Disciple is presented in a positive manner through direct and indirect means of characterization. This pattern continues throughout the remainder of the Gospel. For the reader the importance of this first appearance is immense. Not only does this new character have a high status (v. 23a) but he is a character that hereafter is consistently presented in contrast to Peter.

The "Other" Disciple in John 18:15–18

In this unit, the narrator mentions ἄλλος μαθητής (v. 15a) who, along with Peter, follows Jesus to the high priest. In a parenthetical aside he is mentioned again (μαθητὴς ἐκεῖνος) and presented as one acquainted with the high priest (v. 15b). Unlike the disciple in 1:35–42, there is good reason to suppose that the narrator intends a connection between this disciple and the Beloved Disciple.

In this scene the other disciple is known to the high priest (γνωστὸς τῷ ἀρχιερεῖ, v. 15b). This element of the story is likely not intended to elevate the other disciple at Peter's expense. Instead, like other instances in the Gospel, it appears that the narrator is introducing this facet of the story in order to advance the developing plot. In this regard, Brown writes of the episode, "Certainly the [other] disciple plays no role of theological significance in the scene."[134]

Responding to suggestions that the other disciple is a narrative fiction, generated to explain away problems in the text, both Brown[135] and Dodd[136] suggest the historical plausibility of a relationship between the disciple and the high priest. Historical questions aside, this episode does

134. Brown, *Gospel According to John*, 2:841.

135. Ibid.

136. Dodd (*Historical Tradition in the Fourth Gospe*, 86) writes that the event "is either the product of a remarkable dramatic flair, or it rests on superior information."

little to advance the narrator's portrait of the Beloved Disciple or his ongoing contrast with Peter.

The Beloved Disciple in John 19:25–27

The Beloved Disciple appears again briefly during the crucifixion of Jesus. He is the only disciple present alongside a group of four women. This brief episode is one of the most telling components in the Johannine presentation of the Beloved Disciple. First, he is present at the crucifixion while all the others (including Peter) have abandoned him. He has understood that the willingness to lay down one's life is an implied element in Jesus's commandment to love (13:34–35). In moving toward the cross he runs the risk of laying down his own life. Unlike Peter who denies Jesus three times, the Beloved Disciple shows an unwillingness to renounce his association with Jesus.

More important than his appearance at the foot of the cross, however, is the responsibility given him by Jesus. In a scene that recalls a number of elements from earlier in the story, the Beloved Disciple is entrusted with caring for Jesus's mother. At the end of v. 26, Jesus cries out from the cross saying, γύναι, ἴδε ὁ υἱός σου. The reader learns that the Beloved Disciple takes Jesus's mother to be with him ἀπ᾽ ἐκείνης τῆς ὥρας (v. 27c). The phrase used for John's home is εἰς τὰ ἴδια (v. 27c), recalling the identical phrase in the prologue (1:11). All of this represents a reversal of previous circumstances in the Gospel. Jesus came εἰς τὰ ἴδια but οἱ ἴδιοι did not receive him. Jesus's ὥρα has now arrived and two of οἱ ἴδιοι—his mother and the Beloved Disciple—receive each other at the behest of Jesus. At that moment "a new family of Jesus has been created."[137]

The events recounted in this brief episode highlight the Beloved Disciple's exemplary role in the Fourth Gospel. He is both entrusted with the mother of Jesus and part of a new family of those who belong to Jesus (and by extension, to the Father).

The Beloved Disciple in John 20:3–10

Like 1:35–38 and 13:1–38, this unit has been discussed above in some detail. It was concluded above that these verses draw another series of contrasts between the Beloved Disciple and Peter.

137. Moloney, *Glory Not Dishonor*, 145.

First, during the run to the tomb, the Beloved Disciple overtakes Peter. Some regard this as a "race" reflecting a Johannine-Petrine conflict. While there is not enough internal evidence to arrive at this conclusion, there is clearly a contrast meant to elevate the Beloved Disciple over Peter. The reader should understand this scene as a reflection of the Beloved Disciple's zeal and greater love for Jesus as he moves away from the darkness (associated with Mary's report) and toward the light of Jesus's empty tomb. However, both disciples go to the tomb and thus toward the light. The report of this running to the tomb is not driven by an anti-Petrine polemic, but rather by a desire to elevate the figure of the Beloved Disciple.

Second, the Beloved Disciple stops short of the tomb while Peter arrives and goes directly in. Also, the report of what the Beloved Disciple sees is significantly less detailed than the report of what Peter sees (20:6–7). Thus it seems that "the delay in entering the tomb is in order to make [the Beloved Disciple's] response the climax of the episode."[138]

Third, though the text clearly indicates his lack of understanding (along with Peter's, 20:9) the narrator reports only that the Beloved Disciple believes. This does not suggest Peter's failure to believe but only the narrator's desire that the reader know explicitly that the Beloved Disciple responds properly to the empty tomb. On this intended contrast Lincoln comments,

> It is far more likely that the reader is meant to assume that the Beloved Disciple is the first to believe that Jesus has been raised and that he demonstrates immediate and exemplary faith in contrast to Peter. This is in line with his depiction as the ideal witness who has insight into the key moments of Jesus's passion.[139]

In that light, the Beloved Disciple appears as the prime example of one who comprehends and believes.

There is no doubt an intended connection between the report of the Beloved Disciple's belief and Jesus's words to Thomas in 20:29 (μακάριοι οἱ μὴ ἰδόντες καὶ πιστεύσαντες). Though the Beloved Disciple has seen the empty tomb, he has not seen the resurrected Jesus and in this way he is more like the later readers of the Gospel who will

138. Lincoln, *Gospel According to St. John*, 489.

139. Ibid., 491.

believe without seeing the resurrected Jesus. Again, Lincoln's comments are instructive: "His [i.e., the Beloved Disciple's] response here contrasts with that of Mary Magdalene earlier at the tomb and with that of Thomas later in his demand for visible proof of the bodily reality of the risen Lord. The Beloved Disciple believes on the basis of the empty tomb and without resurrection appearances."[140] Again, the Beloved Disciple emerges as an exemplar for genuine Johannine faith.

The Beloved Disciple Thus Far

In light of the foregoing discussion, it seems prudent to exclude from this summary the unnamed disciple in 1:35–42. The four passages that bear directly upon the present interpretation are 13:21–28; 18:15–18; 19:25–27; and 20:3–10.

In his first four appearances the Beloved Disciple is presented in a substantially positive way. Without question he is the hero figure with whom the Johannine reader is to identify primarily. He consistently "gets it right" in his superior displays of love and insight and in his proper responses to the living and the resurrected Jesus.

Of the Twelve, he stands alone in a number of respects. He alone is privileged to lie at Jesus's side (13:23). He alone is able to ask Jesus directly about the betrayer at dinner (13:25). He alone appears at the foot of the cross (19:25–27). He alone is said to believe in the resurrected Jesus (20:8–9). In each of these ways, the Beloved Disciple contrasts with Peter who has failed to understand Jesus's message and mission (13:6–11, 24, 36–38), resisted Jesus's return to the Father (18:10–11), and denied Jesus three times (18:17, 25–27). In this way, it is clear that the story is meant to evoke in the reader sympathy for the Beloved Disciple while using Peter as a foil. Within the story the Beloved Disciple functions as the disciple par excellence.

Having examined the presentations of Peter and the Beloved Disciple in the Fourth Gospel, it is safe to conclude that Peter, who starts out well in the eyes of the reader, takes a turn where he is depicted as an erring, unfaithful, uncomprehending character. Further, in those areas where Peter is shown to fail, the Beloved Disciple succeeds. This pattern of success and failure is used to create a contrast with which the reader will identify.

140. Ibid.

Before we can offer final thoughts on Peter and the Beloved Disciple, one passage remains to be discussed. Even though the vast majority of scholars believe John 21 is a later addition, much can be gleaned from an understanding of Peter and the Beloved Disciple in that chapter. The present study turns now to an examination of both the Beloved Disciple and Peter in John 21.

Peter and the Beloved Disciple in John 21

Most Johannine scholars believe John 21 is a later addition to the original form of the text.[141] However, this creates a problem for Peter's character (and for the narration of events as a whole) because apart from ch. 21, Peter never fully realizes the promise of Jesus in 1:42. There is in John 21 a concerted effort to restore Peter and, though he is not elevated above the Beloved Disciple, his portrait is improved substantially. In that unit he achieves status as the Johannine "rock" (cf. 1:42) for the early post-resurrection church.[142]

Despite Jesus's reinstatement of Peter in three affirmations meant to overturn his three denials (21:15–17), the Beloved Disciple remains the Johannine hero. He is the first to recognize the risen Jesus (21:7) and is seemingly promised longer life than Peter (21:22).

A great deal can be gleaned from the theory that (1) ch. 21 is not the original ending to the Gospel,[143] and (2) there is in ch. 21 a seemingly conscious attempt to present Peter in a more positive light. Together, these factors suggest that the earliest readers of the Fourth Gospel may have sought to improve Peter's presentation in the story, especially in light of his developing importance in the early church.

The aim of this section is to undertake an exegetical examination of John 21. The following exegesis divides the chapter as follows:

141. Scholars regularly refer to ch. 21 as the "appendix" or the "epilogue" to the Gospel. Notable challenges to this widely accepted position can be found in Smalley, "Sign in John XXI"; and Minear, "Original Functions of John 21."

142. The term "rock" is missing from the chapter, as is an explicit statement about the events of the chapter fulfilling Jesus's earlier statement. However, the closest thing to a fulfillment of Jesus's promise in 1:42 occurs in the reinstatement and special commissioning of 21:15–23.

143. A particularly helpful treatment of the literary and theological reasons behind this assertion can be found in Moloney, *Glory Not Dishonor*, 182–85.

1. Jesus appears in Galilee (21:1–14)
    a. The disciples go fishing (21:1–8)
    b. Breakfast by the shore (21:9–14)
2. Peter is restored (21:15–23)

Jesus Appears in Galilee (21:1–14)

In a peculiar break from the glorious appearance and ministerial commissioning in 20:20–23, the beginning of ch. 21 pictures the disciples as idle and borderline apathetic.[144] The decision to go fishing provides an opportunity for Jesus to appear and to bless the disciples with a miraculous catch of fish. The catch further provides the reader with a symbolic statement on the progress and leadership of the early church. On this Moloney comments,

> The symbolism [during the miraculous catch] is clear. Simon Peter leads, enthusiastically taking action in response to the Beloved Disciple's announcement that the Lord is present (v. 7: *ho kyrios estin*), and at the word of the risen Jesus. Large numbers are drawn into the net, but it is not damaged. The church is a boat under the inspiration of the Beloved Disciple and the leadership of Peter.[145]

In the scene that follows (vv. 15–23) this symbolic statement gives way to a clear delineation of roles for Peter and the Beloved Disciple.

The Disciples Go Fishing (21:1–8)

Using typical Johannine language, the narrator begins with μετὰ ταῦτα (v. 1) and provides details of Jesus's third post-resurrection appearance to the disciples.[146] This appearance occurs in the context of fishing.

144. After reading ch. 20, the reader expects to see the fruit of this apostolic commissioning. However, the abrupt break from 20:31 to 21:1–3 strikes the reader as being rather disjointed.

145. Moloney, *Glory Not Dishonor*, 186.

146. The reader is told in 21:14 that this is Jesus's third appearance, but it is his fourth appearance overall. He appears to Mary Magdalene (20:11–18), to the disciples minus Thomas (20:19–23), and to the disciples including Thomas (20:24–29). The phrase τοῖς μαθηταῖς in 21:14 is likely meant to exclude all but the original Twelve (thus effectively leaving out the first appearance to Mary Magdalene).

Peter, Thomas, and Nathanael (all of whom the reader has met previously), the sons of Zebedee (who are not mentioned in the Fourth Gospel to this point) and two unnamed disciples are together in Galilee.[147] Peter decides to go fishing and the others join him (v. 3). The reader learns in v. 3c that their fishing expedition is a failure. The disciples catch nothing, failing in their endeavor until Jesus comes to assist. After his arrival on the shore they pull in 153 fish (v. 11).[148] Could it be that there is a deeper theological implication behind this turn of events—that their success is wholly dependent upon the presence of Jesus?[149]

Using another typical Johannine literary convention, the narrator provides the temporal setting by informing the reader that Jesus appears πρωΐας δὲ ἤδη γενομένης (v. 4). Jesus stands on the shore and calls out to the disciples but they do not recognize him.[150] They have been unsuccessful in their fishing, but after a strange directive from Jesus (v. 6a), the disciples begin to haul in a massive catch (v. 6b).

Instantly the Beloved Disciple recognizes Jesus and tells Peter ὁ κύριός ἐστιν (v. 7a). Again the Beloved Disciple is elevated as he is the first to recognize Jesus and identify him as κύριος. At this statement, Peter plunges into the water and zealously swims for the shore (v. 8) while the others bring the boat back to the shore.[151] The narrator comments that before jumping into the water Peter girds himself with his outer garment (τὸν ἐπενδύτην διεζώσατο, v. 7c).[152] Apart from this occurrence, the verb διαζώννυμι appears in the NT only in John

147. Is one of these unnamed disciples the same disciple from 1:35–38? Or, is one of these the Beloved Disciple? The appendix is replete with difficult questions about the Beloved Disciple (who is not explicitly identified in this first section of ch. 21).

148. Much discussion surrounds the significance of the number 153. See Brown's detailed analysis (*Gospel According to John*, 2:1074–76).

149. Read in this way, the context recalls the earlier promises of ἄλλος παράκλητος.

150. On two previous occasions the disciples have recognized Jesus immediately. Here, however, they do not. This situation is somewhat similar to the Lukan presentation where Jesus walks on the Emmaus road with two disciples who do not recognize him (cf. Luke 24:13–35).

151. The phrase ὁ κύριός ἐστιν also occurs in the second half of v. 7. There it is preceded by ὅτι and is introducing direct discourse. The repetition of the exact phrase in direct discourse creates a greater vividness in the scene.

152. Among others, Brown (*Gospel According to John*, 2:1072) notes that there are a number of difficulties raised by the donning of more clothes prior to swimming—an act which would surely impede the swimming process.

13:4, 5. In light of the strong connection between Peter's earlier failures elsewhere in the Gospel and his faithfulness in the present pericope, the use of the verb can hardly be regarded as coincidental. In 13:4–5 Jesus "girded himself" in preparation for the footwashing, which Peter misunderstood. Peter's failure to understand that event led consequently to a failure to embrace the teaching of the living Jesus. Here, it is Peter that "girds himself," and he does so in an attempt to embrace the presence of the resurrected Jesus. The circumstances have been reversed.

Peter's action of jumping into the water without waiting for the boat to return to land is an initial indication of his restoration by the narrator. The previous picture of the Beloved Disciple passing Peter on the way to the tomb (20:3–4) suggested that the Beloved Disciple had a greater love for Jesus than did Peter. Here, while the greater insight still belongs to the Beloved Disciple ("It is the Lord," v. 7), the greater zeal for Jesus clearly belongs to Peter. In chapter 2 we established that the narration of actions and direct speech are the primary means of Johannine characterization. The reader is not told that Peter believes, but his actions are evidence of his belief in the resurrected Jesus. As Peter swims, the disciples redirect the boat and head for shore. All the while they are dragging the net full of fish (v. 8).

Breakfast by the Shore (21:9–14)

When the disciples arrive, they find that Jesus has prepared a breakfast of fish and bread (v. 9). He instructs the disciples to bring some of the fish they have just caught (v. 10). Notably, of all the disciples present, it is Peter who pulls the net ashore (v. 11). Again, Peter's actions are a signal to the reader of his faith. They are also to be regarded as a symbolic statement on Peter's role of leadership in the early church—a role that will be elucidated in greater detail in the following pericope.

Jesus beckons the disciples and, though they do not seem to recognize him (οὐδεὶς δὲ ἐτόλμα τῶν μαθητῶν ἐξετάσαι αὐτόν· σὺ τίς εἶ), they are aware that it is the Lord (εἰδότες ὅτι κύριός ἐστιν) (v. 12). As they draw near to eat, Jesus provides the bread and the fish for them. In a narrative aside, the reader is told that this is Jesus's third appearance to the disciples (v. 14).

Peter and the Beloved Disciple (21:15–23)

The most important element of ch. 21 for the present study occurs in this section. Here the reader witnesses the restoration of Peter in a threefold reversal meant to recall Peter's three denials in 18:15–17, 25–27.

Jesus asks Peter three separate times, "Do you love me?"[153] In each instance Peter affirms his love. While it is lost on Peter, the reader perceives the clear link between Peter's three previous denials and his three new opportunities to profess love for Jesus. The coward of ch. 18 is becoming the "rock" of the Johannine church. Whereas the end of the Gospel offered no sweeping image enhancement for Peter, ch. 21 moves toward Peter's full restoration in this conversation with the risen Jesus.

In addition to the three questions by Jesus and professions by Peter, there are three commands for Peter to take care of Jesus's sheep.[154] Peter is not only being restored, he is also being given a position of primacy as regards leadership in the early church. This is made more explicit in the following verses, as is the equally prominent role of the Beloved Disciple.

Jesus utters a puzzling double ἀμήν statement about Peter being bound and led away by others (v. 18). In a typically Johannine aside, the reader learns in v. 19 that this statement is meant by Jesus to indicate the manner of Peter's death.

After this brief exchange with Peter, Jesus utters two important words ἀκολούθει μοι (v. 19). The command leads to another exchange between Peter and Jesus. For now, the manner of Peter's death is ancillary. The mission Peter is given necessitates his following of Jesus.

During the conversation with Jesus, Peter turns and notices the Beloved Disciple, (identified explicitly here as ὃς καὶ ἀνέπεσεν ἐν τῷ δείπνῳ ἐπὶ τὸ στῆθος),[155] and asks Jesus "what about him" (v. 21). Jesus responds with a question of his own: ἐὰν αὐτὸν θέλω μένειν ἕως ἔρχομαι, τί πρὸς σέ; (v. 22b). Jesus then reiterates his earlier words in v. 19, only this time he is more emphatic: σύ μοι ἀκολούθει.[156]

153. Much has been made of the interchange between ἀγαπάω and φιλέω in this section but they should probably be understood as synonyms.

154. βόσκε τὰ ἀρνία μου (21:15); ποίμαινε τὰ πρόβατά μου (21:16); βόσκε τὰ πρόβατά μου (21:17).

155. This phrase recalls the second description of the Beloved Disciple in 13:25 (οὕτως ἐπὶ τὸ στῆθος τοῦ Ἰησοῦ).

156. The addition of σύ is emphatic and could be rendered, "As for you, *you* follow me."

Within the story, Jesus's reply is meant to distinguish clearly for the early readers the roles of Peter and the Beloved Disciple. Jesus has just given to Peter (the "rock") the role of shepherd (i.e., leader) of the church. Peter's question advances the argument of the appendix and provides the Johannine Jesus an opportunity to clarify the role of the Beloved Disciple. Each disciple has a prominent role. Peter is the leader while the Beloved Disciple is the enduring witness. In the end, the supreme role still belongs to the Beloved Disciple. Peter is restored but the Beloved Disciple remains the Johannine hero.[157]

Conclusion

When all of the evidence concerning Peter in the Fourth Gospel has been considered, a mixed portrait emerges. A consistent portrait of Peter is difficult to establish with certainty. His presentation in the Fourth Gospel begins with promise but never fully materializes according to the expectations developed by the reader. Nevertheless, Peter retains a fixed importance in the Gospel and is eventually restored in ch. 21.

The question with which this chapter began was whether the Fourth Gospel can be regarded as anti-Petrine. To that question I answer a qualified "Yes." This is not to suggest that the anti-Petrine hypothesis (as advocated by Titus, Snyder, Maynard, and Droge) is correct, but rather to affirm that in a number of instances Peter is presented in a less-than-flattering light. In the end, however, Peter's character (like Thomas's before him) recovers, and he acquires a privileged status in the Fourth Gospel. In the wake of his consistent portrayal as an uncomprehending disciple, Thomas offers the highest and most complete confession of Jesus in the Gospel (ὁ κύριός μου καὶ ὁ θεός μου, 20:28). Likewise, Peter fails to understand Jesus's words and action in chs. 13 and 18 but recovers in his movement of belief *toward* the tomb in 20:2–3, and is restored to a position of ecclesiastical importance in 21:15–17.

In John 13 and 18 the trait most consistently demonstrated by Peter is a failure to understand Jesus and to respond properly to him.

157. In the final chapter of the Fourth Gospel, Peter is redeemed in a way that the implied reader might expect. There is a narrative cohesion between the promise that he will be "rock" and the threefold charge for Peter to "feed my sheep." However, if we maintain that ch. 21 is a later addition (as most scholars do), then we must assume that the chapter's presentation of Peter is largely a later vision of how the community of faith understood Peter and his role.

In the appendix he is vindicated, though he remains a notch below the Beloved Disciple.

Therefore Peter—like Thomas before him—appears wrong (13:6–11), unbelieving (18:17, 25–27), and ignorant (13:24–25, 36–38; 18:10–11), but is cast in the latter portion of the Gospel in an increasingly positive light (20:2–3; 21:15–17). Also, like Thomas, Peter undergoes a transforming experience from confusion and denial to faith.

For the purposes of this study, the foregoing discussion has established that Peter is another example of an uncomprehending character in the Fourth Gospel. Because his character has more substantial development than Thomas's, Peter has more nuances and multiple rounded edges. However, it is clear that a portion of his characterization in the Fourth Gospel is as one who fails to understand the significance of Jesus's mission and message. In this way, Peter is another example of an uncomprehending character in the Fourth Gospel. But there are still other uncomprehending characters to examine.

This study has already looked at two uncomprehending disciples in detail: Thomas and Peter. I turn now in chapter 5 to a discussion of the remaining uncomprehending disciples in the Gospel of John.

5

Jesus and Other Disciples in the Fourth Gospel

In the previous two chapters we examined in some detail two of Jesus's disciples in the Fourth Gospel: Thomas (ch. 3) and Peter (ch. 4). Those chapters concluded that both Thomas and Peter are good examples of uncomprehending characters in the Fourth Gospel. Despite their eventual redemption in the narrative (Thomas in 20:28 and Peter in 21:15–17), both characters display incomprehension on more than one occasion in the story.

This chapter will focus on some of Jesus's other disciples in order to show that one dimension of their characterization is an inability to comprehend some element of Jesus's presentation in the Fourth Gospel. Specifically, this chapter will consider Andrew (chs. 1, 6), Philip (chs. 1, 6, 14), Judas (not Iscariot) (ch. 14), and the disciples as a representative group (chs. 4, 11).[1]

Admittedly, the role of Andrew, Philip, and Judas (not Iscariot) is rather insignificant in the overall story. However, they are considered here for the sake of thorough investigation. The incomprehension of the disciples as a representative group is clearer and potentially more illuminating for the purposes of the present study. Their role in the Fourth Gospel will also be considered in detail.

1. Several of the passages covered in this chapter have already been examined in detail in previous chapters. Nevertheless, it is important to examine each character on his/her own merits. Therefore, the discussion of this chapter will necessarily contain some repeated material.

Andrew, Philip, and Judas (Not Iscariot) in the Fourth Gospel

Since Andrew, Philip, and Judas (not Iscariot) appear together or in close proximity in several passages (Andrew and Philip in chs. 1, 6, 12; Philip and Judas in ch. 14), all three characters will be considered in this section.

The present discussion begins with an overview of Andrew's role in the Fourth Gospel, followed by an examination of the roles of Philip and Judas, respectively. The exegeses that follow will proceed through the text synchronically, examining first Andrew and Philip in 1:35–42, 43–51, and 6:1–15, then Philip and Judas in ch. 14. The exegetical sections will be followed by a brief discussion of the common elements in their respective presentations.

Andrew in the Fourth Gospel

Other than John the Baptist, who is introduced in the prologue (1:6) and appears in the story's first three scenes (1:19–28, 29–34, 35–42), Andrew is the first minor character to be identified by name in the Fourth Gospel. And though he is only partially correct in his confession to Peter ("We have found the Messiah," 1:41),[2] he is also the first character other than John to confess something of christological import in the Gospel.

Andrew appears three times in the story. He first appears as part of an unnamed twosome on the third day recounted in the narrative (1:35, 37, 39). In 1:40 the reader learns both his name and his status as a follower of John the Baptist (cf. 1:35). He appears a second time just before the bread miracle in 6:8–9, where he questions Jesus about the provision of food for the five thousand. In his third appearance he comes into view briefly assisting Philip in bringing some Greeks to meet Jesus at Passover (12:22).[3] In Andrew's first two appearances the

2. Many commentators regard Andrew's confession as satisfactory. However, not only does Andrew misrepresent the situation by claiming to have "found" Jesus (which the reader knows is untrue), but also he defines Jesus according to Jewish messianic expectations that are absent from the prologue's presentation of Jesus. These elements will be discussed in greater detail below.

3. It is noteworthy that "the Greeks" approach Philip (Φίλιππος) and Andrew (Ἀνδρέας), the only two disciples in the Fourth Gospel whose names are transmitted in Greek form. "Because they are Greek they approach a disciple with a Greek name,

reader hears him speak and witnesses his interaction with others. These two scenes contribute to his overall characterization by the narrator. In ch. 12 Andrew's name is mentioned but there is no recorded speech or focus upon his activity. Therefore, the following study of Andrew will examine his first two appearances in the text while omitting his third and final appearance in ch. 12.

A study of all three units reveals one consistent element of Andrew's presentation in the Fourth Gospel: in each of his appearances he brings someone else to Jesus. The first time he appears he finds his brother Simon and takes him to meet Jesus. The second time he brings a boy with fish and loaves to Jesus during the crisis over feeding the multitude. In his third and final appearance he guides the Greeks to meet Jesus. In these scenes, Andrew is an example of a consistent witness.[4] However, it will be argued below that he never fully grasps the realities set forth in the prologue and thus illustrates the trait of incomprehension. In other words, while Andrew is never the subject of significant character development, it is hoped that an examination of the first two Andrew passages will shed further light on the Gospel's use of uncomprehending characters as foils for Jesus.

Philip in the Fourth Gospel

Philip appears four times in the Fourth Gospel; though he is relatively insignificant in the overall scheme of the story, his presentation is similar to that of Andrew inasmuch as it reveals elements of both spiritual insight and incomprehension. In addition to being one of the first disciples to follow Jesus (1:43–46), Philip appears along with Andrew at Jesus's multiplication of fish and loaves (6:1–15) and in assisting the Greeks in finding Jesus at the feast (12:20–22). In his final appearance

---

Philip, who came from Bethsaida, a town close to the Gentile Decapolis . . . Their Gentile origins are highlighted by Philip's approaching another disciple with a Greek name, Andrew, who comes from the same town as Philip (cf. 1:44; 6:7–8). Together they speak to Jesus" (Moloney, *Gospel of John*, 352).

4. The observation that Andrew is consistently portrayed as bringing someone else to Jesus gives rise to the temptation to label him as a "representative figure" (see the discussion of representative characters in chapter 2). From this perspective one might label Andrew as an example of the consistent witness to Jesus. Therefore, it is interesting that in his detailed study Collins (*These Things Have Been Written*) fails to consider Andrew altogether. He creates space for Philip (pp. 23–25) and Nathanael (pp. 14–16) but Andrew does not make the list.

he is one of three disciples to question Jesus during an early portion of the Farewell Discourse (14:8–10).

In Philip's first, second, and fourth appearances in the story (1:43–51, 6:1–9, and 14:8–10), he contributes to the developing plot in a way that reveals more fully the traits of spiritual insight and naïve misunderstanding. In his third appearance in the narrative (12:20) Philip's presence holds little narrative significance. Like Andrew, he does not speak and his character is not developed in the scene; instead he is little more than an adornment of the narrative, primarily serving to advance the action of the pericope. Therefore in what follows, the discussion will focus on Philip's presentation in 1:43–51, 6:1–9, and 14:8–10.

Judas (not Iscariot) in the Fourth Gospel

Judas (not Iscariot) makes one brief appearance in the story (14:22–24). The reader hears Judas speak in that passage and his few words reveal the static trait of incomprehension.[5] He is one of three disciples to question Jesus in ch. 14 (Thomas and Philip are the others), and his question is part of a literary pattern where an unqualified misunderstanding provides the Johannine Jesus an opportunity to clarify teaching on his return to the Father. Though John 14 was discussed at length in chapter 3, some of that discussion will be reintroduced below in order to validate the consistent presentation of the disciples as uncomprehending across ch. 14.

The focus turns now to each pericope listed above and the resulting presentation of the disciple(s) in view within each unit. As with the exegetical discussions in previous chapters of this study, the reader's awareness of the information provided in the prologue is an essential element of the reading process.

Jesus, Andrew, and Philip in John 1:35–42; 43–51

Andrew appears for the first time in the Fourth Gospel during the early days of Jesus's ministry. As with the previous two days (1:19–28; 29–34) the events of this pericope occur in the physical setting of Bethany be-

5. In chapter 2 I rejected the concrete distinction between "round" and "flat" characters. However, Judas (not Iscariot) is probably the closest thing in the Fourth Gospel to a completely flat character as envisioned by Forster.

yond the Jordan (cf. 1:28).[6] The temporal setting of the pericope is the third day recounted in the story (indicated by the use of τῇ ἐπαύριον in 1:35). The situational setting of this pericope is tied to information revealed in the prologue (1:1–18), and to the events of the previous day (1:29–34).

First, the reader encounters the events and characters in 1:35–42 from the perspective of the prologue's presentation of the λόγος. The implied reader knows of Jesus's heavenly origins (1:1–2) and is also aware that the λόγος (viz., Jesus of Nazareth) has taken on human flesh (1:14, 17). When the story is read from the perspective of that privileged information, the reader senses an ever-increasing tension as the characters struggle to understand what has already been made plain to the reader. Further, this tension leads to instances of dramatized irony and misunderstanding as Andrew (and Philip in the following section) can only partially grasp Jesus's identity.

Second, the events of this pericope are tied to the previous day when John referred to Jesus as "the Lamb of God who takes away the sin of the world" (1:29) and the "Son of God" (1:34). For the two unnamed disciples these events follow those of the previous day and inform the earlier confessions of their rabbi, John the Baptist.

As before, John again calls Jesus the "Lamb of God" (v. 36); this time, however, the reader learns that two disciples are present. Up to now the reader was not aware that John had followers. Here they appear for the first time, and when they hear John's proclamation they move away from John and toward Jesus (v. 37).

An interesting progression takes place as John points his disciples to Jesus. The text indicates that John is in a static position (εἱστήκει, v. 35) and that Jesus is in motion (περιπατοῦντι, v. 36). Presumably, the two disciples are also in a static position as they listen to John. But upon hearing John's proclamation that Jesus is the "Lamb of God," both disciples abandon their static position to follow him (ἠκολούθησαν τῷ Ἰησοῦ, v. 37). The reader understands that their movement from a static position to one of "following" is a positive, early indication of discipleship.[7]

6. There is no indication of a change in physical setting until 1:43, where it is reported that Jesus intends to travel to Galilee. In 2:1 the text indicates explicitly that Jesus is in Cana in Galilee.

7. The language of "following" is explicitly tied to the concept of discipleship in the NT. "The distinctive statistical evidence shows that the special use of ἀκολουθεῖν is

The narrator does not immediately tell the reader who the disciples are, only that they question Jesus (ποῦ μένεις; v. 38d) and follow him to where he is staying (v. 39b).[8] In v. 40 the reader finally meets Andrew by name, as well as his brother Simon Peter (᾿Ανδρέας ὁ ἀδελφὸς Σίμωνος Πέτρου). Though the significance of the scene rests largely with Peter (who goes on to play a much greater role in the events of the Gospel), there are three important elements of Andrew's presentation in this pericope.

First, Andrew follows Jesus without hesitation after hearing the testimony of John, and his immediate response after following Jesus is to find his brother Simon (v. 41a). As stated above, his first inclination is to bring another person to meet Jesus, but this should not be taken as a sign that Andrew fully comprehends who Jesus is.

Second, in his report to Peter, Andrew indicates that he and the other disciple have found Jesus (εὑρήκαμεν τὸν Μεσσίαν, v. 41b), but the reader knows this is not true.[9] This false claim also appears in Philip's words to Nathanael (ὃν ἔγραψεν . . . εὑρήκαμεν, v. 45), which is in the same context as the narrator's comment that Jesus found Philip (εὑρίσκει Φίλιππον, v. 43) and not vice versa. As far as Andrew's statement is concerned, the reader knows that it was John who pointed Jesus out to the two disciples and that he was responsible for "finding" Jesus.

---

strictly limited to discipleship of Christ; apart from a single reference in Revelation it is found exclusively in the four Gospels. To some extent it connotes an external following, as when the multitudes accompany Jesus in Mk. 3:7 and par., Mt. 8:10 and par., or the disciples in a narrower sense in Mt. 8:19 . . . This implies, however, that ἀκολουθεῖν signifies self-commitment in a sense which breaks all other ties. The disciple does what the pupil of the rabbi does, externally in the same forms as the latter, but internally in attachment to Jesus. Hence the word still has the sense of discipleship, but in relation to Jesus it acquires a new content and impress" (*TDNT*, 1:213–14).

8. Though it is not evident at this stage of the narrative, the verb μένω will become an increasingly important term throughout the Fourth Gospel. Since a teacher/rabbi would have a place of instruction in which his followers would gather, the disciples' question makes sense at the level of the events recounted in the pericope. However, behind μένω there is a deeper significance. Barrett (*Gospel According to St. John*, 181) comments, "Nothing is more important than to know where Jesus abides and may be found."

9. Notably, Moloney (*Gospel of John*, 60) regards this claim and the identical one in 1:45 as willful lies by Andrew and Philip. He writes, "The claim on the part of the first disciples to have found Jesus and to have come to a decision about his person and role is a blatant untruth. This is seldom noticed by commentators."

This means that Andrew cannot take credit for initiating his contact with Jesus. On this point Moloney comments,

> The theological point that is made by this untruth is that *true discipleship flows from the initiative of Jesus*. This is the case across both the synoptic and Johannine traditions. For the Johannine Gospel true discipleship involves a correct understanding of who Jesus is. The first disciples fail on both accounts.[10]

A third important element of Andrew's presentation is found in the latter half of his report to Peter. His statement εὑρήκαμεν τὸν Μεσσίαν reveals that he has defined Jesus according to distinctly Jewish expectations. The term Μεσσίας does not appear in the prologue (though χριστός does, cf. 1:17) or in the terminology used by the Baptist in describing Jesus (cf. 1:29, 34, 36). The difference between Μεσσίας and Χριστός also helps to reveal Andrew's initial misunderstanding of Jesus's identity.

The Hebrew term משח and the Greek term χρίω[11] are both translated "to anoint." The participial forms משיח (משיחא in Aramaic) and χριστός became technical terms for "the Messiah" ("the Anointed One") within the different expressions of Judaism and Christianity in the first century CE.[12] The transliterated form Μεσσίας is used only twice in the NT, both in the Fourth Gospel (here and at 4:25). For the implied reader of John's Gospel it is significant that the term appears in contexts dealing with Jewish and Samaritan messianic expectations. This is an indication to the reader that by Μεσσίας, Andrew understands something different from the prologue's use of Χριστός. Against the backdrop of Jesus's description in the prologue, the reader senses that this appellation as applied to Jesus by Andrew is unsatisfactory. Hence, in this first christological confession there is an initial indication that Andrew has not fully understood Jesus.

In this appearance Andrew displays early signs of incomprehension. He appears at first to be characterized by spiritual sensitivity. His willingness to follow indicates a willingness to believe, the central theological

10. Ibid.; emphasis added.

11. BDAG, s.v. χρίω.

12. Of the sixty-nine occurrences of משח in the MT, sixty-one are translated by χρίω in the LXX. For more on the historical, literary, and theological significance of these terms, cf. *TDNT*, 9:93–580.

emphasis of the Fourth Gospel. However, because he has not completely grasped Jesus's identity his belief is defective from the outset.

Since the reader is deeply impacted by the first appearance of any character (however insignificant), Andrew's introduction leaves an impression upon the reader. His partial perception stands out sharply for the reader against the detailed exposition of the prologue. While Andrew's subsequent presentation in the story reveals him to be little more than an agent driving the action of the story, the reader initially recognizes Andrew as a sympathetic character possessing sincerity but an incomplete understanding of Jesus.

In 1:43–51 the reader witnesses a series of events similar to those of the previous day. The reader meets Philip for the first time in 1:43 on the fourth day recounted after the prologue. He is the fourth follower of Jesus to be introduced in the narrative and the third to be named.[13] In some ways this pericope reveals as much about other characters as it does about Philip. Here the reader meets Nathanael for the first time (v. 45a), learns that Jesus is from Nazareth (v. 45b), and learns that Andrew and Peter are from Bethsaida (v. 44). Stibbe comments that in addition to this new information the reader also sees a new facet of Jesus's character in his special γνῶσις about individuals (see especially vv. 47–51).[14]

After the events of 1:35–42 Jesus sets out from Bethany for Galilee. On his way he finds Philip and issues a directive: ἀκολούθει μοι (v. 43b).[15] In the following verse, which is clearly a narrative aside, the reader also learns that Philip is from Bethsaida, the same hometown of Andrew and Peter.[16]

There is no conversation between Jesus and Philip, nor is there a report about Philip following Jesus (though this is assumed). Instead, like Andrew before him, Philip goes directly to another person in order to bring him to Jesus. That person is Nathanael, who appears for the first

13. To this point in the story the reader has met an unnamed disciple (as part of a twosome in 1:35, 37, 39), Andrew (1:40, 42), and Simon Peter (1:41–42). The disciple Philip is also known in the Synoptics and Acts. See Matt 10:3; 14:3; Mark 3:18; Luke 6:14; and Acts 1:13; 8:4–13, 26–40.

14. Stibbe, *John*, 39.

15. It is noteworthy that Jesus commands Peter to follow in 21:19 using this exact phrase.

16. Barrett (*Gospel According to St. John*, 183) writes, "Since [Philip] was a native of Bethsaida it may be inferred that he was in Bethany as an adherent of the Baptist."

time in the story in this pericope. When Philip finds him he confesses, ὃν ἔγραψεν Μωϋσῆς ἐν τῷ νόμῳ καὶ οἱ προφῆται εὑρήκαμεν, Ἰησοῦν υἱὸν τοῦ Ἰωσὴφ τὸν ἀπὸ Ναζαρέτ (v. 45). As with Andrew, Philip's words do not match the reader's experience. In v. 43 the narrator comments that Jesus found Philip on his way to Galilee, but here Philip tells Nathanael that he has found Jesus. As before, this false statement highlights the truth that Johannine discipleship begins at Jesus's initiative—which further highlights Philip's incomprehension.

Apart from the matter of who found whom, Philip's confession of Jesus's identity would still be incomplete. Philip names Jesus's father (Joseph), hometown (Nazareth), and like Andrew before him identifies Jesus according to distinctly Jewish messianic expectations.[17] Each of these elements reveals a failure to grasp what has been revealed to the reader in the prologue.

First, the reader recognizes Philip's identification of Jesus as "the son of Joseph" and "from Nazareth" as falling short of the point of view provided by the prologue. These things may be true where Jesus's historical origins are concerned, but it is more important from the reader's perspective to recognize that Jesus is "the Son of God" (1:34) and that he is from above (1:1–2).[18]

Second, the reader also knows that Jesus is more than a Jewish messianic figure prophesied by the Hebrew Scriptures. He is the unique revealer of the Father (1:18) who possesses the qualities of the Father (1:1c) and brings grace and truth (1:17). Moses may have foretold Jesus's coming, but the reader knows that Jesus has superseded Moses in every way.[19] As with Andrew's messianic confession, the reader senses

17. "Andrew has spoken of him as Messiah. Philip sees him as the one predicted in the Scriptures—both by Moses in the law and by the prophets. The evangelist builds on the early Christian view that the Jewish Scriptures point to Jesus . . . Later the narrative will adduce particular scriptural texts that Jesus fulfils, but here, more generally, passages about the prophet like Moses from the law and Messianic passages from the prophets may well be in view" (Lincoln, *Gospel According to St. John*, 119–20).

18. "There is a profound irony here. The earliest Church recognized Jesus as being 'of Nazareth,' but the Johannine story insists that the believer look beyond his historical origins. In this Nathanael poses a good question. However, the supreme good is the one known to the Christian tradition as 'Jesus of Nazareth.' Yet Philip's mistake, which attempts to understand Jesus in terms of his physical and geographical origins, persists" (Moloney, *Gospel of John*, 55).

19. For an insightful treatment of the role of Moses in the Gospel of John, see Harstine, *Moses as a Character in the Fourth Gospel*, 40–75.

the partial truth of Philip's declaration but realizes that it falls short of encapsulating Jesus's identity as revealed by both the prologue and John the Baptist.

Philip does not figure in the rest of the scene as the focus shifts to an exchange between Jesus and Nathanael. However, in this pericope the reader sees a situation almost identical to that of Andrew in the previous pericope.[20] Philip follows Jesus, at which point he immediately goes to find another and bring him to Jesus while also claiming to have "found" Jesus on his own. Also like Andrew, Philip reveals a Jewish messianic expectation accompanied by a certain level of spiritual insight through his confession. In the end, however, his confession reveals an ultimate failure to grasp the entire truth of Jesus's identity.

Though his words to Nathanael are based upon Jewish theological categories that do not appear explicitly in the prologue, the reader perceives that his confession is at least partially true. Like Andrew, Philip begins his journey in the Fourth Gospel as a sincere character with flawed spiritual perception.

Jesus, Andrew, and Philip in John 6:1–15

The complexities associated with interpreting John 6 have already been discussed in chapter 4. John 6 introduces a number of elements that help to develop significantly the Fourth Gospel's complex Christology. First, the multiplication of fish and loaves (6:10–13) occurs in the narrative around the time of the Jewish Passover (see the narrative aside in 6:4). The Evangelist thus makes a connection between the signs

20. Stibbe (*John*, 39) examines the major elements of 1:35–42 and 1:43–51 side by side. There he notes the following five parallels:

1:35–42	1:43–51
Andrew and Peter from Bethsaida	Philip from Bethsaida
Two disciples find and follow Jesus (one of them is Andrew)	Jesus finds Philip and invites him to follow him
Jesus says, "Come and see" to the two disciples	Jesus says, "Come and see to Nathanael"
Andrew says to Peter, "We have found the Messiah"	Philip says to Nathanael, "We have found the one Moses wrote about"
Jesus calls Simon "Peter," the Rock	Jesus describes Nathanael as "a true Israelite"

and wonders performed by YHWH during the time of Israel's Exodus experience and the signs performed by Jesus (especially the provision of bread).[21] Second, the bread sign is followed by a lengthy theological discourse that pictures Jesus referring to himself as "the bread of life" and "the bread that has come down from heaven" (cf. 6:35, 48, 51). These titles not only allude to YHWH's provision of manna (i.e., "bread from heaven") during Israel's wilderness experience (cf., e.g., 6:31–34) but also provide further insight into the Johannine notion that Jesus supersedes Moses (cf. 1:17). Consequently, the implied reader is aware of the intertextual echoes of Torah that pervade the narrator's description of events in ch. 6.

Andrew and Philip appear early in the chapter, just prior to the bread miracle. This section will examine both the narrator's introduction to the scene (vv. 1–4) and the problem leading to the miracle (vv. 5–9), and will proceed as follows:

1. Temporal, spatial, situational settings (6:1–4)
2. The problem of feeding the crowd (6:5–9)

Temporal, Spatial, Situational Settings (6:1–4)

In characteristic Johannine fashion, 6:1 begins the pericope with a temporal statement (μετὰ ταῦτα) and a statement of the physical setting for the events that are about to unfold (πέραν τῆς θαλάσσης τῆς Γαλιλαίας). These two statements move the reader from the Sabbath events at Bethesda (ch. 5) to a location on the other side of the Sea of Galilee at a time just before the Passover.

In v. 2 the reader learns that a crowd is following Jesus because they have witnessed τὰ σημεῖα ἃ ἐποίει ἐπὶ τῶν ἀσθενούντων.[22] Neyrey comments that Jesus's signs "trigger the crowds to follow Jesus," even though the reader is aware that these signs "prove to be ambiguous or inadequate reasons for discipleship (2:23–25; 3:2; 5:1–15)."[23] This point becomes even more apparent after Jesus's Bread of Life discourse as he

21. On the OT symbolism behind John 6, see the pertinent discussion in Moloney, *Signs and Shadows*, 32–38.

22. In 2:23 the narrator reports that many at the Passover feast believe in Jesus θεωροῦντες αὐτοῦ τὰ σημεῖα ἃ ἐποίει. Though the story presents seven distinct signs, the reader understands that there are other signs performed by Jesus that are not reported by the narrator

23. Neyrey, *Gospel of John*, 117.

is met with the response of the incredulous Jewish leaders (v. 52) and scandalized disciples (vv. 60–66).

The narrator places Jesus with the disciples on the mountainside (v. 3), which creates narrative space between Jesus and the crowd while at the same time allowing Jesus to see the crowd approaching. Seeing the multitude provides Jesus the opportunity to question Philip and eventually perform another sign (which, based upon the description in v. 2, the crowd is likely seeking).

In another parenthetical comment, the narrator informs the reader that the events of John 6 occur near the Passover. Regarding this comment, Lincoln writes, "Like the mention of the mountain, the reference here draws attention to scriptural and Mosaic themes. The Passover is a particularly appropriate setting for the exposition of the exodus events that will follow in Jesus' discourse and for the Eucharistic motifs that emerge at its end."[24]

The Problem of Feeding the Crowd (6:5–9)

The narrative space created by Jesus's location on the mountain not only enables Jesus to see the distant crowd but also provides him the necessary narrative time to pose a question to Philip. The question Jesus asks Philip in v. 5 is πόθεν ἀγοράσωμεν ἄρτους ἵνα φάγωσιν οὗτοι; "Where can we buy bread so that these people may eat?" Inasmuch as this chapter contains explicit links to the Moses traditions, it seems that this question is likely meant to recall Moses's question in Numbers 11:13 (LXX): πόθεν μοι κρέα δοῦναι παντὶ τῷ λαῷ τούτῳ; "Where can I get meat to give to all these people?"

The parallels between these two passages are clear. In John 6:6 and Num 11:13 Jesus and Moses are both facing situations where they are responsible for providing food for a multitude and are in turn trusting in God for the provision; the major difference is that while the context of Num 11 indicates that Moses is sincerely posing the question with a sense of desperation, Jesus is here asking the question for the rhetorical purpose of testing Philip.

In a number of places in the Fourth Gospel, certain characters appear simply, in the words of Barrett, to "advance the argument" of the

24. Lincoln, *Gospel According to St. John*, 211.

text.[25] This same literary technique is at work in the present unit under consideration. As Jesus is about to perform another *semeion*, Philip appears in the narrative and provides Jesus with an opportunity to act miraculously on behalf of the crowd. This point is made even more explicit by the narrator's comment that Jesus questions Philip in order to "test him" and that Jesus "already knew what he was going to do" (v. 6). Within the unfolding story, this is an important indicator that Philip's misunderstanding remains. The reader knows what Jesus is capable of doing, but Philip does not. Consequently, the better-informed reader watches Philip stumble along without the benefit of the information given in the prologue.

In a previous episode with the Samaritan woman, the disciples urged Jesus to eat something. In response Jesus proclaimed, "I have food to eat that you know nothing about" (4:32), and "my food is to do the will of the one who sent me" (4:34). Following this pronouncement the disciples debated the meaning of Jesus's words (4:33) because they were confusing material and spiritual realities. Likewise in 6:7, Philip focuses upon the material provisions necessary for the people to eat (i.e., literal bread and financial resources) rather than the spiritual provisions available in Jesus. His response ("two hundred denarii worth of bread would not be enough for each one to receive a little") shows that he has made no improvement in his understanding from the dialogue in ch. 4.[26] He is simply unaware of who Jesus is and what Jesus can do. Noting Philip's incomprehension, Collins writes that here "Philip represents in fact the misunderstanding of the disciples."[27]

At this point Andrew appears (v. 8) escorting a boy with five loaves and two fish (v. 9a). In contrast to Philip, Andrew's entrance with the boy seems to show greater faith in addition to advancing the action of the story. After he introduces the boy and his provisions he asks Jesus, "but what are these for so many?" (v. 9b). What initially appeared to be a greater faith than that expressed by Philip is instead another misunderstanding. Andrew's question is an indication that he too is un-

25. Though Barrett (*Gospel According to St. John*, 459) uses this phrase to refer to Philip's appearance in ch. 14, this is clearly the case in the present text.

26. "The reader looks forward to a solution to the problem that transcends the limitations of money and quantities of bread, something that Jesus will do (v. 6)" (Moloney, *Signs and Shadows*, 34).

27. Collins, *These Things Have Been Written*, 24.

aware of the resources at Jesus's disposal. In the verses that follow (vv. 10–12) Jesus goes on to provide enough food for the entire multitude; afterward there are twelve baskets full of broken pieces left over (v. 13). Jesus exceeds the expectations of Philip and Andrew, and he does so in a way that they could not anticipate because of their overemphasis on materiality and because of their inability to understand who Jesus is and what he can do.

Though their appearance in this pericope is brief and neither character is developed substantially, each character clearly displays the trait of incomprehension in a way that contrasts with Jesus's divinely assisted actions. Stibbe affirms this when he writes:

> Philip and Andrew are paired together in vv. 5–9, as they are in 12.20–22. Here they are foils for Jesus' multiplication miracle. Philip manifests inadequate faith and understanding in his complaint in v. 7. Andrew reveals more faith in pointing to a small boy with food. However, his question in v. 9, "how far will that go among so many?" shows that he is far from a true appreciation of Jesus' divine resources.[28]

To this point, the reader has seen both Andrew and Philip twice. In each instance both disciples have displayed some form of spiritual incomprehension. Though they appear together once more (12:20–22), that appearance does not serve to deepen their respective portraits. The discussion turns now to the final appearance of Philip in the Gospel and the only appearance of Judas (not Iscariot).

Jesus, Philip, and Judas (Not Iscariot) in John 14:8–10, 22–31

Since a full-scale exegesis of John 14 appears in chapter 3 of this study, it should suffice here to summarize the conclusions offered above. The previous discussion established the presence of a pattern in ch. 14. As Jesus begins to speak of his departure to the Father, his explanation leads to a series of misunderstandings. In the process, Jesus addresses Thomas (vv. 5–7), Philip (vv. 8–10), the disciples minus Judas Iscariot (vv. 11–21), and Judas (not Iscariot) (vv. 22–24). Each disciple asks an uncomprehending question or makes an uncomprehending statement

28. Stibbe, *John*, 83.

that provides Jesus an opportunity to speak more clearly about his return to the Father and the coming of the παράκλητος.

In 14:8 Philip's request (δεῖξον ἡμῖν τὸν πατέρα καὶ ἀρκεῖ ἡμῖν) implies a separation between the Son and Father. This shows a failure to grasp the mutuality of the Father and Son of which the reader is well aware (cf. 1:1–2). Philip's failure to understand this basic element of Jesus's identity leads Jesus to question the nature and content of Philip's belief (v. 10).

The reader meets Judas (not Iscariot) in v. 22.[29] He appears only here in the Fourth Gospel and his only instance of recorded speech continues the pattern of misunderstanding. After the misunderstandings of Thomas and Philip have been addressed, Jesus turns briefly to the entire group before Judas interjects with his question.

When Judas speaks he asks why Jesus intends to reveal himself to the disciples but not to the rest of the world (v. 22). Jesus responds that his commandments are for anyone who loves him and not just the disciples. On this misunderstanding, Moloney notes, "As with earlier questions, Judas asks for information already obvious to the reader."[30] Schnackenburg adds that Judas's question "makes the distance between the disciples and the 'world' quite evident" and "implies a misinterpretation on the part of the disciple."[31] While Judas's misunderstanding is less explicit than the misunderstandings expressed by Thomas and Philip, its presence in the wider literary pattern across John 14 is significant.

In the present chapter both Philip and Judas Iscariot speak to Jesus in an uncomprehending way. Neither Philip nor Judas amounts to more than a minor player facilitating the story's advancement. However, each contributes to the narrator's desired literary effect. The reader understands that the disciples are cast as those who do not fully understand Jesus or appreciate the significance of his words. This failure allows Jesus to speak to the literary audience, providing explanations with authority and clarity.

29. Judas (not Iscariot) also appears in the list of disciples provided in Luke 6:16 and Acts 1:13.

30. Moloney, *Glory Not Dishonor*, 45.

31. Schnackenburg, *Gospel According to St. John*, 3:80.

Andrew, Philip, and Judas as Uncomprehending Characters

It is evident from this examination of the pertinent passages that Andrew, Philip, and Judas (not Iscariot) display the trait of incomprehension in a manner similar to both Thomas and Peter. Though all three disciples are minor characters, each is painted with a hint of incomplete spiritual perception. Their incomprehension is a literary tool used by the narrator to present the Johannine Jesus with opportunities to speak and/or act. In each instance, Jesus's words or deeds confirm a truth already known to the reader while revealing the full extent of the disciple's misunderstanding. In these texts, Andrew, Philip, and Judas are foils for Jesus's words and deeds and should be understood as uncomprehending characters along with Thomas and Peter.

Jesus and the Disciples as a Group in the Fourth Gospel

It has already been argued that a number of individual disciples have an established record of failing to understand properly some element of Jesus's presentation in the Fourth Gospel. Thus far, Thomas, Peter, Andrew, Philip, and Judas (not Iscariot) have appeared in different instances giving evidence of a failure to comprehend Jesus's identity (1:41, 45), intent (13:6–11), mission (11:16; 20:25), and return to the Father (14:5–7, 8–10, 22–24; 18:10). Therefore, it can now be suggested that incomprehension is part and parcel of the Fourth Gospel's presentation of Jesus's disciples. It should come as no surprise then that there are a few instances where the disciples as a group are pictured similarly.

The final section of this chapter will focus on the disciples as a group and their failure to understand Jesus in two passages. The first misunderstanding arises when the disciples cannot comprehend Jesus's words about food in the scene following his discussion with the Samaritan woman (4:27–38). The second misunderstanding is found in the disciples' failure to grasp the simple metaphor that Jesus uses when speaking of Lazarus's death (rather than literal sleep) (11:11–15).

Jesus and the Disciples in John 4:27–38

Throughout the history of exegesis of John 4, a great deal of emphasis has been placed on the misunderstandings that occur across the chapter. However, much of the focus has been on the conversation that occurs between Jesus and the Samaritan woman.[32] But in the events that follow Jesus's interaction with the woman, there is an exchange between Jesus and the disciples that results in their confusion over his words about fulfilling the will of the Father.

In the early part of the conversation between Jesus and the Samaritan woman, their talk revolves around the issue of water. The Samaritan woman is at the well in the middle of the day in order to draw water (v. 6), which provides Jesus an opportunity to make a request of her (δός μοι πεῖν, "give me a drink," v. 7). After this request a strained conversation ensues.

As Jesus speaks metaphorically about water, the woman misperceives his meaning, focusing instead on the literal and material (see the exchange over "living water" in vv. 10–18). The phrase ὕδωρ ζῶν (v. 10) is a euphemism for "running water" and this characteristic Johannine *double entendre* contributes to the Samaritan woman's misunderstanding. She recognizes that running water is necessary for physical sustenance and the prolonging of natural life. Jesus, however, is offering her *living* water that is necessary for spiritual sustenance leading to eternal life. She, like the disciples, overemphasizes the material and initially fails to understand.

The woman eventually progresses toward a partial understanding of Jesus's identity and words, and she returns to town to spread the message (v. 28). Before her departure the disciples arrive on the scene and are surprised to see Jesus speaking with a woman (v. 27). When the Samaritan woman departs, the focus of conversation shifts from "water" to "food" (vv. 31–34). Here the disciples are cast in a manner that reveals their emphasis on the literal and material, and consequently they fail to understand Jesus. The exegesis of this passage will proceed as follows:

1. Return and departure (4:27–30)
2. Jesus and the disciples converse (4:31–38)

Return and Departure (4:27–30)

The reader has neither seen nor heard from the disciples during the episode at the well. The events that begin in v. 5 picture Jesus travel-

32. The conversation between Jesus and the Samaritan woman will be examined in chapter 6 of this study. For the purposes of the present chapter a brief overview of vv. 4–26 will suffice.

ing alone. In v. 8 the reader is informed by means of a parenthetical comment that the disciples have departed into the city to buy food (ἀπεληλύθεισαν εἰς τὴν πόλιν ἵνα τροφὰς ἀγοράσωσιν).[33] Within the story, the absence of the disciples provides the opportunity for an extended conversation between Jesus and the Samaritan woman. As the present scene opens the disciples are returning from their journey to obtain food, while the Samaritan woman is about to depart to the city from which she came.

Upon arrival the disciples are astonished (ἐθαύμαζον) to see Jesus speaking with a woman (v. 27). The term used to express their astonishment is one associated with extraordinary emotion.[34] Their emotional amazement is appropriate when one considers that public interactions between a rabbi and a woman were thought to have quasi-sexual undertones. Such a conversation would bring into question the motives and thus the credibility of the rabbi. The rabbi was warned against having public conversations with women and was equally warned about the propriety of being alone with a woman, even if it was a sister or daughter.[35] Against this backdrop one can appreciate Hoskyns's comment that a public conversation between a rabbi and a woman would have, at the very least, been considered suspicious.[36]

The narrator reports that the disciples are amazed to see Jesus speaking with a woman, but nothing is said of their amazement that she is also a Samaritan. The contentious relationship between Jews and Samaritans was previously noted in the understated phrase from v. 9: οὐ γὰρ συγχρῶνται Ἰουδαῖοι Σαμαρίταις.[37] Kysar comments that the woman's Samaritan identity has already been highlighted in the narrative, implying that within the present scene there is no need

33. The term τροφάς is more properly "nourishment" (BDAG, s.v. τροφή) and is not the same word used by Jesus in vv. 31, 34.

34. BDAG, s.v. θαυμάζω.

35. See the quotations and discussion provided in Morris, *Gospel According to John*, 274, esp. n. 68.

36. Hoskyns, *Fourth Gospel*, 245. See also Barrett, *Gospel According to St. John*, 240, who comments "it was considered undesirable that a Rabbi should speak with women." He supports this claim with a number of rabbinic citations on the subject.

37. Derrett ("Samaritan Woman's Pitcher," 254) notes that συγχρῶνται has been understood in a number of ways. He comments that the term has been thought to refer to the two groups (1) using the same utensils (a point informed by the Mishnah); (2) having business dealings; and (3) having social contact of any kind.

for the narrator to emphasize that point again.[38] That piece of information is already informing the reading experience of the implied reader, who understands that Jesus is crossing multiple cultural boundaries in speaking with a Samaritan who is also a woman.

Despite their astonishment, the disciples do not ask her, "What do you want?" or Jesus, "Why are you speaking with her?" (v. 27cd). This reticence to question Jesus will appear again in 16:5 ("Not one of you asks me, 'Where are you going?'") and 21:12 ("But none of the disciples dared to ask him, 'Who are you?'").

While the disciples arrive and survey the situation, the woman departs to the city and in the process leaves her water jar.[39] By returning to the city rather than going to her husband, she fails to heed Jesus's earlier directive ("Go call your husband and come back here," v. 16).[40] Instead, she goes to a public place and the narrator reports that λέγει τοῖς ἀνθρώποις (v. 28). While the term ἄνθρωπος can be understood in a generic, even gender-neutral sense (i.e., "people"),[41] it seems better to understand that a more specific referent is being implied.

The conversation between Jesus and the Samaritan woman revealed that she had been married five times previously and that her current partner was not her husband (v. 18). In that light, the subtlety of the seemingly generic phrase τοῖς ἀνθρώποις (v. 28) coupled with her report ("Come, see a man who told me everything I have done,"

38. "The shock of his talking with a woman is greater than the fact that the woman is a Samaritan only because John has highlighted the latter already in v. 9" (Kysar, *John*, 68).

39. Much has been made of the water jar throughout the history of exegesis on the Fourth Gospel. Was it left so that Jesus may drink? Should it be read as an indication that she has made a complete break with the past, and is satisfied with "living water"? Is it simply an indication that she ran off in haste and forgot it? Many interpretations abound where the water jar is concerned.

40. Malina and Rohrbaugh (*Social-Science Commentary on the Gospel of John*, 101) comment that this unit is filled with a number of cultural anomalies. Along with the cultural anomalies suggested by the male-female and Jew-Samaritan interactions, they write, "Leaving the water jar indicates that the woman is not going home. Instead she goes to the city. If she has gone to the place in town where people are normally gathered, that is, to the public square, she is in decidedly public, male space. She had been told to go back to private space (her husband), but she goes straight to the most public space available."

41. Lincoln (*Gospel According to St. John*, 179) sees τοῖς ἀνθρώποις as the "citizens of Sychar." Likewise, Moloney (*Gospel of John*, 131) regards them as "fellow-villagers." In addition, the NET renders τοῖς ἀνθρώποις as "the people" in v. 28.

v. 29) suggests a reference to the men to whom she was previously married. The implication may be that she goes first to "the men" who were also mentioned in the conversation with Jesus and that the other townspeople hear and come to Jesus as a result of that conversation.

Her invitation to "Come and see," δεῦτε ἴδετε (v. 29) recalls the words of Philip to Nathanael in 1:46 (ἔρχου καὶ ἴδε). Stibbe regards this "narrative echo effect" as an analepsis that establishes the Samaritan woman as a true disciple of Jesus.[42] Without going too far, it can be affirmed that this echo effect does help establish her status as a disciple. She immediately goes to tell others (as did Andrew and Philip in ch. 1). However, her partial perception of Jesus's identity and her uncertain question (both in v. 29b) reveal that she, like others before her, does not fully understand Jesus. Thus, while she is a disciple in the mold of other Johannine disciples, one should be cautious in using (along with Stibbe) the phrase "true disciple." Within the Fourth Gospel, only the Beloved Disciple can claim that title.

After her report the Samaritan woman asks, μήτι οὗτός ἐστιν ὁ χριστός; (v. 29b).[43] Though Brown regards this question as an expression of "unlikelihood," it should not be regarded as a rejection of Jesus's messianic status.[44] The use of μή (and compound forms) to pose a question in Hellenistic writings generally indicates hesitance and the expectation of a negative answer.[45] Considering the overall context of the Fourth Gospel, which includes a number of conditioned confessions based upon partial insight, it seems best to regard her question as expressing a "cautious opinion."[46] Affirming the uncertainty of the woman's question (rather than its expectation of a negative answer), Lincoln comments that "her lack of certitude does not prevent her from

42. Stibbe, *John*, 67.

43. Historical questions abound over the Samaritan conception of Messiah. The fifth article in the Samaritan creed was the belief in a prophet like Moses. Their Messiah was called *Ta'eb* ("one who returns," from the Hebrew שׁוב, "to turn," "return"). He was to be a successor in the mold of Moses and he was to restore proper worship. Brown (*The Gospel According to John*, 1:172) comments that the scene fits the Samaritan concept of *Ta'eb* as teacher of Torah, "even though the more familiar Jewish designation of Messiah is placed on the woman's lips." For a fuller discussion of the Samaritan concept of Messiah, see Schnackenburg, *Gospel According to St. John*, 1:441.

44. Brown, *Gospel According to John*, 1:172.

45. See BDF, para. 427.

46. Schnackenburg, *Gospel According to St. John*, 1:444.

being an effective witness."[47] The impact of her report is clear as the townspeople begin coming out to meet Jesus.

Across John 4 there are a number of comings and goings that enable the action to continue. At the beginning of the chapter, the disciples left Jesus, which allowed a conversation between Jesus and the woman to take place. When the disciples returned in v. 27, the woman departed. Now that the woman has departed to the city and given her report, the townspeople begin leaving the city and coming toward Jesus (the ἤρχοντο of v. 30 is taken in an ingressive sense). As the townspeople *begin* to move toward Jesus, a "meanwhile" is created in the narration of events that allows the conversation in vv. 31–38 to take place.

Jesus and the Disciples Converse (4:31–38)

Two events are pictured in this unit. The first event is Jesus's conversation with the disciples, which occurs in the narrated time and space of the pericope itself. The second event is the short journey of the Samaritan townspeople to meet Jesus and, though this event is not explicitly narrated, the reader remains aware of it. In vv. 31–34 Jesus and the disciples converse about Jesus's intention to do the will of the Father. While that conversation is taking place, the reader remembers that the citizens of Sychar are making their way to meet Jesus. This remembrance is facilitated by the narrator's use of ἐν τῷ μεταξυ, "in the meantime" (v. 31) and confirmed by Jesus's command for the disciples to "lift up your eyes and see" (v. 35). During the unit's first event there are several elements that point forward to the approaching Samaritans and the imminence of their arrival.[48]

In v. 31 the reader is reminded of the disciples' earlier mission to obtain food (v. 8). Their words to Jesus (ῥαββί, φάγε) bring their mission to completion and create another opportunity for misunderstand-

47. Lincoln, *Gospel According to St. John*, 179. Here the theme of belief in the word continues. The Samaritan townspeople initially believe on the basis of the Samaritan woman's word. However, after hearing Jesus they proclaim that, on the basis of what they have heard, they know him to be "the savior of the world" (v. 42).

48. Moloney (*Belief in the Word*, 158) comments, "[B]ecause of the narrator's report that the Samaritans are coming toward Jesus (v. 30), the reader is aware that the space opened between Jesus and his entourage by the departure of the woman (vv. 27–28) is now being closed. The disciples are told to lift up their eyes, to see the advent of the Samaritans (v. 35)."

ing and correction.[49] Their mention of eating prompts Jesus to reply ἐγὼ βρῶσιν ἔχω φαγεῖν ἣν ὑμεῖς οὐκ οἴδατε (v. 32).[50] Jesus does not have literal food, but his reply allows for a shift from the prominent theme of water in the previous conversation with the Samaritan woman to the theme of food.

In v. 33 the confused disciples do not press Jesus for an explanation. Instead they discuss with one another whether someone has brought Jesus food.[51] As in other instances in the story, the disciples misunderstand Jesus because of their focus on the material rather than spiritual meaning behind his words. Their emphasis on literal food causes them once again to miss Jesus's point.[52]

There is nothing in the prologue that would prepare the reader to understand Jesus's words about food. However, throughout the story thus far the reader has already begun to perceive the shortcomings of the disciples and recognizes this as a moment of confusion that will inevitably lead to Jesus's correction and explanation. Barrett agrees when he writes, "As the woman failed to understand the living water, which is the gift of God, so even the disciples were ignorant of the food by which Jesus lived. The argument moves on (v. 33) by means of their misunderstanding, *as often in John*."[53]

Jesus's clarification begins with an explanation in v. 34 and a further exposition vv. 35–38. He comments that his "food" is to do the will of the one who sent him, and to complete his work (v. 34). The ἵνα of

49. "[T]heir encounter with Jesus is structured according to the pattern of statement-misunderstanding-clarification" (Neyrey, *Gospel of John*, 97).

50. βρῶσις is more properly the *process* of eating, though Barrett (*Gospel According to St. John*, 240) comments that βρῶσις and βρῶμα, "food," are often used interchangeably. This is confirmed by Jesus's use of βρῶμα in the same context (cf. v. 34).

51. Variant textual readings often serve as the earliest commentary on a given text. The text here comments that the disciples spoke πρὸς ἀλλήλους, "to one another" (v. 33), which implies they were not speaking to Jesus directly. Rather, the conversation was restricted to their group. Interestingly, this interpretation is supported by a lesser but more specific variant that has the disciples speaking ἐν ἑαυτοῖς, "among themselves" or "to themselves"(found in D ff^2 q sy^p).

52. "Following a pattern that we have seen in the conversations with the Jews after the temple cleansing, with Nicodemus, and with the woman, the disciples misunderstand Jesus by taking His words in a literal and material fashion . . . [T]he point is that they think only in terms of material food. However, their complete misunderstanding opens up the way for Jesus to impart valuable truths" (Morris, *Gospel According to John*, 277).

53. Barrett, *Gospel According to St. John*, 240; emphasis added.

v. 34 introduces two theologically important purposes clauses, each beginning with a subjunctive verb and connected by καί: (1) ἵνα ποιήσω τὸ θέλημα τοῦ πέμψαντός με, and (2) τελειώσω αὐτοῦ τὸ ἔργον. Jesus's food (or more properly, his purpose, as indicated by the use of ἵνα) is twofold. He must do the will of the Father[54] and he must complete that work. Moloney adds that if we read the καί as epexegetical, "his nourishment is found in his doing the will of the one who sent him, which means he will bring to perfection the work of that person."[55]

The use of the food theme here provides the implied reader with a new insight that will remain throughout the rest of the story: Jesus is sustained by the "food" of performing and completing the work of the Father. The implied reader is hearing this concept for the first time, but not for the last.[56] While Jesus offers to others sustenance in the form of "living water," he finds his own sustenance in the "food" given him by the Father.

In v. 35 Jesus appeals to conventional agricultural wisdom to explain the second event. He asks the disciples, "Don't you say, 'There are four months and then comes the harvest?'"[57] There is a typical process that includes sowing, waiting for a period, and then reaping. However, in this instance Jesus explains that the reaping is going to be immediate (notice the contrast between λέγετε and ἰδοὺ λέγω ὑμῖν in v. 35).[58] His instruction for the disciples to look up and see τὰς χώρας ὅτι λευκαί εἰσιν πρὸς θερισμόν is an initial indication that the seeds sown in his conversation with the Samaritan woman are about to yield an immediate return.

54. Jesus speaks of the Father as "the one who sent me" elsewhere in 5:23, 30, 37; 6:38, 44; 7:16, 18, 28, 33; 8:16, 18, 26, 29; 9:4; 12:44, 49; 13:20; 14:24; 15:21; 16:5.

55. Moloney, *Belief in the Word*, 161.

56. Jesus's work is described as doing and completing the work of God elsewhere in the Fourth Gospel. See, e.g., 5:30, 36; 6:38–39; 9:4; 10:37–38; 17:4.

57. The use of ὑμεῖς λέγετε should most likely be understood in a gnomic sense (i.e., "Is it not commonly stated that? . . ."). For more on the gnomic present, see Wallace, *Exegetical Syntax of the New Testament*, 523–25. On this statement, Schnackenburg (*Gospel According to St. John*, 1:449) writes, "The sentence is Semitic in idiom, and can be either a statement evoked by the occasion or a general proverb."

58. "It is not stated that the harvest is already reaped: the fields are white; the harvest may immediately begin . . . In this crop there will be no interval between sowing and harvest" (Barrett, *Gospel According to St. John*, 241).

In vv. 36–38 Jesus explains that the "harvest" the disciples are about to experience is not rightfully theirs. They have not worked for it but they are receiving the benefits. There is no indication from the narrator as to whether the disciples understand Jesus's words about food or about the harvest. Instead, the townspeople arrive and the scene shifts to an interaction between Jesus and the inquisitive Samaritans.

This first example of the disciples as a representative group complements the reader's developing understanding of Jesus's followers. In this pericope the pattern continues: Jesus speaks, the disciples misunderstand, and Jesus must clarify. The reader witnesses this pattern again in ch. 11.

Jesus and the Disciples in John 11:11–15

A detailed analysis of John 11 was undertaken in chapter 3. While the discussion was primarily focused on the role of Thomas across the chapter, it will suffice here to provide a brief summary of the conclusions offered above.

As the reader approaches this scene, the characters are in place. The disciples have already made their appearance in v. 7 and Jesus is mentioned v. 3. In v. 7 Jesus declares to the disciples his intent to return to Judea. They respond to Jesus's words with an incredulous objection phrased as a question (πάλιν ὑπάγεις ἐκεῖ; v. 8). After speaking of walking in the "daylight" and walking in the "night," Jesus provides a characteristically cryptic answer to the disciples' question in vv. 9–10.

However, their real confusion begins in v. 11a when Jesus comments that Λάζαρος ὁ φίλος ἡμῶν κεκοίμηται. After this Jesus states that he intends to go to Bethany to awaken Lazarus (v. 11b). The reader has already learned of Lazarus's illness (v. 1) and has heard Jesus proclaim that the illness will not result in death (v. 4). But with the simple and common metaphor of sleep in v. 11, the reader understands what the disciples do not: the sickness has indeed caused Lazarus's death. The reader perceives a deeper level of meaning in Jesus's words about the illness not leading to death, but the disciples have once again taken him literally. They consequently misunderstand and reply that he will recover (v. 12).

In v. 13, the narrator turns again to the reader to clarify that Jesus was speaking of death and rather than literal sleep. This explanation further highlights the disciples' misunderstanding and confirms their inability to understand even the most obvious metaphor.

While this is the only scene in the chapter focusing explicitly upon the misunderstanding of the Twelve as a group, there is a series of misunderstandings that begin with Thomas's words, "Let us go also that we may die with him" (v. 16). This statement only increases the impression of the disciples' incomprehension at this stage of the story. On this point, Stibbe comments that the disciples "manifest misunderstanding" throughout ch. 11.[59] He continues,

> They are portrayed as people who are unable to understand even the most transparent of metaphors. When Jesus uses the metaphor of sleep to talk about Lazarus' death (v. 11), the disciples respond with the same superficial literalism which the Pharisees and Jews have shown. They fail to understand a metaphor which was so common it was almost a cliché . . .In what is essentially a comic story, the disciples function as the typical, ignorant buffoons.[60]

As before, a consistent emphasis on the literal or material creates a misunderstanding to which Jesus must respond.

Conclusion: The Disciples as Uncomprehending Characters

The trait of incomprehension has by now become an expected element of the Fourth Gospel's presentation of the disciples. In light of the discussion in the present chapter along with the conclusions of chapters 3 and 4, it can now be suggested that the most consistent trait of the disciples in the Fourth Gospel, both individually and corporately, is their inability to understand Jesus in categories that would be regarded as authentic by the implied reader.

Aside from these specific instances of incomprehension among the disciples as a group, there are other hints in the Fourth Gospel of the disciples' confusion about Jesus. For instance, throughout John 14 and 16 the disciples still do not grasp that Jesus is going away and returning to the Father. They fail to understand both major and minor details on

59. Stibbe, *John*, 125.

60. Ibid.

their way to the events of the passion. Only after the resurrection do they give evidence of any real understanding.

The disciples' persistent inability to understand Jesus is described by Culpepper in an appropriate conclusion to the discussion of this chapter:

> What does emerge about the disciples from their questions is that they have grasped very little of what Jesus has revealed to them. They do know not where he is going. They do not know "the way" to the Father or that they have seen him in Jesus. They have in fact scarcely gotten beyond a "signs" faith. They do not understand what Jesus says about the "little while." Even at the end of the [farewell] discourse, when the disciples think they have got it, they can only parrot proudly what Jesus has just said . . . Only his death and resurrection, his glorification, will enable them to understand what he has revealed.[61]

61. Culpepper, *Anatomy of the Fourth Gospel*, 118–19.

6

Jesus and "Others" in the Fourth Gospel

The last three chapters of this study have focused on the relationship between Jesus and his disciples as envisioned by the narrator of the Fourth Gospel. It has been demonstrated that certain individual disciples and occasionally the corporate body of disciples display a consistent misunderstanding of Jesus's origins, mission, and message. In this chapter the focus shifts from Jesus's disciples to other Johannine characters that display an inability to understand Jesus's words and actions.[1] Specifically, this chapter will examine Nicodemus (3:1–12; 7:45–52; 19:39–42), the Samaritan woman (4:4–42), and the sisters Martha and Mary (11:1–44; 12:1–8).

Jesus and Nicodemus in the Fourth Gospel

Throughout the history of Johannine scholarship few characters have received as much attention as Nicodemus.[2] He has been variously identified as a representative figure,[3] a symbol of incomplete or re-

1. I am making a distinction here between characters directly identified by the term μαθητής and those that are not. Surely other characters in the Gospel that are not identified as a μαθηταί should be regarded as Johannine disciples.

2. "Few of the minor figures in the Gospels have held as much fascination for scholars as John's Nicodemus. The reason for this is not difficult to find: Nicodemus is a puzzling, enigmatic figure" (Bassler, "Mixed Signals," 635).

3. Collins (*These Things Have Been Written*, 14) writes that Nicodemus is "a representative of official Judaism." Schnackenburg (*Gospel According to St. John*, 1:363–64) comments that Nicodemus is "a well-intentioned representative of the ruling classes, a man with religious questions, and one from whom Jesus does not remain totally aloof," but cautions against seeing Nicodemus as a "typical case of the unbelieving Jew." Culpepper (*Anatomy of the Fourth Gospel*, 135) asserts that "Nicodemus seems to represent the many Jews in Jerusalem who believed in Jesus because they saw the signs he was doing, but he quickly takes on a more individual profile." See also the pertinent comments in

luctant faith,[4] a historical individual,[5] the Talmudic figure Naqai[6] (or Naqdimon ben Gorion),[7] and other variations of those suggestions.[8] While there is no consensus on how to identify Nicodemus, virtually all Johannine scholars concede his significance as a crucial character within the Johannine narrative. Whether he is regarded as a representative figure, a historical individual, or a literary symbol, he is a paradigm for the uncomprehending character in the Fourth Gospel.[9] And though the portrait of his incomprehension is almost a caricature in places, he undergoes a transformation that takes him from complete confusion to the edge of authentic discipleship.

Nicodemus appears three times in the Gospel. He makes his first appearance in ch. 3 in what is arguably the best-known passage from the Fourth Gospel. He approaches Jesus initially with a statement of seemingly genuine praise. His approach is followed by an exchange of

---

Brown, *Gospel According to John*, 1:129; Bultmann, *Gospel of John*, 133; Barrett, *Gospel According to St. John*, 204; and Lincoln, *Gospel According to St. John*, 148.

4. Cf., e.g., Martyn, *History and Theology in the Fourth Gospel*, 119–23, 161–63; Moloney, *Belief in the Word*, 120.

5. Morris (*Gospel According to John*, 209) comments that Nicodemus would have been "a typical representative of Pharisaic Judaism" and that he would have "stressed careful observance of the Law and the traditions of the elders." While he does not directly state that Nicodemus was a historical individual, the entire tone of his discussion suggests that he holds that view. See also Carson (*Gospel According to John*, 185–86), who chafes at the suggestion that Nicodemus may not have been a historical individual.

6. "The Babylonian Talmud (*b. Sanh.* 43a) cites a man named Naqai among a group of five disciples of Jesus. Naqai is a shortened form of the Hebrew name Naqdimon, which would be the equivalent of the Greek name which we customarily translate as Nicodemus" (Collins, *These Things Have Been Written*, 57).

7. See, for instance, Büschel, *Evangelium nach Johannes*, 51; and Hoskyns, *Fourth Gospel*, 210–11. In addition, Brown, *Gospel According to John*, 1:30; Barrett, *Gospel According to St. John*, 204; and Carson, *Gospel According to John*, 186, all discuss this suggestion.

8. Sandra Schneiders ("Born Anew," 191) poses a unique understanding of Nicodemus: "No doubt Nicodemus functioned in *John's community* as the hero of its Jewish Christian members, but his primary function in the *Gospel* is to catch the conscience of the reader. Nicodemus is the very type of the truly religious person who is, on the one hand, utterly sincere and, on the other, complacent about his or her knowledge of God and God's will." In John 3 it is difficult to imagine the uncomprehending Nicodemus as the hero of any group within the Johannine community.

9. Stibbe (*John*, 54) writes of him, "Nicodemus is the embodiment of misunderstanding."

three statements or questions from Nicodemus and three answers from Jesus. Here Nicodemus appears as the quintessential uncomprehending character. He understands everything Jesus says within the limits of his own Jewish world and departs in utter bewilderment.

In his second appearance (7:50–51) Nicodemus appears among fellow Jewish leaders, speaking in a manner that indicates a veiled sympathy with Jesus. This appearance represents Nicodemus's gradual progression toward Johannine discipleship.

In his final appearance (19:39–42) Nicodemus assists Joseph of Arimathea in preparing and burying the corpse of Jesus. He does not speak in this final scene, but his actions prove to be an implicit commentary on the extent of his transformation. Despite his journey toward Johannine discipleship, Nicodemus falls just short of the mark.

Jesus and Nicodemus in John 3:1–12[10]

This conversation with Nicodemus is Jesus's first extended discourse in the Gospel. It is also the first conversation between Jesus and one of "the Jews" in the Fourth Gospel. The conversation can be divided into three units, each beginning with a statement or question from Nicodemus followed by an explanation from Jesus. Nicodemus speaks in vv. 2, 4, and 9 and Jesus responds with a double ἀμήν statement in vv. 3, 5, and 11. The conversation proper (vv. 1–12) is then followed by a brief explanation from Jesus (vv. 13–15) and an extended theological explanation from the narrator (vv. 16–21).[11] The following outline provides the structure of this passage:

Nicodemus and Jesus converse (3:1–12)

1. Introduction of Nicodemus (3:1–2a)
2. Conversation (Part 1) (3:2b-3)

10. Commentators on the Fourth Gospel typically cover vv. 13–21 in the section dealing with Nicodemus. However, since the emphasis here is on the characterization of Nicodemus, the present exegesis will focus on the direct exchanges between Jesus and Nicodemus.

11. There is debate about where the words of Jesus end and where the explanation of the narrator begins in John 3. This debate is reflected in the commentary tradition as well as in modern translations. The NRSV, NIV, NASB, NLT, and ESV retain quotation marks throughout vv. 16–21 (indicating that Jesus's words continue), whereas the NAB and NET place quotation marks at v. 15 and leave vv. 16–21 as plain text. Of the two positions I find the latter more convincing.

3. Conversation (Part 2) (3:4–8)
4. Conversation (Part 3) (3:9–12)

Nicodemus and Jesus Converse (3:1–12)

As the reader approaches John 3, many questions about Jesus have been answered, but many still remain. The reader knows that Jesus is the unique representation of God (1:1c) and the revealer of the Father to humanity (1:18), but these truths are still playing out in the story. In ch. 2, Jesus began his public ministry with a unique sign (2:1–11) and an authenticating act in the temple (2:12–22). That chapter ended with the statement that Jesus refused to entrust himself to humans because of his knowledge of humanity (vv. 24–25). This important theological statement leads the reader directly into Jesus's conversation with Nicodemus.

Recalling a number of themes from the prologue, this conversation provides the narrator an opportunity to explain Jesus's mission further to the reader. Reintroducing the themes of spiritual birth (vv. 3–6),[12] life (vv. 15, 16),[13] the world (vv. 16–17),[14] belief (vv. 16, 18),[15] and light (vv. 19–21),[16] Jesus's dialogue with Nicodemus (vv. 1–15) and the explanation that follows (vv. 16–21) give the reader a clear statement of Jesus's mission. In this way, the first Nicodemus episode contains a proclamation of the entire Johannine Gospel message.[17]

Introduction of Nicodemus (3:1–2a)

In 2:23 the narrator provided the reader with a statement of physical setting (Jerusalem) and temporal setting (the time of the Passover). There is no stated change in physical or temporal settings from 2:23 to 3:1, and it is therefore safe to conclude that the events of ch. 3 also occur in Jerusalem around the time of the Jewish Passover.

12. See the discussion about being "born of God" in 1:12–13.

13. Cf. 1:4.

14. Cf. 1:9, 10.

15. Cf. 1:7, 12.

16. Cf. 1:4, 5, 7, 8, 9.

17. On the Johannine Gospel appearing in this passage, see the exegesis given in Collins, *These Things Have Been Written*, 56–67.

The episode begins with the narrator's detailed introduction of a new character. Here four crucial pieces of information are given to the reader. This new character is first identified as a man (ἦν δὲ ἄν-θρωπος), then as a Pharisee (ἐκ τῶν Φαρισαίων).[18] The reader also learns the character's name (Νικόδημος ὄνομα αὐτῷ)[19] and his status as a religious leader (ἄρχων τῶν Ἰουδαίων).[20] These descriptive elements raise questions about the narrator's intended presentation of Nicodemus. Each element is considered below:

1. While the term ἄνθρωπος can be used to refer to a person irrespective of gender, Conway comments that there are two specific reasons for the narrator's identification of Nicodemus as ἄνθρωπος.[21] First, in 2:25 the narrator commented that Jesus needed no testimony περὶ τοῦ ἀνθρώπου because he knew what was ἐν τῷ ἀνθρώπῳ. Thus, the narrator's first piece of information is a subtle sign to the reader that Jesus will not entrust himself fully to Nicodemus.[22] Second, Conway reads the phrase ἄνθρωπος ἐκ τῶν Φαρισαίων proleptically, as a statement pointing forward to the comparisons and contrasts that will be drawn between Nicodemus, a religious Jewish man, and the anonymous Samaritan woman of ch. 4.[23]

2. While the name Νικόδημος does not appear to have a special meaning or importance for the story, it is significant that his

18. The phrase οἱ Ἰουδαῖοι, "the Jews," is most commonly used in the Fourth Gospel to refer to the Jewish leaders. The term Φαρισαῖοι is the second most common term used to refer to Jewish opponents of Jesus. This is one of nineteen occurrences of the term in the Fourth Gospel; the others are in 1:24; 4:1; 7:32, 45, 47, 48, 8:3, 13; 9:13, 15, 16, 40; 11:46, 47, 57; 12:19, 42; 18:3.

19. On the significance of naming in literature, see the comments by Conway, *Men and Women in the Fourth Gospel*, 87–88.

20. Many scholars regard this title as a reference to membership in the Sanhedrin. See, e.g., Bultmann, *Gospel of John*, 133 n. 4; Barrett, *Gospel According to St. John*, 204; Brown, *Gospel According to John*, 1:130 (who translates ἄρχων τῶν Ἰουδαίων as "a member of the Jewish Sanhedrin"); and Schnackenburg, *Gospel According to St. John*, 1:365.

21. See the discussion in Conway, *Men and Woman*, 87.

22. Moloney (*Gospel of John*, 97–98) prefers to translate ἄνθρωπος as "human" in 3:2 but allows for the possibility that "man" may be intended here.

23. See Conway, *Men and Women*, 87. Mary Margaret Pazdan ("Nicodemus and the Samaritan Woman") also sees a series of strong and deliberate comparisons and contrasts in the episodes featuring Nicodemus and the Samaritan woman.

name is provided at all. The discussion of anonymous vs. named characters in chapter 2 concluded that characters that remain nameless in the Fourth Gospel are often presented as models of greater faith than those characters whose names are given. This appears to be the case at least initially with Nicodemus. In ch. 3 he walks away from Jesus in bewilderment while the unnamed Samaritan woman (with whom the reader contrasts Nicodemus) will depart with reluctant faith and unwittingly evangelize her village. However, the reader has not yet made the concrete distinction between named characters as models of lesser faith and anonymous characters as models of greater faith. This distinction emerges only from a synchronic overview of the narrative. In addition, literary critics recognize that the naming of a character is often a signal of their importance and the beginning of their extended characterization in the story. In this regard Sternberg writes, "[T]o bear a name is to assume an identity: to become a singular existent, with an assured place in history and a future in the story."[24]

3. At this stage of the story it is difficult to discern the significance of Nicodemus's designation as ἐκ τῶν Φαρισαίων. While some would argue that the Pharisees are characterized throughout the Gospel as antagonistic toward Jesus, the reader does not yet know enough of the Pharisees to be suspicious. Goulder comments that the word Pharisee "carries hostile overtones throughout the Gospel,"[25] and this is no doubt true in chs. 7, 9, and 11. However, that is hardly the case at this early stage of the story. The Pharisees have appeared only on one occasion prior to Jesus's conversation with Nicodemus, and that was in the context of questions posed to John the Baptist (cf. 1:24). At this stage of the story the implied reader's mind is not made up about the nature and significance of the Pharisees, though a mostly negative impression will crystallize in the mind of the reader as the story moves forward.[26]

24. Sternberg, *Poetics of Biblical Narrative*, 330–31.

25. Goulder, "Nicodemus," 154.

26. Conway (*Men and Women*, 91) argues (in my view unconvincingly) that the term Pharisee brings with it negativity for the reader's perception of Nicodemus. She writes, "To summarize, in general the title Pharisee does not bode well as a character indicator for Nicodemus, in terms of his view of Jesus. In many instances, the Pharisees

4. The phrase ἄρχων τῶν Ἰουδαίων is significant on a number of levels. First, it most likely identifies Nicodemus as a member of the Sanhedrin. Thus, Nicodemus is set apart as one with strong religious and social credentials. Second, and more significant for the developing story, is that ἄρχων (which can be taken as "ruler" or "prince")[27] is used in the Fourth Gospel only of Jewish leaders (7:26, 48; 12:42) and the "prince of this world" (12:31; 14:30; 16:11). In this regard Moloney comments that "[a]s the story unfolds, the leaders of the 'Jews' are increasingly shown to be the historical representatives of the prince of this world."[28] While this is recognizable from a synchronic reading of the whole text, the reader is not yet aware of this connection.

From an examination of these four descriptive elements it appears that the initial presentation of Nicodemus in v. 1 is meant to create sympathy for him on the part of the reader. Nicodemus (whose name is given) is a male member of a respected religious sect (the Pharisees) as well as of the Jewish ruling council (the Sanhedrin). Since the reader is not far enough into the story to be overly suspicious of these credentials, Nicodemus likely begins his journey in a positive light in the eyes of the reader. However, a tension has been created as it has already been suggested that Jesus will not entrust himself to this ἄνθρωπος. This ambiguity creates a necessary ambivalence in the reader.[29]

In v. 2a the reader learns that Nicodemus has come to Jesus by night (οὗτος ἦλθεν πρὸς αὐτὸν νυκτὸς). Through this detail a situational irony emerges, as a supposedly enlightened religious leader seeks Jesus, τὸ φῶς τῶν ἀνθρώπων (see 1:4) while it is dark. As the story progresses the reader understands that Nicodemus's coming by night is

are depicted as opponents and enemies of Jesus." To me this conclusion assumes too much about the development of the reader's understanding at this stage of the narrative. Such a concrete picture does not develop until later in the reading process.

27. BDAG (s.v. ἄρχων) lists the following meanings: (1) "one who has eminence in a ruling capacity, *ruler, lord, prince*"; (2) "one who has administrative authority, *leader, official*."

28. Moloney, *Gospel of John*, 97.

29. It has been suggested that the most identifiable element of Nicodemus's character is ambiguity. Wayne Meeks ("Man from Heaven in Johannine Sectarianism," 54) sees ambiguity as "an important and deliberate part" of the portrait of Nicodemus. In addition, Bassler ("Mixed Signals," 108) comments that "Nicodemus's primary characteristic is ambiguity."

symbolic of his darkened understanding.[30] But at the level of the event itself the phrase indicates Nicodemus's unwillingness to make public his interest in Jesus. There is thus an element of deliberate secrecy on the part of Nicodemus.[31] His attraction to Jesus is at odds with his status in society; again ambiguity emerges.

Conversation (Part 1) (3:2b–3)

Nicodemus's first words to Jesus appear perceptive, but he rapidly descends into confusion from there. He begins by using the honorific term ῥαββί to address Jesus and confesses, οἴδαμεν ὅτι ἀπὸ θεοῦ ἐλήλυθας διδάσκαλος (v. 2b). The plural οἴδαμεν may indicate Nicodemus's status as an official representative of Jewish leadership.[32] More important, however, is the recognition (consonant with the reader's knowledge) that Jesus is "from God." This portion of the initial confession is true from the perspective of the prologue, but as subsequent verses show it is far from a satisfactory Johannine understanding of Jesus's identity.

In the second element of Nicodemus's confession the reader senses his failure to grasp Jesus's identity fully. He continues, οὐδεὶς γὰρ δύναται ταῦτα τὰ σημεῖα ποιεῖν ἃ σὺ ποιεῖς, ἐὰν μὴ ᾖ ὁ θεὸς μετ᾽ αὐτοῦ (v. 2c). Though he correctly identifies Jesus as ἀπὸ θεοῦ, Nicodemus's understanding of this truth is rooted in a signs-based faith, which throughout the Gospel proves to be an inadequate basis for authentic Johannine belief.[33] Neyrey comments that "Nicodemus is only able to name Jesus as 'teacher,' a low-level role, not 'prophet' or 'Messiah.' Although signs can occasion discipleship (2:12; 4:53), Nicodemus never acclaims Jesus as anything but 'teacher.'"[34] Hence what initially seems

30. "The symbolic opposition of light and darkness resurfaces in the *nuktos* of v. 2. Darkness is also mentioned in v. 19 as a symbol of evil, the arena of human sinfulness" (Stibbe, *John*, 55).

31. Brown (*Gospel According to John*, 1:130) affirms both elements of this interpretation: "Darkness and night symbolize the realm of evil, untruth, and ignorance . . . On a purely natural level, the nighttime visit may have been a stealthy expedient for 'fear of the Jews.'"

32. On this suggestion, see Barrett, *Gospel According to St. John*, 205; and Moloney, *Gospel of John*, 97.

33. "The reference to 'signs' points to Nicodemus as representative of those Judeans mentioned in 2:23–24, who believe on the basis of signs, but to whom Jesus would not entrust himself" (Malina and Rohrbaugh, *Social-Science Commentary*, 81).

34. Neyrey, *Gospel of John*, 77. J. D. M. Derrett ("Correcting Nicodemus," 126) notes that the phrase "with God" is common in the OT. He further implies that this phraseol-

like a genuine Johannine perspective on the part of Nicodemus is instead an orthodox theological perspective from first-century Judaism. "He has been well introduced by 2:23: 'Many believed in his name when they saw the signs that he did.'"[35]

Verse 3 contains Jesus's enigmatic answer to Nicodemus's first statement: ἀμὴν ἀμὴν λέγω σοι, ἐὰν μή τις γεννηθῇ ἄνωθεν, οὐ δύναται ἰδεῖν τὴν βασιλείαν τοῦ θεοῦ, "Amen, amen I say to you, unless a person is born from above, he will not be able to see the kingdom of God." For the implied reader this statement stands out as a transparent example of Johannine *double entendre*.

Significant debate centers on the reader's understanding of the phrase γεννηθῇ ἄνωθεν (v. 3). First, some commentators argue that γεννηθῇ should be understood as "be begotten."[36] This however, does not match the contextual emphasis on "rebirth" implied by Nicodemus's misunderstanding (v. 4) as well as Jesus's second explanation about being "born of water and spirit" (v. 5).[37] γεννηθῇ is better understood as "born" in the present context.

Second, a standard conclusion among commentators has been that there is a basic misunderstanding on the part of Nicodemus rooted in the different nuances of ἄνωθεν. The argument states that the implied reader properly understands Jesus's words as "born from above" while Nicodemus understands Jesus to say "born again."[38] Nicodemus's misinterpretation of Jesus's words is confirmed by his question in v. 4.[39] However, the question of Jesus's intended meaning remains.

---

ogy is incorrect with respect to the Johannine Jesus and is evidence of Nicodemus's incomplete understanding of Jesus's identity.

35. Moloney, *Belief in the Word*, 109.

36. "Despite the fact that the Spirit, mentioned in v. 5 as the agent of this birth or begetting, is feminine in Hebrew (neuter in Greek), the primary meaning seems to be 'begotten'" (Brown, *Gospel According to John*, 1:130). See also Beasley-Murray, *John*, 45.

37. "It is better to translate 'born' to maintain the spatial and temporal possibilities of *gennēthȩ̄ anōthen*: rebirth from above" (Moloney, *Gospel of John*, 98).

38. See, e.g., Barrett, *Gospel According to St. John*, 205–6; Brown, *Gospel According to John*, 1:130; Culpepper, *Anatomy of the Fourth Gospel*, 135; Carson, *Gospel According to John*, 189; Hoskyns, *Fourth Gospel*, 212; Lincoln, *Gospel According to St. John*, 150; Malina and Rohrbaugh, *Social-Science Commentary*, 81; Neyrey, *Gospel of John*, 78; Schnackenburg, *Gospel According to St. John*, 1:367; Stibbe, *John*, 57.

39. This is a difficult issue for exegetes as well as translation committees. There is no uniformity among modern English translations when it comes to the rendering of γεννηθῇ ἄνωθεν. The NASB translates γεννηθῇ ἄνωθεν as "born again" without

Arguing against the majority position, Schneiders writes, "At the level of the text, Jesus could *not* have said 'unless one be *born from above*' because this could not have led Nicodemus to think he meant reentry into the maternal womb."[40] Schneiders understands that Johannine misunderstanding is "based on misplaced literalness in interpreting what is said, not on a failure to understand the actual words."[41] In this statement Schneiders is guilty of both creating a false distinction and begging the question.

Here Nicodemus fails to understand the intended nuance of the actual word (ἄνωθεν) *because* of a misplaced literalness. Further examination of the term ἄνωθεν proves to be illuminating on this point. BDAG lists ἄνωθεν as primarily "an adverb of place," and provides the following definitions:

1. In extension fr[om] a source that is above, *from above.*
2. From a point of time marking the beginning of someth[ing], *from the beginning.*
3. For a relatively long period in the past, *for a long time.*
4. At a subsequent point of time involving repetition, *again, anew.*[42]

This list confirms that both "from above" and "again" are acceptable nuances for ἄνωθεν. Further, this means that at the level of the story it is possible for Nicodemus to misunderstand Jesus's use of the actual word (ἄνωθεν), because of a misplaced literal nuance ("born again") rather than the intended spiritual nuance ("born from above"). In light of this

explanation or nuance. The NSRV translates the phrase as "born from above" with a note indicating that "born anew" might also be an appropriate translation. The ESV, NIV, and NLT translate γεννηθῇ ἄνωθεν as "born again" but provide a note indicating it might also be translated "from above." The CEV translates the phrase as "born from above" in vv. 3 and 7 without explanation. The NAB also translates the phrase as "born from above" in vv. 3 and 7 but provides an explanatory note giving the possible meanings for ἄνωθεν.

40. Schneiders, "Born Anew," 192; emphasis added.

41. Ibid. In light of this conclusion Schneiders decides to translate γεννηθῇ ἄνωθεν as "born anew." This is also the conclusion of Bultmann (*Gospel of John*, 135 n. 1), who writes, "Ἄνωθεν can mean 'from above' as well as 'anew', and also 'from the start', 'from the beginning'. In 3.31; 19.11, 23 it means 'from above', whereas in 3.3, 7 it can only mean 'anew'." In light of Bultmann's comments on this issue, it appears that Schneiders's position is heavily reliant upon Bultmann's thinking.

42. BDAG, s.v. ἄνωθεν.

observation, Schneiders's objection is shown to carry little weight in the present discussion.

Though Moloney appears to agree with the distinction between "from above" and "again," he offers a slight departure from the consensus position. He prefers to translate the phrase as "born again from above" or "re-birth from above."[43] In support of this suggestion he argues that "the temporal and spatial dimensions of the word [ἄνωθεν] are called for by its expansion into 'of water (again) and the Spirit (from above)' in v. 5.'"[44] In 1:12–13 the narrator spoke of being "born of God." This birth is not the result of human procreation (ἐξ αἱμάτων), human decision (ἐκ θελήματος σαρκὸς), or the will of a husband (ἐκ θελήματος ἀνδρὸς). It is altogether different from natural birth. The reader understands this critical distinction and also understands that some form of "rebirth" is implied by the use of γεννάω in the present passage. Thus, Moloney's suggestion seems to make "water" and "spirit" too concrete and it appears that the primary distinction in vv. 3, 7 still centers on the difference between "born from above" and "born again."

The interpretation here will argue that these two potential meanings for ἄνωθεν lie at the heart of the misunderstanding in the first exchange between Jesus and Nicodemus. This simple understanding will not only create confusion in Nicodemus but will provide Jesus another opportunity to explain. In the verses that follow, Jesus will draw an even clearer connection between what it means to be born ἐκ θεοῦ (1:13) and born ἄνωθεν (3:3).

Conversation (Part 2) (3:4–8)

Having misunderstood Jesus's statement in v. 3, Nicodemus speaks again, this time posing a question. His first words to Jesus showed an inability to comprehend fully Jesus's identity because his belief was rooted in the signs Jesus performed. In the second stage of their conversation Nicodemus shows an inability to understand Jesus's words about being born ἄνωθεν and he neglects altogether the issue of ἡ βασιλεία τοῦ θεοῦ (which in the Fourth Gospel is a reference to the realization of God's presence in and through Jesus in the present).

43. Moloney, *Gospel of John*, 98.

44. Ibid.

In an absurd instance of Johannine misunderstanding Nicodemus poses two questions. The first is, πῶς δύναται ἄνθρωπος γεννηθῆναι γέρων ὤν; (v. 4a). Without providing Jesus an opportunity to answer, Nicodemus poses his second question: μὴ δύναται εἰς τὴν κοιλίαν τῆς μητρὸς αὐτοῦ δεύτερον εἰσελθεῖν καὶ γεννηθῆναι; (v. 4b). The use of δεύτερον, "a second time," reveals that Nicodemus has understood ἄνωθεν in the strictly temporal sense of "again." Like the disciples, Nicodemus's overemphasis on the literal causes him to miss the point of Jesus's words. Moloney comments,

> [Nicodemus] responds to Jesus in terms he can grasp. The concrete experience of 'a second time' is within his comprehension but physically impossible. A rebirth 'from above' is beyond his control and is thus simply ignored. Jesus' words to Nicodemus combine both the horizontal experience of time and the vertical experience of the inbreak of God. Nicodemus's response is limited to the horizontal, and he does not even raise the question of seeing the kingdom of God.[45]

Thus his failure to understand the first element of Jesus's statement (being born ἄνωθεν) causes him to ignore completely the second element (seeing τὴν βασιλείαν τοῦ θεοῦ). In his second comment to Nicodemus, Jesus continues to emphasize rebirth as a means to experiencing the kingdom of God.

Following the pattern established in vv. 2b–3, Nicodemus speaks (v. 4) and Jesus answers his question with a double ἀμήν statement (v. 5). Here Jesus clarifies his teaching on what it means to be born ἄνωθεν by substituting the phrase γεννηθῇ ἐξ ὕδατος καὶ πνεύματος, "born of water and spirit" (v. 5). With the exception of two phrases, Jesus's first reply to Nicodemus is repeated verbatim. The parallels and differences are listed in the chart below:

45. Moloney, *Belief in the Word*, 130.

Jesus's First Response to Nicodemus John 3:3	**Jesus's Second Response to Nicodemus John 3:5**
ἀμὴν ἀμὴν λέγω σοι	ἀμὴν ἀμὴν λέγω σοι
ἐὰν μή τις γεννηθῇ **ἄνωθεν**	ἐὰν μή τις γεννηθῇ **ἐξ ὕδατος καὶ πνεύματος**
οὐ δύναται **ἰδεῖν**	οὐ δύναται **εἰσελθεῖν εἰς**
τὴν βασιλείαν τοῦ θεοῦ	τὴν βασιλείαν τοῦ θεοῦ

In Jesus's second reply, "born from above" is replaced by "born of water and spirit," and "to see the kingdom of God" is replaced by "to enter into the kingdom of God." While it is generally held among commentators that ἰδεῖν (v. 3) and εἰσελθεῖν (v. 5) are used synonymously here,[46] many questions are raised about the interpretation of the phrase ἐξ ὕδατος καὶ πνεύματος (v. 5).

Some scholars see two different births implied by the phrase ἐξ ὕδατος καὶ πνεύματος. The first birth is thought to be physical and ὕδατος is understood as a reference to either amniotic fluid[47] or semen.[48] The second birth, as implied by πνεύματος, is a spiritual birth. Thus, one must first be born into the world by natural means and then experience a spiritual rebirth. Since the following verse reads "What is born of flesh is flesh and what is born of spirit is spirit," those who argue for this interpretation regard the references to "flesh" and "spirit" as fur-

46. Bultmann (*Gospel of John*, 138 n. 2) flatly asserts that "εἰσελθεῖν is synonymous with ἰδεῖν in v. 3." Carson (*Gospel According to John*, 191) writes that the meaning of ἰδεῖν and εἰσελθεῖν "is much the same." He continues, "inability even to 'enter' may be slightly stronger the inability to 'see' (i.e., experience). But the crucial difference in the wording is the change from 'born *anōthen*' ('from above' or 'again') to *born of water and the Spirit*." In addition, Barrett (*Gospel According to St. John*, 207) comments that "it is impossible to distinguish between" the terms because "'[t]o see' means 'to experience' . . . John often uses synonymous pairs of words, e.g., γινώσκειν, εἰδέναι; ἀγαπᾶν, φιλεῖν." Moloney (*Gospel of John*, 98) dissents: "The verbs must be given the full weight of a physical, historical experience: rebirth in water and the Spirit enables *the sight of* and *entrance into* the Christian community."

47. Carson (*Gospel According to John*, 191) lists this as an interpretive option but does not provide a citation of a particular scholar who advocates the view.

48. See this suggestion in Odeberg, *Fourth Gospel*, 48–71. He marshals an impressive amount of evidence from rabbinic texts as well as Hermetic and Mandaean sources showing that "water" and related terms are used to refer to male semen.

ther confirmation that two births are in view in v. 5. However, there are at least three problems with this view.

First, references to natural birth as "from water" are scarce in ancient sources. Carson comments that texts using water to describe semen are "rare and late."[49] In addition, if natural birth were in view here, one might expect ἐξ αἱμάτων (which clearly refers to natural birth in 1:13) rather than ἐξ ὕδατος.

A second problem for this interpretation is that the passage shifts to a focus on "spirit" in the remaining verses (cf. vv. 6–9) whereas "water" is not mentioned again. This shift indicates that the idea of "spirit" is more prominent for the Evangelist's theological purposes.

A third objection to this interpretation is likely the most decisive. The Greek construction in view here argues against the presence of two distinct ideas. The phrase ἐξ ὕδατος καὶ πνεύματος consists of two anarthrous nouns that are governed by the same preposition and connected by καί. This structure usually indicates a compound object of the preposition, strongly suggesting one idea and therefore a singular birth. In light of these objections it seems best to argue that one birth is envisioned by the phrase "born of water and spirit."

Others have argued that water represents purification or Christian baptism.[50] Notable among those who argue for this interpretation is Bultmann, who suggests that ὕδατος καὶ was added by a later ecclesiastical redactor.[51] There is no textual evidence to support such a claim. However, it is possible that at some stage in the composition history of the Fourth Gospel water references were included to emphasize the importance of water baptism within the Johannine community.[52] There

49. Carson, *Gospel According to John*, 191. Barrett (*Gospel According to St. John*, 209) suggests that the combination of water and spirit could be understood as "spiritual semen."

50. Schnackenburg (*Gospel According to St. John*, 369) is perhaps too extreme in his suggestion that "[e]very Christian hearer or reader of the Gospel must have thought at once of baptism."

51. "The originality of the words ὕδατος καὶ, which link the rebirth with the sacrament of baptism, is at the least very doubtful. Admittedly they are found throughout the tradition (by contrast with v. 8, which is only infrequently found and is certainly an interpolation), but they are, in my opinion, an insertion of the ecclesiastical redaction, which in 6.51b–58 has also forged the link with the Last Supper. The meaning of baptism is not only not mentioned in the following passage, but if mentioned could only confuse the ideas in v. 6 and v. 8" (Bultmann, *Gospel of John*, 138–39 n. 3).

52. "[T]he community's break with the synagogue and a growing awareness of its uniqueness led to the introduction of the reference to water, to make an explicit refer-

seems to be baptismal significance at some level behind the phrase ἐξ ὕδατος.[53] But at the level of the story, there is more here than simply a veiled reference to the importance of baptism for John's community (not to mention that this interpretation also suggests two births—one by means of baptism and the other by means of spiritual renewal).

The best interpretation of this verse understands the phrase "born of water and spirit" as a reference to new birth where cleansing and renewal are emphasized. The connection between spirit and water has already been hinted at in the words of John the Baptist regarding baptism by water and the spirit (cf. 1:26, 32–33). Here the connection between water and spirit is made more concrete. In this way, the rebirth envisioned by Jesus reflects some of the eschatological traditions of the OT. Carson expresses this view succinctly:

> Far more important is the Old Testament background to 'water' and 'spirit'. The 'spirit' is constantly God's principle of life, even in creation (e.g. Gn. 2:17; 6:3; Jb. 34:14); but many Old Testament writers look forward to a time when God's 'spirit' will be poured out on humankind (Joel 2:28) with the result that there will be blessing and righteousness (Is. 32:15–20; 44:3; Ezk. 39:29), and inner renewal which cleanses God's covenant people from their idolatry and disobedience (Ezk. 11:19–20; 36:26–27). When water is used figuratively in the Old Testament, it habitually refers to renewal or cleansing, especially when it is found in conjunction with 'spirit'.[54]

Hence, birth by means of "water and spirit" is characterized by inner cleansing, spiritual renewal, and the ability to experience the kingdom in the present through association with Jesus.[55] All of this imagery comes from the OT and should be embraced readily by the learned Jewish

ence to the ritual of water baptism, a public sign that *externally* marked the *internal* experience and commitment to the beliefs of the Johannine community" (Moloney, *Gospel of John*, 99).

53. "John neither ignores nor repudiates the Christian rite, but sees it as a rite that is separable from its meaning, an outward that is separable from its inward, and thus issues the warning against a sacramentarian misapprehension of the eucharist" (Barrett, *Gospel According to St. John*, 208).

54. Carson, *Gospel According to John*, 195.

55. Emphasizing the widely recognized Johannine realized eschatology, Malina and Rohrbaugh (*Social-Science Commentary*, 83) argue that the "kingdom of God" in this passage is not a reference to something future but something to be experienced through Jesus in the present.

leader. However, Nicodemus fails to understand once again, as the third stage of his conversation with Jesus will reveal (cf. v. 9).

From a literary perspective this interpretation makes the most sense in the context of Jesus's first conversation with a member of the Jewish leadership. Jesus speaks to Nicodemus in terms he cannot understand (born ἄνωθεν) and in terms he should understand but does not (born of water and spirit). That Nicodemus fails to understand the imagery of his own Hebrew Scriptures further heightens the portrait of his incomprehension.

In the end several factors suggest that vv. 3 and 5 should be regarded as true parallels, thus strengthening the connections between ἄνωθεν and ἐξ ὕδατος καὶ πνεύματος (as well as ἰδεῖν and εἰσελθεῖν). First, the structure of the two is identical and there is variation in the actual wording in only two places. Second, a common element of Johannine discourse is the use of synonyms (e.g., ἀγαπάω/φιλέω, ἀποστέλλω/πέμπω, βλέπω/θεωρέω, etc.),[56] or similar language to describe the same realities. This flexibility in the content of Johannine discourse is evidence of the Evangelist's predilection for saying the same thing in multiple ways, as noted by Barrett:

> It is reasonable to assume that John is still speaking of the same [birth], that is, that the adverb and the adverbial phrases are substantially equivalent to each other, though the introduction of 'water and spirit' suggests fresh, and more precise, ideas.[57]

Third, Jesus's teaching in v. 5 clarifies and expands but does not change the content or context of his previous comment in v. 3. All of this suggests an agreement between vv. 3 and 5 where Jesus teaches Nicodemus about one spiritual rebirth.

Jesus continues his explanation to Nicodemus by commenting that τὸ γεγεννημένον ἐκ τῆς σαρκὸς σάρξ ἐστιν, καὶ τὸ γεγεννημένον ἐκ τοῦ πνεύματος πνεῦμά ἐστιν (v. 6). Rather than drawing a contrast

56. On this topic see most recently Gignac, "Use of Verbal Variety in the Fourth Gospel," 191–200. See also Tarelli, "Johannine Synonyms"; McKay, "Style and Significance in the Language of John 21:15–17." Among those who argue for a concrete distinction behind Johannine synonyms are Mercer, "*APOSTELLEIN* and *PEMPEIN* in John"; idem, "Jesus the Apostle." See also Abbott (*Johannine Vocabulary*, 103) who writes, "The whole of this Gospel is pervaded with distinctions of thought, represented by the subtle distinctions of word or phrase—words and phrases so far alike that at first the reader may take the thought to be the same, though it is always really different."

57. Barrett, *Gospel According to St. John*, 208.

between "water" and "spirit" as some have suggested, this verse contrasts natural birth and spiritual birth. Nicodemus has failed to understand that birth from above is different from natural birth. Natural birth was described in the prologue as ἐκ θελήματος σαρκὸς (see 1:13), and therefore it is significant that the term σαρκὸς is used here to connote natural birth once again. It is unlikely that "flesh" is used here in the characteristically negative sense found in the Pauline writings.[58] Here σάρξ refers to the natural course of human activity and judgments (see its use in 7:24; 8:15). In the Johannine economy there are only two births: a natural birth characterized by human volition and insight, and a spiritual birth characterized by renewal and cleansing.

In v. 7 Jesus continues his second reply to Nicodemus, saying, "Do not be amazed that I said to you (sg.), 'you (pl.) must be born from above.'"[59] In vv. 3, 5 Jesus spoke to Nicodemus exclusively in the singular. Here, however, Jesus switches from the singular to the plural second person pronoun, indicating that he is speaking to Nicodemus about the implications of this teaching for a wider group. While this statement may have carried significance for the original readers of the Fourth Gospel, within the story the switch to ὑμᾶς likely reflects Jesus's definitive reply to Nicodemus's earlier use of the plural in v. 2a (οἴδαμεν, "we know"). Therefore the necessity of spiritual rebirth is not for Nicodemus alone but for those he claims to represent. As the story advances it becomes clear that Nicodemus moves closer and closer to this spiritual rebirth while those he represents (οἱ Ἰουδαῖοι, οἱ ἄρχοντες, and οἱ Φαρισαῖοι) move further and further away.

Inasmuch as Jesus uses imagery that should be familiar to Nicodemus, there is an expectation that he ought to understand Jesus's words about being born of water and spirit. However, there is also a sense in which this birth is shrouded in mystery. This recognition brings about the wordplay in Jesus's enigmatic statement about the blowing

58. This observation is strengthened by the recognition that Jesus is presented as becoming "flesh" (1:14).

59. Some commentators argue that a concrete distinction in translation should be maintained between μή followed by the present imperative ("stop doing") and μή followed by the aorist subjunctive ("do not start"). However, this distinction can be discerned only a fraction of the time in Hellenistic Greek. For more on the history of this discussion see McKay, "Aspect in Imperatival Constructions." There is also a helpful discussion of prohibitions in Wallace, *Exegetical Syntax of the New Testament*, 714–17. In this verse, μὴ θαυμάσῃς is simply a general prohibition.

of the wind: τὸ πνεῦμα ὅπου θέλει πνεῖ καὶ τὴν φωνὴν αὐτοῦ ἀκούεις, ἀλλ' οὐκ οἶδας πόθεν ἔρχεται καὶ ποῦ ὑπάγει (v. 8ab). Just as the blowing of the wind (τὸ πνεῦμα) is unpredictable and mysterious, so it is with those who are born of the Spirit (τὸ πνεῦμα). Their origins and destination are unpredictable and mysterious to those who are born ἐξ αἱμάτων and perceive only from the perspective of σάρξ. According to Moloney the sound generated by the wind may also be an implicit reference to the Spirit's voice.[60] This observation deepens the sense of mystery drawn by the connection between the blowing of the wind and those born of the Spirit.

Conversation (Part 3) (3:9–12)

In v. 9 Nicodemus speaks for the third and final time in this conversation. As in v. 4, Nicodemus responds with an uncomprehending question: πῶς δύναται ταῦτα γενέσθαι; "How can these things be?" With this question the initial portrait of Nicodemus's incomprehension is complete. He began with sincere but contrived praise (v. 2b), progressed to a clarifying question (v. 4), and here expresses complete bewilderment. The question shows that Nicodemus still perceives Jesus from the perspective of the flesh. There is an irony here for the perceptive reader who understands that the very thing Nicodemus needs is the thing he is unable to grasp. The narrator and the implied reader can understand what a leading religious authority within Israel cannot.

As in the previous two instances, Jesus answers Nicodemus's question with a double ἀμήν statement, but not before expressing wonderment at Nicodemus's incomprehension. Jesus asks Nicodemus, σὺ εἶ ὁ διδάσκαλος τοῦ Ἰσραὴλ καὶ ταῦτα οὐ γινώσκεις; Jesus's identification of Nicodemus as "*the* teacher of Israel" is both a reminder to the reader that Nicodemus holds a significant place in the religious hierarchy of Israel and an ironic reversal of Nicodemus's earlier confession that Jesus is ἀπὸ θεοῦ ἐλήλυθας διδάσκαλος.

Following the pattern of vv. 3 and 5, Jesus responds to Nicodemus for a third time in v. 11 using the double ἀμήν formula: ἀμὴν ἀμὴν λέγω σοι ὅτι ὃ οἴδαμεν λαλοῦμεν καὶ ὃ ἑωράκαμεν μαρτυροῦμεν, καὶ τὴν μαρτυρίαν ἡμῶν οὐ λαμβάνετε. Considering the composition history of the Fourth Gospel, the use of the plural here may reflect

60. Moloney, *Gospel of John*, 99.

the interests and perspectives of the Evangelist and his community.[61] However, the plural plays a more important role in the story. Like the reference to Nicodemus being ὁ διδάσκαλος τοῦ Ἰσραὴλ, Jesus's use of οἴδαμεν is another ironic reversal of Nicodemus's earlier confession in v. 2. In this way, the plural is similar to the Pauline use of "we" in an editorial fashion.[62]

Nicodemus does not comprehend the substance of Jesus's testimony and therefore fails to receive his teaching. Likewise, Nicodemus's fellow Jewish leaders will fail to receive Jesus's teaching, confirming what the reader has already learned in the prologue: εἰς τὰ ἴδια ἦλθεν, καὶ οἱ ἴδιοι αὐτὸν οὐ παρέλαβον (1:11).

To this point, Jesus has been speaking of elemental earthly matters (τὰ ἐπίγεια, v. 12a). If Nicodemus has been unable to grasp these basic truths, how will it be possible for him to grasp τὰ ἐπουράνια (v. 12b), about which Jesus has yet to speak? This master of the Torah has failed to appreciate Jesus's teaching on what it means to be spiritually reborn. With this question Jesus states explicitly what the reader has witnessed throughout the pericope. The educated and respected Jewish leader who should be a sympathetic hero in the reader's estimation is instead shown to be the picture of incomprehension.

Jesus and Nicodemus in John 7:45–52

Nicodemus makes his second appearance in ch. 7 just following a controversy over Jesus's identity. Throughout John 7 Jesus is confronted by the opinions of different groups, and in 7:25–36 he answers the questions and addresses the speculations from the residents of Jerusalem (τινες ἐκ τῶν Ἱεροσολυμιτῶν, v. 25), the crowds (ἐκ τοῦ ὄχλου δὲ πολλοὶ, v. 31), and the Jewish leaders (represented by οἱ ἀρχιερεῖς καὶ οἱ Φαρισαῖοι [v. 32], οἱ ὑπηρέται [v. 32], and οἱ Ἰουδαῖοι [v. 35]). In vv. 40–44, some confess that Jesus is ὁ προφήτης (v. 40) and some confess that he is ὁ χριστός (v. 41a), while others fail to believe that he is the Messiah because he is from Galilee (vv. 41b–42)—an ironic misunderstanding of Jesus's origins from the perspective of the prologue. After this division among the crowds the story returns to focus on the Jewish leaders and their desire to entrap Jesus.

61. Lincoln, *Gospel According to St. John*, 152.

62. See, for instance, the consistent use of the editorial "we" in 2 Corinthians 4–5.

In vv. 45–52 the Jewish leaders discuss Jesus with the temple officers who have been sent to apprehend him. A polemical response from the leaders toward the temple officers leads Nicodemus to caution the group by reminding them of their obligation to Torah. The response of the Jewish leaders to Nicodemus carries the same polemical tone as their response to the temple officers, and the reader senses in Nicodemus a sensitivity that was not present in his first appearance. This sensitivity is offset by the unbridled hostility of the Jewish leaders. The unit can be divided into the following sections:

1. The Jewish leaders discuss Jesus (7:45–49)
2. Nicodemus addresses the group (7:50–52)

The Jewish Leaders Discuss Jesus (7:45–49)

In v. 30 the reader learned that some of the Jerusalem residents wanted to seize Jesus (ἐζήτουν οὖν αὐτὸν πιάσαι) but did not because his hour had not yet come. Then in v. 32 temple officers (ὑπηρέται) are sent to seize Jesus (ἵνα πιάσωσιν αὐτόν) but they too fail to capture him. In v. 44 the debate about Jesus's identity concludes with the statement that some in the group likewise want to seize him (τινὲς δὲ ἤθελον ἐξ αὐτῶν πιάσαι αὐτόν) but they also fail to capture him. As v. 45 begins, "[t]he narrator now returns to the more official attempts to arrest Jesus which he had introduced in v. 32."[63]

In v. 45 the temple officers return to the chief priests and Pharisees empty-handed. The narrator does not report directly that the officers have failed to apprehend Jesus. Rather, this is implied by the question of the chief priests and Pharisees: "Why did you not bring him back?" (v. 45b).

The officers' reply reflects the ambivalence of the crowds that have just been debating Jesus's identity in vv. 40–44. They respond by saying οὐδέποτε ἐλάλησεν οὕτως ἄνθρωπος, "No one ever spoke like this man" (v. 46).[64] With this response the officers reveal that they have been persuaded or at least swayed by the teaching of Jesus. The incredulous response of the Jewish leaders follows: μὴ καὶ ὑμεῖς πεπλάνησθε; "You have not been deceived also, have you?" (v. 47). The reply of the offi-

63. Lincoln, *Gospel According to St. John*, 259.

64. Another acceptable translation of this verse could be "No *man* ever spoke like this," where the emphasis is placed on "man" rather than the speech.

cers creates an interesting link with vv. 50–52 as both the ὑπηρέται in this section and Nicodemus in the next section identify with Jesus. The hostility of the Jewish leaders toward Jesus allows this connection to emerge more clearly.

Here the educated Jewish leaders compare themselves to the members of the ignorant ὄχλος who do not know the Law. They ask, "None of the rulers or the Pharisees have believed in him, have they?" Again, the ἄρχων Ἰουδαίων (v. 48) function as the historical representatives of ὁ ἄρχων τοῦ κόσμου (12:31; 14:30; 16:11). The self-righteous leaders condemn the crowd as an accursed rabble, ignorant of the Jewish law (v. 49).[65]

Nicodemus Addresses the Group (7:50–52)

At this point Nicodemus steps onto the narrative stage once again and is reintroduced by two descriptive phrases. The narrator reminds the reader that he came to Jesus previously (ὁ ἐλθὼν πρὸς αὐτὸν [τὸ] πρότερον) and that he is one of the leaders (εἷς ὢν ἐξ αὐτῶν) (v. 50). While the reader will sense his sympathy toward Jesus in the following verse, the identification of Nicodemus as εἷς ὢν ἐξ αὐτῶν is an indication that Nicodemus's journey toward authentic Johannine belief remains incomplete. As before the reader's experience with Nicodemus is accompanied by a sense of ambiguity. His sympathies lie with Jesus, but as "one of them" his loyalties remain with his fellow Jewish leaders. Nevertheless, it is ironic that a representative of the characteristically hostile "Jews" has come forward in defense of Jesus.

The statement in v. 51 reminds the Jewish leaders of their responsibility to obey Torah: μὴ ὁ νόμος ἡμῶν κρίνει τὸν ἄνθρωπον ἐὰν μὴ ἀκούσῃ πρῶτον παρ᾽ αὐτοῦ καὶ γνῷ τί ποιεῖ; "Our law does not condemn a man unless it first hears from him and learns what he is doing, does it?" It is possible that Deut 1:16–17 (with its injunction to provide a fair hearing) is in view here. This possibility is stated by a num-

65. "Behind the Greek phrase lies the rabbinic technical term *'am ha-aretz*, which literally means 'people of the land' and was a derogatory, bitterly hostile designation for all Jews who did not observe the extensive prescriptions of the Law, especially with regard to tithes and Levitical cleanliness. The expression is connected with עמי הארץ, the term for the mixed pagan-Jewish population in the books of Ezra-Nehemiah, where it means those ignorant of the Law as such, those who did not really belong to Israel" (Schnackenburg, *Gospel According to St. John*, 2:160).

ber of commentators.[66] In addition to Deut 1:16–17, Talbert cites Deut 17:2–5; 19:15–19, *m. Sanh.* 5.4, and *Exod Rabbah* 21:3 as background to Nicodemus's comment.[67] Moloney argues that "[n]o legal precept in the Old Testament or in rabbinic Judaism demands that the accused be heard and that the accuser come to know what he does. Nicodemus enunciates a new understanding of the Law here."[68] Without quibbling too much about a specific OT referent, it should be noted that at the level of the story Nicodemus's appeal to his understanding of Torah (ὁ νόμος ἡμῶν) in defense of Jesus is highly significant for his overall characterization. This shows movement from judgments that are associated with the flesh (cf. 7:24; 8:15) to those characterized by spiritual insight. He uses the source of his religious authority (Torah) to come to Jesus's aid.

At this point in the story the Jewish leaders have established a reputation as those who are consistently hostile toward Jesus. Thus their response to Nicodemus who shows sympathy toward Jesus is predictable. Subtly castigating Nicodemus, they ask if he is also from Galilee (v. 52a). Admonishing him to investigate the Scriptures, the leaders comment, ἐκ τῆς Γαλιλαίας προφήτης οὐκ ἐγείρεται (v. 52b).[69] The leaders mistakenly believe that Jesus is from Galilee. This is true where his earthly origins are concerned, but the reader knows that Jesus's origins are heavenly. He is from above. The Jewish leaders revile him because they do not know where he is from.

The reply that "no prophet comes from Galilee" brings the scene to an abrupt end. Nicodemus's failure to respond to the identification of Jesus as ἐκ τῆς Γαλιλαίας is a subtle indication that he still fails to perceive properly Jesus's identity.

---

66. Among others see Bauer, *Johannesevangelium*, 115; Brown, *Gospel According to John*, 1:325; Lincoln, *Gospel According to St. John*, 259; Schnackenburg, *Gospel According to St. John*, 2:160.

67. Talbert, *Reading John*, 151.

68. Moloney, *Signs and Shadows*, 92.

69. One important witness ($\mathfrak{P}^{66*}$) includes the article before προφήτης. This reading likely reflects an addition, clarifying the text to indicate that the "prophet like Moses" (Deut 18:15) is in view. Since religious leaders would be aware that at least one OT prophet came from Galilee (see 2 Kgs 14:25), it is possible to take the anarthrous προφήτης in a qualitative sense and understand that the prophet like Moses is implied even without the article. For more on the qualitative sense in anarthrous constructions see Wallace, *Exegetical Syntax of the New Testament*, 244–45.

By the very fact that Nicodemus advocates for Jesus, he is separating himself from his fellow Jewish leaders. In addition, their abuse of him is also an indication that they are separating themselves from him. He has taken a step away from his previous posture of incomprehension but he has not yet made a definitive break from the Jewish leadership. In this way the characteristic of ambiguity emerges once again. Nicodemus actively positions himself against the group of which he remains a part.

In the end neither the ὑπηρέται nor Nicodemus can be classified as genuine Johannine believers, but their support for Jesus is a pervasive element of this brief scene. Nicodemus has been identified as a member of the Jewish leadership and for now he remains "one of them."

Jesus and Nicodemus in John 19:39–42

Nicodemus appears for a final time in this unit. He does not speak but the narrator's description shows that while he has made progress, his journey toward authentic belief will remain incomplete.

In his second appearance Nicodemus was reintroduced as the one who had previously come to Jesus and as one of the Jewish leaders. Here the narrator refers to him as Νικόδημος, ὁ ἐλθὼν πρὸς αὐτὸν νυκτὸς τὸ πρῶτον, "Nicodemus, who first came to him by night" (v. 39a). Absent from this description is any reference to Nicodemus being one of the Jewish leaders. Further, Nicodemus now comes accompanying Joseph, who in v. 38 is described as μαθητὴς τοῦ Ἰησοῦ. Whereas Joseph had previously kept his affection for Jesus secret "for fear of the Jews" (v. 38), he and Nicodemus now come to Pilate publicly to ask for the body of Jesus. These appear to be positive signs for the presentation of Nicodemus.

In v. 39b Nicodemus is pictured bringing a large mixture of myrrh and aloes for Jesus's body, a description that has raised a host of questions about how to understand this final scene. Is this to be understood as a royal burial?[70] Is this an indication that Nicodemus has misunderstood life after death?[71] Culpepper comments that Nicodemus "expresses his grief by bringing expensive spices, but finds no life in Jesus'

70. See Schnackenburg, *Gospel According to St. John*, 3:296–97, for this suggestion.

71. See Sylva, "Nicodemus and His Spices."

death."[72] Those characters in the Fourth Gospel who are associated with the body of Jesus on the cross (19:25–27) and in the events that follow (19:38; 20:1–9) are surely to be regarded as true disciples. And it seems that Nicodemus through his associations with Joseph (identified as a disciple) and the body of Jesus has himself become an authentic disciple. However, in v. 38 the narrator not only described Joseph as a disciple of Jesus but also commented that he asked for the body of Jesus secretly διὰ τὸν φόβον τῶν Ἰουδαίων. Like the parents of the young man born blind (9:20–23) and those in the crowd (12:42), Joseph (and Nicodemus by association) represent those who come to terms with Jesus's identity but allow their faith to lurk behind the scenes for fear of reprisal by the Jewish leaders.

In vv. 40–42 Joseph and Nicodemus take the proper steps (in accord with Jewish burial customs, τοῖς Ἰουδαίοις ἐνταφιάζειν) to embalm and bury Jesus. After this section Nicodemus disappears from the story. The narrator does not stop to comment further, but the reader realizes that although Nicodemus has come a long way, he still judges from the perspective of the flesh. He remains sympathetic to Jesus but still comes secretly "for fear of the Jews." He entered the narrative as the picture of ambiguity, and though he has come a long way, some of that ambiguity remains as he departs.

Conclusion

In these three passages the reader has witnessed Nicodemus's transition from confusion at Jesus's words, to sympathy with Jesus's plight, to affection for Jesus himself. He does not attain to complete Johannine discipleship, as he is still associated (through Joseph of Arimathea) with a "fear of the Jews" (19:38). Nicodemus remains shrouded in ambiguity. He wants to identify with Jesus but, as in ch. 3, he continues to approach Jesus secretly for fear of the Jews. Nicodemus has come a long way but cannot be considered a true Johannine disciple. In the words of Culpepper, "He remains, therefore, 'one of them,' not one of the children of God."[73]

72. Culpepper, *Anatomy of the Fourth Gospel*, 136.

73. Ibid.

Jesus and the Samaritan Woman in John 4:4–42

The next individual in the story to interact with Jesus after his conversation with Nicodemus is the unnamed woman of Samaria. The episode with the Samaritan woman presents the reader with a number of striking contrasts to the first Nicodemus episode.[74] The first and most obvious contrast is their difference in gender. In addition, Nicodemus is identified by name while the woman remains anonymous throughout her interaction with Jesus. Nicodemus is a religious leader of some standing, while she is a Samaritan and therefore considered a religious and ethnic half-breed.[75] He approaches Jesus at night while the unnamed woman approaches the well (not Jesus) at noon. Like Nicodemus, the woman initially misunderstands Jesus's enigmatic speech. However, the outcome of the two episodes is quite different. While Nicodemus leaves his first encounter with Jesus in absolute confusion, the woman of Samaria walks away with a reluctant faith (cf. 1:29). But, despite her positive outcome in the eyes of the reader, the woman of Samaria, like others before her, initially fails to understand Jesus at several turns in their conversation. These points of misunderstanding will be examined in the present discussion.[76]

Johannine scholars have recognized that the episode with the Samaritan woman follows the pattern of OT betrothal scenes (e.g., Isaac and Rebekah in Gen 24; Jacob and Rachel in Gen 29; Moses and Zipporah in Exod 2).[77] An awareness of the episode's parallels to OT betrothal scenes creates expectations in the reader that go unfulfilled.

74. "He was learned, powerful, respected, orthodox, theologically trained; she was unschooled, without influence, despised, capable only of folk religion. He was a man, a Jew, a ruler; she was a woman, a Samaritan, a moral outcast. And both needed Jesus" (Carson, *The Gospel According to John*, 216).

75. "A number of references in the Gospels view them as neither fully Jewish nor fully Gentile, as straddling the borders between the Jewish and Gentile worlds (cf., e.g., Matt. 10.5–6). The origins of the Samaritans and the time of their increased divergence from elements of mainstream Judaism are shrouded in obscurity because of the sparsity of the sources and their predominantly polemical nature" (Lincoln, *Gospel According to St. John*, 172).

76. For a creative and thorough examination of the Samaritan woman from a number of perspectives including historic interpretation, art, and modern interpretive methods, see Day, *Woman at the Well.*

77. See, e.g., Neyrey, "What's Wrong with This Picture? 83; idem, *Gospel of John*, 91; Lincoln, *Gospel According to St. John*, 170; Conway, *Men and Women in the Fourth Gospel*, 106–9.

An interesting sexual tension also arises that likewise results in the reader's unfulfilled expectations. Overall this episode provides a number of twists that create surprises for the reader.[78] The betrothal expectations and sexual tension are ultimately abandoned within the story and the initially unsympathetic Samaritan woman becomes a sympathetic Johannine insider. Throughout her conversation with Jesus, the Samaritan woman manifests misunderstanding, but her departure to Sychar brings with it a reluctant acceptance that Jesus is not only prophet (4:19) but also Messiah (4:29). The passage can be read in four parts:

1. Jesus travels through Samaria (4:4–6)
2. Jesus and the woman converse (4:7–26)
    a. Exchange over water (4:7–18)
    b. Exchange over worship (4:19–26)
3. Conversation with the disciples (4:27–38)[79]
    a. Return and departure (4:27–30)
    b. Exchange over food (4:31–38)
4. Jesus and the citizens of Sychar (4:39–42)

Jesus Travels through Samaria (4:4–6)

In the preceding unit (4:1–3) the narrator explained that Jesus left Judea for Galilee because the Pharisees had learned of his success in making and baptizing disciples. This section begins by providing the reader with information about Jesus's response to the knowledge of the Pharisees.

In v. 4 the narrator comments, ἔδει δὲ αὐτὸν διέρχεσθαι διὰ τῆς Σαμαρείας. It is commonly argued that the trip through Samaria was the shortest route to Galilee and that ἔδει should be understood as an indicator of geographical necessity.[80] Evidence from Josephus is often presented to support the claim that it was necessary for travelers to pass through Samaria on their way to Galilee.[81] However, the trip through

78. "Indeed, a major element in the account's literary structuring is the way it builds on but subverts the betrothal type-scene" (Lincoln, *Gospel According to St. John*, 170).

79. Since this unit was examined in detail in chapter 5 I will provide here only a summary of the exegesis offered above.

80. Among others see Bultmann, *Gospel of John*, 176.

81. E.g., Barrett (*Gospel According to St. John*, 230) writes that the necessity of passing through Samaria is "confirmed by Josephus." He then cites Vita 269: "Samaria was

Samaria was not geographically necessary, as Brown has pointed out: "[T]he *main route* from Judea to Galilee was through Samaria, [but] if Jesus was in the Jordan valley (iii 22) he could easily have gone north through the valley and then up into Galilee through the Bethshan gap, avoiding Samaria."[82]

The term ἔδει (δεῖ) is used elsewhere in the narrative in reference to the will of the Father (cf. 3:14, 30; 4:20, 24; 9:4; 10:16), indicating that it is an expression of theological import in the Fourth Gospel. Hence, it appears that ἔδει should be read in the present context as a reference to the constraining will of God. In what follows the reader will understand that Jesus has been compelled by the Father to pass through Samaria for the purpose of meeting the woman.

The following verses add greater specificity to the physical setting of the episode. On his way through Samaria Jesus reaches a town called Sychar (v. 5a), which is further described by the narrator as being "near the tract of land that Jacob gave to his son Joseph" (v. 5b). There are a number of questions surrounding both Jacob's well and the city of Sychar.

Though there is a site known as "Jacob's Well" explicitly linked to the patriarch through tradition, the Jacob texts in Genesis never picture Jacob digging a well. However, there are passages in Genesis that picture Jacob acquiring the land of Shechem (Gen 33:19) and giving that land to Joseph (Gen 48:22).[83] The area previously known as Shechem is close to modern Askar. Some scholars equate Sychar with Askar, "which lies close to the site identified by continuous tradition with the 'Jacob's Well' of antiquity."[84] Therefore, a tenuous connection can be made between Sychar and Shechem, though scholars are divided on this point.[85]

Historical questions aside, for the purposes of the unfolding story it is significant that Jesus's location is explicitly associated with the pa-

now under Roman rule and, for rapid travel it was essential (ἔδει) to take that route (sc. through Samaria), by which Jerusalem may be reached in three days from Galilee."

82. Brown, *Gospel According to John*, 1:169; emphasis added.

83. Gen 48:22 reads, "I give you one portion (שכם) more than your brothers which I took from the hand of the Amorites by my sword and bow." Notably, the LXX translates the Hebrew noun שכם with the proper name Σικιμα (= Shechem).

84. Barrett, *Gospel According to St. John*, 231.

85. Schnackenburg (*Gospel According to St. John*, 1:421–23) embraces this connection while Brown (*Gospel According to John*, 1:169) rejects it, writing that it is "probably wrong on several counts."

triarch Jacob. Neyrey is persuasive in his argument that this account cannot be understood properly apart from an awareness of the Jacob traditions.[86] Those traditions not only inform the background of the episode but also provide a foundation for the reader's expectation of a betrothal scene. During the course of the conversation several comparisons are drawn between Jesus and Jacob that result in the conclusion that Jesus has superseded the patriarchs. This theme appears several times in the Fourth Gospel.[87]

Lincoln points out that the standard features of a "betrothal type-scene" are: (1) a potential bridegroom or his representative travels to a foreign land, (2) he encounters a woman at a well, (3) there is a dialogue about water in which water is asked for or offered, (4) the woman hurries home to report the stranger's arrival, (5) the bridegroom is then invited to the future father-in-law's home where a betrothal is arranged at a meal.[88] As this scene opens Jesus is traveling through foreign territory (feature 1), and in the following section he encounters a woman at the well (feature 2) where water will become the first major topic of discussion (feature 3). The woman eventually departs to her home (feature 4), but by that point in the story the reader's expectations have been undermined and replaced with new expectations. In addition to the parallel features already listed, the explicit mention of Jacob and Joseph along with Jacob's well (πηγὴ τοῦ Ἰακώβ, v. 6a) helps the reader recall the betrothal traditions and heightens the expectation of such a scene in this passage.

The physical setting of this episode has now been established precisely. The reader knows that Jesus is in the *region of Samaria* (v. 4), outside the *town of Sychar* (v. 5), and by the *well of Jacob* (v. 6). This "public space" becomes the setting for Jesus's conversation with the Samaritan woman.[89] After establishing the physical setting the narrator provides

86. Neyrey, "Jacob Traditions and the Interpretation of John 4:10–26."

87. In 4:12 the woman asks Jesus, "You are not greater than our father Jacob, are you?" Then in 8:53 the Jewish leaders ask Jesus, "You are not greater than our father Abraham who died, are you?" Neyrey ("Jacob Traditions," 419) comments that these questions "belong to a theme in the Gospel which asserts Jesus's superiority to the founding fathers of traditional Jewish religion." The theme of Jesus's superiority to Moses is also present in the Fourth Gospel (see, e.g., 1:17).

88. Lincoln, *Gospel According to St. John*, 170. For similar comments, see also Alter, *Art of Biblical Narrative*, 52.

89. Neyrey ("What's Wrong With This Picture?" 78) argues that though this episode

the situational and temporal settings for the episode. Tired from his journey, Jesus sits down beside the well (ἐκαθέζετο οὕτως ἐπὶ τῇ πηγῇ, v. 6b)[90] "at about the sixth hour" (ὥρα ἦν ὡς ἕκτη, i.e., noon, v. 6c).[91] Now that the reader is aware of the what, where, and when of this episode, the stage is set for Jesus's interaction with the woman.

Jesus and the Woman Converse (4:7–26)

To this point in the Gospel the reader has witnessed only one interaction between Jesus and a female character. In 2:1–11 Jesus and his mother have a brief, and some argue tense, exchange over the need for more wine at the wedding in Cana. The mother of Jesus instructs the waiters at the banquet to do whatever Jesus tells them and then she leaves the scene (v. 5). With this command she becomes the first Johannine believer to exercise faith in the word (rather than the works) of Jesus.[92]

In his question to her in 2:4, Jesus addresses his mother as "woman," γύναι. Echoes of that conversation appear in the present unit, as the narrator continually reminds the reader that the Samaritan is a woman (vv. 7, 9, 15, 17, 19, 25) and as Jesus directly addresses as γύναι (v. 21). Like Jesus's mother, the Samaritan woman will eventually come to terms with Jesus's identity on the basis of his words (vv. 19, 29) rather than his works.

The Samaritan woman enters the scene in v. 7 and the conversation begins with Jesus's request for water. His request provokes the woman,

occurs in public space, "the author intends the scenario described there to be perceived as the 'private' world of kinship groups." He continues, "They may be narrated as occurring 'out of doors,' but the meetings of Jesus and the woman (4:7–26) and the woman and the villagers (4:39–42) should ultimately be seen as the formation of fictive kinship groups, and so they are governed by the customs of the 'private' rather than 'public.'"

90. Moloney (*Gospel of John*, 121) suggests that this phrase implies a "genuine settling down for rest." In addition, Stephen Moore argues that this passage is as much about the needs of Jesus (i.e., the need for rest, the need for water, the need for her to need his gift, etc.) as the spiritual needs of the woman. See Moore's interesting study, "Are There Impurities in the Living Water? 208.

91. But see Culpepper (*Anatomy of the Fourth Gospel*, 219), who suggests that the phrase should be understood as 6:00 p.m. While it is generally held that "the sixth hour" corresponds to midday, Johannine scholars have not settled definitively the issue of reckoning time in the Fourth Gospel.

92. On this see Moloney, *Gospel of John*, 66–70. In opposition to this view, Stibbe (*John*, 62) remarks that the episode with the Samaritan woman "is the first narrative in John's story which portrays women in a more favourable light than men."

and the resultant conversation moves through topics as diverse as Jewish-Samaritan relations (v. 9), Jesus's identity (vv. 10–12), the background of the woman (vv. 16–18), and the nature of true worship (vv. 20–24).

Exchange over Water (4:7–18)

Jesus is seated by the well exhausted from his journey when "a woman of Samaria" comes to draw water. The narrator's initial description of the woman creates the first contrast with the Nicodemus episode in ch. 3. He was introduced as ἄνθρωπος ἐκ τῶν Φαρισαίων (3:1), while she is introduced as γυνὴ ἐκ τῆς Σαμαρείας (v. 7a).[93] In addition, whereas the reader learns more about the status and identity of the "man of the Pharisees" (e.g., Νικόδημος ὄνομα αὐτῷ and ἄρχων τῶν Ἰουδαίων), the description of the woman ends here. The reader is aware only of her gender (female), her home (Samaria), and her purpose in coming to the well (to draw water), and therefore must read further to learn more about her. As it stands, her credentials are much less impressive than those of Nicodemus. As a woman from Samaria without a name in the story, her journey begins in an unflattering light in the eyes of the reader, and therefore she is not initially a sympathetic character with whom the reader will identify.

As the woman approaches the well, Jesus makes a polite request of her: δός μοι πεῖν (v. 7b).[94] In the eyes of a pious Jew it would have been as scandalous for Jesus to speak with a woman as with a Samaritan.[95] Jesus's request of the Samaritan woman is followed by a narrative aside to the reader explaining that the disciples had gone off to buy food (v. 8). The purpose of this parenthetical comment is twofold. First, it explains

93. Some argue that the woman is a representative of all Samaritans, but more convincing is the argument of Moloney (*Gospel of John*, 121) that "the thrust of 4:7–30 is to show the response of this woman to the word of Jesus. The passage as a whole (i.e., vv. 1–42) is directed to the response of Samaritans, representatives of the world beyond the borders of Israel, but this becomes clear only at the end of the passage when Samaritans make a confession of faith in Jesus."

94. This use of the imperative likely falls into the category of "polite request" (see Wallace, *Exegetical Syntax of the New Testament*, 487–88) and should not be read with the force of a command.

95. That Jesus crosses two cultural boundaries in speaking with a woman and a Samaritan is widely recognized in the commentary tradition. Talbert (*Reading John*, 112–13) provides a helpful background discussion on the two elements of a man speaking with a woman and a Jew interacting with a Samaritan.

to the reader why Jesus is asking the woman rather than the disciples to assist him in getting a drink. Second, it both anticipates and answers the reader's question concerning the whereabouts of Jesus's disciples who have just been mentioned in v. 2. Their absence from the scene provides the occasion for this interaction to take place.[96]

In ch. 3, Nicodemus initiated the discussion and Jesus responded. Here Jesus initiates the discussion with his request and the woman responds indignantly: πῶς σὺ Ἰουδαῖος ὢν παρ᾽ ἐμου πεῖν αἰτεῖς γυναικὸς Σαμαρίτιδος οὔσης; (v. 9a). This abrasive response contains the only instance in the Fourth Gospel where Jesus is identified as Ἰουδαῖος. The woman's reply is indicative of the realism with which her portrait is drawn in this opening section.[97] This realism is further highlighted by the second narrative aside in these two verses, οὐ γὰρ συγχρῶνται Ἰουδαῖοι Σαμαρίταις, "For Jews do not share things in common[98] with Samaritans" (v. 9b).[99]

Historically, tensions between Jews and Samaritans developed around the time of Israel's return from exile. During that period most Jews "viewed the Samaritans not only as the children of political rebels but as racial half-breeds whose religion was tainted by various unacceptable elements."[100] Among those elements were the rival temple built on Mt. Gerizim and the acceptance of the Pentateuch alone as authoritative

96. "From a narrative point of view, the mention of [Jesus'] thirst—along with the absence of the disciples—is a literary ploy by the narrator to engage Jesus in conversation with the woman" (Lee, *Flesh and Glory*, 73).

97. "The woman in John 4 is first of all presented *realistically*; she is certainly no cardboard stereotype. When Jesus asks her for a drink of water, she responds with indignation: 'How can you, a Jew, ask me for a drink'. When Jesus points out that she is acting in ignorance, that she does not recognize the living water which Jesus as to offer, she replies with sarcasm" (Stibbe, *John*, 66).

98. This translation is suggested by David Daube ("Jesus and the Samaritan Woman") who argues that the background of the term in this context is the assumption that the Samaritans were ritually impure.

99. Addressing the *Sitz im Leben* of the Fourth Gospel in relation to this passage, Collins (*These Things Have Been Written*, 16–17) writes, "Underlying the story there lies quite clearly the issue of the relationship between the Jews and the Samaritans, but in the situation of the Christian church in which this account took shape there was the more urgent issue of the relationship between Jewish Christians and Samaritan Christians . . . [I]t would appear that in v. 9 John is not so much concerned with showing that Jesus was willing to break a ritual prohibition imposed by the Pharisees, but that he destroyed the basis for any hatred between Jew and Samaritan."

100. Carson, *Gospel According to John*, 216.

Scripture. These features of Samaritan religious life were abhorrent to Jews and greatly contributed to the enmity that developed between the two groups.

In the previous chapter the reader witnessed an initially sympathetic character in Nicodemus who walked away from Jesus without spiritual understanding. In each instance where Nicodemus posed a question (vv. 4, 9) he began with πῶς, "how?" and each question revealed further the extent of his incomprehension. Here the reader is presented with an *unsympathetic* character who likewise begins her first question with πῶς. Thus it appears as though the narrator is baiting the reader into a false expectation that this conversation will run its course in a manner similar to the first Nicodemus episode. In any case, the normal course of an expected betrothal scene has been interrupted by the woman's abrasive reply.

Here Jesus abandons the double ἀμήν formula that was so pervasive in the first Nicodemus episode and answers the woman's question directly. He tells her that if she had known the gift of God and who it is that speaks to her, she would have asked him for a drink and he would have provided ὕδωρ ζῶν (v. 10). At least three elements of Jesus's reply to the woman deserve greater attention.

First, Neyrey has argued that the background to Jesus's use of τὴν δωρεὰν τοῦ θεοῦ is informed significantly by a knowledge of the targumic expansions of Numbers 21:18–19. It takes some work to draw the connection between Jacob and the well in Num 21, but Neyrey fits the pieces of the puzzle together:

> The trend of some traditions was not to associate Jacob with any particular well, but to link him with the traveling well tradition (see 1 Cor 10:4) . . . The legend of the traveling well should, of course, be linked primarily with Miriam's well in Numbers 21. But as the Targums on Numbers 21 indicate, Miriam's well was itself simply the old patriarchal well which had been lost and was only then rediscovered . . . Hence, while there is nothing in the legends to suggest why Jacob specifically should be associated with a given well at Bethel or Shechem, he is linked to the general well tradition.[101]

101. Neyrey, "Jacob Traditions," 420.

I suggest, therefore, that the reader aware of the cultural script will recognize the subtle connection between the patriarch Jacob and the Pentateuchal well traditions.

In Num 21:16 it is reported that when the children of Israel arrived at Beer, YHWH promised Moses, "I will give them water." Then in vv. 18–19 the Hebrew text includes two references to the region of Mattanah. In the MT Num 21:18 reads, "And from the wilderness they went to Mattanah" (מתנה). In the LXX the text was mistranslated as καὶ ἀπὸ φρέατος εἰς Μανθαναιν, "and from *the cistern* into Mattanah." The reading morphed again in the targumic literature where the name מתנה came to be associated with the Hebrew root for "gift," נתן. The Targums read, "And from the wilderness it was *given* to them as a *gift*."[102] Hence, the miraculous well provided by YHWH throughout the Pentateuch was associated (at least in the targumic literature) with the "gift of God."[103] This connection would likely have informed the original reader's experience with the Fourth Gospel in the present passage and therefore sheds some light on our understanding of the implied reader's experience.

Second, there is some debate over whether Jesus himself is the gift or whether some other gift is to be understood by τὴν δωρεὰν τοῦ θεοῦ.[104] In the present context it seems best to take the genitive in the objective sense and understand that Jesus is the gift from God. This interpretation emerges even more in the second part of Jesus's response: καὶ τίς ἐστιν ὁ λέγων σοι. Taken epexegetically, the καί here links the "gift of God" with "the one who is speaking." As in 3:16, Jesus is God's gift and he offers himself to the woman.

Third, the phrase ὕδωρ ζῶν was a common euphemism for "flowing water" (as opposed to stagnant cistern water).[105] This double meaning gives rise to the Samaritan woman's first misunderstanding.

102. *Tg. Neo,* Num 21:18 reads, "And from the wilderness it was *given* to them as a *gift*." *Tg. Yer 1* Num 21:18 reads, "And from the desert it was *given* to them." *Tg. Yer 2* Num 21:18 reads, "And from the desert it was *given* to them as a *gift*."

103. Schnackenburg (*Gospel According to St. John*, 1:426) regards δωρεά as a much broader term in this context, arguing that it is "a comprehensive term for everything that God bestows on man for his salvation."

104. Brown, *Gospel According to John*, 1:170.

105. The phrase "living water" in religious writings has a history of pointing to a reality beyond the literal and material realities of water. For examples from Jewish, Christian, and Hellenistic texts, see Barrett, *Gospel According to St. John*, 233–34.

Like those characters already discussed in this study, she perceives only the literal meaning of Jesus's words and misses the point that Jesus is offering cleansing, life-giving water. Again, as with the first Nicodemus episode, the peculiar image of water is introduced to signify spiritual cleansing and renewal.[106]

The woman's failure to understand is revealed in v. 11 by her observations (κύριε, οὔτε ἄντλημα ἔχεις καὶ τὸ φρέαρ ἐστιν βαθύ) and her question (πόθεν οὖν ἔχεις τὸ ὕδωρ ζῶν;). The comment that Jesus has nothing with which to draw water presupposes the woman's misunderstanding of τὸ ὕδωρ ζῶν. Also the use of κύριε, "sir," by the Samaritan woman is ironic in light of the reader's awareness of Jesus's divine origins. Jesus is ὁ κύριος but in a sense different than she perceives. Her polite addressing of Jesus with κύριε also signals a slight movement from the abrasiveness of σὺ Ἰουδαῖος ὢν (v. 9) to a more polite discourse, though a mocking tone remains in the words of v. 12.

The interrogative term πῶς (v. 9a) is now replaced by πόθεν (v. 11b). The woman continues questioning Jesus as she struggles to come to terms with his identity. However, the change from πῶς to πόθεν alerts the implied reader to another subtle but nonetheless important difference between this conversation and the first Nicodemus episode. Nicodemus's response to Jesus's teaching remained static, and he departed in confusion. This subtle change represents a growth in the woman's understanding of and approach to Jesus.

A comparison between Jesus and Jacob has been lurking beneath the surface of this pericope, and in v. 12 the woman makes it explicit by drawing a direct comparison between Jesus and the patriarch. In a question that expects a negative answer, the woman asks Jesus if he is greater than τοῦ πατρὸς ἡμῶν Ἰακώβ. Her question to Jesus is ironic inasmuch as it unwittingly affirms what the reader knows to be true. Jesus was with God in the beginning. He is indeed greater than Jacob. There is thus a tension between the knowledge of the reader who has read the prologue and the knowledge of the woman who has not.

In and of itself the woman's question could be considered sincere, but the string of clauses that follows, introduced by the relative ὅς, appears to be an attempt at denigrating Jesus. According to the woman, the well was built by Jacob (1) who drank from it himself (αὐτὸς ἐξ

106. See Lee, *Flesh and Glory*, 65–87, for an insightful treatment of the Johannine water symbol both in ch. 4 and throughout the Gospel.

αὐτοῦ ἔπιεν), (2) whose sons drank from it (καὶ οἱ υἱοὶ αὐτοῦ), and (3) whose livestock drank from it (καὶ τὰ θρέμματα αὐτοῦ). This string of clauses is governed by one relative pronoun and connected by καί in three places. The resultant force is a comparison between Jesus and Jacob, Jesus and Jacob's sons, and Jesus and Jacob's livestock. For the Samaritan woman, all things associated with the patriarch (including his sons and his livestock) are superior to this man with whom she is conversing. Even in light of the woman's use of κύριε, the tone of her reply remains one of mockery.

Again Jesus abandons the double ἀμήν formula and answers the woman directly. He distances himself from the woman's direct comparison to Jacob and instead draws a comparison between the water from Jacob's well and the water he offers. Speaking from the perspective of literal water, Jesus states that everyone who drinks from Jacob's well will thirst again (v. 13). This is a self-evident principle based upon natural laws governing human need. On the other hand, there are two lasting implications of drinking the "water" Jesus provides. First, whoever drinks (ὃς δ᾽ ἂν πίῃ)[107] Jesus's water will never again experience thirst (οὐ μὴ διψήσει εἰς τὸν αἰῶνα, v. 14a). Second, whoever drinks the water Jesus gives will experience within a fountain springing up to eternal life (πηγὴ ὕδατος ἀλλομένου εἰς ζωὴν αἰώνιον). The eternal implications of drinking the water Jesus offers are signaled by the use of αἰών/αἰώνιος in both halves of the verse.

The use of οὐ μή plus the aorist subjunctive in v. 14a functions in the same manner as other instances of emphatic negation already discussed in this study. This construction is the most emphatic way to negate something in Hellenistic Greek; here (as in 13:8) the construction is followed by εἰς τὸν αἰῶνα—intensifying the rhetorical impact of the phrase.[108]

Neyrey draws another connection between the Jacob traditions and Jesus's words that is especially pertinent to this stage of the conversation:

107. The change from πᾶς ὁ πίνων in v. 13 to ὃς δ᾽ ἂν πίῃ in v. 14 "points to a universal, once-for-all drinking, eliminating a continual need to return to the source of the water" (Moloney, *Gospel of John*, 123).

108. As noted in chapters 3 and 4, the combination of οὐ μή plus the aorist subjunctive is used to deny the potentiality of an action. For more on this see Wallace, *Exegetical Syntax of the New Testament*, 468.

> In the legends about Jacob mention is made of a miracle whereby water would automatically surge to the top of Jacob's well and overflow, a phenomenon well-attested in the Targums of Genesis 28 and in other Midrashic accounts: "Five miracles were wrought for our father Jacob at the time that he went forth from Beersheba . . . The fourth sign: the well overflowed, and the water rose to the edge of it, and continued to overflow all the time he was in Haran."[109]

The woman's understanding of the well is likely informed by a tradition such as this one, which helps to explain the significance of the phrase πηγὴ ὕδατος ἀλλομένου εἰς ζωὴν αἰώνιον.[110] The comparison is subtle but striking: Jacob's presence caused his well to overflow while he was in the region. Jesus is in the region but the water he offers will overflow even after he is gone. The water he offers will spring up eternally. This subtle point again contrasts Jesus with Jacob and reminds the implied reader that Jesus is greater than the fathers of the Jewish religion (cf. 1:17).

A role reversal has been developing throughout the conversation and it reaches its culmination in v. 15. The woman began as a potential giver (v. 7) and here becomes the potential receiver. Noting this reversal, Lee writes, "Ignoring the obstacles and the woman's objection, Jesus reverses the roles of giver and receiver, presenting himself as the water-giver and the woman the one who is thirsty and lacking the means of slaking her thirst."[111] In v. 7 Jesus said to her, "give me a drink." Here in v. 15 she says to Jesus, "Sir, give me this water." The reversal can be outlined in the following way:

Jesus speaking, v. 7b:	δός	μοι	πεῖν
Woman speaking, v. 15b:	δός	μοι	τοῦτο τὸ ὕδωρ

What was previously a posture of mockery has now become a posture characterized by openness. The woman persists in her overly literal interpretation of Jesus's words, but she is at least open to receiving what he has to offer. Her language (δός μοι) recalls Jesus's earlier discussion

109. Neyrey, "Jacob Traditions," 420.

110. The text uses two words for well/cistern: πηγή (vv. 6, 14) and φρέαρ (vv. 11, 12). While some commentators argue that there is an intended theological difference, I find it more convincing that this is yet another instance where Johannine synonyms are being used.

111. Lee, *Flesh and Glory*, 72.

of τὴν δωρεὰν τοῦ θεοῦ (v. 10). At the level of the story her openness is driven by a desire to avoid returning to the well (v. 15c). Significant, however, is the fact that she is no longer questioning Jesus but making a request of him. As before (v. 11) the woman shows a slight progression in her response to Jesus, unlike Nicodemus who remained consistently confused and questioning.

Perhaps more than any other verse in this pericope, v. 16 suggests the woman's role as a foil. In John 6 Jesus asks Philip a question for the express purpose of testing him because, according to the narrator, Jesus "already knew what he was going to do" (6:6). Though not explicitly stated by the narrator, the same dynamic is at work in 4:16. Jesus places one requirement on the woman's reception of ὕδωρ ζῶν. He instructs her, ὕπαγε φώνησον τὸν ἄνδρα σου καὶ ἐλθὲ ἐνθάδε. As will be revealed in the following verse, Jesus already knows the details of her home situation, and it therefore becomes clear that he says this with the purpose of testing her. This request is a narrative ploy to advance the plot (by informing the reader of the woman's background) and to make the woman a foil. She is shown to be a foil as her answer (v. 17b) and Jesus's subsequent correction of her answer (v. 17c) create an opportunity for Jesus to clarify the nature of true worship (vv. 21–23) and his identity (v. 26; cf. v. 10: τίς ἐστιν ὁ λέγων σοι).

When Jesus tells her to call her husband she responds, οὐκ ἔχω ἄνδρα (v. 17b). In affirming her words Jesus replies καλῶς εἶπας ὅτι ἄνδρα οὐκ ἔχω (v. 17c). The ὅτι in this sentence is introducing direct discourse, but Jesus's reply does not reflect the woman's exact wording, as one would typically expect in instances of direct discourse. Instead Jesus's reply places the word ἄνδρα at the front rather than the back of the phrase, subtly indicating that Jesus aims to emphasize what the woman has attempted to deemphasize (viz., the presence or absence of an ἄνδρα in her life).[112] While she admits that she does not have a husband the woman is not forthcoming about what (or whom) she does have. She leaves out the five previous husbands and her current paramour.

112. Word order in Hellenistic Greek is quite flexible. Therefore, it is not uncommon to see the direct object at multiple places in the sentence. However, here the word order in both instances seems to reflect deliberate attempts at de-emphasis (the woman's words) and emphasis (Jesus's words).

If the reader's expectations of a betrothal scene had not been dashed to this point, they are dashed definitively in v. 18. Jesus's directive to "go call your husband" has resulted in her frank but incomplete admission that she has no husband. After Jesus affirms this he adds, πέντε γὰρ ἄνδρας ἔσχες καὶ νῦν ὃν ἔχεις οὐκ ἔστιν σου ἀνήρ. There is no longer reason to suspect that this will end in betrothal. Her scandalous past is now on display and there can be no pretense to chastity.[113] On this facet of the interaction with the woman vis-à-vis betrothal scenes Neyrey comments,

> Because the key element of a worthy wife is virginity or sexual exclusivity, the narratives all insist that the social intercourse at the well be strictly in accord with cultural customs. Females are shy and defensive of their virtue, speak respectfully to males, and obey when commanded. They then seek the shelter of the 'private' world as soon as possible. But the Samaritan woman is hardly "sexually exclusive," not with five husbands and still another male in her life. Her appearance at noon independent of the company of other women suggests an outcast.[114]

Jesus's knowledge astounds the woman, and as she struggles to come to terms with his identity the conversation shifts abruptly from the topic of "living water" to the topic of true worship.

Exchange over Worship (4:19–26)

Jesus's three imperatives in v. 16 (ὕπαγε, φώνησον, ἐλθέ) redirect the conversation from the gift of ὕδωρ ζῶν to the woman's personal life. In v. 19 the woman in turn redirects the conversation from Jesus's revelations about her marital status to the locale (and ultimately the nature) of worship.

From a literary perspective the purpose of the woman's confession, κύριε, θεωρῶ ὅτι προφήτης εἶ σύ (v. 19) is twofold.[115] First, this statement brings about a comedic moment as the reader witnesses

113. Feminist critics have been quick to point out that the woman's situation should not be regarded as evidence of the woman's unrighteousness or wanton promiscuity. See, for instance, Conway, *Men and Women in the Fourth Gospel*, 117–18.

114. Neyrey, *Gospel of John*, 91.

115. θεωρέω in this instance should probably be understood in the sense of coming to an intellectual understanding. See BDAG, s.v. θεωρέω.

a gratuitous change of subject by the Samaritan woman.[116] Second, in light Jesus's insightful words to the woman, her confession is also an affirmation of his knowledge. Her conception of προφήτης is likely that of the "prophet like Moses" from Deut 18:15–18 and includes some element of knowledge that is not accessible to the average individual. She has not yet arrived at Johannine faith, but she has already made it further than Nicodemus who was only able to confess Jesus as ῥαββί. The woman successfully redirects the focus of the conversation, and her speculations on the identity of Jesus serve as a segue to her questions about worship.

Since there is enough evidence to regard Jesus as a prophet the woman decides to discuss with him the ideas of worship that have historically divided Jews and Samaritans. Drawing a distinction between Samaritan religious practice (οἱ πατέρες ἡμῶν . . . προσεκύνησαν) and Jewish religious teaching (καὶ ὑμεῖς λέγετε), the woman raises the question of the proper place of worship.[117] Samaritan tradition held that Mt. Gerizim was the proper place of worship and the place where YHWH dealt with his people. Reading OT passages through the grid of their own religious interests, the Samaritans "continued to use this mountain in northern Palestine for their rites even after the destruction of their temple by Hyrcanus."[118] The Jewish temple was located in Jerusalem; since the Deuteronomic code mandated one place of worship, a division emerged between Jews and Samaritans. The woman's observation (and implied question) is solely related to the proper locale of worship, and Jesus's answer corresponds to her understanding of προφήτης and answers the "how" of worship rather than the "where."

The previous universal offer of cleansing water to "anyone who drinks" (v. 14a) is recalled by Jesus's teaching on the universality of worship. In a response that reemphasizes her gender and recalls the prior conversation with his mother, Jesus begins his reply with the words πίστευέ μοι, γύναι. This introductory formula is the closest thing in

116. Moloney (*Gospel of John*, 128) argues that she "raises the question of Gerizim and Jerusalem (v. 20) not to steer Jesus away from her personal secrets but, on the basis of her perception that Jesus is a prophet, to delve into 'an age-old problem debated between Samaritans and Jews.'" However, the abrupt change in subject matter suggests the woman's deflection of attention from her personal life.

117. Technically speaking, the woman makes a direct statement, but a question is clearly implied by her comparison of Jewish and Samaritan approaches to worship.

118. Barrett, *Gospel According to St. John*, 236.

the conversation to the double ἀμήν formula used in each response to Nicodemus in ch. 3.[119] It is significant that πιστεύω is used inasmuch as belief is the central theological emphasis of the Fourth Gospel. In the end the woman's belief will move beyond simple statements about the place and nature of worship. For now, however, the focus is on the distinction between Jewish and Samaritan approaches to worship.

In answer to the woman's proposed alternative (Mt. Gerizim or Jerusalem), Jesus answers by speaking of a time (lit. "hour," ὥρα) when neither locale will serve as the place for worshiping the Father. Here Jesus envisages an eschatological period when there will be no temple and the debate between Jew and Samaritan will become irrelevant. It is noteworthy that Jesus speaks of worshiping "the Father" (v. 21) rather than simply God. The word πατήρ appears throughout the woman's conversation with Jesus. In v. 12 the woman spoke of Jacob as τοῦ πατρὸς ἡμῶν. In v. 20 she proclaimed that οἱ πατέρες ἡμῶν worshiped on Mt. Gerizim. Here Jesus speaks not of worshiping God but of worshiping the Father (προσκυνήσετε τῷ πατρί). Hence, her concepts of Jacob and the gift of his well, her patriarchal religious ancestors, and the following of Samaritan rituals are "eclipsed by Jesus's words on the worship of God as worship of 'the Father.'"[120]

Jesus makes no attempt to distance himself from the enmity that exists between Jews and Samaritans and further castigates the Samaritans for worshiping what they do not know (v. 22a). His words widen the divide between Jew and Samaritan by immediately contrasting their approach with the Jews who not only worship according to knowledge (v. 22b) but also are the source of salvation (v. 22c). The use of "you" (ὑμεῖς) and "we" (ἡμεῖς) not only creates a sharp contrast between the practices of Jew and Samaritan but also locates Jesus within his religious tradition. As the woman earlier noted (σὺ Ἰουδαῖος ὢν, v. 9b), Jesus is a Jew and as such is part of the faith community from whom God's salvation flows.[121]

119. Bultmann (*Gospel of John*, 189 n. 5) affirms this reading: "It [viz., Jesus's answer] is introduced by the singular πίστευέ μοι, which clearly stands in the place of ἀμὴν ἀμ. λέγω σοι (the latter occurs nowhere in ch. 4)."

120. Moloney, *Gospel of John*, 128.

121. "This is an encounter between Jesus and the non-Jewish world (cf. vv. 4, 7, 9), and thus the traditions of Judaism, culminating in the salvation that Jesus brings, and the traditions of Samaritanism are contrasted. Jesus is revealing himself and the way to the Father to a non-Jewish world" (Moloney, *Gospel of John*, 128).

The phrase ἔρχεται ὥρα is repeated in v. 23 (cf. v. 21), but this time it is followed by καὶ νῦν ἐστιν. Here the widely recognized concept of Johannine realized eschatology emerges. Whether some are worshiping in ignorance (v. 22a) or according to knowledge (v. 22b), Jesus points to a time both future and partially inaugurated (ἔρχεται ὥρα καὶ νῦν ἐστιν, v. 23a) when worship will take place ἐν πνεύματι καὶ ἀλήθειᾳ (v. 23b). These are two key terms that have appeared several times to this point in the story (πνεῦμα appears in 1:32, 33; 3:5, 6, 8, 34; ἀλήθεια and cognate forms appear in 1:9, 14, 17; 3:3, 5, 21). "Spirit" and "truth" move the woman's understanding of worship beyond the traditional categories of "where" (Mt. Gerizim or Jerusalem) to "how" (out of the depths of one's existence). These are the kind of worshipers whom the Father seeks (ὁ πατὴρ τοιούτος ζητεῖ, v. 23d). ζητέω implies not a passive idea such as "these are the kind of worshipers God desires," but rather an active idea such as to "ask for, request, [or] demand" something.[122]

In v. 24 Jesus further explains the phrase ἐν πνεύματι καὶ ἀληθείᾳ by stating what would have been a given for both Jews and Samaritans: πνεῦμα ὁ θεός. Thus, if one desires to worship God properly, it is necessary (δεῖ) to do so in Spirit and in truth. On this teaching Moloney comments,

> The basis for all that Jesus has taught the Samaritan woman is the way God acts. *God is not a mountain, a place, or a sanctuary. God is spirit* (v. 24a), an all-pervading personal presence to the believer. This may be remarkable language for the Samaritan woman but it has appeared in earlier treatments of Jesus's creative life-giving presence (cf. 1:12–13; 3:3–8). The hour has now come when the only acceptable act of worship (*dei proskunein*) is the total orientation of one's life and action toward the Father, sharing already in the gift of the Father (*en pneumati*), a gift that is all that it claims to be (*kai alethēia*).[123]

It is impossible to tell from the woman's response how much she comprehends of Jesus's words. It is safe to conclude that she is somewhat captivated by Jesus's enigmatic words about worship along with his previous insights about her personal life. Possibly drawing upon the traditional Samaritan idea of *ta'eb*[124] the woman responds to Jesus's

122. BDAG, s.v. ζητέω.

123. Moloney, *Gospel of John*, 129; emphasis added.

124. See the discussion of *ta'eb* in n. 44 of chapter 5.

teaching by telling him of her expectation that Μεσσίας ἔρχεται (v. 25). She adds to this the further expectation ἀναγγελεῖ ἡμῖν ἅπαν–τα. It is uncertain whether she envisions her conversation with Jesus as similar to what will happen when Messiah comes. What is certain is that her statement about Messiah provides Jesus the opportunity to make his identity explicitly known.

In a statement that is often mistranslated Jesus tells the woman ἐγώ εἰμι, ὁ λαλῶν σοι (v. 26). Three things are accomplished by Jesus's use of this phrase. First, Jesus answers the question of his identity. He is the Messiah, which is affirmed in the plainest sense of ἐγώ εἰμι following the woman's statement about the Messiah. Second, Jesus alludes to the fact that he is the unique representation of the Father, which is affirmed in the wider theological sense of ἐγώ εἰμι, a title that becomes clearer throughout the course of the story.[125] Third, Jesus draws this section to a close by recalling the words of v. 10 (τίς ἐστιν ὁ λέγων σοι). Jesus, the one who has been speaking with her, is both Μεσσίας and κύριος ("I am"/"YHWH").

Before the woman can respond to Jesus's revelation another abrupt transition occurs. The disciples arrive and the woman eventually departs to her city, expressing wonderment at her conversation with Jesus. Though the narrator does not explicitly call her a believer, the events that transpire in the following scenes show that she has had a genuine Johannine conversion.

Conversation with the Disciples (4:27–38)

This scene was examined in detail in chapter 5 under the discussion of the disciples as a representative group. Therefore, it should suffice here to provide a summary of the exegesis offered above.

This unit contains two scenes. The first scene pictures the simultaneous arrival of the disciples and departure of the Samaritan woman (vv. 27–30). The second scene consists of a conversation between Jesus and the disciples about "food" (vv. 31–38), which leads to their primary misunderstanding in the pericope. The conversation in the second scene also creates a "meanwhile" that allows the citizens of Sychar to travel the short distance from town to the well.

125. For more on the theological significance of ἐγώ εἰμι in the Fourth Gospel refer to the discussion of John 13:18–20 in chapter 4.

In the first scene the disciples return and are amazed at the sight of Jesus conversing with a woman (v. 27). As they approach, the woman departs to Sychar and immediately tells "the men" (τοῖς ἀνθρώποις)[126] about her conversation with Jesus. She beckons them with the words, δεῦτε ἴδετε ἄνθρωπον ὃς εἶπέν μοι πάντα ὅσα ἐποίησα (v. 29). This is followed by her reluctant question: μήτι οὗτός ἐστιν ὁ χριστός; "This is not the Christ, is it?"[127] On this scene Stibbe comments,

> This action symbolizes the development of the woman into a witness for Jesus (*marturousēs*, v. 29). Having become a disciple, she now invites others to come to Jesus . . . [S]he testifies to the people of Samaria, and through her word (*dia ton logon*, v. 29) many come to faith. This process symbolizes the woman's development from disciple to disciple-maker. Having become a witness, she helps others to become disciples.[128]

In this way the Samaritan woman becomes a model for the reader inasmuch as she moves from misunderstanding and mockery to spiritual comprehension and evangelism.[129]

Her reluctant question reveals that her interaction with Jesus has had a different outcome from the first Nicodemus episode. Whereas Nicodemus started with praise (3:2b) and left in utter confusion (3:9), she begins with scorn (vv. 11–12) followed by confusion (v. 15), but eventually leaves to tell others about Jesus (v. 29). Her reluctant acceptance of Jesus's messianic status is a sign to the reader that she has achieved genuine Johannine belief.

When she tells the citizens about Jesus they begin coming out to meet him (v. 30) and while the citizens are on their way to meet Jesus, he converses with his disciples about "food." Whereas Jesus and the Samaritan woman have just spoken about water (vv. 7–18), a topic that

126. In chapter 5 I argued that τοῖς ἀνθρώποις is first a reference to the men to whom she had been married, and second a reference, by implication, to the citizens of Sychar.

127. I understand μήτι as an indicator of the woman's hesitance, but see Elizabeth Danna ("Note on John 4:29") who argues that the woman clearly expects "no" as the answer to the question μήτι οὗτός ἐστιν ὁ χριστός.

128. Stibbe, *John*, 67.

129. Moloney (*Gospel of John*, 157) disagrees, arguing that "[d]espite the progress she makes in her approach and understanding of Jesus, she remains a model of imperfect or partial belief in Jesus."

led to her initial misunderstanding, here Jesus and the disciples discuss "food," βρῶμα, a topic that likewise leads to the disciples' misunderstanding (vv. 32–33). Jesus explains that his "food" (i.e., his spiritual sustenance) is to do the will of the Father and to complete it (v. 34).

Using language related to agriculture, Jesus tells the disciples that they are about to reap a spiritual harvest for which they have not worked (vv. 36–38). As he completes his teaching on this topic the citizens of Sychar arrive on the scene. Through his harvest metaphor Jesus has implicitly informed the disciples (as well as the reader) that the Samaritans will manifest genuine belief.

Jesus and the Citizens of Sychar (4:39–42)

In v. 39 the narrator makes it clear that the woman's report is the impetus for the belief of many Samaritans (ἐκ δὲ τῆς πόλεως ἐκείνης πολλοὶ ἐπίστευσαν εἰς αὐτὸν τῶν Σαμαριτῶν διὰ τὸν λόγον τῆς γυναικὸς). Her status as a Johannine evangelist was already established by her report (v. 29) and the subsequent journey of her fellow citizens to see Jesus (v. 30). With this explicit statement her journey in the narrative is complete. The report of her successful testimony only serves to contribute further to the narrator's intended characterization of the woman as one who has progressed from hostility and incomprehension to proclamation and understanding. She is pictured not only as a reluctant (but genuine) believer but also as a faithful witness to Jesus's messianic status.

The citizens of Sychar ask Jesus to stay with them for a few days (ἠρώτων αὐτὸν μεῖναι παρ᾽ αὐτοῖς, v. 40). The term μένω gains theological significance as the story moves forward culminating in ch. 15. Here the Samaritans who will go on to express belief on the basis of Jesus's word begin by asking Jesus to "abide" with them. The narrator reports that Jesus remains two days (v. 40b).

While Jesus remains with the citizens, many more believe in him because of the word he preaches. The citizens of Sychar are said to believe initially because of the woman's word (διὰ τὸν λόγον τῆς γυναικὸς, v. 39), and then more express belief because of Jesus's word (διὰ τὸν λόγον αὐτοῦ, v. 41). Use of the identical phrase (διὰ τὸν λόγον) should be regarded as evidence of the woman's faithfulness in spreading Jesus's word.

In v. 42 the woman's fellow citizens tell her that they now believe not because of her report (διὰ τὴν σὴν λαλιὰν) but because they have heard for themselves. Some argue for a distinction between διὰ τὸν λόγον τῆς γυναικὸς and διὰ τὴν σὴν λαλιὰν, but this is a false distinction. The variation from λόγος to λαλιά is most likely another instance of Johannine synonymy. Again the woman's status as a faithful witness to Jesus's messianic status is confirmed.

This episode climaxes as non-Jews proclaim Jesus to be the universal savior (v. 42). This is another in the growing list of christological confessions throughout the Fourth Gospel and, like that of the woman, the confession of the Samaritans is also born out of belief in the word of Jesus.

Conclusion

The Samaritan woman is a model of Johannine transformation. She initially misunderstands Jesus's offer of living water by asking how he expects to retrieve it (v. 11), and then by asking him to give it to her (v. 15). She follows this performance by introducing her town to Jesus, thereby becoming both a believer and evangelist (v. 29). Her steady progression from incomprehension to belief is evident in her words to Jesus and her fellow citizens as she goes from πῶς, "how" (v. 9), to πόθεν, "where" (v. 11), to δός μοι, "give me" (v. 15), to δεῦτε ἴδετε, "come and see" (v. 29).

Like Peter and Thomas, the Samaritan woman experiences both incomprehension and redemption as part of her characterization in the story. The woman begins as a foil for Jesus's teaching on spiritual renewal (vv. 7–18), true worship (vv. 19–24), and his identity as the Messiah and revealer of the Father (vv. 24–25). She ends with the recognition that Jesus is ὁ χριστός. Like the disciples she overemphasizes the literal and material associated with Jesus's words but eventually emerges with the knowledge that Jesus is the Messiah, which has already been revealed in the prologue (Ἰησοῦ Χριστοῦ, 1:17). That she comes to terms with this element of Jesus's identity on the basis of his words attests to her comprehensive Johannine makeover.

Jesus, Martha, and Mary in the Fourth Gospel

The final characters to be considered in this study are the sisters Mary and Martha. The argument set forth in this section sees the sisters as uncomprehending figures throughout ch. 11. They fail to recognize not only Jesus's power over death in the present (rather than ἐν τῇ ἐσχάτῃ ἡμέρᾳ, cf. 11:23–25) but also his intent in visiting Lazarus's tomb (cf. 11:39–40).[130] Even their christological confessions reveal a failure to grasp fully Jesus's identity and abilities.

That both Martha and Mary would be included in a list of uncomprehending characters goes against the grain of traditional Johannine scholarship. Most modern exegetes regard both sisters as examples of satisfactory Johannine faith.[131] A fresh reading of the more subtle nuances of ch. 11 reveals that the sisters are initially characterized by incomprehension, though Mary eventually moves forward in her understanding of Jesus in ch. 12.

Jesus, Martha, and Mary in John 11:1–44

Three new characters are introduced in John 11: Martha, Mary, and Lazarus, the siblings from Bethany. The three are not known to the reader, though their introduction is accompanied by the comment that Jesus loves them (ἠγάπα δὲ ὁ Ἰησοῦς τὴν Μάρθαν καὶ τὴν ἀδελφὴν αὐτῆς καὶ τὸν Λάζαρον, v. 5). Through this comment and other noted elements of their presentation, the sisters are initially cast in a very positive light. However, their conversations with Jesus each reveal incomplete understanding of his identity and abilities. An analysis of 11:1–44 yields the following three units:

1. Jesus and the disciples by the Jordan (11:1–16)
2. Jesus and the sisters in Bethany (11:17–37)
    a. Jesus arrives in Bethany (11:17–19)
    b. Jesus and Martha (11:20–27)

---

130. "Their misunderstanding is that they do not see that Jesus himself is now the resurrection and the life for those who believe. Their misunderstanding lies in their failure to relinquish or modify the traditional futuristic eschatology for the Johannine realized eschatology" (Culpepper, *Anatomy of the Fourth Gospel*, 140).

131. Neyrey (*Gospel of John*, 197), comments that Martha is part of an inner-circle elite who "should be evaluated as a singularly blessed person . . . because of her revelations, she enjoys a very high status." Among other modern commentators who regard Martha and/or Mary as subjects of fully Johannine confession are Barrett (*Gospel According to St. John*, 388, 397–403) and Carson (*Gospel According to John*, 414, 428–30). For more on this, see the compiled list and accompanying comments in Moloney, "Can Everyone Be Wrong?" 515 n. 36.

c. Jesus and Mary (11:28–37)

3. Jesus and Lazarus at the tomb (11:38–44)

Since 11:1–16 was examined in detail in chapter 3, I will not provide an in-depth exegesis of those verses here. Instead the discussion will begin with a summary of vv. 1–16 before proceeding to a full exegesis of 11:17–44.

At the outset of John 11 the reader is presented with important information about the siblings from Bethany. The reader hears the name of Lazarus for the first time while learning simultaneously of his illness (v. 1a). Following the mention of Lazarus the reader is introduced to his sisters Mary and Martha (v. 1b) and is "reminded" that Mary is the one who anointed Jesus's feet and wiped them with her hair (v. 2). This "reminder" grabs the reader's attention because the event described has not yet taken place in the story (it occurs in 12:3). The narrator's proleptic comment in v. 2 creates a narrative gap that elevates Mary and beckons the reader to keep close watch on her.[132]

In v. 3 the sisters send a message to Jesus regarding their brother's illness, creating the problem for which Jesus's journey to Bethany will be the solution. Upon learning of Lazarus's situation, Jesus comments that the illness will not lead to death but rather will result in God's being glorified (v. 4). This is followed by the parenthetical comment about Jesus's love for Martha, Mary, and Lazarus (v. 5). It is important here to remember that the Beloved Disciple is the only other character in the story to be described in this manner.

These first few verses accomplish a great deal in terms of the characterization of Mary and Martha. The reader understands from the description provided here that a mutual love exists between Jesus and the siblings. Also in mentioning Mary first and recounting her good deed, the narrator singles her out, beckoning the reader to pay special attention to her. These elements of the narrative create an initially positive impression of all three characters.

After the siblings are introduced, Jesus has a discussion with his disciples about returning to Judea. The disciples misunderstand Jesus's

132. "The naming of Mary before her sister Martha (v. 1), and the indication that she was the one who anointed Jesus and wiped his feet with her hair (v. 2), instruct the reader on the importance of Mary for the story that is being introduced. The reader must keep an attentive eye on Mary. She is an important character" (Moloney, "Can Everyone Be Wrong?" 510).

desire to return to Judea to "awaken Lazarus" (vv. 6–13), after which Jesus tells them plainly that Lazarus has died (v. 14). However, even though Lazarus has died Jesus says that he rejoices (χαίρω, v. 15) in anticipation that God will engender belief in the disciples through this situation. The scene concludes with Thomas's words, "Let us go also in order that we may die with him" (v. 16). Thomas's unintentionally ironic statement ends the conversation and the scene comes to a close. The following verse transports Jesus and the disciples to Bethany.

Jesus and the Sisters in Bethany (11:17–37)

In this section Jesus arrives in Bethany and the remainder of ch. 11 takes place in and around that region. On one level the journey to Bethany is about the raising of Lazarus, but at a deeper level it pictures the beginning of the events that will lead up to Jesus's final week. The trip to Bethany signals Jesus's nearness to Jerusalem and "leads the reader to wonder if the time of Jesus's passion and death is near at hand."[133] This section consists of three units detailing Jesus's arrival in Bethany (vv. 17–19) and his conversations with Martha (vv. 20–27) and Mary (vv. 28–37).

Jesus Arrives in Bethany (11:17–19)

The discussion between Jesus and the disciples (vv. 11–16) ends abruptly as the narrator reports their arrival near Bethany (v. 17a, see the mention of Βηθανία in v. 18a). Upon arrival Jesus learns that Lazarus has already been in the tomb for four days (v. 17b). Later rabbinic texts reflect a Jewish belief that an individual's soul hovered around the body for three days after death looking for an opportunity to reenter the body. It was believed that after those three days, when the soul became aware of the body's decomposition, it would depart for good.[134] Thus the mention of four days suggests that Lazarus's death is permanent and irreversible. In a forthcoming climactic scene Jesus will reverse this seemingly permanent situation in a resurrection that symbolizes God's granting of resurrection life to everyone who believes.

Another narrative aside (v. 18) tells of the short distance between Jerusalem and Bethany (ὡς ἀπὸ σταδίων δεκαπέντε, approximately

133. Moloney, "Faith of Martha and Mary," 473.

134. See the discussion of these texts in Carson, *Gospel According to John*, 411. See also the exposition in Strack-Billerbeck, *Kommentar zum Neuen Testament*, 2:544.

1.75 miles), a distance that has allowed many fellow Jews (πολλοὶ δὲ ἐκ τῶν Ἰουδαὶων) to come and console the sisters (v. 19).[135] With the arrival of the Jewish people all of the players in this episode have been introduced. The action of the story can now proceed unimpeded by the introduction of new characters or information.

Jesus and Martha (11:20–27)

Martha hears that Jesus has arrived in Bethany and goes out to meet him while her sister remains seated (ἐκαθέζετο) in the house (v. 20).[136] Mary has already been highlighted by her description in v. 2 and the reader is carefully watching her behavior. From this scene it becomes immediately clear that the two women will respond to Jesus in different ways.

Martha's initial words to Jesus reveal her fundamental belief in him and his healing abilities (κύριε, εἰ ἦς ὧδε οὐκ ἂν ἀπέθανεν ὁ ἀδελφός μου, v. 21), though the rest of the scene will be dominated by Martha's proclamation of what she *knows* rather than what she *believes*. She recognizes (οἶδα ὅτι) the special relationship Jesus has with the Father and comments that God will grant to Jesus whatever he asks (v. 22). Like Nicodemus (3:2) and the man born blind (9:31–33), Martha confesses her belief that Jesus is a miracle worker with a special relationship to God. However, several elements of her confession suggest (at least initially) that Martha has more than just a signs faith but rather a profound understanding of Jesus's identity.

First, she uses the term κύριε in addressing Jesus, but not in the same manner as the Samaritan woman (cf. 4:11, 19). Martha's use of the term is a confession of Jesus's christological status. Second, her recognition of the relationship between Jesus and the Father is congruent with the prologue's statement that Jesus was "face to face" with God (πρὸς τὸν θεόν) in the beginning (1:1b, 2). Third, she recognizes Jesus's power over death, which also coincides with the description of Jesus found in the prologue (ἐν αὐτῷ ζωὴ ἦν, 1:4). Even in the face of this seemingly profound confession, the reader will ultimately recognize that Martha

135. Cf. Barrett (*Gospel According to St. John*, 394), who speaks to the duty of caring for the bereaved within Judaism.

136. This is the same word used of Jesus while he is seated at the well in 4:6. Bernard (*Critical and Exegetical Commentary*, 1:135) notes that the term καθέζομαι carries a durative sense in the in NT.

believes in Jesus as a miracle worker in a traditional Jewish sense. Further she fails to understand that he is the purveyor of life who possesses power over death even in the present.

Jesus answers Martha by assuring her that Lazarus will live again (ἀναστήσεται ὁ ἀδελφός σου, v. 23). The reader has been anticipating Jesus's intervention in the death of Lazarus since his comment to the disciples in v. 14 and also senses that Jesus is about to act in this regard. On the other hand, Martha seems blissfully unaware.

Typical instances of Johannine misunderstanding revolve around a character's overly literal interpretation of Jesus's spiritual language. Here that situation is reversed. Jesus tells Martha what will literally occur in the near future (viz., "Your brother will rise again") but Martha's response is overly spiritual and theological (οἶδα ὅτι ἀναστήσεται ἐν τῇ ἀναστάσει ἐν τῇ ἐσχάτῃ ἡμέρᾳ, v. 24). Again, as in v. 22, Martha interjects with a statement of knowledge (οἶδα ὅτι) rather than belief. Martha's misunderstanding of Jesus's intent to raise Lazarus in the present is at odds with her confession that God will grant to Jesus whatever he asks (v. 22). It becomes clear that she has a futuristic eschatological expectation consonant with Pharisaic Jewish thinking on the issue. She has therefore missed the reality of God's presence and power through Jesus in the present. Her comment in v. 24 not only betrays her inability to comprehend the powers at Jesus's disposal but also errs by looking exclusively to the future rather than the present for the glorious inbreak of God in and through Jesus.

The exchange between Martha and Jesus has gotten nowhere and leads Jesus to a direct statement of self-identification: ἐγώ εἰμι ἡ ἀνάστασις καὶ ἡ ζωή (v. 25b). This is another in a string of predicated ἐγώ εἰμι statements throughout the Gospel.[137] There is little need for speculation about the meaning of this statement because Jesus continues by explaining what it means for him to be "the resurrection and the life." The one who believes in Jesus will live, even if the believer dies (v. 25c), as this has already been spelled out for the reader in 5:21–25. The statement in v. 25c is not so difficult to interpret. Those who die physically will know eternal life through belief in Jesus.

137. For a comprehensive discussion of predicated and unpredicated ἐγώ εἰμι statements in the Fourth Gospel, see Ball, *'I Am' in John's Gospel*. Refer also to my previous discussion in nn. 23 and 24 of chapter 3.

The continued explanation in v. 26 is not as easy to understand. Commentators disagree over how to understand the statement, "Everyone who lives and believes in me will never die" (v. 26).[138] Specifically at issue is the phrase ὁ ζῶν. Is this a reference to physical life? Is this a reference to spiritual life? Is there an intentional ambiguity that shrouds the meaning of this statement? Martha has confused future and present eschatological realities and Jesus seems to blur the distinction between the two in v. 26. Moloney writes that "[t]he blending of realized and traditional eschatology, familiar to the reader from 5:24–29 (see also 6:40, 54), returns. People die physically (v. 25b), but faith in Jesus assures a life that transcends death."[139] The distinction between vv. 25 and 26 can therefore be explained in the following way: everyone who believes in Jesus and dies physically will still live spiritually (v. 25), and the believer who lives spiritually will never die (οὐ μὴ ἀποθάνῃ εἰς τὸν αἰῶνα) spiritually (v. 26).[140]

Early in the conversation Martha was forceful and clear about what she knew (cf. οἶδα in vv. 22, 24), providing Jesus little room for explanation. Now that Jesus has had an opportunity to explain, he asks her not about what she knows but what she believes (πιστεύεις τοῦτο; v. 26b). This is key moment in the conversation because it forces Martha to reckon with Jesus's claims about himself rather than with her own understanding of who Jesus is. Her response shows that though she claims to believe in Jesus, she still does not understand who he is. Furthermore, she has refused to have her present beliefs subjected to the truth Jesus has shared.

She responds with the substance of her belief. Martha begins her answer with πεπίστευκα, "I have believed." Understood as a perfect with an intensive force (i.e., "I have believed and continue to believe that . . ."), this word is a subtle indication that whatever the content of her belief, she has held it for some time.[141] Her confession thus begins with

138. Beasley-Murray (*John*, 190–91) provides a helpful overview of the scholarly discussion on this point.

139. Moloney, *Signs and Shadows*, 161.

140. Brown (*Gospel According to John*, 1:425) also takes this interpretation.

141. Barrett (*Gospel According to St. John*, 397) denies that this form indicates a "primitive confession of faith" and instead argues that this is a characteristically Johannine form. I am not persuaded by this argument. Inasmuch as it accompanies some of the other subtle nuances in Martha's confession, I believe the perfect should be given its normal grammatical emphasis here. For more on the intensive use of the perfect tense, see Wallace, *Exegetical Syntax of the New Testament*, 574–76.

a subtle clue to the reader that her mind is made up about the nature of resurrection and has been for awhile.[142]

She goes on to confess that Jesus is ὁ χριστὸς ὁ υἱὸς τοῦ θεοῦ ὁ εἰς τὸν κόσμον ἐρχόμενος (v. 27). Throughout this study I have argued that the prologue sets the theological and literary agenda for the remainder of the Gospel. I have also sought to read the text closely, paying careful attention to the story's recurring allusions to the prologue. Martha is an exceptional character in the Fourth Gospel in that her words agree fully with the prologue's description of Jesus, but her confession nevertheless falls short of satisfactory Johannine belief.

On the surface of things, each element of Martha's confession is supported by the prologue. Jesus is ὁ χριστὸς (cf. 1:17), ὁ υἱὸς τοῦ θεοῦ (implied by ὁ ὢν εἰς τὸν κόλπον τοῦ πατρὸς in 1:18), and ὁ εἰς τὸν κόσμον ἐρχόμενος (cf. 1:9). However, it is not the content of Martha's confession that reveals her incomprehension, but the context.

From a Johannine perspective the theology of Martha's confession is fully orthodox. But the careful reader will see that Martha answers Jesus in a way that is not demanded by his question. In the light of Martha's agreement with 1:1–18 and 20:31, many regard her confession as complete, but it fails to answer the substance of Jesus's question. When Jesus asks Martha if she believes τοῦτο (v. 26b), the understood referent is his self-identification (v. 24) and explanation about present and future eschatological realities (vv. 25–26a). Martha responds to Jesus's question with a statement of belief, but that belief is not in Jesus's ability to raise her brother in the here and now. Neither is it a belief that Jesus is "the resurrection and the life." Instead, she confesses that Jesus is "the Christ" in a manner similar to the confession of Jesus's earliest disciples in ch. 1. Her perspective is one informed by traditional Jewish expectations and unmoved by Jesus's self-identification. Because of this she misses his point completely. Regarding her misunderstanding Moloney comments,

> Jesus has asked whether she believes that he is the resurrection and the life (v. 26). She has responded in terms that can be regarded as acceptable messianic categories: the Christ, the son of God (see Ps 2.7; 2 Sam 7.14), the one who is to come into the world. Earlier uses of these expressions (see 1.49; 6.14) have al-

142. Moloney (*Signs and Shadows*, 162) calls her belief a "long-held conviction."

> ready reflected the limited faith of those who confess their belief in these terms.[143]

After her answer there is no further explanation from the narrator nor is there further conversation in this exchange. Martha does not answer the question Jesus has asked her in vv. 25–26. She departs in the following verse to retrieve her sister without having grasped Jesus's identity or his intent in coming to Bethany to raise Lazarus.

This initial scene presents Martha as an uncomprehending character who misunderstands on two counts. She perceives Jesus as a miracle worker and she believes in him from a perspective influenced by traditional Jewish beliefs. She fails to understand Jesus's abilities both prior to and after his assurance about the raising of Lazarus (v. 23) and his own self-identification (v. 25). Her view of Jesus is about to be challenged by the events at Lazarus's tomb.[144]

Jesus and Mary (11:28–37)

The initial verse of this section is a bridge passage that links the appearances of Martha and Mary. The two have already been mentioned together (vv. 1, 5, 19) but they have not yet appeared in the same scene. They appear together briefly in this verse before Mary's departure to meet Jesus.

After her initial exchange with Jesus, Martha goes to call for Mary (v. 28a), telling her privately that ὁ διδάσκαλος is asking for her. Martha's very first word in the text was κύριε, "Lord," but here she regresses in referring to Jesus as simply "the teacher." The term "teacher" given in two forms in the Gospel (ῥαββί and διδάσκαλος) has consistently signaled an incomplete understanding of Jesus (e.g., the unnamed disciples in 1:38; Nathanael in 1:49; Nicodemus in 3:2). In each of these instances the belief is "conditioned by religious and cultural

143. Moloney, "Can Everyone Be Wrong?" 514.

144. Unlike many commentators, Brown (*Gospel According to John*, 1:434) recognizes the shortcomings in Martha's confession and comments that the reader should "understand her outlook in much the same way that we understood that of the Samaritan woman in ch. iv." In addition, he writes, "to make Martha understand that he has the power to give life now, [Jesus] will act out a drama of the gift of life by raising Lazarus."

circumstances."[145] Therefore, as in her conversation with Jesus, Martha's display of partial faith continues in her report to Mary.

Attention remains fixed on Mary, a character who has already been elevated in the reader's eyes. She responds appropriately to Martha's report about Jesus and she arises quickly to see him (v. 29). Once again the narrator speaks to the reader through a narrative aside, commenting that Jesus has not yet entered the town but has stayed in the place where he and Martha have just met (v. 30). Jesus remains where he is and the result is that Mary comes out to meet him just as Martha had. This state of affairs creates a parallelism in the scenes involving both sisters. They come out to meet Jesus in the same place, and both respond to him initially by uttering the same words, "If you had been here, my brother would not have died."

As Mary leaves, the Jewish consolers mistakenly believe she is going to mourn at the tomb and they follow her (v. 31). Their misunderstanding leads them to the scene of the conversation between Mary and Jesus, and ultimately to the scene of Lazarus's resurrection.

The reader first met Mary through the narrator's proleptic reminder of her good deed, where she is positioned at the feet of Jesus (v. 2). Here for a second time the reader sees Mary at the feet of Jesus, only this time it occurs in a display of grief (v. 32a). Mary's first words to Jesus are nearly identical to those of Martha in v. 21 (κύριε, εἰ ἦς ὧδε οὐκ ἄν μου ἀπέθανεν ὁ ἀδελφός, v. 32c), but gone is any reference to Jesus's special relationship with God (as in v. 22). Could this be a sign of good things to come for Mary? Does she possess more than the simple signs faith of her sister? The reader waits to see what will come of Mary's confession.

Thus far the responses of the two women have differed significantly. Mary moved quickly to meet Jesus (v. 29), prostrated herself (v. 32a), and confessed her belief in him (v. 32b). Her response seems to signal a move in the right direction away from the limitations of Martha's faith. This positive step, however, is halted by Jesus's awareness of Mary's response. She, along with the group of Jewish mourners, is weeping (v. 33ab). The combined group (including Mary) is viewing events from the perspective of death and has, like Martha, missed the power of God that is present in Jesus. At this stage of the narrative Jesus becomes

145. Moloney, "Can Everyone Be Wrong?" 516.

angered (ἐνεβριμήσατο τῷ πνεύματι)[146] and distressed (ἐτάραξεν ἑαυτόν) (v. 33c).

The verb ἐμβριμάομαι expresses anger and displeasure.[147] Though this is not a commonly recognized element of modern readings of Jesus's response to Mary, it should be. Jesus is perturbed and distressed by the group's disturbing lack of faith.[148] His intent all along has been to raise Lazarus, but everywhere he is surrounded by a lack of faith in his ability to do so. In this conclusion I am following Moloney's departure from the majority position, which sees Jesus expressing compassion or grief. Moloney observes,

> The narrative is designed to lead the reader away from mourning and weeping toward faith in Jesus as the resurrection and the life (vv. 25–26; see v. 26b: πιστεύεις τοῦτο;). Anything short of this is not good enough, but 'the Jews' are portrayed as characters who oppose Jesus (v. 8) and who go to Mary and Martha that they might console them over the loss of Lazarus (v. 19). In v. 33, Mary, despite her good start, called by Jesus, prostrating herself at his feet, and modifying Martha's understanding of Jesus (vv. 28–32), has joined the weeping Jews.[149]

Therefore Jesus's response to their collective tears is not one of compassion or grief as some have proposed, but one of indignant consternation. Mary was initially elevated in the reader's eyes but the reader sees that her belief is as incomplete as Martha's signs faith.

In his highly emotional state Jesus asks where Lazarus has been laid (v. 34a). The reader has been anticipating Jesus's intervention in the situation and this question allows Jesus and the crowd to move toward the tomb. The crowd responds to Jesus's question with the words, κύριε, ἔρχου καὶ ἴδε (v. 34b). Earlier in the story Jesus used this very phrase

146. I find convincing Moloney's argument (see "Can Everyone Be Wrong?" 517–18) that many commentators have missed the nuances associated with Jesus's response in this pericope. The verb ἐμβριμάομαι is often rendered (in my estimation, incorrectly) in a way that indicates deep sorrow or distress. Perhaps more appropriate is the NLT's rendering which pictures Jesus as "deeply indignant."

147. BDAG, s.v. ἐμβριμάομαι.

148. "The depth of Jesus' disturbance is indicated by the use of another verb denoting a powerful emotional response, ταράσσω, and the locating of this anger and emotion at the depths of his being, τῷ πνεύματι. Jesus is angered and deeply disturbed emotionally—even to the points of tears—by the universal lack of faith" (Moloney, "Can Everyone Be Wrong?" 518).

149. Ibid., 517–18.

when beckoning the early disciples to follow him, the source of light and life (cf. 1:39). Here the crowd uses the phrase to beckon Jesus to the place of darkness and death.[150]

Without commenting further the narrator simply reports that Jesus wept (ἐδάκρυσεν ὁ Ἰησοῦς, v. 35).[151] This response heightens the emotional scene that has been taking place. Jewish mourners have gathered to console the sisters. Mary has been weeping. Jesus has expressed anger and distress at the universal lack of faith in his ability to raise Lazarus, and all of this is topped off by Jesus's display of grief. That Jesus's tears are understood to be an indication of his grief is signaled by the first comment of the crowd, ἴδε πῶς ἐφίλει αὐτόν (v. 36b).

Others in the mixed crowd remember that Jesus caused the man born blind to see (cf. 9 1–7). If Jesus is indeed the healer they know him to be, could he not have done something to change Lazarus's fate? (v. 37). They too fail to see his intent in coming to the tomb. He is not there to mourn a death but to raise a life. With this comment the scene ends on an ironic note. The reader knows that the movement to the tomb is a sign of positive things to come. Jesus intends to raise Lazarus from the dead, a point everyone else has missed.

This scene reveals that Mary, like her sister, has an incomplete faith. Martha's tone was more aggressive and forceful while, Mary's prostration and tears have unveiled a more passive posture. Nevertheless, both sisters completely miss the point of Jesus's presence in Bethany and respond to him from the perspective of signs faith (cf. vv. 21, 32). Jesus is the resurrection and the life. He has come to show forth God's power in the present by raising Lazarus from the dead and bringing glory to the Father and Son. All have misunderstood, but they will see the truth when they gather at the tomb of Lazarus.

Jesus and Lazarus at the Tomb (11:38–44)

The scene now changes locale and shifts to the tomb, but there remains an emotional continuity with the previous section. Jesus again appears

150. This is noted by Lightfoot, *St. John's Gospel*, 223.

151. δακρύω is a *hapax legomenon* in the NT. This is a significant element informing the reader that the source of Jesus's tears is not that of the crowd (whose weeping is referred to with the verb κλαίω). Their tears are tears of mourning. On the other hand, Jesus's tears are borne out of consternation at their failure to understand that he is "the resurrection and the life."

as highly indignant (ἐμβριμώμενος ἐν ἑαυτῷ, v. 38), perhaps at the foolish speculations of the crowd in v. 37. Both sisters have failed to believe in Jesus's word and the characteristically hostile and unbelieving Ἰουδαῖοι have retained their typical posture. Jesus will now support his failed word with miraculous deeds in hopes that this might engender belief in those who witness Lazarus's resurrection (cf. v. 42).

In v. 38b the narrator turns to the reader once again, describing the tomb as a cave over which a boulder has been placed (ἦν δὲ σπήλαιον καὶ λίθος ἐπέκειτο ἐπ' αὐτῷ). Jesus's command that the boulder be removed is again met with an ironic comment. The reader understands that removal of the boulder will culminate in the raising of Lazarus, but Martha objects. It is noteworthy that Martha is described here as the "sister of the deceased," ἡ ἀδελφὴ τοῦ τετελευτηκότος (v. 39b). This phrase highlights the reversal that is about to occur. In what follows, Lazarus will be transformed from "the one who had died" to the one who has been raised.

Before the stone can be rolled away Martha tells Jesus, "Lord, already he stinks for he has been there four days" (v. 39c). As noted above, many scholars have argued that Martha's confession of faith in v. 27 was satisfactory. If that is the case, then it is difficult to account for her objection in v. 39. If she has truly grasped the truth that Jesus is the resurrection and the life, she should be eager with anticipation. Instead, she objects that there will be an odor due to advanced decomposition.[152] Here is yet another element of this pericope that suggests that Martha has not understood Jesus as "the resurrection and the life."

Read in the context of Martha's persistent misunderstanding and Jesus's second indignant display, the rhetorical question of v. 40 (οὐκ εἶπόν σοι ὅτι ἐὰν πιστεύσῃς ὄψῃ τὴν δόξαν τοῦ θεοῦ;)[153] should be read as a "harsh rebuke" suggesting that "she has not arrived at an expression of perfect Johannine faith."[154] Though there are a number of semantic categories for the third-class conditional statement, its use

152. "Martha is still locked within her own world, that of tombs, death and sorrow" (Moloney, "Can Everyone Be Wrong?" 520).

153. Brown (*Gospel According to John*, 1:427) notes that this is not a direct citation of anything Jesus has already said but rather the general import of Jesus's words to Martha.

154. Ibid., 521.

here indicates a "more probable future occurrence."[155] The crowd will see the glory of God displayed in a deed that foreshadows Jesus's own resurrection.

The stone is removed (v. 41a) and Jesus thanks the Father for listening to him (v. 41b). During his prayer Jesus also affirms his knowledge that the Father has always listened to him, but acknowledges that this statement is uttered so that the crowd might believe. Throughout the episode in Bethany, Jesus's word has failed, but perhaps his word accompanied by his miraculous deed will have an impact upon the unbelieving crowd (a crowd that includes Martha and Mary). Jesus expresses a desire that his forthcoming sign will cause the crowd to believe that God has sent him (v. 42b).

In the climactic moment of this scene Jesus, with a great shout (φωνῇ μεγάλῃ ἐκραύγασεν), calls Lazarus to come forth from the grave. This loud cry is an indication of Jesus's authority and power over death. Brown also notes that this term is used four times throughout chs. 18–20 to describe the clamor of the crowds to crucify Jesus. He writes, "Thus a contrast might be drawn between the crowd's shout that brings death to Jesus and Jesus's shout that brings life to Lazarus."[156]

Earlier Lazarus was called "the deceased," τοῦ τετελευτηκότος (v. 39), and here he is called "the one who had died," ὁ τεθνηκὼς (v. 44). These terms create a sharp contrast between Lazarus's state both prior to after Jesus's intervention as "the resurrection and the life." Lazarus is no longer the one who had died. He has been raised to newness of life and, ironically, his life will shortly becomes the impetus for the taking of Jesus's life (cf. 11:49–53).

When Lazarus comes out of the grave he is still encumbered by his grave cloths. After a description of Lazarus from the narrator that points forward to several elements of Jesus's resurrection scene,[157] Jesus speaks, commanding the crowd to loose the revivified man from the bonds of death. Lazarus has been raised and is ready to be unveiled. Jesus has confirmed his role as the resurrection and the life.

155. On the nuances of the third-class condition, see Wallace, *Exegetical Syntax of the New Testament*, 696.

156. Brown, *Gospel According to John*, 1:427.

157. The verbal and conceptual parallels have already been discussed in the examination of Peter and the Beloved Disciple (20:3–10) in chapter 4.

In this scene Martha is again depicted as an uncomprehending character. Her inability to confess Jesus as "the resurrection and the life" in her previous appearance is confirmed again in her protest at the tomb. Even as Jesus is about to raise Lazarus from the dead, her mind is still fixed on things associated with death and the grave. She has again failed to believe in Jesus's word. The final appearance of the two sisters will reveal that while Mary moves forward significantly in their understanding of Jesus's identity, Martha remains in her signs faith.

Jesus, Martha, and Mary in John 12:1–8

This brief scene begins with the characteristic statement of temporal and physical settings. It is six days before the Passover (πρὸ ἓξ ἡμερῶν τοῦ πάσχα)[158] and Jesus has returned to Bethany (v. 1a). All three siblings are present at a meal that has been prepared for Jesus. Lazarus, designated as ὃν ἤγειρεν ἐκ νεκρων' Ιησοῦς in v. 1b, is present at the table (v. 2c) and Martha is pictured as serving (διηκόνει) (v. 2b). The scene shifts from Lazarus and Martha to Mary's anointing of Jesus's feet. That the narrator moves forward without returning to comment on Martha is significant. Her previous failure to believe Jesus's word has persisted even in the wake of her brother's resurrection. For Martha, Jesus remains a miracle worker in the traditional Jewish sense and she remains an uncomprehending character.

The narrative gap that was created by the first mention of Mary's anointing of Jesus's feet (11:2) is now filled by the narrator's account of that deed (v. 3). The description of Mary's deed is meant to evoke a picture of extravagance.[159] She anoints Jesus with λίτραν μύρου νάρδου πιστικῆς πολυτίμου, "a pound of expensive aromatic oil made from pure nard,"[160] which leads to the house being filled with an aromatic

158. The reader should not understand these six days in a symbolic sense but rather that these events begin roughly a week before the events of Passover.

159. "The gesture is a demonstration of love and dedication, and the spreading of the odor indicates extravagance" (Moloney, "Can Everyone Be Wrong?" 523).

160. This description raises a few issues. First, the word λίτραν is a Latin loanword (*libra*) referring to a Roman pound, the equivalent of twelve ounces. Modern English readers should be careful to avoid reading this in the modern sense (i.e., 16 oz). Second, there is some question about whether πιστικῆς should be understood as "pure" (from πιστός, meaning "genuine" or "faithful") or as "pistic" (from either a place or trade name, or associated with the pistachio nut). On this, see Carson, *Gospel According to John*, 428. Of the two I opt for "pure" as it seems more appropriate to the context.

scent. The anointing fills the earlier narrative gap but more importantly draws a contrast between the responses of Mary and Martha. Martha has not properly perceived Jesus's words and deeds. On the other hand, Mary's deed shows a growth in her understanding. This is clarified by Jesus's answer to the protest of Judas (cf. v. 7b).

Judas protests the extravagance of Mary's deed and asks why the oil was not sold for three hundred denarii and the money given to the poor (v. 5). This objection is both preceded and followed by important elements in the characterization of Judas. In v. 4 the narrator uses three descriptive phrases to fill out the initial portrait: ὁ Ἰσκαριώτης (his surname), εἷς ἐκ τῶν μαθητῶν αὐτοῦ (his status as a disciple), and ὁ μέλλων αὐτὸν παραδιδόναι (his role in the story). That the individual presented as "the betrayer" would speak up against Mary's deed is a telling element of this pericope. The narrator is drawing a contrast between devotion to and betrayal of Jesus. Significantly, in the present passage both devotion and betrayal are connected to the death of Jesus. Mary's devotion has prepared Jesus for death where Judas's betrayal leads to Jesus's death.

In the verse following Judas's objection (v. 6) the narrator speaks to the reader in a narrative aside that gives direct information about the betrayer. Judas's statement is driven by greed and not by a genuine concern for the poor. In his role as keeper of the money box he has regularly stolen from the contents of the bag. With this description Judas "dons the black hat" even more. As "the betrayer," he is not characterized as one who begins positively and progresses to that role. Rather, he is presented from the outset as a picture of evil and his character continues on that trajectory even to the end.

As stated above, Jesus confirms the importance of Mary's act by commanding Judas to leave her alone (ἄφες αὐτήν, v. 7a). He continues by explaining that her deed was performed ἵνα εἰς τὴν ἡμέραν τοῦ ἐνταφιασμοῦ μου τηρήσῃ αὐτό (v. 7b). There is some discussion as to how the ἵνα clause should be read.

One option is to connect it with ἄφες αὐτήν so that it reads "leave her alone so that she might keep it for the day of my burial." Here αὐτό would refer to the aromatic oil. Carson notes that it can be understood with an imperatival force: "Leave her alone. Let her keep it for the day of my burial."[161] In addition, Brown suggests that the notion "is not that

161. Carson, *Gospel According to John*, 429.

she is to keep the perfume for some future use, but that (unknowingly) she was keeping it until now to embalm Jesus."[162] In support of this reading Brown translates the ἵνα clause as a free standing sentence that begins, "The purpose was that . . ."[163] Moloney argues that this solution "brings its own difficulties, but it seems to suit the context better, as the day of preparation for burial is symbolically fulfilled at Bethany."[164] He continues,

> The passion is in view, and the anointing is seen as a preparation for Jesus's death. In the context, the symbol is clear: Mary's long-awaited anointing of his feet (see 11.2) is the day of preparation for the burial of Jesus . . . Jesus' supportive explanation of Mary's gesture in v. 7 indicates that, at last, one of the characters in the story has 'got it right'.[165]

Mary thus shines forth as a model of Johannine belief, and a critical contrast is created between her role and the role of Martha, whose depiction has already been abandoned within the story.

This section concludes with Jesus's comment that the people will always have the poor but they will not always have him (v. 8). This statement foreshadows the gruesome events of the coming week as Jesus begins his steady movement toward the cross.

Conclusion

The sisters of Bethany begin as sincere followers and friends of Jesus who do not fully comprehend his identity or abilities. Throughout chs. 11 and 12 Martha remains an uncomprehending character who views Jesus as a miracle worker from a Jewish perspective, and from this perspective understands resurrection as something in the future. Ironically, she has "the resurrection and the life" standing before her but continues to look forward to the future for resurrection, thereby missing out on the truth of Jesus's identity.

Mary, on the other hand, begins with a signs faith but moves forward in her ability to comprehend the significance of Jesus's death. Her

162. Brown, *Gospel According to John*, 1:449. This option is similar to Carson's "elliptical" reading (*Gospel According to John*, 429).

163. Ibid.

164. Moloney, "Can Everyone Be Wrong?" 525.

165. Ibid.

anointing of Jesus's feet reveals that she has gained an appreciation for the connection between Jesus's approaching death and his identity as the resurrection and the life. Like Thomas, Peter, and the Samaritan woman, she leaves the story a redeemed character in the eyes of the reader.

Conclusion

The issue of John's relation to the *Gospel of Thomas* is an important one with potentially far-reaching implications. Questions about the relationship between the two gospels necessarily incorporate historical, literary, and theological considerations, many of which lie beyond the scope of the present study. The focus of this study has been intentionally narrow, seeking to challenge one key element of the theory that the Fourth Gospel contains a theological response to the *Gospel of Thomas* or the traditions contained therein.

The view I have designated as the community-conflict hypothesis relies heavily upon the supposed polemical characterization of Thomas in the Fourth Gospel. The argument for a conflict between the communities associated with John and Thomas cannot be made apart from the supposition that Thomas is the subject of a significant Johannine polemic. Throughout this study I have sought to demonstrate that Thomas is one among a number of uncomprehending characters in the Fourth Gospel. I have also sought to demonstrate that the portrait of Thomas as uncomprehending is no more or less extreme than John's other uncomprehending characters. It has been my aim to show that Thomas is merely one stitch in a wider literary pattern where uncomprehending characters serve as foils for Jesus's words and deeds.

The conclusion of this study can be divided into three sections: (1) a summary of the literary purposes of uncomprehending characters in the Fourth Gospel, (2) a summary of the theological purposes behind John's uncomprehending characters, and (3) the implications of this study for the community-conflict hypothesis.

Literary Purposes of John's Uncomprehending Characters

In this study I have grouped the Fourth Gospel's uncomprehending characters into two categories: Jesus's disciples and "others." The former group includes Thomas, Peter, Andrew, Philip, Judas (not Iscariot), and the disciples as a representative group. The latter includes Nicodemus, the Samaritan woman, Martha, and Mary. The central argument of the previous four chapters is that all the characters in both of these groups consistently fail to understand Jesus's identity, teaching, or actions, and these misunderstandings provide the Johannine Jesus an opportunity to clarify some element of his identity or mission.

After an examination of each character in detail in chapters 3 through 6, it can now be concluded that there is a conscious effort on the part of the Evangelist to present these characters as foils for Jesus. There are, of course, varying levels of incomprehension in the narrative. For instance, Nicodemus's inability to understand ("How can these things be?" 3:9) is much more explicit than the incomprehension displayed in the confessions by Andrew ("We have found the Messiah," 1:41), and Martha ("I have believed that you are the Christ, the son of God who was to come into the world," 11:27). Each character is given different nuances by the narrator and these add to the overall literary effect. Nevertheless, there is a consistent pattern that drives the episodes containing these uncomprehending characters. The pattern consists of (1) a statement or action by Jesus, followed by (2) a misunderstanding from the character in question, and typically (3) a clarification by Jesus through explanation, action, or both. In each instance of incomprehension the implied reader's knowledge of the prologue informs and highlights the given character's misunderstanding.

The misunderstandings that arise in these various passages serve the literary purposes of the narrator at two levels of the story. The first area is the development of the plot and the second is the story's approach to characterization.

(1) Plot Development

When literary critics refer to a story's "plot" they are addressing the structure of the action of a story, specifically as the action is ordered and focused toward achieving emotional and rhetorical effects. Throughout the story John's uncomprehending characters contribute to the narrator's desired emotional and rhetorical effect by pointing the reader both backward and forward.

The reader must continually return to the information revealed in the prologue in order to evaluate each character's response to Jesus.

Therefore, uncomprehending characters advance the plot by causing the reader to look back at what has been revealed, which in turn points forward to the cumulative effect of the story to that point. In each instance of incomprehension the reader must remember what information has already been given about Jesus and also how each character in the story has received him thus far. This constant back-and-forth movement helps contribute to the narrator's desired effect on the reader by not only keeping the reader aware of what has transpired but also by building anticipation in the reader for what will take place. In this way, John's uncomprehending characters help to advance the action of the story while emphasizing Jesus's role as the revealer of the Father.

(2) Characterization

In chapter 2 I addressed the classic distinction between round and flat characters and argued (following more recent literary critics) that characters in the Fourth Gospel are to be categorized on a continuum that includes full-blown characters, types, and agents (or actants). While Jesus is the only example of a full-blown character in the Gospel, he is not the only character to contribute to the overall rhetorical effect of the story. John's uncomprehending characters constitute a character group that demonstrates a dominant trait, thereby allowing Jesus to preach, teach, heal, or simply emote (cf. e.g., John 11). Jesus's response to these characters confirms the reader's impression of their incomprehension and assists the reader's evaluation of each. This allows a contrast to emerge between the reader's expectation of Jesus (based upon the information provided in the prologue and the cumulative reading experience) and a given character's expectation of Jesus (based upon an incomplete understanding).

In addition, the consistent incomprehension of these characters allows the reader to see another contrast in the actions and confessions of the Beloved Disciple. Whereas the disciples and others respond inappropriately to Jesus, the Beloved Disciple consistently responds to Jesus in the right way, creating a literary environment that elevates the Beloved Disciple to an exalted status among Johannine characters.

Within the narrative the narrator draws the contrast between the Beloved Disciple and the uncomprehending characters, but the narrator also envisions the reader outside the narrative as a potential comprehending or uncomprehending character. Thus, through the agency of (1) incomprehension, (2) the prologue, (3) the Beloved Disciple, and (4) the Gospel's stated aim (20:31), the narrator challenges the reader to evaluate Jesus properly and to respond appropriately (that is, by believing). In this way the reader has the potential to avoid incomprehension like the failing characters and can become, like the Beloved Disciple, one who grasps Jesus's identity and believes in him. Since proper belief is the primary Johannine theological category, this insight serves as the perfect segue to an examination of the theological significance of John's uncomprehending characters.

Theological Purposes of John's Uncomprehending Characters

John's uncomprehending characters help to clarify the presentation of several interwoven Johannine theological themes. The identity of Jesus is laid out for the reader in the prologue and a proper or improper understanding of Jesus's identity has implications for the reader's view of belief, Christology, and the Johannine theology of the cross (viz., Jesus's mission). These related themes come to the forefront of the narrative every time an uncomprehending character fails to understand Jesus.

The implied reader (who already knows the story of Jesus but is reading the Johannine version for the first time) understands that Jesus is from above and that he is the revealer of the Father who will eventually die on a Roman cross. An understanding of Jesus's identity informs the Gospel's christological presentation. Furthermore, an understanding of John's Christology clarifies Jesus's mission toward the cross, which in turn clarifies the nature of authentic Johannine belief. Whether explicit or implicit, these themes are present in the reader's every encounter with an uncomprehending character. The confessions of characters like Andrew, Philip, and Nicodemus are based upon a failure to grasp Jesus's identity as the one who is from above. Through their words they reveal a fundamental misunderstanding of Jesus's identity (i.e., the Gospel's Christology) and thereby exercise inauthentic Johannine belief. The questions of characters like Thomas, Peter, and Judas (not Iscariot) reveal a fundamental misunderstanding of Jesus's mission (i.e., John's theology of the cross), which shows a failure to grasp Jesus's identity (i.e., John's Christology).

A synchronic reading of the narrative provides the reader with the knowledge that Jesus is the Christ, the Son of God, and the revealer of the Father who has come from above, to be glorified on the cross and at the tomb. For one to believe in Jesus, an understanding of these truths must be present. Through the uncomprehending characters the narrator illustrates improper belief in Jesus and beckons the reader to believe from an informed perspective.

Critique of the Community-Conflict Hypothesis

In light of the literary and theological purposes behind John's uncomprehending characters it seems valid, though perhaps too simplistic, to suggest that the community-conflict hypothesis fails in the face of (1) Thomas's relative unimportance in the overall narrative scheme of the Johannine story, and (2) the presence of many other similarly uncomprehending characters.

If indeed an early Christian debate was the impetus for the composition of all or part of the Fourth Gospel, should we not expect to find additional and more explicit evidence of John's polemic against Thomas in particular? Should we not also expect Thomas to appear more often and in a more substantive role than he actually does? He appears four times in the narrative (11:16; 14:5; 20:24–31; 21:2) and only one of the four appearances (20:24–31) has him speaking in a way that holds any real theological substance. Thomas's relative insignificance in the overall narrative is an important area of critique, but it ultimately fails to address the assertions of Riley, DeConick, and Pagels. I conclude this volume by returning once more to the community-conflict hypothesis.

In their publications on the John-*Thomas* relationship, Riley, DeConick, and Pagels are concerned with the history of early Christianity and what they regard as its multiform development. All three scholars rely heavily upon source-, form-, and redaction-critical criteria to explain the conflict they envision. Elements of historical inquiry also factor into their discussions. Then, after developing a picture of the John-*Thomas* conflict using a complex set of different historical-critical elements, each scholar introduces one narrative critical insight to validate their view—the characterization of Thomas. This leads to a truncated reading of the Johannine narrative that drastically overemphasizes the significance of one minor character. The hermeneutic that emerges is an amalgam of loosely connected methodological assumptions forced together to paint a picture that is unsupported by the available information. Through this approach they reveal that their greater concern is to mine the text for insights that will assist their revaluation of early Christianity and gospel origins. Or, to say it more succinctly, in the character of Thomas they simply find what they are looking for. Because of this they generate incomplete, superficial readings of the Fourth Gospel that subjugate the interests of careful reading to those of historical speculation and reconstruction.

Their approach forsakes a great deal of the Fourth Gospel's content and ultimately robs the Johannine narrative of the opportunity to say anything affirmative, declarative, or genuinely didactic to the Johannine reader. The practical outworking of their theory leads to the inevitable conclusion that John's story of Jesus is simply a vehicle for polemic and apologetic in the wider context of theological bickering. However, questions that are raised of Thomas must necessarily be raised of other characters in the narrative, and this is where the community-conflict hypothesis fails. A closer examination of the Gospel reveals a spate of similarly uncomprehending characters, several of whom carry greater theological and narratival significance than Thomas.

Our awareness of this literary trend brings to mind the tongue-in-cheek questions raised earlier by Dunderberg.[1] For instance, after seeing the presentation of Philip in the Fourth Gospel, should we examine the *Gospel of Philip* for possible areas of polemic and/or apologetic? Is it possible that there exists—somewhere yet undiscovered—a "Gospel of Andrew" or maybe an "Acts of the Samaritan Woman" in which we should expect to find ideas that compete with the teachings of John 4? Or perhaps there lies dormant a literary strand of "Marthanite" Christianity that reveals the expectation of future resurrection in a way that dismisses the bodily resurrection of Lazarus? Were we to rely upon the foundational assumptions of the community-conflict hypothesis we might be tempted to answer "yes" to these questions. However, a closer reading of the Johannine narrative reveals that this is not necessary. Thomas is not the target of a Johannine polemic but rather is one of many foils for the narrator of the Fourth Gospel.

The Fourth Gospel presents the reader with an impressive array of characters, each of which contributes to the story in a way that serves

1. See especially Dunderberg, *Beloved Disciple in Conflict?* 66.

the Evangelist's stated purpose in 20:31: "These things have been written that you might believe that Jesus is the Christ, the son of God, and believing, you might have life in his name." The reader learns about the nature of true belief in Jesus by watching the foibles, frustrations, and failures of these characters. Thus, from a methodological standpoint, it is more appropriate to examine the Fourth Gospel carefully as an autonomous narrative, rather than mining the text for details that will assist the development of theories related early intra-Christian relationships.

After everything has been examined carefully, a consistent literary analysis of characters in the Fourth Gospel reveals a pattern where uncomprehending characters provide the Johannine Jesus with opportunities to speak authoritatively to the literary audience. Thomas is one of these characters, and should not be regarded as the target of a Johannine polemic; nor should he be regarded as the impetus for the Fourth Gospel's composition. While this study has not solved the larger question of John's relationship to the *Gospel of Thomas*, the realization of literary trends and theological emphases in the Fourth Gospel raises serious problems for the community-conflict hypothesis.

Bibliography

Reference Works and Sources

Aland, Kurt, Matthew Black, C. M. Martini, Bruce M. Metzger, and Allen Wikgren, editors. *The Greek New Testament*. 3rd ed. Stuttgart: United Bible Societies, 1975.

Bauer, Walter, Fredrick William Danker, W. F. Arndt, and F. W. Gingrich. *A Greek-English Lexicon of the New Testament and Other Early Christian Literature*. 3rd ed. Chicago: University of Chicago Press, 2000.

Blass, F., A. Debrunner, and R. W. Funk. *A Greek Grammar of the New Testament and Other Early Christian Literature*. Chicago: University of Chicago Press, 1979.

Brown, Colin, editor. *The New International Dictionary of New Testament Theology*. 4 vols. Grand Rapids: Zondervan, 1986.

Brown, Francis, S. R. Driver, and Charles A. Briggs. *A Hebrew and English Lexicon of the Old Testament*. Oxford: Clarendon, 1907.

Crum, Walter E. *A Coptic Dictionary*. 1939. Reprinted, Ancient Language Resources. Eugene, OR: Wipf & Stock, 2005.

Elliger, K., and K. Rudolph, editors. *Biblia Hebraica Stuttgartensia*. Stuttgart: Deutsche Bibelgesellschaft, 1983.

Green, J. B., and S. McKnight, editors. *Dictionary of Jesus and the Gospels*. Downers Grove, IL: InterVarsity, 1992.

Kittel, Gerhard, and Gerhard Friedrich, editors. *Theological Dictionary of the New Testament* Translated by Geoffrey W. Bromiley. 10 vols. Grand Rapids: Eerdmans, 1964–76.

Metzger, Bruce M. *A Textual Commentary on the Greek New Testament*. 2nd ed. Stuttgart: United Bible Societies, 1994.

Nestle, Eberhard, Erwin Nestle, K. Aland, and B. Aland, editors. *Novum Testamentum Graece*. 27th ed. Stuttgart: Deutsche Bibelgesellschaft, 1994.

New Testament: New English Translation / Novum Testamentum Graece. Stuttgart: Deutsche Bibelgesellschaft; Dallas: NET Bible Press, 2004.

Rahlfs, A., editor. *Septuaginta: id est Vetus Testamentum Graece iuxta LXX Interpretes*. Stuttgart: Württemburgische Bibelanstalt, 1965.

Strack, H. L., and P. Billerbeck. *Kommentar zum Neuen Testament aus Talmud und Midrasch*. 6 vols. Munich: Beck, 1922–61.

Wallace, Daniel B. *Greek Grammar Beyond the Basics: An Exegetical Syntax of the New Testament*. Grand Rapids: Zondervan, 1996.

Commentaries

Barrett, C. K. *The Gospel According to St. John*. 2nd. ed. London: SPCK, 1978.

Bauer, Walter. *Das Johannesevangelium*. HKNT 6. Tübingen: Mohr, 1933.

Beasley-Murray, George R. *John*. Waco, TX: Word, 1987.

Bernard, J. H. *A Critical and Exegetical Commentary on the Gospel According to St. John*. 2 vols. ICC. Edinburgh: T. & T. Clark, 1928.

Boismard, M. E., and A. Lamouille. *L'Evangile de Jean*. Synopse des Quatre Evangiles en Francais 3. Paris: Cerf, 1977.

Brown, Raymond E. *The Gospel According to John*. 2 vols. AB 29, 29a. Garden City, NY: Doubleday, 1966, 1970.

Bultmann, Rudolf. *The Gospel of John*. Translated by George. R. Beasley–Murray. Oxford: Blackwell, 1971.

Büschel, F. *Das Evangelium nach Johannes*. NTD 4. Göttingen: Vandenhoeck & Ruprecht, 1949.

Carson, D. A. *The Gospel According to John*. Grand Rapids: Eerdmans, 1991.

Culpepper, R. Alan. *The Gospel and Letters of John*. Interpreting Biblical Texts. Nashville: Abingdon, 1998.

Haenchen, Ernst. *John*. 2 vols. Translated by R. W. Funk. Hermeneia. Philadelphia: Fortress, 1984.

Hoskyns, Edwyn Clement. *The Fourth Gospel*. London: Faber, 1947.

Keener, Craig S. *The Gospel of John*. 2 vols. Peabody, MA: Hendrickson, 2003.

Kysar, Robert. *John*. ACNT. Minneapolis: Augsburg, 1986.

Lightfoot, R. H. *St. John's Gospel*. Oxford: Oxford University Press, 1956.

Lincoln, Andrew T. *The Gospel According to St. John*. BNTC 4. Peabody, MA: Hendrickson, 2005.

Lindars, Barnabas. *The Gospel of John*. NCB. London: Oliphants, 1972.

MacRae, George W. *Invitation to John: A Commentary on the Gospel of John with Complete Text from the Jerusalem Bible*. Doubleday New Testament Commentary Series. Garden City, NY: Image, 1978.

Malina, Bruce J., and Richard L. Rohrbaugh. *Social-Science Commentary on the Gospel of John*. Minneapolis: Fortress, 1998.

Marsh, John. *The Gospel of John*. Pelican Gospel Commentaries. Harmondsworth, UK: Penguin, 1968.

Moloney, Francis J. *Belief in the Word: Reading the Fourth Gospel, John 1–4*. Minneapolis: Fortress, 1993.

———. *Glory Not Dishonor: Reading John 13–21*. Minneapolis: Fortress, 1998.

———. *The Gospel of John*. SP 4. Collegeville, MN: Liturgical, 1998.

———. *Signs and Shadows: Reading John 5–12*. Minneapolis: Fortress, 1995.

Morris, Leon. *The Gospel According to John*. NICNT. Grand Rapids: Eerdmans, 1995.

Neyrey, Jerome H. *The Gospel of John*. New Cambridge Bible Commentary. New York: Cambridge University Press, 2007.

Odeberg, Hugo. *The Fourth Gospel: Interpreted in its Relation to Contemporaneous Religious Currents in Palestine and the Hellenistic–Oriental World*. Amsterdam: Grüner, 1974.

Ridderbos, Herman N. *The Gospel According to John*. Grand Rapids: Eerdmans, 1997.

Schnackenburg, Rudolf. *The Gospel According to St. John*. Translated by C. Hastings. 3 vols. HTCNT 4. New York: Crossroad, 1968–82.

Smith, D. Moody. *John*. ANTC. Nashville: Abingdon, 1999.

Stibbe, Mark W. G. *John*. Readings. Sheffield: JSOT, 1993.

Talbert, Charles H. *Reading John: A Literary and Theological Commentary on the Fourth Gospel and the Johannine Epistles.* New York: Crossroad, 1992.

Other Literature

Abbott, Edwin. *Johannine Vocabulary: A Comparison of the Words of the Fourth Gospel with Those of the Three.* London: Black, 1905.

Adam, A. K. M. *What is Postmodern Biblical Criticism?* Guides to Biblical Scholarship. Minneapolis: Fortress, 1995.

Allison, Dale C., Jr. "Peter and Cephas: One and the Same." *JBL* 111 (1992) 489–95.

Alter, Robert. *The Art of Biblical Narrative.* New York: Basic Books, 1981.

Ashton, John. "The Transformation of Wisdom: A Study of the Prologue of John's Gospel." *NTS* 32 (1986) 161–86.

Attridge, Harold A. "'Seeking' and 'Asking' in Q, Thomas, and John." In *From Quest to Q: Festschrift James M. Robinson,* edited by Jon Ma. Asgeirsson, Kirstin de Troyer, and Marvin W. Meyer, 295–302. BETL 146. Leuven: Peeters, 2000.

Baarda, T. "John 1:17b: The Origin of a Peshitta Reading." *ETL* 77 (2001) 153–62.

Bacon, B. W. "The Motivation of John 21:15–25." *JBL* 50 (1931) 71–80.

Ball, David Mark. *"I Am" in John's Gospel: Literary Function, Background and Theological Implications.* JSNTSup 124. Sheffield: Sheffield Academic, 1996.

Bar-Efrat, Shimon. *Narrative Art in the Bible.* JSOTSup 70. Sheffield: Almond, 1989.

Bassler, Jouette M. "Mixed Signals: Nicodemus in the Fourth Gospel." *JBL* 108 (1989) 635–46.

Bauer, Walter. *Orthodoxy and Heresy in Earliest Christianity.* Edited by Robert A. Kraft and Gerhard Kroedel. Philadelphia: Fortress, 1971.

Beck, David R. *The Discipleship Paradigm: Readers and Anonymous Characters in the Fourth Gospel.* BIS 27. Leiden: Brill, 1997.

———. "The Narrative Function of Anonymity in the Fourth Gospel." *Semeia* 63 (1993) 143–58.

Berlin, Adele. *Poetics and Interpretation of Biblical Narrative.* Bible and Literature Series. Sheffield: Almond, 1983.

Best, Ernest. "1 Peter and the Gospel Tradition." *NTS* 16 (1969) 95–113.

Black, Matthew. "Does an Aramaic Tradition Underlie John 1:16?" *JTS* 42 (1941) 69–70.

Blomberg, Craig L. *The Historical Reliability of John's Gospel: Issues & Commentary.* Downers Grove, IL: InterVarsity, 2002.

Boismard, M. E. "Le lavement des pieds." *RB* 71 (1964) 5–24.

———. *Moïse ou Jésus: Essai de Christologie Johannique.* BETL 84. Leuven: Leuven University Press, 1988.

Boisson, Nathalie, and Anne Boud'hors. *Actes du huitième Congrès international d'ètudes coptes.* 2 vols. OLA 163. Leuven: Peeters, 2007.

Booth, Wayne C. *The Rhetoric of Fiction.* Chicago: University of Chicago Press, 1961.

Borgen, Peter. "Observations on the Targumic Character of the Prologue of John." *NTS* 16 (1969) 288–95.

Boyarin, Daniel. "The Gospel of the Memra, Jewish Binitarianism and the Prologue to John." *HTR* 94 (2001) 243–84.

Broadhead, Edwin K. "An Authentic Saying of Jesus in the Gospel of Thomas?" *NTS* 46 (2000) 132–49.

Brown, Raymond E. *The Community of the Beloved Disciple*. New York: Paulist, 1979.

———. *The Death of the Messiah. From Gethsemane to the Grave: A Commentary on the Passion Narratives of the Four Gospels*. ABRL. New York: Doubleday, 1994.

———. "The Gospel of Peter and Canonical Gospel Priority." *NTS* 33 (1987) 321–43.

———. "The Gospel of Thomas and St. John's Gospel." *NTS* 9 (1962) 155–77.

———. *An Introduction to the Gospel of John*. Edited and updated by Francis J. Moloney. ABRL. Garden City, NY: Doubleday, 2003.

———. "The Prologue of the Gospel of John: John 1:1–18." *RevExp* 62 (1965) 429–39.

———. "Roles of Women in the Fourth Gospel." *TS* 36 (1975) 688–99.

Brown, Raymond E., Karl P. Donfried, and John Reumann, editors. *Peter in the New Testament: A Collaborative Assessment by Protestant and Roman Catholic Scholars*. Minneapolis: Augsburg, 1973.

Bultmann, Rudolf. *The History of the Synoptic Tradition*. New York: Harper & Row, 1957.

Burnett, Fred W. "Characterization and Reader Construction of Characters in the Gospels." *Semeia* 63 (1993) 4–28.

Cameron, Ron. *Sayings Traditions in the Apocryphon of James*. HTS 34. Philadelphia: Fortress, 1984.

Carson, D. A. "The Purpose of the Fourth Gospel: John 20:31 Reconsidered." *JBL* 106 (1987) 639–51.

———. "Syntactical and Text-Critical on John 20:31: One More Round on the Purpose of the Fourth Gospel." *JBL* 124 (2005) 693–714.

———. "Understanding Misunderstandings in the Fourth Gospel." *TynBul* 33 (1982) 59–91.

Carter, Warren. "The Prologue of John's Gospel: Function, Symbol and the Definitive Word." *JSNT* 39 (1990) 35–58.

Cassidy, Richard J. *John's Gospel in New Perspective: Christology and the Realities of Roman Power*. Maryknoll, NY: Orbis, 1992.

Charlesworth, James H. *The Beloved Disciple: Whose Witness Validates the Gospel of John?* Valley Forge: Trinity, 1995.

Chatman, Seymour Benjamin. *Story and Discourse: Narrative Structure in Fiction and Film*. Ithaca: Cornell University Press, 1978.

Chennattu, Rehka M., and Mary L. Coloe, editors. *Transcending Boundaries: Contemporary Readings of the New Testament, Essays in Honor of Francis J. Moloney*. Biblioteca di Scienze Religiose 187. Rome: Liberia Ateneo Salesiano, 2005.

Collins, Raymond F. "From John to the Beloved Disciple: An Essay on Johannine Characters." *Int* 49 (1995) 359–69.

———. "The Representative Figures of the Fourth Gospel." *DRev* 94 (1976) 26–46.

———. *These Things Have Been Written: Studies on the Fourth Gospel*. Louvain Theological & Pastoral Monographs 2. Louvain: Peeters, 1990.

Coloe, Mary. "The Structure of the Johannine Prologue and Genesis 1." *ABR* 45 (1997) 40–55.

———. "Welcome into the Household of God: The Foot Washing in John 13." *CBQ* 66 (2004) 400–15.

Conway, Colleen M. *Men and Women in the Fourth Gospel: Gender and Johannine Characterization*. SBLDS 167. Atlanta: Scholars, 1999.

———. "The Production of the Johannine Community: A New Historicist Perspective." *JBL* 121 (2002) 479–95.

———. "Speaking through Ambiguity: Minor Characters in the Fourth Gospel." *BibInt* 10 (2002) 324–41.

Cotterell, F. Peter. "The Nicodemus Conversation: A Fresh Appraisal." *ExpTim* 96 (1985) 237–42.

Cullman, Oscar. *Peter; Disciple, Apostle, Martyr: A Historical and Theological Essay.* Translated by Floyd V. Filson. Philadelphia: Westminster, 1953.

Culpepper, R. Alan. *Anatomy of the Fourth Gospel: A Study in Literary Design*. FF. Philadelphia: Fortress, 1983.

———. "The Johannine *hypodeigma*: A Reading of John 1." *Semeia* 53 (1991) 132–52.

———. "The Pivot of John's Prologue." *NTS* 27 (1981) 1–31.

———. "The Plot of John's Story of Jesus." *Int* 49 (1995) 347–58.

Culpepper, R. Alan, and C. Clifton Black, editors. *Exploring the Gospel of John: In Honor of D. Moody Smith*. Louisville: Westminster John Knox, 1996.

D'Angelo, Mary Rose. "Intimating Deity in the Gospel of John: Theological Language and 'Father' in 'Prayers of Jesus.'" *Semeia* 85 (1999) 59–82.

Danna, Elizabeth. "A Note on John 4:29." *RB* 106 (1999) 219–23.

Daube David. "Jesus and the Samaritan Woman: The Meaning of συγχράομαι [Jn 4:7ff.]." *JBL* 69 (1950) 137–47.

Davies, Stevan. "The Christology and Protology of the Gospel of Thomas." *JBL* 111 (1992) 663–82.

———. *The Gospel of Thomas and Christian Wisdom*. NewYork: Seabury, 1983.

———. "Mark's Use of the Gospel of Thomas." *Neot* 30 (1996) 307–34.

———. Review of *Resurrection Reconsidered: Thomas and John in Controversy*, by Gregory J. Riley. *RBL*, June 26, 2000, n.p. Online: http://www.bookreviews.org/pdf/2219_1329.pdf.

Day, Janeth Norfleete. *The Woman at the Well: Interpretation of John 4:1–42 in Retrospect and Prospect*. BIS 61. Leiden: Brill, 2002.

de Boer, Martinus C. "John 4:27: Women (and Men) in the Gospel and Community of John." In *Women in the Biblical Tradition*, edited by George J. Brooke, 208–30. Studies in Women and Religion 31. Lewiston, NY: Mellen, 1992.

DeConick, April D. "'Blessed Are Those Who Have Not Seen' (Jn 20:29): Johannine Dramatization of an Early Christian Discourse." In *The Nag Hammadi Library after Fifty Years: Proceedings of the 1995 Society of Biblical Literature Commemoration*, edited by John D. Turner and Anne McGuire, 381–98. NHMS 44. Leiden: Brill, 1997.

———. "John Rivals Thomas: From Community Conflict to Gospel Narrative." In *Jesus in the Johannine Tradition*, edited by Robert T. Fortna and Tom Thatcher, 303–12. Louisville: Westminster John Knox, 2001.

———. "The Original Gospel of Thomas." *VC* 56 (2002) 167–99.

———. *The Original Gospel of Thomas in Translation: With a Commentary and New English Translation of the Complete Gospel.* LNTS 287. Edinburgh: T. & T. Clark, 2007.

———. *Recovering the Original Gospel of Thomas: A History of the Gospel and Its Growth*. LNTS 286. Edinburgh: T. & T. Clark, 2005.

———. *Seek to See Him: Ascent and Vision Mysticism in the Gospel of Thomas*. VCSup 33. Leiden: Brill, 1996.

de Jonge, Martinus. "Nicodemus and Jesus: Some Observations on Understanding and Misunderstanding in the Fourth Gospel." *BJRL* 53 (1971) 337–59.

Derrett, J. D. M. "Correcting Nicodemus (John 3:2, 21)." *ExpTim* 112 (2001) 126.

———. "The Samaritan Woman's Pitcher." *DR* 102 (1984) 252–61.

Dodd, C. H. *Historical Tradition in the Forth Gospel*. Cambridge: Cambridge University Press, 1965.

———. *The Interpretation of the Fourth Gospel*. Cambridge: Cambridge University Press, 1953.

Donahue, John R., editor. *Life in Abundance: Studies of John's Gospel in Tribute to Raymond E. Brown, S.S.* Collegeville, MN: Liturgical, 2005.

Doresse, J. *L'Évangile selon Thomas*. Paris: Plon & Rocher, 1959.

Drijvers, Jan J. W. "Fact and Problems in Early Syriac-speaking Christianity." *SecCent* 2 (1982) 173–75.

Droge, Arthur. "The Status of Peter in the Fourth Gospel: A Note on John 18:10–11." *JBL* 109 (1990) 307–11.

Duke, Paul D. *Irony in the Fourth Gospel*. Atlanta: John Knox, 1985.

Dunderberg, Ismo. *The Beloved Disciple in Conflict? Revisiting the Gospels of John and Thomas*. Oxford: Oxford University Press, 2006.

———. "Beloved Disciple in John: Ideal Figure in an Early Christian Controversy?" In *Fair Play: Diversity and Conflicts in Early Christianity, Essays in Honour of Heikki Räisänen*, by Ismo Dunderberg, Christopher Tuckett, and Kari Syreeni, 243–69. NovTSup 103. Leiden: Brill, 2001.

———. "John and Thomas in Conflict?" In In *The Nag Hammadi Library after Fifty Years: Proceedings of the 1995 Society of Biblical Literature Commemoration*, edited by John D. Turner and Anne McGuire, 361–80. NHMS 44. Leiden: Brill, 1997.

———. "Thomas and the Beloved Disciple." In *Thomas at the Crossroads: Essays on the Gospel of Thomas*, edited by Risto Uro, 65–88. Studies of the New Testament and Its World. Edinburgh: T. & T. Clark, 1998.

———. "Thomas' I-Sayings and the Gospel of John." In *Thomas at the Crossroads: Essays on the Gospel of Thomas*, edited Risto Uro, 33–63. Studies of the New Testament and Its World. Edinburgh: T. & T. Clark, 1998.

Dunderberg, Ismo, Christopher Tuckett, and Kari Syreeni. *Fair Play: Diversity and Conflicts in Early Christianity, Essays in Honour of Heikki Räisänen*. NovTSup 103. Leiden: Brill, 2001.

Edwards, Hubert E. *The Disciple Who Wrote These Things: A New Inquiry Into the Origins and Historical Value of the Gospel According St. John*. London: J. Clark, 1953.

Ehrman, Bart. "Cephas and Peter." *JBL* 109 (1990) 463–74.

Evans, Craig A. *Noncanonical Writings and New Testament Interpretation*. Peabody, MA: Hendrickson, 1992.

———. "'Peter Warming Himself': The Problem of an Editorial 'Seam.'" *JBL* 101 (1982) 245–49.

Fee, Gordon D. "On the Text and Meaning of John 20:30–31." In *To What End Exegesis? Essays Textual, Exegetical, and Theological*, 29–42. Grand Rapids: Eerdmans, 2001.

Fennema, D. A. "John 1:18: 'God the Only Son.'" *NTS* 31 (1985) 125–26.

Filson, Floyd V. "Who Was the Beloved Disciple?" *JBL* 68 (1949) 83–88.

Fitzmyer, Joseph A. *Essays on the Semitic Background of the New Testament*. Sources for Biblical Study 5. Missoula, MT: Scholars, 1974.

———. *To Advance the Gospel: New Testament Studies*. New York: Crossroad, 1981.

Fokkelman, J. P. *Reading Biblical Narrative: An Introductory Guide*. Louisville: Westminster John Knox, 1991.

Forster, E. M. *Aspects of the Novel*. New York: Harcourt, Brace, 1927.

Fortna, Robert T. *The Fourth Gospel and Its Predecessors: From Narrative Source to Present Gospel*. Philadelphia: Fortress, 1988.

Fortna, Robert T., and Tom Thatcher, editors. *Jesus in the Johannine Tradition*. Louisville: Westminster John Knox, 2001.

Freed, Edwin D., and Russell B. Hunt. "Fortna's Signs-Source in John." *JBL* 94 (1975) 563–79.

Gaertner, Bertil. *The Theology of the Gospel according to Thomas*. Translated by Eric J. Sharpe. New York: Harper, 1961.

Garitte, Gerard. "Les 'Logoi' d'Oxyrhynque sont traduits de copte." *Muséon* 73 (1960) 335–49.

Gignac, Francis T. "The Use of Verbal Variety in the Fourth Gospel." In *Transcending Boundaries: Contemporary Readings of the New Testament, Essays in Honor of Francis J. Moloney*, edited by Rekha M. Chennattu and Mary L. Coloe, 191–200. Biblioteca di Scienze Religiose 187. Rome: Liberia Ateneo Salesiano, 2005.

Goguel, Maurice. *La Foi à la résurrection de Jésus dans le Christianisme primitif: étude d'histoire et de psychologie religieuses*. Paris: Leroux, 1933.

Goulder, Michael. "Nicodemus." *SJT* 44 (1991) 153–68.

Grant, Robert M., with David Noel Freedman. *The Secret Sayings of Jesus*. Garden City, NY: Doubleday, 1960.

Grenfell, Bernard P., and Arthur S. Hunt. *Logia Iesou, Sayings of Our Lord: From an Early Greek Papyrus*. London: Frowde, 1897.

Grese, William C. "'Unless One is Born Again': The Use of Heavenly Journey in John 3." *JBL* 107 (1988) 677–93.

Guillamont, Antoine. "Les sémitismes dans l'Évangile selon Thomas: Essai de classement." In *Studies in Gnosticism and Hellenistic Religions: Presented to Gilles Quispel on the Occasion of His 65th Birthday*, edited by R. van den Broek and M. J. Vermaseren, 190–204. Etudes préliminaires aux religions orientales dans l'Empire romain 91. Leiden, Brill 1981.

———. "Sémitismes dans les logia de Jésus retrouvés *à* Nag-Hammadi." *JA* 246 (1958) 113–23.

Guillamont, Antoine, et al., editors and translators. *The Gospel according to Thomas: Coptic Text Established and Translated*. Leiden: Brill, 1959.

Gundry, Robert. "In My Father's House Are Many Mansions." *ZNW* 58 (1967) 68–71.

Hamid-Khani, Saeed. *Revelation and Concealment of Christ: A Theological Inquiry into the Elusive Language of the Fourth Gospel*. WUNT 120. Tübingen: Mohr/Siebeck, 2000.

Hanson, A. T. "John 1:14–18 and Exodus 34." *NTS* 23 (1977) 90–101.

Harstine, Stan. *Moses as a Character in the Fourth Gospel.* JSNTSup 229. Sheffield: Sheffield Academic, 2002.

Hays, Richard B. "Reading Scripture in Light of the Resurrection." In *The Art of Reading Scripture*, by Ellen F. Davis and Richard B. Hays, 216–38. Grand Rapids: Eerdmans, 2003.

Hayward, C. T. R. "The Holy Name of the God of Moses and the Prologue of St. John's Gospel." *NTS* 25 (1978) 16–32.

Heil, John Paul. *Blood and Water: The Death and Resurrection of Jesus in John 18–21.* CBQMS 27. Washington, DC: Catholic Biblical Association, 1995.

Hooker, Morna D. "The Johannine Prologue and the Messianic Secret." *NTS* 21 (1974) 40–58.

Hulen, Amos B. "The Call of the Four Disciples in John 1." *JBL* 67 (1948) 153–57.

James, Henry. "The Art of Fiction." *Longman's Magazine* 4 (1844) n.p.

Johnson, Stephen R. "The Gospel of Thomas 76:3 and Canonical Parallels: Three Segments in the Tradition History of the Saying." In *The Nag Hammadi Library after Fifty Years: Proceedings of the 1995 Society of Biblical Literature Commemoration*, edited by John D. Turner and Anne McGuire, 308–24. NHMS 44. Leiden: Brill, 1997.

Kasser, Rodolphe. *L'Évangile selon Thomas: Présentation et commentaire théologique.* Biliothèque Theologique. Neuchâtel, Switzerland: Delachaux & Niestlé, 1961.

Kermode, Frank. *The Genesis of Secrecy: On the Interpretation of Narrative.* Cambridge: Harvard University Press, 1979.

Koester, Craig. *Symbolism in the Fourth Gospel: Meaning, Mystery, and Community.* 2nd ed. Minneapolis: Fortress, 2003.

———. "The Savior of the World (John 4:42)." *JBL* 109 (1990) 665–80.

Koester, Helmut. "Dialog und Spruchüberlieferung in den gnostischen Texten von Nag Hammadi." *EvT* 39 (1979) 532–56.

———. "The Extracanonical Saying of the Lord as Products of the Christian Community." *Semeia* 44 (1988) 57–77.

———. "Gnostic Sayings and Controversy Traditions in John 8:12–59." In *Nag Hammadi, Gnosticism and Early Christianity*, edited by Charles W. Hedrick and Robert Hodgson Jr., 97–110. 1986. Reprint, Eugene, OR: Wipf & Stock, 2005.

———. "Gnostic Writings as Witnesses for the Development of the Sayings Tradition." In *The Rediscovery of Gnosticism: Proceedings of the International Conference on Gnosticism at Yale*, edited by Bentley Layton, 238–61. Leiden: Brill, 1980.

———. "ΓΝΩΜΑΙ ΔΙΑΦΟΡΟΙ: The Origin and Nature of Diversification in the History of Early Christianity." *HTR* 58 (1965) 279–318.

———. "One Jesus and Four Primitive Gospels." *HTR* 61 (1968) 203–47.

———. "Written Gospels or Oral Tradition." *JBL* 113 (1994) 293–97.

Koester, Helmut, and Stephen J. Patterson. *Ancient Christian Gospels: Their History and Development.* Philadelphia: Trinity, 1991.

Köstenberger, Andreas. "Seventh Johannine Sign: A Study in John's Christology." *BBR* 5 (1995) 87–103.

Kysar, Robert. "The Background of the Prologue of the Fourth Gospel: A Critique of Historical Methods." *CJT* 16 (1970) 250–55.

Lake, Kirsopp. "Simon, Cephas, Peter." *HTR* 14 (1921) 95–97.

La Potterie, Ignace de. "Structure du Prologue de Saint Jean." *NTS* 30 (1984) 354–81.

Layton, Bentley. *The Gnostic Scriptures: A New Translation with Annotations and Introductions*. Garden City, NY: Doubleday, 1987.

———, editor. *The Rediscovery of Gnosticism: Proceedings of the International Conference on Gnosticism at Yale, New Haven, Connecticut, March 28–31, 1978*. 2 vols. SHR 41. Leiden: Brill, 1980–81.

Lea, Thomas D. "The Reliability of History in John's Gospel." *JETS* 38 (1995) 387–402.

Lee, Dorothy. *Flesh and Glory: Symbolism, Gender and Theology in the Gospel of John*. New York: Crossroad, 2002.

Lehtipuu, Outi. "Characterization and Persuasion: The Rich Man and the Poor Man in Luke 16.19–31." In *Characterization in the Gospel: Reconceiving Narrative Criticism*, edited by David Rhoads and Kari Syreeni, 73–105. JSNTSup 184. Sheffield: Sheffield Academic, 1999.

Leipoldt, Johannes. *Das Evangelium nach Thomas Koptisch und Deutch*. TUGAL 101. Berlin: Akademie-Verlag, 1967.

Leon-Dufour, Xavier. "Towards a Symbolic Reading of the Fourth Gospel." *New Tesatment Studies* 27 (1981) 439–56.

Leroy, H. *Rätsel und Missverständnis. Ein Beitrag zur Formgeschicthe des Johannesevangeliums*. BBB 30. Bonn: Peter Hanstein, 1968.

Lewis, F. Warburton. *Disarrangements in the Fourth Gospel*. Cambridge: Cambridge University Press, 1910.

Lieu, Judith M. "The Mother of the Son in the Fourth Gospel." *JBL* 117 (1998) 61–77.

Lozada, Francisco, and Tom Thatcher, editors. *New Currents through John: A Global Perspective*. Atlanta: SBL, 2006.

Maccini, Robert Gordon. "A Reassessment of the Woman at the Well in John 4 in Light of the Samaritan Context." *JSNT* 53 (1994) 35–46.

Mahoney, Aidan. "A New Look at an Old Problem [John 18,12–14, 19–24]." *CBQ* 27 (1965) 137–44.

Malbon, Elizabeth Struthers. "The Major Importance of Minor Characters in Mark." In *The New Literary Criticism and the New Testament*, edited by Elizabeth Struthers Malbon and Edgar V. McKnight, 58–86. JSNTSup 109. Sheffield: Sheffield Academic, 1994.

Marcovich, M. "Textual Criticism on the Gospel of Thomas." *JTS* 20 (1969) 53–74.

Martyn, J. Louis. *History and Theology in the Fourth Gospel*. 2nd ed. Nashville: Abingdon, 1979.

Maynard, Arthur H. "The Role of Peter in the Fourth Gospel." *NTS* 30 (1984) 531–48.

McKay, K. L. "Aspect in Imperatival Constructions in New Testament Greek." *NovT* 27 (1985) 201–26.

———. "Style and Significance in the Language of John 21:15–17." *Novum Testamentum* 27 (1985) 319–33.

McKnight, Edgar V. *Postmodern Use of the Bible: The Emergence of Reader-Oriented Criticism*. 1988. Reprint, Eugene, OR: Wipf & Stock, 2005.

McRae, George W. "Gnosticism and the Church of John's Gospel." In *Nag Hammadi, Gnosticism and Early Christianity*, edited by Charles W. Hedrick and Robert Hodgson Jr., 89–96. 1986. Reprint, Eugene, OR: Wipf & Stock, 2005.

Meagher, John C. "John 1:14 and the New Temple." *JBL* 88 (1969) 57–68.

Meeks, Wayne. "The Man from Heaven in Johannine Sectarianism." *JBL* 91 (1972) 44–72.

Meier, John P. "The Circle of the Twelve: Did it Exist During Jesus' Public Ministry?" *JBL* 116 (1997) 635–72.

Mercer, Calvin. "APOSTELLEIN and PEMPEIN in John." *NTS* 36 (1990) 619–24.

———. "Jesus the Apostle: 'Sending' and the Theology of John." *JETS* 35 (1992) 457–62.

Meyer, Marvin. *The Gospel of Thomas: The Hidden Sayings of Jesus*. San Francisco: HarperSanFrancisco, 1992.

Minear, Paul S. "The Original Functions of John 21." *JBL* 102 (1983) 85–98.

Moloney, Francis J. *Beginning the Good News: A Narrative Approach*. Collegeville, MN: Liturgical, 1992.

———. "Can Everyone Be Wrong? A Reading of John 11.1—12.8." *NTS* 49 (2003) 505–27.

———. "The Faith of Martha and Mary: A Narrative Approach to John 11,17–40." *Bib* 75 (1994) 471–93.

———. "The Fourth Gospel and the Jesus of History." *NTS* 46 (2000) 42–58.

———. "The Function of Prolepsis for the Interpretation of John 6." In *The Gospel of John: Text and Context*, 169–92. BIS 72. Leiden: Brill, 2005.

———. *The Gospel of John: Text and Context*. BIS 72. Leiden: Brill, 2005.

———. *A Hard Saying: The Gospel and Culture*. Collegeville, MN: Liturgical, 2001.

———. *The Johannine Son of Man*. 2nd ed. Biblioteca di Scienze Religiose 14. Rome: Libreria Antoneo Salesiano, 1978.

———. "Narrative Criticism of the Gospels." *Pacifica* 4 (1991) 181–201.

———. "Telling God's Story: The Fourth Gospel." In *The Forgotten God: Perspectives in Biblical Theology, Essays in Honor of Paul J. Achtemeier on the Occasion of his Seventy-Fifth Birthday*, edited by Andrew A. Das and Frank J. Matera, 107–22. Louisville: Westminster John Knox, 2002.

———. "Who Is 'the Reader' in/of the Fourth Gospel?" *ABR* 40 (1992) 20–33.

Moore, Stephen D. "Are There Impurities in the Living Water That the Johannine Jesus Dispenses? Deconstruction, Feminism and the Samaritan Woman." *BibInt* 1 (1993) 207–27.

Mowley, Henry. "John 1:14–18 in the Light of Exodus 33:7—34:35." *ExpTim* 95 (1984) 135–37.

Mudrick, Marvin. "Character and Event in Fiction." *Yale Review* 50 (1961) 202–18.

Munro, Winsome. "The Pharisee and the Samaritan in John: Polar or Parallel?" *CBQ* 57 (1995) 710–28.

Neirynck, Frans. "The Anonymous Disciple in John 1." *ETL* 66 (1990) 5–37.

Neyrey, Jerome H. "Jacob Traditions and the Interpretation of John 4:10–26." *CBQ* 41 (1979) 419–37.

———. "The 'Noble Shepherd' in John 10: Cultural and Rhetorical Background." *JBL* 129 (2001) 267–91.

———. What's Wrong with This Picture? John 4, Cultural Stereotypes of Woman, and Public and Private Space." *BTB* 24 (1994) 77–91.

O'Day, Gail R. "Toward a Narrative-Critical Study of John." *Int* 49 (1995) 341–46.

O'Rourke, John J. "Asides in the Gospel of John." *NovT* 21 (1979) 210–19.

Pagels, Elaine H. *Beyond Belief: The Secret Gospel of Thomas*. San Francisco: HarperCollins, 2003.

———. "Exegesis of Genesis 1 in the Gospels of Thomas and John." *JBL* 118 (1999) 477–96.

———. *The Gnostic Gospels*. New York: Random House, 1979.

Painter, John. "John: Christology and the Fourth Gospel—A Study of the Prologue." *ABR* 31 (1983) 45–62.

Pamment, Margaret. "Focus in the Fourth Gospel." *ExpTim* 97 (1985) 72–73.

Parker, Pierson. "John the Son of Zebedee and the Fourth Gospel." *JBL* 81 (1962) 35–43.

Patterson, Stephen J. *The Gospel of Thomas and Jesus*. FF. Sonoma: Polebridge, 1993.

Patterson, Stephen J., James M. Robinson, and Hans-Gebhard Bethge. *The Fifth Gospel: The Gospel of Thomas Comes of Age*. Harrisburg, PA: Trinity, 1998.

Pazdan, Mary Margaret. "Nicodemus and the Samaritan Woman: Contrasting Models of Discipleship." *BTB* 17 (1987) 145–48.

Perrin, Nicholas. "NHC II,2 and the Oxyrhyncus Fragments (P.Oxy. 1, 654, 655): Overlooked Evidence for a Syriac Gospel of Thomas." *VC* 58 (2004) 138–51.

———. *Thomas and Tatian: The Relationship between the Gospel of Thomas and the Diatessaron*. Atlanta: SBL, 2002.

Petersen, Norman R. *The Gospel of John and the Sociology of Light: Language and Characterization in the Fourth Gospel*. Valley Forge, PA: Trinity, 1993.

Poirier, Paul-Hubert. "The Writings Ascribed to Thomas and the Thomas Tradition." In *The Nag Hammadi Library after Fifty Years: Proceedings of the 1995 Society of Biblical Literature Commemoration*, edited by John D. Turner and Anne McGuire, 295–307. NHMS 44. Leiden: Brill, 1997.

Powell, Mark Allan. *What Is Narrative Criticism?* Guides to Biblical Scholarship. Minneapolis: Fortress, 1990.

Pryor, John W. "Jesus and Israel in the Fourth Gospel—John 1:11." *NovT* 32 (1990) 201–18.

———. *John, Evangelist of the Covenant People: The Narrative & Themes of the Fourth Gospel*. Downers Grove, IL: InterVarsity, 1992.

———. "Of the Virgin Birth or the Birth of Christians? The Text of John 1:13 Once More." *NovT* 27 (1985) 296–318.

Puech, H. Ch. "Une Collection des paroles de Jésus récemment retrouvée: L'Évangile selon Thomas." In *Comptes rendus de l'Academie des Inscriptions et Belles Lettres*, 146–67. Paris: Institut de France: 1957.

Quispel, Gilles. "L'Évangile selon Thomas et le Diatessaron." In *Gnostic Studies II*, 31–55. Istanbul: Nederlands Historisch-Archaelogisch Institut te Istanbul, 1975.

———. "The Gospel of Thomas and the New Testament." *VC* 11 (1957) 189–207.

———. *Makarius, das Thomasevangelium und das Lied von der Perle*. NovTSup 15. Leiden: Brill, 1967.

———. "Qumran, John and Jewish Christianity." In *John and the Dead Sea Scrolls*, edited by James H. Charlesworth, 137–55. New York: Crossroad, 1991.

———. "Some Remarks on the Gospel of Thomas." *NTS* 5 (1959) 276–90.

———. *Tatian and the Gospel of Thomas: Studies in the History of the Western Diatessaron*. Leiden: Brill, 1975.

Rena, John. "Women in the Gospel of John." *EgT* 17 (1986) 131–47.

Rensberger, David. *Johannine Faith and Liberating Community*. Philadelphia: Westminster, 1988.

Rhoads, David, and Kari Syreeni, editors. *Characterization in the Gospel: Reconceiving Narrative Criticism*. JSNTSup 184. Sheffield: Sheffield Academic, 1999.

Richard, Earl. "Expressions of Double Meaning and Their Function in the Gospel of John." *NTS* 31 (1985) 96–112.

Ridderbos, Herman. "The Structure and Scope of the Prologue to the Gospel of John." *NovT* 8 (1966) 180–201.

Riddle, Donald W. "The Cephas–Peter Problem and a Possible Solution." *JBL* 59 (1940) 169–80.

Riley, Gregory J. *Resurrection Reconsidered: John and Thomas in Controversy*. Minneapolis: Fortress, 1995.

Rimmon-Kenan, Shlomith. *Narrative Fiction: Contemporary Poetics*. 2nd. ed. New York: Routledge, 2002.

Robbins, Vernon K. "Rhetorical Composition and Sources in the Gospel of Thomas." *Society of Biblical Literature Seminar Papers* (1997) 86–114.

Robinson, John A. T. "The Relation of the Prologue to the Gospel of St. John." *NTS* 9 (1963) 120–29.

Robinson, James M., editor. *The Nag Hammadi Library in English*. 3rd rev. ed. San Francisco: Harper & Row, 1988.

Robinson, James M., and Helmut Koester. *Trajectories through Early Christianity*. Philadelphia: Fortress, 1971.

Schenke, Hans-Martin. "The Function and Background of the Beloved Disciple in the Gospel of John." In *Nag Hammadi, Gnosticism and Early Christianity*, edited by Charles W. Hedrick and Robert Hodgson Jr., 111–25. 1986. Reprint, Eugene, OR: Wipf & Stock, 2005.

Schlatter, Adolph von. *Der Evangelist Johannes, Wie er spricht, denkt und glaubt: Ein Kommentar zum vierten Evangelium*. Stuttgart: Calwer, 1958.

Schneemelcher, Wilhelm, editor. *New Testament Apocrypha*. 2 vols. Translated by R. McL. Wilson. Louisville: Westminster John Knox, 1991.

Schneiders, Sandra. "Born Anew." *ThTo* 44 (1987) 189–96.

———. "Death in the Community of Eternal Life: History, Theology, and Spirituality in John 11." *Int* 41 (1987) 44–56.

———. "The Foot Washing (John 13:1–20): An Experiment in Hermeneutics." *CBQ* 43 (1981) 76–92.

———. "History and Symbolism in the Fourth Gospel." In *L'Évangile de Jean: Sources, Rédaction, Théologie*, edited by Martinus de Jonge, 371–76. BETL 44. Louvain: Louvain University Press, 1977.

———. *The Revelatory Text: Interpreting the New Testament as Sacred Scripture*. San Francisco: HarperSanFrancisco, 1991.

———. "Women in the Fourth Gospel and the Role of Women in the Contemporary Church." *BTB* 12 (1982) 35–45.

Scholer, David M. "Bibliographia Gnostica: Supplementum II/1." *NovT* 40 (1998) 73–100.

———. "Bibliographia Gnostica: Supplementum II/2." *NovT* 41 (1999) 58–93.

Scholes, Robert. *Elements of Fiction*. New York: Oxford University Press, 1968.

Schwartz, Eduard. *Aporien im vierten Evangelium*. Berlin: n.p., 1907.

Segovia, Fernando F. "John 13:1–20, The Footwashing in the Johannine Tradition." *ZNW* 73 (1982) 39–42.

Segovia, Fernando F., and Mary Ann Tolbert, editors. *Reading from This Place: Social Location and Biblical Interpretation in the United States.* Minneapolis: Fortress, 1995.

Seim, Turid Karlsen. "Roles of Women in the Gospel of John." In *Aspects on the Johannine Literature: Papers Presented at a Conference of Scandinavian New Testament Exegetes at Uppsala, June 16–19, 1986*, edited by Lars Hartman and Birger Olsson, 56–73. ConBNT 18. Stockholm: Almqvist & Wiksell, 1987.

Sell, Jesse. "Johannine Traditions in Logion 61 of the Gospel of Thomas." *PRSt* 7 (1980) 24–37.

———. "A Study of the Self-Predication Statements Attributed to 'Jesus Christ' in the Naga-Hammadi Coptic 'Gnostic' Corpus." Ph.D. diss., Duke University, 1976.

Sellew, Philip. "The Gospel of Thomas: Prospects for Future Research." In *The Nag Hammadi Library after Fifty Years: Proceedings of the 1995 Society of Biblical Literature Commemoration*, edited by John D. Turner and Anne McGuire, 327–46. NHMS 44. Leiden: Brill, 1997.

Sevrin, Jean-Marie. "L'Interprétation de L'Évangile selon Thomas, Entre Tradition et Rédaction." In *The Nag Hammadi Library after Fifty Years: Proceedings of the 1995 Society of Biblical Literature Commemoration*, edited by John D. Turner and Anne McGuire, 347–60. NHMS 44. Leiden: Brill, 1997.

Siverstev, Alexei. "The Gospel of Thomas and Early Stages in the Development of the Christian Wisdom Literature." *JECS* 8 (2000) 319–40.

Skinner, Christopher W. "Another Look at the Lamb of God." *BSac* 141 (2004) 89–104.

Smalley, Stephen S. "The Johannine Son of Man Sayings." *NTS* 15 (1968) 278–301.

———. "The Sign in John XXI." *NTS* 20 (1974) 275–88.

Smith, J. Z. "The Garments of Shame." *HR* 5 (1966) 217–38.

Snyder, Graydon F. "John 13:16 and the Anti-Petrinism of the Johannine Tradition." *BRev* 16 (1971) 5–15.

Staley, Jeffrey L. *The Print's First Kiss: A Rhetorical Investigation of the Implied Reader in the Fourth Gospel.* SBLDS 82. Atlanta: Scholars, 1988.

———. "The Structure of John's Prologue: Its Implications for the Gospel's Narrative Structure." *CBQ* 48 (1986) 241–64.

———. "Subversive Narrator/Victimized Reader: A Reader Response Assessment of a Text-Critical Problem, John 18,12–24." *JSNT* 51 (1993) 91–98.

Sternberg, Meir. *The Poetics of Biblical Narrative: Ideological Literature and the Drama of Reading.* Indiana Literary Biblical Series. Bloomington: Indiana University Press, 1985.

Stibbe, Mark W. G. *John.* Readings. Sheffield: Sheffield Academic, 1993.

———. *John as Storyteller: Narrative Criticism and the Fourth Gospel.* SNTSMS 73. Cambridge: Cambridge University Press, 1992.

———. *John's Gospel.* New Testament Readings. New York: Routledge, 1994.

Summers, Ray. *The Secret Sayings of the Living Jesus: Studies in the Coptic Gospel according to Thomas.* Waco, TX: Word, 1968.

Sylva, Dennis D. "Nicodemus and His Spices." *NTS* 34 (1988) 148–51.

Tarelli, C. C. "Johannine Synonyms." *JTS* 47 (1946) 175–77.

Tenney, Merrill C. "The Footnotes of John's Gospel." *BSac* 117 (1960) 350–64.

Thatcher, Tom. "A New Look at Asides in the Fourth Gospel." *BSac* 151 (1994) 428–39.

Tilborg, Sjef van. *Imaginative Love in John*. BIS 2. Leiden: Brill, 1993.

Titus, Eric Lane. "The Identity of the Beloved Disciple." *JBL* 69 (1950) 323–28.

———. *The Message of the Fourth Gospel*. New York: Abingdon, 1957.

Tobin, Thomas H. "The Prologue of John and Hellenistic Jewish Speculation." *CBQ* 52 (1990) 252–69.

Tolmie, D. F. *Narratology and Biblical Narratives: A Practical Guide*. San Francisco: International Scholars Publications, 1999.

Tuckett, Christopher. "Thomas and the Synoptics." *NovT* 30 (1988) 132–57.

Turner, H. E. W., and Hugh Montefiore. *Thomas and the Evangelists*. SBT 1/35. Naperville, IL: Allenson, 1962.

Turner, John D., and Anne McGuire. *The Nag Hammadi Library after Fifty Years: Proceedings of the 1995 Society of Biblical Literature Commemoration*. NHMS 44. Leiden: Brill, 1997.

Urban, Christian. *Das Menschenbild nach dem Johannesevangelium: Grundlagen johanneischer Anthropologie*. WUNT 2/137. Tübingen: Mohr/Siebeck, 2001.

Valantasis, Richard. *The Gospel of Thomas*. New Testament Readings. New York: Routledge, 1997.

Van der Watt, J. G. "The Composition of the Prologue of John's Gospel: The Historical Jesus Introducing Divine Grace." *WTJ* 57 (1995) 311–32.

Viviano, Benedict T. "The Structure of the Prologue of John (1:1–18): A Note." *RB* 105 (1990) 176–84.

Von Wahlde, Urban C. "Literary Structure and Theological Argument in Three Discourses with the Jews in the Fourth Gospel." *JBL* 103 (1984) 575–84.

Waetjen, Herman C. "Logos προς τον θεον and the Objectification of Truth in the Prologue of the Fourth Gospel." *CBQ* 63 (2001) 265–86.

Watty, William. "The Significance of Anonymity in the Fourth Gospel." *ExpTim* 90 (1979) 209–12.

Weiss, Herold. "Footwashing in the Johannine Community." *NovT* 21 (1979) 298–325.

———. "The Sabbath in the Fourth Gospel." *JBL* 110 (1991) 311–21.

Wendling, Emil. *Die Entstehung des Marcus-Evangeliums: Philologische Untersuchungen*. Tübingen: Mohr/Siebeck, 1908.

Williams, Joel F. *Other Followers of Jesus: Minor Characters as Major Figures in Mark's Gospel*. JSNTSup 102. Sheffield: Sheffield Academic, 1994.

Wilson, R. McL. *Studies in the Gospel of Thomas*. London: Mowbray, 1960.

Wojciechowski, Michal. "La source de Jean 13.1–20." *NTS* 34 (1988) 135–41.

Woll, D. Bruce. "The Departure of 'The Way': The First Farewell Discourse in the Gospel of John." *JBL* 99 (1980) 225–39.